UNIX®:
The Complete Reference
System V Release 3

UNIX®:
The Complete Reference

System V Release 3

Stephen Coffin

Osborne **McGraw-Hill**
Berkeley, California

Osborne **McGraw-Hill**
2600 Tenth Street
Berkeley, California 94710
U.S.A.

For information on translations and book distributors outside of the
U.S.A., write to Osborne **McGraw-Hill** at the above address.

A complete list of trademarks appears on page 689.

UNIX®: The Complete Reference

234567890 DODO 898

ISBN 0-07-881299-2

CONTENTS

ELEVEN   **UNIX System Administration**   **311**

Developing a book is impossible without the help of a great many people, only a few of whom can be mentioned here. Jim Farber and Fred Hicinbothem provided outstanding technical reviews. John Moran, Jeff Pepper, and Alex Gillon were especially helpful in the administrative area. Special thanks to Pat Somers for her patience. And, of course, thanks to the many giants of the UNIX system, whose broad shoulders provide an excellent view.

ACKNOWLEDGMENTS

Introduction

O N E

The UNIX Operating System has evolved in the past twenty years from its invention as an experiment in computer science to become one of the most influential and popular computer environments in the world. Today more than two hundred thousand computers ranging in size from microcomputers with limited resources to the largest mainframes and supercomputers, use the UNIX system. This growth is accelerating ever faster as more and more users succumb to the amazing flexibility, power, and elegance of the UNIX system.

These unique features of the UNIX system have led to this growth:

• *Software Tools* The UNIX system introduced a new idea in computing: that problems can be solved and applications created by interconnecting a few simple parts. These parts are usually off-the-shelf components that are designed to do a single job, and do it well. Large applications can be built from simple sequences of commands. This philosophy also extends to the development domain, where packaged subroutines are combined into new executable programs. This basic concept of *software reuse* is a major reason why the UNIX system is such a productive environment in which to work.

• *Portability* The UNIX system has been ported to nearly every moderate and large computer ever built. Now that microcomputers are beginning to have the processing power that was once reserved for mainframes costing millions of dollars, the UNIX system is a natural evolution for these inexpensive but powerful machines. Only a few minor changes and adaptations have been required to make the UNIX system available on these new microcomputers, and it is now agreed that no more portable operating system exists. The value of this portability cannot be overestimated, because software development is expensive and tedious. Major applications such as word processors, databases, and graphics systems can take many years to develop. Once an application is completed, the only way to give it a future beyond the lifespan of the hardware it was designed for is to either re-create it for a new machine or to retain the same operating system on new generations of computers. It is generally agreed that the UNIX system provides an environment that allows easy movement of applications from microcomputers to mainframes.

• *Flexibility* A major attraction of the UNIX system to software and hardware developers is its flexibility. It has been adapted to applications as divergent as factory automation, telephone switching systems, and personal games and toys. New functions and commands are being added at a fast pace, and most developers prefer to use the UNIX system as a "workbench" for their applications. It is so easy to extend the basic UNIX system that some turnkey application packages are barely recognizable as being based on it.

- *Power* The UNIX system is one of the most powerful operating systems available for any computer. Its clean and terse command syntax allows users to do many things quickly and simply that are not even possible with other operating systems. Users can take advantage of built-in UNIX system services and commands that would be expensive add-ons (if they existed at all) in other systems. No operating system is richer in its capabilities than the UNIX system.

- *Multiuser and Multitasking* Because the UNIX system is a time-sharing multitasking environment, it can easily do more than one thing at a time. In a personal UNIX system a user may be simultaneously editing a file, printing a file on a printer, sending electronic mail to another machine, and using an electronic spreadsheet. The UNIX system is designed to effortlessly handle a user's multiple simultaneous needs. It is also a multiuser environment, supporting the activities of more than one person at a time. It is not unusual for large mainframe versions of the UNIX system to support several hundred users at once, and all these users have the same "private" view of their system as does a single user on a microcomputer.

- *Elegance* The UNIX system is widely regarded as one of the most elegant computer operating systems. Once users understand some of the basic concepts of the UNIX system, they can do a great many things in a beautiful and simple way. UNIX system users who move to other operating systems often wonder why the things that seemed so simple under the UNIX system are not even possible in other environments. Developers of other operating systems and applications often borrow ideas and themes from the UNIX system to enrich their own systems.

All these things, and many others, help to account for the rapid surge of popularity that the UNIX system has enjoyed in recent years. These factors make it clear that the UNIX system will continue to grow and develop, and most computer users will eventually meet it in one place or another. Many will have their own UNIX system on their own personal microcomputer.

Who Should Read This Book

This book is intended for the new user of the UNIX system — someone who probably uses a general-purpose multiuser UNIX system or who owns a personal UNIX system. It will help you learn to navigate in the UNIX system environment, teach you how to use the most useful commands, and prepare you to go as far as you wish with the UNIX system on your own.

In this book we assume that you have some experience with computers and computer operating systems, perhaps with MS-DOS or another microcomputer operating system or perhaps with a mainframe. However, most people with no previous computer experience can use this book to learn the fundamentals of the UNIX system.

It is oriented toward the System V, Release 3 (also known as SVR3 or 5.3) version of the UNIX system. The descriptions and examples here are taken from this release. However, because most versions of the UNIX system available today act similarly in the basic to intermediate level of command usage, the book will be helpful even if you have an older (or newer!) version.

How to Read This Book

It is desirable that you read this book in conjunction with hands-on access to a UNIX system so that you can try the examples and see the results for yourself, on your own machine and with your own user identification. You can customize the system's operation to meet your own needs and experiment with the commands and functions as your interests lead you. If you try the examples on your own system, maybe you'll find some bugs; if so, please send them to us.

We begin each chapter with the most generally useful and least complex material on the chapter's topic. You can become a competent user of the UNIX system just by reading the first half of each chapter. However, if you desire more information or need reference material as you become more skilled at using the UNIX system, the second half of each chapter can help you. Each chapter ends with a section called "Going Further" that introduces more difficult or more esoteric aspects of the topic. Remember, the UNIX system is a big place, and whole books could (and often do) follow after the end of each "Going Further" section.

This book does not exhaustively describe every command or every possible option for each command that it does discuss. You should use the *UNIX User's Manual* along with this book for more detailed and exact reference materials. In addition to learning more about the UNIX system, you will eventually have a thorough knowledge of the standard reference documentation.

So dive in! Maybe you will write the next book on the UNIX system!

The Lore and Controversy of the UNIX System

The UNIX system is unique in the computer world in that it has attracted both intensely loyal defenders and intensely critical detractors. Almost no one who has used the UNIX system is indifferent to it. Its fans tend to wax profound about its elegance, power, and flexibility, while its enemies wax profane about its terse syntax and strange command names, its sparse documentation, and its complexity to administer. Computer experts usually fall into the "fan" category, while beginners fall into the "foe" category. (We hope that this book will help you leap directly over the "foe" stage to defender status.)

Like the pocket calculator, the UNIX system was originally developed by experts for their own use; so, in the early days, the needs of the beginning user were ignored in favor of speed and accuracy from the experts' point of view. Again, like the pocket calculator, the advantages of the UNIX system have helped it move quickly from the expert to the novice, bringing with it some of the expert features and unconcern for the novice.

Happily, recent releases have been aimed at the less skilled user, without reducing the system's power and other advantages. Now, with SVR3, nearly anyone can administer and use their own UNIX system and can go as far as they wish with it. These improvements have primarily occurred in the following areas:

- *Bulletproofing* The UNIX system has been hardened so that very little routine software maintenance is required to keep the system tuned and running at peak performance. Many formerly routine jobs of an administrator, such as periodically deleting log files or rebooting the system, have become automatic or unnecessary.

- *Consistency* Almost all commands have evolved over the years to follow a more consistent command syntax, so that the confusingly inconsistent usage of different commands has been reduced. There are still plenty of inconsistencies, but things are moving in the right direction.

- *Documentation* The standard documentation (the *UNIX User's Manual*), while still intended as terse reference material, has evolved to be more consistent, with more examples of command usage and more explanatory material than in older releases. You may not notice this in your first perusal of the *User's Manual*, but it's true!

• *User Agents* Most implementations now provide simplified tools (even expert systems in some cases) to aid in the configuration and administration of the UNIX system.

• *New Features* Many new capabilities and commands have entered the UNIX system in the last few releases. Most of these have been aimed at bringing some of the ideas of BSD (Berkeley Software Distribution) and XENIX into the AT&T System V products. The **uucp** file transfer subsystem has been substantially improved, there are new features to support networking with the **streams** mechanism, the development environment has been enhanced, and there are many other features. A new online **help** facility can make life easier for the beginner, though it still needs enhancement in future releases.

• *Operating System Sharing* Modern microcomputer versions allow the machine and its files to be shared between the UNIX system and the MS-DOS system. This feature will soon be extended to the new MS-OS/2. Operating system sharing means that the multitasking capabilities of the UNIX system can be used to execute MS-DOS as a process under the UNIX system, allowing all the "background" functions of the UNIX system to execute at the same time that the machine might be used for MS-DOS programs. This feature is currently restricted to versions of the UNIX system running on the Intel 80286 and 80386 machines.

Because of these and other changes, many of the old criticisms of the UNIX system are no longer really valid. Make no mistake, the UNIX system is still a powerful and complex operating system, but over time it has become much more regular, controllable, and friendly.

But because of this history as an experts' system, a definite mystique and a great deal of lore have grown up around the UNIX system. Historically most "gurus" learned their skills by word of mouth, by sitting at the knee of an already knowledgeable expert. Even today it helps to have a more knowledgeable person to answer questions and to explain some of the more esoteric aspects of the UNIX system.

The UNIX system was invented in large part in reaction to the large and clumsy computer operating systems available in the late 1960s. Foremost goals in its design were to make it wide in scope and to design commands that didn't attempt to solve all possible problems. On the contrary, a fundamental guiding principle of the earliest development was to design commands that did only one thing but did that thing simply, quietly, and very well. For example, a command designed to concatenate and display files should not try to paginate the output or print the files on a printer. Those tasks should be left to other programs that could do those things without the burden of concatenation.

This insistence on a "small is beautiful" philosophy had several major effects. First, a new requirement appeared that was not apparent before: the output of some of these *tools*, as these single-purpose commands were called, must be channeled into the input of other tools. The results were the concepts of command pipelines and standard input and output, which we will examine in detail later. Second, the development of new commands and other applications was much less difficult than it was in other operating systems, so the UNIX system experienced substantial growth and advancement, which continues today. The ease of software development and maintenance was a direct result of the UNIX system philosophy of making tools. Third, the UNIX system contains a great number of single-purpose commands. This is a mixed blessing for users, because you must learn a lot of command names for functions that might be combined into a single command in other operating systems. However, most users agree that the difficulties associated with the many commands are more than counterbalanced by the flexibility and power that the tools approach provides.

The Modern UNIX System — Pro and Con

The UNIX system remains somewhat controversial, though its multiuser and multitasking features are becoming more widely respected in the microcomputer community than ever before. Compared to MS-DOS, for example, the UNIX system is much larger and more complex. In return, it offers many features not available to MS-DOS. The new MS-OS/2 multitasking (but single-user) operating system may give the UNIX system its strongest challenge, though the long-range impact of MS-OS/2 is yet to be felt.

The original "do one thing well" philosophy of the early UNIX system has been somewhat lost in modern releases, and today's commands contain a great number of options and controls. This is a mixed blessing, because now commands can be more difficult to use. However, they can also be adapted to new situations without contortions. By and large, the key concepts of the early philosophy, such as pipelines, have been retained, while the capabilities of the commands have been expanded to meet new needs.

The UNIX system is primarily oriented to *character-based* terminals and devices. Special add-on software is needed to make the UNIX system work with bit-mapped graphics displays. This historical dependence on and support for ASCII terminals is another mixed blessing. On the one hand, the nifty graphics of modern microcomputers are not as widely available for UNIX machines as might be desired. On the other hand, the UNIX system allows users to call a remote machine with an inexpensive terminal, over inexpensive dial-up telephone lines. This makes the system ideal for *server* applications, in which the primary user interface is not associated with the centralized UNIX machine but executes directly on a remote "intelligent" terminal. This is a modern architecture for local area network environments in small- to moderate-sized business offices. The new X windowing system is a good example of the use of intelligent terminals with centralized servers.

The UNIX system runs counter to the current trend of making operating systems "invisible" to the user. Many operating systems have attempted to create user interfaces that eliminate the operating system from the user's view. The Macintosh Finder, for example, is really an operating system with relatively simple functions. The window- and menu-oriented user interface helps to hide the commands, file system, and administrative tools from the user. In using the UNIX system, however, the more aware you are of the internal functions of the system, the more you can control it to your benefit and improved productivity. This fact arises mainly from its creation as an experts' system, in which most users were well aware of the internals of the system as they used it. Now that the UNIX system has been adopted by a larger user community, tools such as user agents have been provided to insulate the user from many of the subtleties and complexities of the operating system. However, even though you can now use the system without extensive understanding of its complexities, you still can benefit substantially from more knowledge about what it's really doing when you use a command.

UNIX System History

Even though the UNIX system originated in AT&T Bell Laboratories, one of the largest and most well-funded research institutions in the United States, its history is almost unique in comparison to other major computer operating systems because advances are largely the results of individual people with unique creative ideas. A joke with more than a grain of truth among developers goes like this: "To get a new release of the UNIX system, you lock a bunch of hackers up in a closed room (or on a single UNIX machine!) and every year or so you take the software that more than one half of them are using, and that is the next release of the UNIX system." The implication is that advances have come not primarily from bureaucratic decision making but rather directly from the needs and the creativity of the users. This is still true today, making the UNIX system one of the most fertile gardens for the creation of new concepts in computing.

The UNIX system was designed by a group of people who were AT&T representatives on the development of one of the seminal influences in modern computing, the MULTICS Operating System, developed at MIT in the late 1960s. As one of the early time-sharing systems, MULTICS embodied most of the ideas in today's multitasking systems. Unfortunately, MULTICS suffered as a result of its innovative role and was much more complex and clumsy than was necessary. In the late 1960s, AT&T withdrew most of its participation in the MULTICS project, leaving a group of talented but frustrated people with plenty of ideas for what a time-sharing system *should* be like. Without access to the MULTICS system, these people were left without a modern operating system to work with, so they created a new one. Original designers Ken Thompson and Dennis Ritchie built the system based on a design worked out with Rudd Canaday. They were soon joined by several other able computer scientists, among them J. F. Ossanna and R. Morris. After a period of discussion and proposals, they managed to acquire a castoff DEC PDP-7 and set to work. Like a great many of the best projects, this one started with the creation of a game: Thompson and Ritchie developed a space travel game for the PDP-7. Following this experience, they turned to more mundane pursuits and soon created a new file system structure and software that is very similar to the modern file system. A process environment with scheduling was added, and the rest of a rudimentary operating system followed. The name UNIX was soon applied to the results because their work was a simplification of the MULTICS system. The system was running on the PDP-7 at the beginning of 1970, and by mid-1970 they had moved the project to the newly introduced DEC PDP-11 machine. Many of the key ideas of the modern UNIX system were present in the earliest implementations, including the file system, the implementation of processes, and the command line structure still used today.

The original implementation was coded in assembly language, but the C programming language was soon developed within the group, beginning in 1971. The C language was almost immediately used in the continuing development of the UNIX system, and in 1973 the kernel was recoded in C. Today only a very few high-performance kernel subroutines are written in assembly language. This was the first attempt at coding an entire operating system in a high-level language, and the portability it provided is widely regarded as a major reason for the popularity that the UNIX system enjoys today.

At the same time, the text processing tools that later became **troff** were begun, and the first real customer of a UNIX system was the Bell Laboratories Patent Attorney's Office, which began to use the **roff** program in the fall of 1971.

The UNIX system immediately captured the imagination of the computer scientists at Bell Laboratories, and after only two or three years, there were about a dozen UNIX systems running on several different machines. Major software enhancements came frequently, and AT&T began supporting the system as an internal product within Bell Laboratories. The **troff** program appeared during this period, among many other innovations.

However, the UNIX system came into its own with the development of larger PDP-11 machines, such as the PDP-11/45 and PDP-11/70 in the early to mid-1970s. The UNIX system fitted naturally into the DEC architecture, and the UNIX system resulted in the sale of many hundreds of PDP-11 machines over the years. Developers within Bell Laboratories began using UNIX machines for their word processing work, and Bell System product designers began using PDP-11s with the UNIX system for turnkey systems within the telephone business.

Simultaneously, AT&T released many copies of the UNIX system to universities around the world, and a whole generation of computer scientists in the late 1970s learned their trade with the UNIX system. This resulted in another fertile wave of innovation, and the widely used BSD (Berkeley Software Distribution) implementation appeared from the University of California at Berkeley. As AT&T moved to harden the UNIX system and optimize it in the direction of business computing, the BSD releases became dominant in the university and engineering communities. Compatibility between AT&T and BSD versions remains somewhat questionable, and today's users usually belong to one camp or the other. The BSD versions stand on an equal footing with AT&T versions, though teams on both sides are scurrying to bring the best innovations of the other system into their new releases.

During the late 1970s, AT&T began a new naming scheme for their version of the UNIX system. Formerly the major releases were named for new versions that came out of the research area, and two of the most popular releases were named Sixth Edition and Seventh Edition. Following an internal reorganization of UNIX system support, AT&T changed its numbering to System III and System V. Actually these new releases were direct descendants of the Seventh Edition, and System V superseded System III in the mid-1980s. System IV was used internally in Bell Laboratories, but was regarded as a transition product that was not publicly supported. Now, in the late 1980s, AT&T has standardized on its System V name, and its recent releases are called system V Release 2 and System V Release 3, which are often abbreviated to SVR2 and SVR3, respectively.

During the late 1970s and early 1980s, one or both of the BSD and AT&T releases were ported to nearly every computer with the power to support it. This usually meant at least high-speed disk units and built-in memory management support in the CPU, though experimental versions have been adapted to ROM-based machines with no hard disk at all. Today you can buy versions of the UNIX system for the largest supercomputers, the widely used mainframe machines, and nearly all minicomputers sold.

As the microcomputer has developed in speed and power, and its cost has dropped, these machines have moved into range of the UNIX system. The original 8088 machines were nearly powerful enough to support the UNIX system, and a few implementations could run on these machines. The popular XENIX operating system is a streamlined version of the UNIX system for the IBM PC, but it is really at or over the edge of the machine's capability, and has only come into its own with the 80286 and 80386 machines.

Recently, AT&T Bell Laboratories has developed a new generic version called the Eighth Edition, or the Research UNIX system. Though not sold commercially, this release has been widely distributed to universities.

The descendents of the BSD releases are being constantly improved, and agreements between AT&T and Microsoft, AT&T and Sun, and AT&T and Amdahl are further integrating the microcomputer and supercomputer versions. Eventually it is expected that the SVR3, BSD, and XENIX releases will converge into a single version of the UNIX system that can run in almost any hardware environment. This combined product may also allow object-code compatibility between different releases for the same machine.

The SVR3 Release

The SVR3 release is the most up-to-date version of the AT&T UNIX system. It has been ported to most host machines and is the current standard for the AT&T line. It has been significantly enhanced over older releases, and many changes have been made. The major changes at the user level include more online help, significantly improved (and simplified) system administration tools, and better resistance to damage from power outages and other inadvertent system crashes. At the lower levels of the UNIX system, the major changes have been support for shared libraries, much improved virtual memory support, and new tools for integrating local area networks with the kernel. Of course, there have been extensive smaller changes and optimizations throughout the system.

SVR3 Versus BSD and SVR2

The SVR3 system is becoming significantly more bug-free than the BSD releases and incorporates many of the innovations that originated in BSD systems. Overall, there is better support for SVR3 than for BSD releases, and the BSD versions are fragmenting as different vendors enhance the system in their own ways. Almost all commercial systems use SVR3, while scientific and technical systems tend to build from the BSD base. Compared to its immediate predecessor, the AT&T SVR2 release, SVR3 has several new features, but it is larger and often slower. That is, SVR3 requires significantly more real memory and a larger hard disk than SVR2. In return, the SVR3 user gets a state-of-the-art system, new networking features, and better support from documentation and administration tools.

Microcomputer Requirements

At present the UNIX system can run on nearly any computer that contains sufficient real memory and a fast hard disk. However, UNIX machines require much more hardware support than MS-DOS, though not much more than MS-OS/2. Generally, at least 2.0 megabytes of random access (real) memory (RAM) are required in an SVR3 machine, and at least 40 megabytes of fast hard-disk space are required.

A fast disk is necessary because multiple tasks may need to be stored temporarily while another task uses the real memory. This temporary storage is usually done by "swapping" inactive tasks out of real memory to disk, and this task swapping can happen more than once a second. Implementations of the UNIX system that use only floppy disks usually perform poorly and are generally viewed as toys.

The large size of the hard disk arises from the very large number of commands and functions supported with the standard UNIX system. A fully configured system can contain more than 20 megabytes of stored programs. There are more than 400 separate user commands and over 2600 files and directories in SVR3! Of course many of these can be eliminated when the system is configured for a special purpose; the standard UNIX Development Set, used for programming under the UNIX system, contains nearly one half of the total. If you are not doing programming, these files are unnecessary. However, it is wise to have at least 40 megabytes of hard-disk space before loading a UNIX system.

The large amount of real memory required results from some of the powerful yet subtle traits of the UNIX system. The lowest level of the operating system, the *kernel*, which resides in memory at all times and mediates all connections between user programs and the machine hardware, takes more than one half of a megabyte all by itself. The architecture also includes many *buffers* which act much as a RAM disk acts under single-tasking operating systems. Much of the observed speed comes from these built-in buffers, but they also take a great deal of real memory. Then, of course, the executing programs need memory for their own use. Some large UNIX systems configured for high performance with many simultaneous users have more than 16 megabytes of real memory. Smaller personal systems can of course get by with much less than that, but at least 2.0 and preferably 2.5 or 3.0 megabytes are usually recommended for fast performance.

Going Further

The information presented in each chapter is organized by level of difficulty. The easiest and most useful material appears in the first part of each chapter, while the real "meat" of the commands and tools appears in the middle section. The last part of each chapter, under the heading "Going Further," is devoted to the more difficult but still very important information that expert users need, but not every day. In subsequent chapters we will assume a familiarity with the material in the "Going Further" sections of previous chapters, but you should probably read only the first half of each chapter the first time through. As you gain experience with the UNIX system, you can go back to the more difficult material as you need it.

Assembling a UNIX System

Most users are not long content with the basic package purchased from a computer dealer. As with MS-DOS, there are a great many add-on software products available for most UNIX systems. Some of these are oriented toward a specific business need such as spreadsheet programs, word processors, or high-quality graphics packages. An operating system is usually chosen based on the available applications. However, the UNIX system environment encourages modifications and enhancements to some of the basic system software, and many software packages are available that substitute for the major subsystems. For example, enhanced print spoolers and communication packages are available, as are several additional *shell* programs, which supply the user interface to the operating system.

Also, individual vendors have frequently added to or modified the system either to customize their product or simply because some command or subsystem can be improved. This is most likely to occur in two areas. First, many different variants of the commands exist, as they have grown and changed through the history of the UNIX system. Individual developers and users tend to collect the versions of commands that they like better than the standard ones. Such custom programs often appear in releases that you can buy, such as commands from BSD releases in SVR3. Many times the command's behavior on a specific release will differ slightly from the SVR3 standards. Second, vendors of UNIX systems often provide customized tools for administering the system. Such user agents can make the job of managing a system much easier, though usually at a cost of some of the flexibility and power that is built into the subsystems. These user agents often differ remarkably from each other. In this book we will discuss the official SVR3 commands and system administration tools.

Tutorial

As an introduction we will walk through a short session with the UNIX system, introducing some basic concepts along with some examples of how a user interacts with the UNIX system. At the end of this chapter, you should be able to get into and out of the UNIX system without difficulty.

We will assume that you have already attached a terminal to a UNIX machine that has been set up by someone else and is used by others. Most beginners with the UNIX system start on machines administered by someone else. After learning the basics and exploring an existing system, it is much easier to set up a machine of your own. If you are starting with a brand-new machine, however, you should probably read Chapter 21, Configuring a System, first, and then look at the opening pages of Chapter 19, Boot and Shutdown. When the system is up and running, you can return to this chapter.

Your terminal might be a system console, a character-oriented terminal attached directly to an RS232 port on the machine, or a remote terminal connected via a telephone line and modem. It doesn't matter which type you are using, since the system will usually act the same for all of these terminal types. Terminals and their configurations are discussed in detail in Chapter 11.

This basic access is completely character oriented; no graphics or icons will appear. Because the UNIX system was originally developed for "dumb" printing terminals, much of the system still assumes character-oriented terminals.

The version of the UNIX system available in English-speaking countries uses the American Standard Code for Information Interchange (ASCII) character set. Thus IBM 3270-style terminals will usually not work with the UNIX system, and graphics terminals must provide an ASCII mode.

Logging In

Once your terminal is attached to the UNIX machine, you may have to press a RETURN or two to wake up the UNIX system. When you do, you will see the "login prompt."

```
Welcome to the "my_sys" System.
login:
```

Because UNIX is a multiuser system, your first task is to identify yourself to the system so that it can respond to you in an individual way. This gives you access to your files and establishes your session according to preferences you have established. A unique *login id* identifies each user who is connected to the system. Usually your login id will be your name or initials or some whimsical identification that you choose. The only requirements are that the login id be fewer than eight characters long and consist only of letters and numbers. In this scheme uppercase and lowercase characters are distinguished, so that the login id "STEVE" is not the same as the id "steve."

All login id's should have a lowercase character first—if your login id begins with an uppercase character, the system will think that you are calling in from a terminal that has only uppercase, and will treat you very differently. The login id must be unique; that is, no other user on the machine can have the same one.

If you have established your login id as "steve," for example, you would respond to the "login" prompt with "steve"

```
Welcome to the "my_sys" System.

login: steve
```

and end your entry by pressing RETURN.

Unlike most text entry under the UNIX system, you usually cannot correct typing errors at the login prompt by backing up with the BACKSPACE key, because the system has not yet identified you. Use of the BACKSPACE key to delete a character is treated as a user preference.

After you have entered your login id, the system requests your individual password:

```
Welcome to the "my_sys" System.

login: steve
Password:
```

The system wants you to verify that you are the person authorized to use that login id. After all, your login id is usually public information, and the system wants to protect your files and other private data from others.

So enter your individual password, ending with RETURN. Unlike the login id, the system will not display (*echo* in UNIX system jargon) the characters of your password as you type them. This additional security measure prevents someone looking over your shoulder from discovering your password.

If you enter either your login id or password incorrectly, or if you are not an authorized user of the machine, the system will respond as follows:

```
Welcome to the "my_sys" System.

login: steve
Password:
Login incorrect
login:
```

The system will not tell you if the login id was entered incorrectly or the password was wrong, but it will give you a second chance. Start over by entering your login id and then entering your password when prompted.

When your login id and password pair have been accepted, you will see some initial banners and messages:

```
UNIX System V Release 3.1
System my_sys
Copyright (c) 1987 AT&T
All Rights Reserved

The my_sys system will be down for software installation
from 6:00 to 7:00 PM tonight.   =pat


news: new_user

You have mail.

$
```

These messages will probably differ on your system, but this example is typical of an active multiuser UNIX system. The first message

```
UNIX System V Release 3.1
```

is simply a banner that identifies the system in use. Next comes the identification of the machine, **my—sys**. Each UNIX system has a unique identifying name.

Next come some copyright notices for the software installed on the machine. These notices may differ depending on who is marketing the specific UNIX system version in use and on what added software is installed on the machine.

Then comes a message placed by the system administrator called the "message of the day." Your system may or may not have a message because it is usually used only to announce information of current interest.

The next line

```
news: new_user
```

comes from another feature of the UNIX system called *news*. This feature is usually used by the system administrator to announce information of longer useful life than messages given by the message of the day, and once you read the news, you will no longer see the prompt at login time. The message of the day, however, will be displayed every time you log in until it is changed or deleted by the system administrator. The "news" prompt also gives the subject of the news: "new—user" in this case.

Next is

```
You have mail.
```

This is a reminder that a message from another user (*electronic mail*) is waiting for you in your mailbox. You will see this prompt each time you log in until you delete the mail. Unlike news, just reading your mail will not necessarily cause the "You have mail." prompt to disappear when you log in.

Finally, the login process is completed, and the system turns control over to you by printing the "$" prompt. Whenever you see the "$," the system is waiting for your input; you will be talking to the command processor, the *shell*.

Read the News

You might first read the news because it may affect your subsequent use of the system.

Read the news by entering

```
$ news
```

followed by RETURN. Because the system prints the "$," you

don't need to enter it. Remember that uppercase and lowercase characters are different in the UNIX system; **news** and most other command names are entered in lowercase characters only. You are actually instructing the command processor (the shell) to execute a command called **news**, which looks in a standard place for news items that you have not yet seen, and then prints those messages at your terminal. When you enter **news**, the response might be as follows:

```
$ news
new_user (pat) Mon Jun 22 08:26:47 1987
The 'my_sys' system has a new user!  Welcome "steve"....    =pat
$
```

Each item starts with a banner line that shows the name of the news item, the login id of the author (in parentheses), and the date the item was created. When all news items have been displayed, the **news** program ends, and control returns to the shell: another "$" prompt reminds you that the shell is ready for your commands.

List Your Files

Next you might look at the files that exist in your private data storage area. The UNIX system has an excellent *file system* for storing files and commands. After logging in, you are at a specific place in that file system, called your *home directory*, which is usually where you keep your private files and data. Because each user has a personal home directory, the files of other users are not shared with yours. This segregation of users' data means that others can have files with the same names as your files without causing problems. (We will examine the file system in more detail in Chapter 4.)

You can list the names of your private files with the **ls** (for list) command.

```
$ ls
note
README
$
```

Again, enter the command name at the shell prompt "$," and the **ls** command will execute. When finished, control returns to the shell for your next command.

In this case there are two files, named **note** and **README**. Recall that uppercase and lowercase differ, so **README** is not the same as **readme**. Because you are a new user, this small number of files is not unusual, but it would not be unusual to see up to a hundred file names when you enter the **ls** command. There is no limit to the number of files allowed in a directory.

In many cases a new user would find no files in the home directory, and the output from the **ls** command would look a bit different:

```
$ ls
$
```

Here **ls** would print exactly nothing, returning directly to the shell for your next command. This illustrates a rather general feature of the UNIX system: if there is nothing to say, the system usually says nothing. Although this might seem a bit terse, if not rude, we will see good reasons for this silence in the next few chapters.

Actually, like most commands, **ls** has several other options and features. For example, you might try the following:

```
$ ls -l
```

Adding the −l (minus ell) tells the **ls** command to generate a "long" listing, one that gives much more information about a file than the simple version described above. You tell a command that you want it to do something a little different than usual by giving it an *argument*. Arguments are sometimes signaled by the presence of a − (minus) sign before the argument. Such an argument is called a *flag* or *option*. Leave a space after the command name but none between the − sign and the argument letter. The results of this command might be as follows:

```
$ ls -l
total 2
-rw-rw-rw-  1 steve    users       138 Apr  5 19:34 README
-rw-rw-rw-  1 steve    users       227 Apr  5 19:33 note
$
```

This reveals several other facts about files. The first thing on the left, "-rw-rw-rw-," tells the *permissions* of the file, while "steve" is the *owner* of the file, who belongs to the *group* "users." The file size, in bytes, comes next, and the last thing on the line is the filename. (These and other attributes of files will be discussed in Chapter 4.)

Arguments in the UNIX system are similar in function to those in MS-DOS and other operating systems: they modify the function of the command. In contrast to MS-DOS arguments, however, UNIX system command arguments begin with the − (minus) character rather than the / (slash). The / character has another use in the UNIX system.

Commands usually allow many arguments, which help provide a great deal of the flexibility and power of the system. You can consult the *UNIX User's Manual*, the major reference document for the UNIX system, to learn the exact syntax for all arguments to all commands. (We will discuss the *UNIX User's Manual* in Chapter 8.)

Display a File

Now that you know that your home directory contains two files, you can display their contents. The **cat** (for concatenate files) command is provided to display files.

```
$ cat note
```

This command illustrates another general aspect of commands: filenames are usually arguments with no − or other argument marker.

The following command causes the contents of the file **note** to be displayed on your terminal:

```
$ cat note
Hello, steve, and welcome to the 'my_sys' system.  We all wish
you well in your exploration of the UNIX system, and we hope that
soon you'll be giving us advice on how to better use the
UNIX system                            =pat
$
```

There are several things to note here. First, the **cat** command displays the file and then returns directly to the "$" prompt for the next command. Second, the file is displayed without any extraneous headers or other material that was not in the file. Again, this is an attribute of the terse nature of the UNIX system that you will find very handy later on.

Delete a File

The **cat** command did not change the file, so it is still present. You can now delete the file if you wish with the **rm** (for *remove*) command.

```
$ rm note
$
```

The **rm** command silently deleted the file and then returned to the shell. If you try **ls** again, you will see that the file is gone:

```
$ ls
README
$
```

Under the UNIX system, you cannot recover a file once it is deleted with **rm**. Because the **rm** command is so powerful, you might wish that it prompt you for confirmation before it deletes a file. You can use the modified command **rm −i note** instead (the −i is for interactive):

```
$ rm −i note
note:
```

Here **rm** is prompting you to decide whether you really want the file **note** to be deleted. Enter y if you want to delete the file; enter anything else if you don't.

```
$ rm −i note
note: y
$
```

Once again the file is deleted. If you are deleting more than one file with a single invocation of **rm −i**, you will be prompted for confirmation before each file is deleted.

You can *interrupt* execution of the command while it is waiting for your input if you wish to return to the shell directly. Press DEL or BREAK on your keyboard to interrupt the execution of the command and return to the shell.

```
$ rm −i note
note:
$
```

In this case any files that you selected for deletion (by answering Y to the confirmation prompt) before you pressed the DEL key will be removed, but the rest will not.

You can take this *break* action with nearly all commands while they are waiting for your input. You can also use this technique to stop commands that are producing too much output or seem to be "hung." What do you think will happen if you press DEL while the shell is waiting for your input (at the "$" prompt)?

Read Your Mail

Recall that when you logged in, you saw the following message:

```
You have mail.
```

This prompt informs you that another user on the machine has sent you some electronic mail. If no mail was waiting, you would not have seen that prompt when you logged in.

Electronic mail is similar in function to mail that you get from the post office: it provides communications between users, everyone has a unique mailing address, and each message has an envelope and contents. You can read your mail with the **mail** command:

```
$ mail
```

This simply instructs the shell to run the **mail** command, which looks in your mailbox and displays each item in turn at your terminal.

```
$ mail
From jim Mon Apr  6 18:24 EST 1987
Hello, steve, welcome to the UNIX system. Why don't we go out to
lunch today and discuss your new computer system?    -Jim

?
```

The first line of this mail item is called the *postmark*. It tells you that the message is from "jim" and was sent on Mon Apr 6 18:24 EST 1987. You usually won't care about when the message was sent, but the postmark can be useful, as you will see in Chapter 13.

After the message is displayed, the **mail** program pauses for your input, prompting with "?" to let you know that it is waiting for a decision about that mail message. You can delete the message, skip to the next message (if there is one), save the message in a file, or take one of several other actions. You can delete the message by pressing d, followed by a RETURN, to tell the **mail** program that you're through with the message:

```
$ mail
From jim Mon Apr  6 18:24 EST 1987
Hello, steve, welcome to the UNIX system. Why don't we go out to
lunch today and discuss your new computer system?    -Jim

? d
$
```

The **mail** program silently and obediently deletes the message.

Because there is no more mail, the program ends and you are returned to the shell for your next command. If you had more messages in your mailbox, the next would have been displayed after you took some action with the first. Likewise, you could read, and dispose of in one way or another, each message in your mailbox.

The **mail** command includes some built-in help to remind you of all the options available at the "?" prompt. If you have not deleted a mail message, you can try entering ? instead of **d**, as shown in Figure 2-1. We will discuss these options later, but you can see that the **mail** command provides a rich set of operators for dealing with mail messages.

```
$ mail
From jim Mon Apr  6 18:24 EST 1987
Hello, steve, welcome to the UNIX system.  Why don't we go out to
lunch today and discuss your new computer system?   -Jim

? ?
#                    display message number #
-                    print previous
+                    next (no delete)
! cmd                execute cmd
a                    position at and read newly arrived mail
dq                   delete current message and exit
d [#]                delete message # (default current message)
h a                  display all headers
h d                  display headers of letters scheduled for deletion
h [#]                display headers around # (default current message)
m user               mail (and delete) current message to user
n                    next (no delete)
p                    print
q                    quit
r [args]             reply to (and delete) current letter via mail [args]
s [file]             save (and delete) current message (default mbox)
u [#]                undelete message # (default current message)
w [file]             save (and delete) current message without header
x                    exit without changing mail
y [file]             save (and delete) current message (default mbox)
?
```

Figure 2-1.   Help from the **mail** command

Send Mail

Since you received a mail message from another user, you can
send a message back. The **mail** command is used to send as well
as to read mail:

```
$ mail jim
```

In this case you give the **mail** command an argument. Unlike
the flag arguments signified by —, this argument is used to tell
mail the major target of the action that the command will take.

Here it is the addressee. The command **cat note** takes a file-name as a major argument, because the major function of **cat** is to concatenate and display files. But the **mail** command is used to communicate with other users, so its major argument is logically the login id of the user (or users) who will receive the mail. Like most other commands, **mail** allows more than one argument. You could enter

```
$ mail jim steve
```

to send the same message both to the login id "jim" and to yourself.

If you enter the above command, the **mail** program will begin executing and will pause while you type in your message. Enter the following message:

```
$ mail jim steve
Jim-- thanks for your welcome and lunch invitation.
I'd love to join you for lunch.
lets get together around noon.
See you then;  Steve
```

Type in as many lines as you wish. If you make a mistake, you can back up as many characters as needed with the BACKSPACE key, up to the beginning of the line. Once you press RETURN, however, the UNIX system (and the **mail** program in this case) will have accepted your input, and you cannot easily erase it. As usual, if you wish to stop the program and return to the shell without sending the message, press DEL. What happens if you do this?

Assuming that you do not abort the command with the DEL key, you will eventually need to tell **mail** that you have finished entering text. Do this by pressing CTRL-d. This tells the **mail** program that you are through entering the message:

```
$ mail jim steve
Jim-- thanks for your welcome and lunch invitation.
I'd love to join you for lunch.
lets get together around noon.
See you then;  Steve
CNTRL-d
You have mail.
$
```

The **mail** program will silently send the message (if there are no errors), and return to the shell for the next command.

Generally, this silent and terse behavior of commands holds true only if there are no errors in the command execution. No news is usually good news, and you can assume that if the command acts silently and returns to the shell without some error message, it probably completed successfully.

In the example above, you see that the shell has given you another prompt: it has repeated "You have mail." Because you sent a copy of the mail message to your own login id, the shell will prompt you that new mail has arrived. You will see this prompt only once until the next time you log into the system. You can choose to not read the mail immediately (especially if you just sent it!). Because the **mail** program sends the message before returning to the shell, and the shell looks at your mailbox to determine if any new mail has arrived, the "You have mail." prompt is sent to your terminal. This happens after the **mail** program completes but just before the shell returns with the "$" prompt for another command. The UNIX system often provides services like this, and you will occasionally see messages from the shell or from other programs that may be running in the system simultaneously. Remember, the UNIX system is a multitasking system, so several other things might be going on in the system at the same time as your session.

The UNIX system has many powerful tools for communications, both between users and between different machines. We will discuss these tools in Chapters 13 and 14.

Who's Logged In

Because it is a multiuser system, other people may be sharing the system with you, using other terminals attached to the machine. Normally you will not see these other users because the system makes you think that you have the machine all to yourself. However, there are tools to let you see who else is logged into the machine and to give you some idea of what they are doing.

Another theme that runs through the design of the UNIX system is that the users of a machine form a relatively friendly group of people who can easily communicate with each other and share files if needed. The UNIX system delicately balances the freedom of all users to wander around in the machine as a whole and the restrictions dictated by security considerations. The system provides excellent tools to identify the security status of user login id's, system-wide administrative files and programs, and your private files. (We will discuss this topic in more detail in Chapter 11.)

You can see who else is currently logged into the machine by using the **who** command.

```
$ who
```

Enter the command name as usual at the shell prompt "$" and press RETURN.

```
$ who
jim          console      Apr   7  14:05
steve        tty00        Apr   7  16:41
$
```

The results come to your terminal, and the **who** command ends, returning you to the shell prompt.

The output tells you that two users are currently logged into the system, "jim" and your own login id "steve." Some other information is also available. First is the terminal you are using. Your terminal, tty00, refers to a remote terminal known as tty00. The other user, "jim," is using the system console that is directly attached to the computer. The rest of the line shows you the date and time that the user logged into the system: "steve" logged in at 4:41 P.M. local time.

In a large UNIX system there may be more than one hundred users logged in at once, while in smaller machines there may be only one. It doesn't matter; the system lets each user behave as if she or he had the entire use of the machine.

Changing Your Password

You can accomplish one more chore—changing your password—before you end this session by logging out. The login id and password pair form the key to security in the UNIX system. If unfriendly hands gain access to these items, they can log into the system as you and do great damage to your files. They could even change your password, preventing you from logging in again until the system administrator patched up your login id. Therefore, you should keep your password a secret and change it frequently. Of course, you want everyone to know your login id so that they can send you mail and so on. But your password is like the key to your home: if it falls into the wrong hands, you might be in trouble.

As a new user of this machine, you expect that the system administrator created your login id with a preassigned sample password. This is already a potential security breach because most system administrators use a simple rule to generate passwords for new users. Your login id, or some such easily detected word, will often be given as a beginning password, so you should create your own private password as soon as you can.

If your new login id was established with no password by your system administrator, you probably will not see the "password:" prompt, but you will gain access to the system directly from the "Please login:" prompt. You should add a password as soon as possible.

The user password system is designed so that no one can figure out your password unless you tell them. That is, after you create your own private password, it is not available in the file system. It is *encrypted* such that if you forget it, no one can tell you what it is. The only thing that the system administrator can do is to delete the password and assign you a new one. So you should make every effort to remember your password. Of course some ways of remembering your password are not as wise as others. Don't, for example, write it on a slip of paper and attach it to your terminal.

Think of a new password for yourself, one that you can remember easily but will be difficult for someone else to figure out. The system usually demands that the password be at least six characters long and contain at least one digit or other nonalphabetic character. These rules, which have evolved from many years of security considerations, provide a large and complex range of passwords, making it difficult for someone else to determine yours.

Once you have decided on a new password, you can tell the system to use it from now on with the **passwd** command. Notice the peculiar spelling of this command name.

```
$ passwd
Old password:
```

The system will not let you change a password so easily. You must first enter your current (old) password to convince the **passwd** program that you're really who you claim to be. Type in your current password, and you'll notice that the characters are not echoed as you type. The UNIX system treats all passwords this way. If you make a mistake, the **passwd** program will exit, returning you to the shell to try again. When you enter your current password correctly, **passwd** will let you enter a new one:

```
$ passwd
Old password:
New password:
```

Type in your new choice; again, it will not be echoed.

```
$ passwd
Old password:
New password:
Re-enter new password:
```

Now **passwd** wants you to type in your new password a second time, just to verify that you entered it correctly. If the two entries do not match, the **passwd** command will complain and then let you try again.

```
$ passwd
Old password:
New password:
Re-enter new password:
They don't match; try again.
New password:
```

You didn't hurt anything, and you can enter the password again (twice!). If you press DEL now, **passwd** will exit with your old password still in force. If you have entered the password the same both times, the **passwd** command will change the system's idea of your password and then return to the shell as usual for your next command.

Logging Out

When you are through with your session, you should tell the system that you are finished by *logging out*. When you log out, the UNIX system will free the terminal for someone else, or you can log in again immediately if you choose, perhaps with a different login id. Logging out also prevents unfriendly people from using your terminal and user id to cause potential mischief. You should log out whenever you are away from the terminal, especially if the terminal is in a public place, such as a business office. The two most important factors for maintaining the security of a UNIX system are keeping the passwords secure and logging out whenever you are away from your terminal. If your machine is physically secure in a room that only you have access to, these rules are not as significant. However, you should learn good security practices early and continue to observe them as long as you are using the system.

The UNIX system provides two different procedures for

logging out. First, the **exit** command will log you off the machine.

```
$ exit

Welcome to the "my_sys" System.
Please login:
```

The UNIX system stops execution of your shell, resets itself, and returns the terminal to the initial "login" prompt. You can now turn off the terminal or log in again.

Instead of using the **exit** command, you could have logged off the machine by pressing CTRL-D. This is the *end-of-file* mark, and the shell takes it as a signal to log off. We will discuss the use of the end-of-file mark in Chapter 3.

Some UNIX systems are configured so that turning off the power on your terminal or console will also log you off the system. Terminals connected to the machine through dial-up telephone lines and modems usually act this way. However, until you are sure of the behavior of your machine, you should always log off explicitly before hanging up the telephone line or turning off the power on the terminal.

Going Further

At a terminal, you end commands or other text lines by pressing RETURN or entering NEWLINE. In UNIX system jargon the symbol used to end a line of text is the NEWLINE character. At a terminal, the RETURN or ENTER key usually acts like NEWLINE, but in fact the ASCII character for NEWLINE is the *linefeed* character. Experiment with your terminal and system by ending a line of text with linefeed (CTRL-j) instead of RETURN. Does the system act the same?

The Shell I

The *shell* is the software that listens to commands typed in at the terminal and translates them into instructions in the system's internal syntax. The name *shell* really describes the function: it is hard material that stands between the core of the system and the outside world, providing a robust *user interface* for the operating system. The shell includes an unusually large number of functions; in fact, it implements some of the most powerful and elegant concepts in the UNIX system. Much effort has been dedicated to improving the shell and creating new versions of it for special purposes. The shell is so vital that it usually isn't considered apart from the system as a whole. Many capabilities and functions come from services provided by the shell. In this chapter we will examine more functions of the UNIX system, focusing primarily on those services provided by the shell.

Commands in the UNIX System

Commands are usually separate executable programs that the shell finds and executes in response to typed instructions, such as **mail** and **who**. But the shell is actually much more powerful and useful than just a means of passing commands to the system for execution.

The shell helps you use the machine. First and foremost, the shell is a *command interpreter* that can expand and change the command (according to built-in rules) before it is executed. Equally important are the *wild-card* and *command connection* operators, which can make a command line more general and flexible. Also, commands can take advantage of conditions in the current user *environment*, managed by the shell, to modify the way they work.

Command Structure

When you type a command such as **cat** to the shell, you will frequently add *command line arguments*. These are the modifying *flags* that usually begin with a − (minus) sign as well as major arguments such as filenames or other user login id's. Commands are of this form:

```
$ pr -d note
```

The **pr** command is used to print files. Actually the output goes to the terminal rather than to a printer, so **pr** is something like the **cat** command. While **cat** is better at concatenating multiple files, **pr** is better at paginating and columnizing files.

In the UNIX system command syntax, flags follow the command name and precede the major arguments. The command given above tells **pr** to copy the file **note** to the terminal, making a double-spaced copy of the input file. A filename is given as a major argument, and the function of the command is modified with the flag (−**d** in this case, to indicate double spacing). Neither the flag nor filename argument is required for most commands.

If you wish, you can add a second flag to the **pr** command:

```
$ pr -n -d note
```

This tells **pr** to generate both double-spaced (−**d**) and line-numbered output (−**n**). All flags precede all filename arguments. An equivalent form of this command is the following:

```
$ pr -nd note
```

You can combine flags with a single − to mark the beginning of the flags.

The example given above produces a double-spaced listing at the terminal with line numbers beginning "1, 2, 3, 4...." You can use the same command to produce output with line numbers beginning "1, 3, 5, 7...."

```
$ pr -n2 -d note
```

The −**n** flag of the **pr** command can have an argument of its own, which signifies the interval between the numbers it puts onto each line. So you say **pr** −**n2** to count lines by twos rather than by ones. You could also use one of these alternate forms:

```
$ pr -n2 -d note
$ pr -d -n2 note
$ pr -d -n 2 note
$ pr -d        -n 2      note
$ pr -dn2 note
```

They are all equivalent because the system cares neither about

the order of flag arguments, nor whether each flag has its own
— sign, nor about extra spaces between the flags.

The following forms, however, would not do what you
expect:

```
$ pr - n2 -d note
$ pr -nd2 note
$ pr note -nd2
```

You need to place the — sign directly in front of the flag argument, with no intervening space, and you must place the flags
(if any) before the filename(s). Also, you must make sure that
the argument modifying a flag, such as the 2 in this example, is
next to the flag it modifies. Generally, when you make a mistake the command will respond with a message reminding you
of the correct form, though sometimes the mistake will be
subtle and the command will execute incorrectly. That doesn't
usually hurt anything.

You can add a second filename to the **pr** command if you
wish.

```
$ pr note README
```

The list of filenames is given on the same command line, separated with *white space*, which is simply any spaces or tab characters. You always need at least one white space character to
separate arguments, though more is also acceptable.

In these commands

```
$ pr -dl note README
$ cat note
$ pr -d -l 2 README
```

the first has three arguments and the second has one. Arguments are counted from the command, **pr** in this case. The
command name is called *argument zero* of the command
entered to the shell, —**dl** is the first argument, and the two
filenames are the second and third, respectively. The third
command above is **pr** with four arguments, even though the
2 is associated with the —**l** flag. Arguments are separated by
white space, so the command

the −l flag. Arguments are separated by white space, so the command

```
$ pr -d -l 2 README
```

is a **pr** command with four arguments, of which two are flags, one is associated with a flag, and the last is a filename.

Many commands accept multiple filenames as arguments. Compare the output from the **pr** command given above with the output from the following:

```
$ cat note README
```

The differences arise from the different functions associated with the two commands. The **cat** command is designed to concatenate files together, so the two files seem to run together in the output, while **pr** is intended primarily to paginate files, so the header material is associated with each filename in turn.

Command Line Expansion

The shell provides tools that make it easy to specify multiple filenames as command arguments. Two special characters, called wild-card characters, can substitute for filenames or parts of filenames.

In the sample directory containing the files **note** and **README**, the command

```
$ cat *
```

is equivalent to **cat note README**. That is, the * (asterisk) character tells the shell to "take all the files in the directory." Actually the shell looks at the filenames, rebuilds the command line with the full names in place of the wild-card characters, and then executes the command.

The * wild-card character can also be embedded within a partial filename. For example,

```
$ cat RE*
```

will concatenate all files that begin with *RE*, while

```
$ cat *AD*
```

will concatenate all files that contain *AD* in their names. Unlike the * wild-card character in MS-DOS file naming, which can only substitute for the name section of the filename or the extension section, the * in the shell substitutes for any character sequence in the command.

The second wild-card character is the ? (question mark), which substitutes for any single character in a filename. For example,

```
$ cat ?EADME
```

would display the **README** file, as would the following command:

```
$ cat ?E?DME
```

However,

```
$ cat R?DME
```

would not find the file because the ? can only substitute for one character.

You can also mix these two wild-card characters in the same command. For example,

```
$ ls ??A*
```

would list the names of all the files with *A* in the third position in the filename.

The example given above would also find a file named **REA**. Actually the wild-card character * tells the shell to "substitute all strings of zero or more characters." On the other hand, the ? must match a real character in the filename. For example,

```
$ ls README?
```

would not find the file **README**, but

```
$ ls README*
```

would find it.

Environment Variables

Another service provided by the shell is the maintenance of *environment variables*, which are character strings of the form *name=value*, where "name" can be any character string that does not include the $ (dollar) sign and does not have embedded white space, and *value* can be any character string including spaces. Many environment variables are usually associated with your login id, and they vary depending on the system, the installed software, and your personal preferences.

You set an environment variable by giving the name=value pair to the shell:

```
$ SAMPLE="hello world"
```

The shell recognizes this command as the definition of an environment variable, and it remembers the name and value. Notice that the convention is to name environment variables in uppercase characters, but this is not required. Immediately after the name, without intervening white space, add the = (equal) sign, and then enter the value you wish. You must *quote* the value section of this assignment by surrounding it with the "(double quote) character because it includes a space. We will discuss this further below.

You needn't predefine or declare the name of an environment variable before you use it. The shell will determine if the name is already in use. If it is, the shell will change the value of that environment variable to the new value and discard the old value. If the name is not already in use, the shell will create it for you.

When you want the value of an environment variable, name it beginning with the $ (dollar) sign. This tells the shell to recognize the following string as an environment variable, and to take its value; otherwise, the shell would interpret the string as a simple character string.

You can use the **echo** command to display the value of an environment variable.

```
$ echo $SAMPLE
```

The following command tells the shell to write the value of the environment variable to the terminal.

```
$ echo $SAMPLE
hello world
$
```

What happens if you enter the following command?

```
$ echo SAMPLE
```

You can use environment variables as command names or as command arguments as you wish. For example:

```
$ XYZ="cat note"
$ $XYZ
Hello, steve, and welcome to the 'my_sys' system.  We all wish
you well in your exploration of the UNIX system, and we hope that
soon you'll be giving us advice on how to better use the
UNIX system                            =pat
$
```

Before executing your command, the shell substitutes the value associated with the name into your command as entered. You can use this mechanism to assign long but frequently used commands to a short environment variable; then you can enter only the environment variable (beginning with $ so that it is interpreted by the shell!), and the shell will execute the assigned value.

You can also use the **echo** command to echo arbitrary strings to the terminal.

```
$ echo hello $SAMPLE world
hello hello world world
$
```

You could also embed the environment variable inside another character string.

```
$ echo hello${SAMPLE}world
hellohello worldworld
$
```

Because the shell doesn't know if you meant the environment variable *$SAMPLE* or *$SAMPLEworld*, you must *protect* the name SAMPLE when it is not surrounded by white space. The *curly brackets* do this when they immediately follow the **$**. Undefined environment variables are usually ignored by the shell. What happens if you enter the following?

```
$ echo hello$SAMPLEworld
```

There are usually 10 to 30 more-or-less permanent environment variables associated with your login id. They are usually assigned by the system when you log in and are maintained by the shell until you log off. Some of these permanent environment variables are used directly by the shell, while others may be used by specific application packages for their own purposes. You can look at all your currently assigned environment variables with the following command:

```
$ env
```

The **env** command will display a complete list, each of the form name=value.

```
$ env
LOGDIR=/usr/steve
HOME=/usr/steve
SHELL=/bin/sh
MAIL=/usr/mail/steve
EDITOR=/usr/bin/vi
LOGNAME=steve
UMASK=00
TERM=ansi
PATH=:/usr/steve/lib:/bin:/usr/bin:/usr/lbin:/etc
TZ=EST5EDT
$
```

You may have many more than these.

Add or change environment variables as you wish, but be careful not to change the value of existing environment variables because they may be used in commands or applications. Before you use an environment variable name for the first time, check to see whether it is already in use. If you try to echo the value of a nonexistent environment variable, the shell will display nothing.

```
$ echo $ISANY
$
```

This tells you that you can use the environment variable for your own purposes.

Quoting Command Line Arguments

The shell will interpret a character string with embedded white space as multiple arguments because it uses the white space as delimiters to divide up the command line. For example:

```
$ SAMPLE=hello world
world: not found
$
```

The error message following the assignment of the environment variable *SAMPLE* occurs because the shell interpreted the string *hello world* as two separate arguments. Because the name=value pair of the environment variable assignment requires the value to be a single argument, the shell assigns it the value *hello*. Then the shell tries to interpret the next argument, **world**, as a command to execute; however, because there is no command named world, the shell complains that it cannot find the command. The command line is discarded.

You solve this problem by *quoting* the value, that is by surrounding the string you wish to protect with the " (double quote) character. For example:

```
$ SAMPLE="hello world"
$ echo $SAMPLE
hello world
$
```

You made the string a single argument when you quoted it. You can do this for any argument to a command because command line arguments are processed by the shell, and the shell interprets the quote operator ".

The double quote operator does not protect the quoted string from interpretation of environment variables. You can use this property to construct command line arguments with both environment variables and embedded white space.

```
$ SAMPLE="My login id is $LOGNAME"
$ echo $SAMPLE
My login id is steve
$
```

On the other hand, you may wish to prevent evaluation of environment variables but include their name in a command line. The shell allows this; use ' (single quote) instead of the double quote. For example:

```
$ SAMPLE='Use $LOGNAME to determine my login id'
$ echo $SAMPLE
Use $LOGNAME to determine my login id
$
```

You can also quote your command line arguments with the single quotes if you wish to have an embedded " character:

```
$ echo '"hello world"'
"hello world"
$
```

In this example the double quotes are no longer shell operators because they are protected by the single quotes. Thus they are treated as part of the character string you wish to echo.

PS1

Some environment variables are used by the shell but may not appear in the output of the **env** command. One of these, *PS1* (for prompt symbol, level one), is the value of your shell prompt, which until this point has been "$" (dollar). You can look at its value with the **echo** command.

```
$ echo $PS1
$
$
```

In this example the **echo** command has displayed the value of the prompt; then the shell has printed it to signal that it is ready for the next command.

You can change the value of *PS1* just like any other environment variable.

```
$ PS1="hello: "
hello:
```

Now the shell prompt is no longer "$" but the value that you just assigned, *hello:*. You can make your prompt be any character string that you wish.

Environment variables are evaluated when they are entered, not when they are executed. For example:

```
$ SAMPLE="Your command master: "
$ PS1=$SAMPLE
Your command master: SAMPLE=hello
Your command master: echo $SAMPLE
hello
Your command master:
```

PS1 was set to the value of *$SAMPLE*, but as you change *$SAMPLE* again, *$PS1* does not change. The command to set *PS1* to *$SAMPLE* was evaluated when *$SAMPLE* was "Your command master:", so that becomes the new value of *PS1*, not the value of *$SAMPLE* when *$PS1* is printed.

Standard Input and Output

So far you have entered commands by typing them at the terminal, and the output of the commands has been displayed at the terminal. Actually most commands take input from any *input stream* and write their output on an *output stream*. That is, commands are implemented such that they read a sequence of characters as input and produce a sequence of characters as output. These input and output character sequences are called streams because there is really no internal structure in the character strings. The command just sees a long sequence of characters as input. Even the NEWLINE character is not treated differently, although some commands (like the shell!) take action on character sequences ending with NEWLINE. The input stream for a command is called *standard input* and the output stream is called *standard output*. For example, the command

```
$ echo $PS1
```

writes to standard output.

The shell usually arranges things so that the standard input of a command comes from the terminal keyboard and standard output goes to the terminal display. However, you can redirect standard input and standard output to files. For example:

```
$ cat note > n.copy
$
```

The > (right arrow) character tells the shell to redirect standard output to a file, in this case one named **n.copy**. The shell will create the file if it does not exist or will empty an existing file before writing the command output to the file. You can easily destroy an existing file in this way, so be careful before redirecting output.

You can also redirect standard input to come from a file instead of from the terminal by using the < (left arrow) symbol.

```
$ mail jim < note
$
```

In this example the contents of the file **note** are used as input to the command **mail jim**. The result will be that Jim will receive the file in his electronic mail. This has the same effect as if you executed the command **mail jim** and typed the contents of the file **note** at the keyboard.

You can combine redirection of both standard input and standard output at the same time. For example:

```
$ pr < note > n.copy
$
```

This example causes the shell to execute the command **pr** with the file **note** as input, with output going to the file **n.copy**. Notice that the shell requires the command name to be first on the line, with the redirection operators following. You can also write any of the following commands:

```
$ pr > n.copy < note
$ pr >n.copy <note
$ pr <note >n.copy
$ pr >n.copy<note
```

but the form

```
$ n.copy > pr < note
```

is incorrect. It is good practice to separate redirection operators from command names and arguments with blanks, but this is not required. Notice that you could have used an environment variable if you wished.

```
$ SAMPLE=note
$ pr < $SAMPLE > n.copy
$
```

Standard input/output (I/O) and stream redirection are some of the most general and powerful features of the UNIX system, and they have some important implications. First, most commands are designed to work with simple byte streams as input and output in order to make redirection most powerful. Almost all files are simple streams of bytes, with no internal structure such as seen in record-oriented file systems. The meaning of a file is determined solely by the application or user who uses the file and is not enforced by any property of the UNIX system. Because most commands use standard input and output, there are consistent and reliable ways of using I/O. You can usually interchange the keyboard, files, and hardware devices in your commands.

Some commands allow you to give filenames as arguments instead of requiring you to redirect standard input from a file to the command. This is a property of the commands and is not enforced by the operating system or the shell, so it does not always work. For example, the two commands

```
$ cat < note
$ cat note
```

are equivalent, because the **cat** command operates on a file or on its standard input. Like many commands, **cat** lets you mix both files and standard input in the same command. The following forms are also equivalent:

```
$ cat note README n.copy
$ cat note - n.copy < README
```

The — (minus) alone as an argument, with no attached flag letter, is often used by commands to signify "take the standard input at that point." In the second example above, **cat** processes the file **note**, takes standard input that was redirected from the

file **README**, and then processes the file **n.copy**.
Similarly, the command

```
$ cat note - n.copy > output
```

would process the file **note**, wait for your input from the keyboard, and then process the file **n.copy**. Because you did not
redirect standard input, the shell leaves it attached to the
keyboard.

The End-of-File Mark

If you use the keyboard as standard input, you must tell commands like **cat** that you are through entering characters and
that it should continue its work as if the file you entered
through the keyboard had ended. The UNIX system provides a
special character that is used as the *end-of-file mark* when it is
the first character on a line. This character does not appear at
the end of a disk file because the system can tell when a disk file
ends. However, when you are using the keyboard as a file, the
system doesn't know when you are through unless you tell it.
The CTRL-D key combination is used as the end-of-file mark
when entered from the keyboard. You form this character by
holding down the CTRL key on the keyboard and pressing the D
key.

In the command

```
$ cat note - n.copy > output
```

cat will process the file **note**, wait for input from the terminal,
and read your typed input until you press CTRL-D, and then go
on to process the file **n.copy**. All three sources of input will be
joined in the file output.

Appending Standard Output to a File

Because the > operator causes an existing file to be emptied and re-created, all the old contents of the file will be lost. Sometimes you would like to have the output of a command added to the end of an existing file. There are several ways to accomplish this. The command sequence

```
$ pr < note > n.copy
$ cat note n.copy > dup.note
$ rm n.copy
$
```

will make the file **dup.note** contain both the original **note** and the one produced from the **pr** command. Another way to accomplish the same thing is with the >> operator, which tells the shell to redirect standard output to a file but to just add the new characters onto the end of the file instead of truncating it first. This command sequence

```
$ cat note > dup.note
$ pr note >> dup.note
$
```

will produce the same result as the example given above but with one less command. If the file given as target to the >> operator does not exist, it will be created for you. Note that the >> operator can contain no white space between the > characters. There is no equivalent << operator for standard input.

Standard Error

We have discussed standard input and output of commands, but the system also provides a third stream, *standard error.*

Most commands use the standard error stream to display any error messages or unusual output that you don't want in the standard output stream. You don't want error messages mixing with normal output, so the system will write these messages on another stream. You can see standard error in operation if you intentionally create an incorrect command. For example, if you try to **cat** a file that does not exist, you see an error message.

```
$ cat no.file
cat: cannot open no.file
$
```

If you now redirect the standard output of the **cat** command,

```
$ cat no.file > output
cat: cannot open no.file
$
```

the results are the same. The error message still appears at the terminal. You can redirect standard error by using the operator **2>** or **2>>**, depending on whether you want to create a new file or *append* data to an existing file, respectively:

```
$ cat no.file 2> output
$ cat output
cat: cannot open no.file
$
```

The peculiar notation **2>** is used because standard I/O channels are assigned numbers: 0 refers to standard input, 1 refers to standard output, and 2 refers to standard error. These numbers are used primarily by programmers in developing software, but in this case the number 2 has crept into the user-level access to the shell.

Pipes

You will often wish to take the output of one command and use it as the input to another. For example, you might use the following command sequence:

```
$ cat note README > temp
$ pr < temp
$ rm temp
$
```

You may not be very interested in saving the intermediate file, but you want the output of the **cat** command to be used as the input to the **pr** command. While the command sequence given above will work, the shell provides a more powerful and elegant operator for this purpose, the |(pipe) operator. A command line built with the pipe operator is known as a *pipeline*. Use the | operator to tell the shell that you wish the output of one command to be used as the input to another command. For example,

```
$ cat note README | pr
$
```

will concatenate the files **note** and **README**, and use the standard output as the standard input of the **pr** command. The standard output of **pr** will come to the terminal, but you could redirect it with the following:

```
$ cat note README | pr > output
$
```

There are other command lines that accomplish the same function. You could have redirected the input to **cat** with the following:

```
$ cat - README < note | pr > output
$
```

Read this last example as two separate commands separated with the | operator: **cat − README < note** and **pr > output**. The standard output of the first command is attached to the standard input of the second. Redirection is local to the part of the pipeline where it appears, so this command is not equivalent to the previous one:

```
$ cat - README | pr > output < note
$
```

In most cases standard input goes into the beginning of a pipeline (reading from left to right on the command line), and standard output emerges from the end or right-hand side of the pipeline. However, a command line must always begin with a legal command. The following command line is incorrect:

```
$ note > cat - README | pr > output
```

Also, the | operator only connects commands; you must use the > and < operators to signify redirection of data files. This is also incorrect

```
$ note | cat - README | pr > output
```

unless you have a command named **note** in your system!

Filters

The pipeline is not limited to only two commands. You can build up pipelines of arbitrary length just by attaching the standard output of one command to the standard input of the next. The

UNIX system has many commands that are intended to be used in this way. These commands are often called *filters*, because they pass their input to their output, changing it on the way through the program. The changes made by the filter program will depend on the specific program.

The **tr** (for translate characters) program is a classic example of a filter. It takes two arguments, which are interpreted as sets of characters (not character strings this time). The **tr** program copies its standard input to its output, but for each character in the character set given as first argument, **tr** will replace that character with the character in the same position in the second argument.

```
$ echo "hello world" | tr e 3
h3llo world
$
```

The **tr** command is unusual because it will not take a filename for its input; it only reads its standard input. A little trickier is the following:

```
$ echo "hello world" | tr eo 34
h3114 w4rld
$
```

Fields and Delimiters

A more useful command that is often used as a filter is **cut**. The **cut** command is used to copy only some parts of each line of its standard input to its output. A *field* of a line is a string of characters separated by a fixed *delimiter* character. The UNIX system uses several different field delimiter characters in different situations, though three commonly used delimiters are the *tab* character, the *space*, and the *colon*.

The form \t signifies the tab character when printing it in text like this book, but to create it, you press the TAB key on the keyboard. The idea of the line consisting of fields is similar to the way you counted arguments in commands to the shell, but in that instance the field delimiter was any white space character. In many other situations the **:** (colon) is used as a delimiter.

The **cut** command is used to copy only some fields of an input line to the output. In creating a command line for the **cut** command, you must tell it which field or fields to copy to the output and what delimiter character will separate the fields on the input line. You might consider the following file as a set of data *records*, with one record per line:

```
$ cat datafile
123:543:654:234
987:753:123:765
435:765:135:963
$
```

Each record in this example consists of four fields separated by the **:** delimiter; the end of the line delimits each record. If you had needed to use the **:** as a character within a field you would have chosen a different delimiter character. You must select the delimiter carefully to be sure that it is not used in the data.

You can use the **cut** command to show only part of the data in this simple *database*. If you want to see only the second field on each line, the following command line is appropriate:

```
$ cut -f2 -d: < datafile
```

Use the **−d** (for delimiter) argument to tell the **cut** command to use the **:** character as a delimiter, and use the **−f** (for field) argument to tell the **cut** command that you wish to copy only the second field to the output.

```
$ cut -f2 -d: < datafile
543
753
765
$
```

Notice that the delimiter character is not included in the output and that each line of input produces one line of output.

The **cut** command also lets you save more than one field of your input lines.

```
$ cut -f1,2,4 -d: < datafile
123:543:234
987:753:765
435:765:963
$
```

Fields 1, 2, and 4 of the input file are selected in this example, cutting out field 3. The fields are selected with the −**f1,2,4** argument, with each field that you wish to copy listed, separated with commas. In the output the fields are separated with the original delimiter, the colon.

You could also change the delimiter character. What happens if you use the character 3 as a delimiter? The system lets you do this if you wish, because there is nothing special about any of the characters; you just made the **:** the delimiter in the example above as a *convention*, or an agreement to be consistent in some area to make life easier. Many commands use **:** as a delimiter, but you will often find reasons to use different or multiple delimiters.

```
$ cat datafile
123:543:654:234
987:753:123:765
435:765:135:963
$ cut -f2 -d3 < datafile
:54
:12
5:765:1
$
```

The output looks a little confusing, but you can understand it if you read the line

```
123:543:654:234
```

as four fields separated by the **3** character: 12, :54, :654:2, and 4. In the UNIX system files are just streams of characters; the system does not enforce any special structure on data.

The **cut** command can also cut its input lines based on the *columns* that a field falls into. The word *column* is a holdover from the days when data was stored on punched cards, each of which had 80 columns (which accounts for most terminals having 80 character positions on a line). We still refer to lines of input as having columns, even though the system treats data as a stream of characters with no intrinsic column positions. As another convention, we agree that the NEWLINE character in the input stream tells us to begin counting columns until we see the next NEWLINE character.

You can create a **cut** command that operates on fields in columns.

```
$ cut -c5-8 datafile
```

Notice that the **cut** command can also take a filename or list of filenames as command line arguments, as well as reading its standard input. The example given above uses the −**c5−8** (for column) argument to select columns 5 through 8 of the input file as one field. We mark the *range* of a field with a − (dash).

```
$ cat datafile
123:543:654:234
987:753:123:765
435:765:135:963
$ cut -c5-8 datafile
543:
753:
765:
$
```

Again, the **cut** command is counting column positions in each line of the file, so the **:** has no special meaning in this example.

Another commonly used filter is the **sort** command. The **sort** command is used to rearrange its input lines into an alphabetic or numeric sequence.

```
$ sort < datafile
123:543:654:234
435:765:135:963
987:753:123:765
```

The **sort** command does not change the contents of each line, but it will rearrange the lines into alphabetic or numeric order. By default, **sort** will sort the file by using the beginning of the line as the *key* field, the character string that is used to alphabetize the lines. However, **sort** lets you use any field in the file, and the field detection rules are similar to those used with the **cut** command. (We will discuss **sort** in more detail in Chapter 6.)

You can combine **cut** and **sort** in a pipeline for many purposes. You can use it, for example, to look at all the names of your environment variables, in alphabetical order.

```
$ env | cut -f1 -d= | sort
EDITOR
HOME
LOGDIR
LOGNAME
MAIL
PATH
SHELL
TERM
TZ
UMASK
$
```

The = (equal) sign was used as a field delimiter, and the command cut the name part out of each name=value environment variable and then sorted the names into alphabetical order. The output came to standard output, the terminal, because it was not redirected.

Many filters are intended as the last element of a pipeline. A good example is the **pg** (for pager) command. This command will prevent output that is directed to the screen from scrolling off the screen too fast to view. The function of the **pg** filter is to break up the output into screen-sized chunks. It will display a screenful and then pause, displaying a : (colon) at the bottom of the screen. When you press the RETURN key, it will display another screenful. This process will continue until the output reaches its end-of-file, when **pg** will return to the shell for the next command. The **pg** command was adapted from an older command called **more**, and some systems still use the older name. You can see it in action if you try to display a file that is longer than a single screenful. Try the following command:

```
$ echo /etc/profile | pg
```

If you want to stop the **pg** program before its output is completed, you can press the DEL key to return to the shell immediately, whenever **pg** has paused.

You can make a pipeline as long as you wish. Many examples of pipelines contain more than five or six commands, and a great many commands are designed to be used as filters.

Fairly sophisticated applications can be developed using only sequences of pipelines, but the major benefit of the ideas of stream files, standard I/O, redirection of I/O, and command pipelines is to allow you to create solutions to file-related or data-related problems easily and quickly at the terminal. The example above, of listing, cutting, and sorting your environment variables, might have required the development of an application program in BASIC, C, or Pascal in another operating system. In the UNIX system many of your ad hoc questions and problems can be solved with pipelines of commands that operate on data files consisting of character streams and ASCII text lines.

Return Values from Commands

In addition to their standard output and standard error, commands return a numeric *return code* invisibly to the shell. This value is usually zero if the command completes successfully and some nonzero value if the command fails for any reason. The nonzero values are command dependent. These values can range from 0 through 255; and the different possible failures of a command are usually associated with different return codes. You can see this value with the variable *$?* (dollar question mark). This value is reset after each command to be the return value of that command. So if you wish to save it, you must assign it to a new environment variable. This assignment actually causes the value of *$?* to change, but luckily not until after it has been assigned to your "safe" new environment variable. For example:

```
$ cat no.file
cat: cannot open no.file
$ SAVE=$?
$ echo $?
0
$ echo $SAVE
2
$
```

Only the return value from the very last command that is executed is saved in the *$?* variable.

The *$?* variable is not actually an environment variable like those discussed above but belongs to another class of object called *shell variables*. This is because the shell variables are not available to executed commands like the true environment variables but rather are maintained internally by the shell. The shell variables are single character names, but as usual, when you want to see their value, you must precede the name with *$*. There are several other shell variables as well as *?*, including # (gives the number of command line arguments for this shell) and *$* (gives the *process number* of this shell). The value of the shell variable *$* is accessed by *$$*. (We will discuss these shell variables in more detail in Chapter 7.)

The Grave Operator

You can also take the standard output of a command and assign it to an environment variable. You must take care when you do this because the length of the value part of the name=value pair that makes up an environment variable is limited, usually to 256 characters. The ` (grave or backquote) operator is used.

```
$ SAMPLE=`echo $LOGNAME`
```

This assigns the standard output of the command **echo $LOGNAME** to the environment variable *SAMPLE*.

```
$ SAMPLE=`echo $LOGNAME"`
$ echo $SAMPLE
steve
$
```

Note that the grave character is not the single quote character but is another character on the ASCII keyboard.

A good example of how to use the ` operator to advantage involves the command **wc** (for word count). This is a filter that reads its standard input (or a filename given as argument) and produces a count of the number of lines, words, and characters in the input. Words are character strings surrounded by white space. For example:

```
$ wc note
     4      44     227 note
$
```

The file **note** contains four lines, with 44 words and a total of 227 characters. The command

```
$ wc < note
```

or

```
$ cat note | wc
```

would give the same result, except that because no filenames were given as arguments to **wc**, the output will not include the filename.

```
$ cat note | wc
     4      44     227
$
```

The **wc** command can take three arguments, −l, −w, and/or −c, to limit the output to lines, words, or characters, respectively. For example:

```
$ wc -w < note
      44
$
```

You might use this form as the end of a pipeline and assign the result to an environment variable for later use.

```
$ ALLWORDS=`cat * | wc -w`
$ echo $ALLWORDS
73
$
```

In this example you created the pipeline **cat** * | **wc** −**w** and assigned the standard output to the environment variable *ALLWORDS*. Recall that the * character is expanded by the shell to refer to all filenames in the relevant directory before the command is executed.

Going Further

The functions of the shell discussed here include most of the fundamental tools that the shell provides to the user. However, the shell is really a very useful and powerful programming language that lets you easily build useful tools from the commands. Shell programming is often used both by users and to implement key operating system functions. We will discuss using the shell as a programming language in Chapter 7, after a detour for a discussion of the file system and some more of the user commands.

Command Sequences

The shell offers several more operators for combining commands into a command line. You can use the **;** (semicolon) operator to put two or more commands on the same command line. Unlike the pipe operator, the **;** doesn't connect the commands together; it just separates independent commands that happen to be on the same command line. For example:

```
$ ls ; echo hello
README
note
hello
$
```

The output of the **echo** command directly follows the output from the **ls** command at your terminal.

You might also use the following:

```
$ SAMPLE=`ls ; echo hello`
$ echo $SAMPLE
README note hello
$
```

In this example the environment variable _SAMPLE_ will contain a list of the names of your files, and **echo** will add a name that is not an existing file. The return value from a command sequence separated with the **;** operator is the value of the last command entered, in this example the **echo** command. There are a great many uses for command sequences, as we will see in later chapters.

Shell Redirection

The shell is known by the name **sh** (for shell). Because **sh** is a normal command, you can execute it just like any other command. The instance of the shell that is listening to your commands as you type them is called your _login shell_ because it starts when you log in and ends when you log out. Its standard input is attached to your keyboard when you log in, and its standard output is attached to your terminal's display. If you wish, you can execute another instance of the shell as a command.

```
$ sh
```

If you do this, you have *recursively* created a second copy of the shell that is now listening to commands and executing them. However, the login shell is still around, waiting patiently for the command (another instance of the shell!) to end so that it can go back to work. You can end the second shell with the **exit** command, and then you'll return to the original shell, or you can end it by pressing CTRL-D as the end-of-file mark for the input to that shell. Then you must kill your login shell when you want to log off. When you have a second shell, it will still print the PS1 prompt, and it can be very difficult to determine which shell is in control (unless you change your PS1 prompt). You can take advantage of this feature if you wish to use a different shell than the one you get when you log in, perhaps a shell that allows editing of command lines before you hit the RETURN key to execute it. We'll see an example of this later.

Another use of the shell as a normal executable command is very widely used. Imagine that instead of typing your commands directly to the shell, you make a file that contains some commands, perhaps some commonly used sequence of commands that you execute regularly. You might create this list of commands with a text editor, or simply by entering the following:

```
$ cat > cmds
```

Then you can type in your commands until you press CTRL-D to signal end of file to **cat**, and instead of being executed as you type, the commands are saved in the file **cmds**, to which you have redirected the output of **cat**.

Now you can take that file of commands and use it as redirected standard input to a **sh** command.

```
$ sh < cmds
```

This executes a second copy of the shell, giving it the file **cmds** as input. The shell (not your login shell, remember) will read and execute the commands in the file, writing the results to the standard output, which is your terminal. If you also redirect the output from this command, you can save the results in a file:

```
$ sh < cmds > output
```

You might also wish to save the standard error output in another file, in case something goes wrong.

```
$ sh < cmds > output 2> errors
```

The shell uses these concepts, though in a form that is much easier to use, to implement *shell programs.*

The File System

**F
O
U
R**

Another major contribution of the UNIX system to computing technology is the *file system*. File management in the UNIX system is extremely flexible and powerful, so much so that the file system concepts have been widely adopted in other operating systems, notably MS-DOS. The UNIX system provides a *hierarchical directory* scheme. A directory is a "container" for a group of files, and directories can be included in other directories, resulting in a large structure that can be drawn as a *tree*. Commands, data files, other directories, and even hardware *devices* can be represented as directory entries. The UNIX system provides a powerful but simple way to name a specific file or directory within the file system, so that commands can easily understand where to find the things you enter as filenames on the command line.

In this chapter we will introduce files and directories and look at some of the commands that manipulate them.

Files and Directories

A *file* is a sequence of bytes of data that resides in semipermanent form on some stable medium such as a magnetic disk or tape. This file can contain anything that you can represent as a stream of bytes, including executable programs, such as commands; text, such as mail messages or book manuscripts; databases; bit-maps that might be screen images or pictures; and so forth. If you can put it onto a disk or tape and can name it, then it can be a file. Although the system considers any file to be a simple, undifferentiated sequence of bytes, a user or application program may impose additional structure on the contents of a file to give it more meaning.

Text files are a simple example of this additional structure. In text files a special ASCII character called NEWLINE is used to delimit lines, which creates a logical "text" structure on a file. Another example is the binary data contained in an executable program like **cat** or **wc**. You can find files with these names in the file system and can use the **wc** tool to count the characters in them, just as you do in text files. The **cat** command is seldom useful for files that do not contain text, but there is no reason why you can't use it to display a *binary* (or non-ASCII) file or any other file. In fact you will occasionally use **cat** or **wc** in a pipeline when you're doing some operation on a non-ASCII file. For example, you can sometimes **cat** binary files directly to some printers or graphics terminals for output.

One type of file that is of interest is the *directory*, which contains not text or an executable program but a list of filenames and some other information related to these files. A directory is a file like any other but is used differently than other types of files.

Directories have names just like other files, and these names obey the same naming rules as normal files: any ASCII characters are allowed, up to a maximum of 14 characters. In naming a file or a directory it is unwise to include the shell wild-card operators or other characters that are treated as special by the shell. For example, avoid the $ (dollar), ; (semi-colon), \ (backslash), & (ampersand), ! (exclamation point), * (star), and | (pipe). You may use these characters in file or directory names if you wish, but it can become confusing, because whenever you mention these names to the shell, you must quote them to keep the shell from treating them as operators instead of normal characters. One character, the / (slash), is reserved for use in making filenames and cannot be used within a name.

A directory is a place within the file system as a whole that contains files. This place is analogous to a file drawer in your desk, where you can put things. In the UNIX system you put files in directories. Because the system treats all files as a sequence of data bytes, you can put any type of file in any directory; in fact you can put a directory into another directory. This helps you understand the file system as a whole, because it is a hierarchy of directories and subdirectories, with no limit on the depth of nested subdirectories.

Figure 4-1 provides an example. A directory named **steve** might contain the files **note**, **README**, and **dir1**. The files **note** and **README** are normal text files, but **dir1** is another directory, which in turn may contain the files **hello**, **goodbye**, and **dir2**. If **dir2** is a directory as well, it could contain more files, such as **up** and **down**. You can usually think about (and draw) directories in a hierarchy of subdirectories.

When you execute the command **ls** to list your filenames, it does not list the names of all the files available in the system, only those in a specific directory. You cannot tell from the

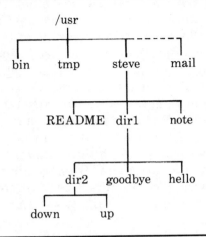

Figure 4-1. A sample directory hierarchy

simple listing of filenames whether a name is associated with a file or a directory, but you see the names of all the entries in the *current directory.* You can give an argument to the **ls** command, such as the following:

```
$ ls note
note
$
```

If the argument refers to a file, **ls** will only write the name to the standard output. If the argument refers to a directory, **ls** will look in the directory and write the names of all the files in the directory:

```
$ ls dir1
hello
goodbye
dir2
$
```

There are other ways to distinguish files and directories, as you will see.

Directory Naming

You can construct filenames that include a directory as part of the name. The / (slash) character is used to separate the different *components* of a filename of this form. For example, the name **dir1/goodbye** refers to the file **goodbye** in the directory **dir1**, **dir1/dir2** refers to the file (a directory in this case) **dir2** in directory **dir1**, and **dir1/dir2/down** refers to the file **down** in directory **dir2**, which in turn is found in directory **dir1**. These filenames can be as long as you wish, as long as no single part is longer than 14 characters. Only the last component of a file named this way is allowed to be a file, though it can be either a file or a directory, depending on how you you use it. All the intermediate components must be directories.

This type of name is called a *path* or a *pathname*, because the listing of the directories and subdirectories in the name describes a path through the large hierarchy of subdirectories in the system.

The Working Directory

When you give the command **ls** with no arguments, it lists the contents of the *current directory*. You are always logically located at (or in) a directory, which is called the current or *working directory* and is a reference point or base point in constructing pathnames. For example, the pathname **dir1/goodbye** refers to a directory **dir1**, which is located in the current directory, and to the file **goodbye** in the directory **dir1**.

The command **pwd** (for print working directory) will tell you what directory you are currently in.

```
$ pwd
/usr/steve
$
```

The **pwd** command returns the pathname of the current directory on its standard output. A common use of **pwd** is in an assignment to an environment variable, to help you remember a directory as you move around the file system.

```
$ HERE=`pwd`
$ echo $HERE
/usr/steve
$
```

Use the ` (grave) character to assign the standard output of the command to the variable.

Moving Around in the Directory Hierarchy

You can move around in the directory hierarchy with the **cd** (for change directory) command.

```
$ ls
README
dir1
note
$ cd dir1
$ ls
dir2
goodbye
hello
$ pwd
/usr/steve/dir1
$
```

The current directory has changed.

The current directory is also known by the directory name **.** (dot). You can use the pathname **./note** to refer to the file **note** in the current directory or **./dir1/goodbye** to refer to the directory **dir1** in the current directory.

```
$ pwd
/usr/steve/dir1
$ cd ./dir2
$ pwd
/usr/steve/dir1/dir2
$
```

The presence of the dot at the beginning of a pathname is usually redundant, because the system begins interpreting a path at the current directory, but sometimes the dot is needed.

You have moved down in the file system to a subdirectory in these examples using the **cd** command. You can also move up in the file system to a *parent directory* of the current directory. Use the special operator .. (dot-dot) to refer to the parent of the current directory:

```
$ pwd
/usr/steve/dir1/dir2
$ cd ..
$ pwd
/usr/steve/dir1
$
```

You can move downward, toward subdirectories, as far as directories exist. At the bottom of the directory hierarchy, there will be no more subdirectories, only files. You can go downward no further without creating a new directory at the lowest level. What happens if you continue to move upward, toward parent directories?

```
$ pwd
/usr/steve/dir1
$ cd ..
$ pwd
/usr/steve
$ cd ..
$ pwd
/usr
$ cd ..
$ pwd
/
$
```

Eventually you reach the top of the directory hierarchy, beyond which no more directories exist. This top directory is an anchor point for the file system and is called the *root directory*, or the *root*, of the file system. It has a special status because you can find all files in the system by starting at the root directory and working downward to more and more subdirectories.

If you construct a pathname beginning with the / (slash) character, the system understands that the pathname starts at the root directory. If the pathname has no leading slash, the system assumes that you are starting at the current directory.

```
$ pwd
/usr/coffin
$ ls dir1
dir2
goodbye
hello
$ ls /usr/coffin/dir1
dir2
goodbye
hello
$
```

These two command forms refer to the same directory; one is constructed by beginning at the current directory and the other by beginning at the root directory. The former is usually called a *relative pathname*, while the latter is called a *complete pathname* or an *absolute pathname*. You will use both types when you construct filename arguments for commands; sometimes one or the other is easier.

You can use a pathname in a command argument whenever you can use a simple filename. This command argument

```
$ cat /usr/steve/note
```

is equivalent to

```
$ cat note
```

if your current directory is **/usr/steve**. This is a very general property of the UNIX system. In fact the full pathname is the unique identifier for all files. The short, simple filename is just a convenient shorthand that you use, but the system always understands a full pathname when you enter a filename.

Changing the Directory Hierarchy

You can create new directories as you wish and delete others that you no longer need. The **mkdir** (for make a directory) command is used to create a new directory.

```
$ ls
README
dir1
note
$ mkdir new.directory
$ ls
README
dir1
new.directory
note
$
```

The **mkdir** command takes a list of pathnames as arguments and will create the directory or directories that you name. As usual, if the name is a full pathname, the new directory will be created at the bottom of the path specified. If it is a simple name, the new directory will be created as a subdirectory of the current directory. Directory names follow the same rules as other files; you cannot create a directory with the same name as another file or directory in the same parent directory. When a new directory is created, it is *empty*, with no files in it.

Use the command **rmdir** (for remove directory) to delete a directory.

```
$ rmdir new.directory
$ ls
README
dir1
note
$
```

The **rmdir** command will fail and give an error message if you try to delete a directory that is not empty.

```
$ pwd
/usr/steve
$ rmdir dir1
rmdir: dir1 not empty
$
```

This prevents you from deleting a directory somewhere in the middle of the file system, possibly leaving as orphans some files in the directory you are attempting to delete.

However, you may delete a directory and everything in it, including any subdirectories and the files in them. Needless to say, this is a very dangerous procedure because you must be certain that you really want to delete everything below a point in the directory hierarchy. Use the **rm** command with the argument **−r** (for recursive) to do this, not the **rmdir** command.

```
$ rm −r dir1
$
```

Note that if everything goes correctly, **rm** will silently do its job, deleting **dir1** and everything in it. To repeat, this can be a very dangerous operation. Take care that you really mean it!

Your Home Directory

When you log into a UNIX system, you start at a specific place in the file system that is your own private, or home, directory. You can freely create files and subdirectories in this directory, and the UNIX system and other users will not touch them. Most users usually work in their home directory or in subdirectories that they create within their home directory. The home directories of other users do not conflict with yours.

No matter where you are in the file system, you can return to your home directory at any time with the **cd** command. In the preceding examples **cd** was used with an argument to refer to the full or relative file system location you wished to change directories to. If you give the command **cd** with no arguments, you return immediately to your home directory.

```
$ pwd
/usr/steve/dir1/dir2
$ cd
$ pwd
/usr/steve
$
```

The system provides an environment variable, called *HOME*, that contains the pathname for your home directory, and it is used by a great many commands that create files.

```
$ echo $HOME
/usr/coffin
$
```

The following two commands

```
$ cd
$ cd $HOME
```

will have the same effect.

Every system will define the *HOME* environment variable for you, and you should not change it. Because some commands and applications use this variable, some systems may prevent you from changing it to protect the integrity of the system.

File-Oriented Commands

The system provides many commands to manipulate files and move them around within the file system. Use the **cp** (for copy) command to make an exact copy of a file.

```
$ ls
README
dir1
note
$ cp note note.copy
$ ls
README
dir1
note
note.copy
$
```

The first argument is the existing file; the second is the new file to create. As usual, you can give a pathname instead of a simple filename.

```
$ cp ./note /usr/steve/note.cp
```

This has the same effect as the previous example. If the *target* file or pathname already exists, **cp** will delete the old file and then make the copy, without complaining, so you must take care that the target filename is correct.

If the target pathname is an existing directory instead of a filename, the copy will be put into the directory named, using the same name as the *source* filename:

```
$ pwd
/usr/steve
$ ls dir1
dir2
goodbye
hello
$ cp note dir1
$ ls dir1
dir2
goodbye
hello
note
$
```

The **cp** command will also take a list of filenames as the source and copy all the files to the destination. When multiple names are given, it is an error if the target is a filename and not a directory. The **cp** command will complain and refuse to take any action. However, if the target is a directory, **cp** will copy all the files named as sources into the target directory.

```
$ pwd
/usr/steve/dir1
$ ls dir2
down
up
$ cp hello goodbye dir2
$ ls dir2
down
goodbye
hello
up
$
```

You cannot use a directory as a source name. If you wish to copy the contents of a directory to a new directory, you must name each file that you wish to copy, either explicitly or with a wild-card operator.

```
$ pwd
/usr/steve
$ cp dir1/* .
$
```

If **cp** can complete its work successfully, it will return silently to the shell. Only if there is some problem will **cp** complain on its standard error output.

A similar command is **mv** (for move), which obeys the same command line rules as **cp**. This command moves the file from one place to another, or changes the file's name.

```
$ ls
dir1
goodbye
hello
$ mv hello welcome
$ ls
dir1
goodbye
welcome
$
```

You can move a file into an existing directory, with the same name, or you can change the name of a file as you move it, depending on whether the target argument is an existing directory or a filename.

```
$ pwd
/usr/steve
$ mv note dir1/try
$ ls dir1
dir2
goodbye
hello
note
try
$
```

Again, the source can be a list of files or pathnames, and the target is the last argument. In this case you usually make the target a directory, which must exist because neither **cp** nor

mv will create it.

Finally, the **ln** (for link) command also acts in a similar way, except that its function is to make the same file appear under two different names.

```
$ ls
dir1
goodbye
hello
$ ln hello hhh
$ ls
dir1
goodbye
hello
hhh
$
```

In this example you did not make a copy of the file **hello**, you simply created a second filename that refers to the same physical file. If you edited or changed the file **hello**, the changes would also appear in the file **hhh**, which would not be the case if you actually made a copy of the file with **cp**. The **ln** command is usually used to make the same file appear in more than one directory.

As with **cp** and **mv**, you can use **ln** with a list of filenames as source arguments and a single existing directory as the target (the last argument on the command line). You cannot use a directory as the source argument without naming each file to be linked.

When you create another name for a file with **ln**, the file acquires an additional *link*. If you delete one of the files with **rm**, you don't actually delete the file; you just remove the link from the name to the file. The file is actually deleted from the system only when you have removed the last link, or deleted the last name that the file was known by in the file system.

A file is always a member of a directory. If the file has multiple links, it may be in more than one directory at the same time (with the same or different names). However, this is not true of directories because you cannot **ln** a directory by name. Because the file system is a strict hierarchy, a directory must have a fixed location within the hierarchy, with a parent and possibly some subdirectories. A file can be in two places at once, but a directory cannot.

Options for the ls Command

When **ls** was used to display the contents of a directory in the preceding examples, the files were listed on the screen in alphabetical order, one name per line of output. This display format is seldom useful for listing to the terminal, because the names quickly scroll off the top of the screen in large directories. The **ls** command provides several options that control the display of the output, as well as others that control what files or directories are selected for display. If you use −**C** (for columns) as a flag to **ls**, the output will be displayed in a more compact form for the display.

```
$ ls
dir1
README
note
$ ls -C
dir1         README         note
$
```

This form is usually much better for the terminal, but using −**C** when the output of **ls** is redirected to a pipeline or environment variable will rarely be what you want. Some versions of **ls** on different systems are smart enough to display output to the terminal in columns by default and will use the one-per-line format if the output is redirected. Also, the order of files in the columnar display will vary widely among systems, and the display format may depend on how many files are listed. Test your own system to see how it acts.

Another useful option for **ls** is −**a**. Actually **ls** has been lying to you all along, not really listing the names of *all* the files in the directory. By default, **ls** will not display any files in the named directory that begin with . (dot). You can see all the files in the directory with the following command argument:

```
$ pwd
/usr/coffin
$ ls -C
dir1         README         note
$ ls -aC
   .            .profile       dir1
   ..           README         note
```

You can see several files that were not shown before.

Most systems maintain several hidden files in your home directory, and this will vary depending on the system and on any application software you have installed. However, the files shown above are of special interest: the . (dot) is the current directory, and the .. (dot-dot) is the parent directory. Actually these are real entries in each directory, because each directory includes a pointer for finding itself and its parent directory. This is a *linked list* implementation of directories in the file system. In every directory you can find the . and .. directories, displayed with **ls** −**a**. What does .. refer to in the root (slash) directory, given that the root has no parent? The answer is that the root is a special case, where the .. and . directories are the same.

The **ls** command will mark the type of each file that it displays in a directory listing if you use the −**F** argument, adding / (slash) to the end of each directory and * (star) to the name of each executable file. These extra characters are not part of the filename.

```
$ pwd
/usr/steve
$ ln /bin/cat .
$ ls -F -C
README          cat*        dir1/           note
$
```

In this directory **cat** is marked as executable, and the subdirectory **dir1** is displayed with the / (slash) character.

Another useful option of the **ls** command is −**R** (for recursive). Use capital *R* here because there is another option for **ls** with lowercase *r*, to reverse the order of output. The **ls** −**R** command will search through the directory hierarchy from the directory named as argument (default to the current directory) and display all the files and subdirectories.

```
$ pwd
/usr/steve
$ ls -RCF
README          cat*        dir1/           note

dir1:
dir2/           goodbye     hello

dir2:
down            up
$
```

You can redirect the output to a file or use it as standard input to a file manipulation command if you wish. The UNIX system provides another command, **find**, that is often used when a complete list of filenames in a directory *substructure* is desired, for example to back up a portion of the file system to floppy disk. We will discuss **find** in detail in Chapter 6.

File Permissions

Each file and directory in the file system has many attributes in addition to its name. You can see some of them with **ls** −l (for long listing). For example:

```
$ pwd
/usr/steve
$ ls -1
total 3
-rw-rw-rw-   1 steve      users        138 Apr  5 19:34 README
drwxrwxrwx   3 steve      users         80 Apr  5 19:43 dir1
-rw-rw-rw-   1 steve      users        227 Apr  5 19:33 note
$
```

The filename is given at the far right, and each name in the directory has its own line in the output. The next section to the left, for example, "Apr 5 19:34," is the date and time that the file was last changed. This *time stamp* is often used when you compare files or back up your data.

The next column to the left, containing "138" or "227," gives the size of the file in bytes, which can range from zero bytes, for a newly created file, to 1 megabyte or larger. The system provides a system-wide variable called *ulimit* to control the maximum file size, though it is often set at 1 megabyte. Recall that a directory is a file, so it also has a size in bytes, but this size is seldom useful.

Because the UNIX system is a multiuser system, files can be created by individual users, who then "own" the files until they delete them or give them to another user. Each user also belongs to a group and can share files with other users in the group, but not with other users. In the output from **ls** −l you can see the user and group who own the files: "steve" is the file owner, and "users" is the name of the group to which "steve" belongs. When you create a file, the system gives the file to the group of which you are a member. However, you can change the ownership and group assignment of a file independently, so that the user listed in the output from **ls −l** may not actually belong to the group listed. We will review groups in more detail in Chapter 20.

Moving one more column to the left, you see a column of single-digit numbers. This is the number of links that the file has. When you use **ln** to create another name for the file, this count goes up by one; when you delete a filename with **rm**, the count goes down by one. When the count is zero, the actual file is deleted.

Finally, the leftmost column of the output, "-rw-rw-rw-", gives the *permissions* or *mode* of the file. The leftmost position in the output is "−" (dash) if the file is a normal file and "d" if it is a directory, although "b" and "c" can also appear in this position if the file is a *special* file. Special files are used to control hardware devices.

The next three positions in the output give the permissions for the owner of the file; the next three give the permissions for the group that owns the file; and the final three give the permissions for all other users in the system. Each of these three groups has three parts: (1) *read* access to the file, (2) *write* access, and (3) *execute* access. Read access means that the subject (the owner, the group, or all others) may read the file, for example, with **cat**. Write access means that the subject may write the file, such as by editing it or by redirecting output to it. Execute access means that the subject may execute the file as a command, by naming it as we have been doing with **ls** or **rm**. For a directory, the meanings are slightly different. Read access means that the subject may look at the contents of the directory, for example, with **ls**. Write access means that the user may create a file in that directory, and execute access means that the user may pass through the directory in searching for subdirectories.

These access forms are shown in the output from **ls −l** as "r" for read access, "w" for write access, and "x" for execute access. For example, the output "-rw-r-----" means that the owner can read and write the file, members of the group can read but not write or execute the file, and others have no access. The output "-r----x--x" means that the owner can read but not write or execute the file, while group members and all others can execute but not read or write it.

There is one more important option for **ls**. If you request **ls** −l for a file, you see the information for that file, but if you give the same command for a directory, the output is the listing for the files in the directory.

```
$ ls -l dir1
total 1
drwxrwxrwx  2 steve     users       64 Apr 18 12:43 dir2
-rw-rw-rw-  1 steve     users        0 Apr 17 17:42 goodbye
-rw-rw-rw-  1 steve     users        0 Apr 17 17:42 hello
$
```

This is normally what you want because you usually want information about the contents of a directory.

But how do you get information about the permissions of the directory itself? One way is to **cd** to the parent directory and issue the **ls** −l command, as the preceding example gives the information for the directory **dir2**. To get information about directory **dir1** when you're in your home directory, use the following:

```
$ cd ..
$ ls -l steve
```

The **ls** command provides a more efficient way to do this that does not require you to change directories.

```
$ ls -ld dir1
drwxrwxrwx  3 steve     users       80 Apr 18 12:43 dir1
$
```

Use **ls** −d (for directory listing) to list the name of a directory rather than its contents. Combined with the −l option, you can see the status of the directory.

The system provides several commands designed to manipulate the ownership and permissions of files and directories. If the file is yours to give, you can give ownership away with the **chown** (for change owner) command.

```
$ ls -l note
-rw-rw-rw-  1 steve     users       227 Apr  5 19:33 note
$ chown note jim
$ ls -l note
-rw-rw-rw-  1 jim       users       227 Apr  5 19:33 note
```

The **chown** command takes a filename or list of filenames as argument, and the login id of the user to whom you wish to give the file. The target user is always the last argument. The user to whom you try to give the file must be a legal login id for someone on the system. Once you have given the file away, you cannot use **chown** to get it back.

Similarly, use the **chgrp** command to change the group that owns a file, if you own the file and are a member of the group that owns it:

```
$ ls -l note
-rw-rw-rw-  1 steve     users       227 Apr  5 19:33 note
$ chgrp note bin
$ ls -l note
-rw-rw-rw-  1 steve     bin         227 Apr  5 19:33 note
```

Again, when you have given the file to someone else, you no longer own it, so you cannot get it back. Of course, if you have read permission on the file, you can copy it with

```
$ cat note > my.note
```

or a similar command. You will own the new file that you create.

Finally, you can change the permissions of a file that you own by using the **chmod** (for change mode) command. A file may have three sets of permissions: user, group, and other. These are known as **u**, **g**, and **o**, respectively, and correspond to the three permission categories listed with **ls** −**l**. Each category of user can have read, write, or execute access to a file, known as **r**, **w**, and **x**, respectively. You can use this shorthand to create a **chmod** command:

```
$ ls -l note
-rw-rw-rw-  1 steve      users         227 Apr  5 19:33 note
$ chmod -w note
$ ls -l note
-r--r--r--  1 steve      users         227 Apr  5 19:33 note
$ chmod +w note
$ ls -l note
-rw-rw-rw-  1 steve      users         227 Apr  5 19:33 note
$
```

In the first case you gave the flag argument −**w** to **chmod**, which tells it to remove write permissions for the file. The second example adds write permissions again. The use of + (plus) as a flag is an exception to the normal use of −, but you can understand the meaning: in this case you use − to remove a permission and + to add a permission.

You can change more than one of the three permissions in the same command if you wish.

```
$ chmod -w+x note
$ ls -l note
-r-xr-xr-x 1 steve      users         227 Apr  5 19:33 note
$ chmod -wx note
$ ls -l note
-r--r--r-- 1 steve      users         227 Apr  5 19:33 note
$
```

In all these examples **chmod** has changed the permission for all three classes of users. You can also make changes for any single class by adding a letter before the − or +.

```
$ ls -l note
-rw-rw-rw-  1 steve      users         227 Apr  5 19:33 note
$ chmod u-w note
$ ls -l note
-r--rw-rw-  1 steve      users         227 Apr  5 19:33 note
$ chmod go+wx note
$ ls -l note
-r--rwxrwx  1 steve      users         227 Apr  5 19:33 note
$
```

The syntax for **chmod** is user class (**u**, **g**, or **o**), followed by the action to take (− or +), followed by the permission to change (**r**, **w**, or **x**). The list of file or directory names to change follows at the end of the command line.

The **chmod** command can also take a numeric argument that describes the user class and permission to change as a sequence of bits.

```
$ chmod 0466 note
```

This usage, however, is more error prone than the one given earlier. The number is an octal representation of the permissions described here. Also, **chmod** can set permissions **s** and **t** as well as **r**, **w**, and **x**. The **s** and **t** permissions are used by some executable programs to modify their execution environments and may appear in **ls −l** output for some system files; they are not used by individual users.

Going Further

Many of the interesting features of the file system are associated with execution of commands, such as the **s** permission. Some are designed to improve the linkage between a filename in a directory and the actual physical storage of data on the disk (or other medium). The system allows *mounting* additional file systems at arbitrary places in the directory tree. You can even configure the system to use a local area network such that a file may reside on a different machine's disk. Most of these capabilities are associated with system administration and configuration, which we will discuss in Chapters 11 and 21.

The basename and dirname Commands

The UNIX system provides commands to construct file and directory names from complete pathnames, and vice versa. For example, you may have an environment variable that contains a complete pathname, and you might wish to know only the name of a specific file.

```
$ echo $EDITOR
/usr/bin/vi
$ MYEDIT=`basename $EDITOR`
$ echo "My editor is $MYEDIT"
My editor is vi
$
```

Use the command **basename** to return the last component of a full pathname on its standard output. This usually gives you the name of a file with the directory path stripped off. The command **dirname**, on the other hand, gives only the directory section with the filename stripped off.

```
$ EDDIR=`dirname $EDITOR`
$ echo "My editor $MYEDIT is in the directory $EDDIR"
My editor vi is located in the directory /usr/bin
$
```

You will find many uses for these pathname manipulation tools when we discuss *shell programming* in Chapter 7.

Device Files

So far we have discussed regular files and directories, but you can observe a third type of file with the **ls** command. These are *device files*, *special files*, or simply *devices*. The UNIX system provides a standard interface between hardware peripherals and the operating system that acts just like a normal file. That is, all I/O to hardware is done by writing to a file. This is not a disk file such as we have discussed but a special pathname that refers the I/O channel to the hardware. Just like redirecting standard I/O to a normal file, you can redirect output to a hardware device from the shell level without fanfare or confusion. This is a complex subject of interest to system designers and developers, and only a brief introduction will be given here.

The command **tty** (for teletype, a throwback to when terminals were slow printers often manufactured by the Teletype Corporation) will return the pathname associated with your terminal.

```
$ tty
/dev/tty00
$
```

Your terminal can be accessed through the file /**dev/tty00**; in fact the standard input for the shell that is listening to your commands (the login shell) was attached to this file when you logged into the system. The device pathnames vary on different systems and change when you log into different terminals on a system, so always use the **tty** command if you need to determine your login device. The directory /**dev** contains many other device files in addition to terminal devices. You can use this pathname just like any other in the file system.

```
$ ls -l /dev/tty00
crw-rw-rw-  1 steve  users      7,  2 Apr 19 13:21 /dev/tty00
$
```

The first character in the output, "c", tells you that this is neither a normal file nor a directory but a *character special* file, designed to move data character by character, like a terminal, modem, or printer. Another type of special file is the *block special* device, marked with "b" in the first position, which is designed to move large chunks of data at once, like disk drives and some tape devices. You can use a block device as a file system.

Device files have permissions just like any others, and some are owned by the current user. In the example given here, you may read and write the file, which allows data into and out of your terminal, and other users may read the file, allowing them to "listen in" on your terminal session if they wish. What command line would you use to listen in on the device?

```
$ cat - < /dev/tty00
```

Try this on your own device, with the following:

```
$ cat - < `tty`
```

What is happening? You can hit the DEL key to kill the **cat** command and restore your terminal to sanity. Try **cat** − > **tty**   . What happens?

The mesg Command

In the preceding example you could directly read and write to the device file that represents your terminal. If the permissions output from **ls—l`tty`** shows that other users can also read and write your device file, then they can either eavesdrop on your session or write directly to your terminal by redirecting I/O. This is a potential security risk. However, the system administrator, or the system itself through software, sometimes needs to send a message directly to your terminal. This might happen when the system is being turned off and the administrator would like to warn you before the machine goes dead so that you can save your files and log off cleanly. The **wall** (for write to all users) and the **write** (for writing messages between users) commands use this direct I/O to your terminal for communications. We will discuss the use of these commands in Chapter 13.

You can control the access of others to your terminal simply by changing the permissions on this device file. You can do this directly with the **chmod** command, but the system provides a command expressly to allow or prohibit messages like this. Use the **mesg** (for message) command to allow or refuse others to write to or read from your terminal device. This command takes one argument, **y** or **n** to accept or reject messages, respectively. For example:

```
$ ls -l /dev/tty00
crw-rw-rw-  1 steve    users       7,  2 Apr 20 18:37 /dev/tty00
$ mesg n
$ ls -l /dev/tty00
crw-r--r--  1 steve    users       7,  2 Apr 20 18:38 /dev/tty00
$ mesg y
$ ls -l /dev/tty00
crw-rw-rw-  1 steve    users       7,  2 Apr 20 18:37 /dev/tty00
$
```

The **mesg** command just changes the permissions on your device file.

In addition to the **tty** devices, there are many other device files in the /**dev** directory. One of the most interesting of these is

/**dev** /**null**, which is an infinitely large wastebasket that you can use to redirect output that you wish to discard. For example:

```
$ cat /etc/passwd > /dev/null
$
```

The output is discarded.

Another device file of interest is /**dev/kmem** (for kernel memory), which is a representation of the real memory in the machine. Special programs such as debuggers can read /**dev/kmem** to see how the system is using memory at any time. However, normal users are prohibited from peeking (or writing!) /**dev/kmem**, because it would be a security violation if the system's memory were accessible.

In addition, all the hardware devices attached to the system, such as terminal ports, printer ports, and disk drives, have representations in the /**dev** directory. We will discuss these as needed.

Browsing the File System

Our discussion in this chapter has focused mostly on your home directory and the files and directories that you create in it for your own use. Of course this is only a small part of the file system, which is a large and complex structure. In fully configured SVR3 systems there are more than 2200 files and 400 directories, though more than one fourth of the total is in the Software Development Set, which may not be installed on your system. About 450 of these files are commands. Further, individual users and application software can substantially add to this total. Most of these files have specific purposes for the operation of the system, and if they are not present or if the permissions are wrong, then something will not work correctly, with extremely variable results. When something like this goes wrong, it can test the skills of the best "guru" to find and fix the problem without reloading the system. Usually you must be very careful when you change or delete a file that is not in your home directory, even more so when you change the permissions of an existing system file.

On the other hand, browsing through the file system can be a source of great entertainment and insight into the system's inner workings. Only a few files are not readable, and those can be made readable if security considerations are not foremost in your machine.

Starting in the root directory, there are several important files and subdirectories, as shown here:

```
$ ls -FC /
bin/        etc/        lib/         mnt/       tmp/       usr/
dev/        install/    lost+found/  shlib/     unix*
$
```

The file /**unix** is the disk file that contains the executable program for the UNIX kernel, which is always loaded and running while the system is up. Most of the other contents of the root directory are subdirectories. The UNIX system has evolved some relatively standard conventions for naming directories, and different applications and even individual users usually follow these conventions in their own home directories. The directory names **bin** (for binary), **lib** (for library), **src** (for source), **man** (for manual), **usr** (for users), and **etc** (for et cetera) appear widely. Most executable programs reside in a **bin** directory, most development libraries and other supporting material reside in a **lib** directory, most source code for applications and commands resides in a **src** directory, most documentation resides in a **man** directory, most of the items associated with users reside in a **usr** directory, and most of the supporting material resides in an **etc** directory. You don't need to use these names in your own home directory as long as you don't change the names of the directories that the UNIX system expects.

You can see many of these names in the root directory. The **bin** directory contains many of the commands. Most of the rest are in the directory /**usr**/**bin**, and some are in the directory /**usr**/**lbin** (for local bin). The oldest commands are in /**bin**, which, in the history of the UNIX system, overflowed quickly into /**usr**/**bin**, where users once set up their own personal commands. Many of these commands were eventually included in the standard system, and users began putting their personal commands into the directory /**usr**/**lbin**. This in turn became part of the system, and executable programs now reside in all three of these directories. You can get a feel for the history of the UNIX system by looking at which commands are in which of these directories. Many systems now include another directory, /**usr**/**local** (or sometimes /**local**/**bin**), which contains commands that are owned by individual users. In a later release of the UNIX system perhaps one of these will be included in the standard system. One complicating factor here is that /**usr** and its subdirectories are often on a separate mountable file system from the /**bin** directory, and some commands have moved in one direction or the other based on their importance. If a command cannot be unmounted, it is usually in the /**bin** directory.

The /**etc** directory contains a large number of commands, files, and tools that are used in the administration of the UNIX system as a whole. For example, /**etc**/**rc2.d** is a directory that contains files that are used when the system *boots*, and /**etc**/**passwd** is a file that contains the list of authorized users on the machine. The pieces of the UNIX operating system that make up the kernel are kept in /**etc**/**conf** or /**etc**/**atconf**. These materials are used to build a new kernel when you add new hardware that includes device drivers to your machine. Your machine will have only one of these directories, and you should never manually change or delete the contents, even though they may occupy a considerable amount of disk space.

The /**lib** directory contains subroutine libraries and tools used in software development. There may be no /**lib** directory on your machine. The /**dev** directory contains the files that link to hardware devices, while /**tmp** is used for temporary storage of files by applications, especially during software development. You can use /**tmp** for your own temporary files if you wish. Such files are deleted when the system is rebooted.

The /**usr** directory contains much more than /**usr**/**bin**, because this is where all user-related materials are usually kept. Besides /**usr**/**bin** and /**usr**/**lbin**, there is usually a /**usr**/**lib** and a /**usr**/**src**, which contain libraries and source code for the system, respectively. The source code for the complete UNIX system is usually kept in /**usr**/**src** and its subdirectories, although this is rarely present on microcomputers. The /**usr**/**lib** directory includes directories for the **uucp** communications subsystem in /**usr**/**lib**/**uucp**, while /**usr**/**lib**/**terminfo** contains descriptions of specific features of different terminals that may be attached to the system. The /**usr**/**lib**/**cron** directory contains files associated with the timing and scheduling functions of the system; /**usr**/**lib**/**tmac** and /**usr**/**lib**/**spell** contain files and tools for word processing functions; and /**usr**/**man**, if present, contains documentation including the text of the *UNIX User's Manual.*

The /**usr** directory contains many other directories: /**usr**/**games** contains games and toys; /**usr**/**adm** contains files used by the system administration tools; /**usr**/**mail** is used by the electronic mail system; /**usr**/**include** is used by software developers; and /**usr**/**spool** contains *spool* directories for I/O jobs that are queued for later action, such as print jobs in /**usr**/**spool**/**lp** and data communications in /**usr**/**spool**/**uucp**.

The home directories for individual users are usually located in the /**usr** directory, though some systems define a special directory for users that is named /**u**. This convention, which comes from the BSD version of the UNIX system, may be the origin of a new directory substructure that will eventually be as standard as the /**usr** directory.

Finally, application developers usually carve out a piece of this directory hierarchy for the exclusive use of their applications. Your system may have many more directories in the file system than we have mentioned, but in every system the basic /**usr**, /**etc**, /**bin** type structure is preserved. Browse your own system and consider the layout; we will meet many of these files and directories in later chapters.

Editing and
Regular Expressions

Basic Editing with ed
Regular Expressions
The grep Command
The sed Stream Editor
The vi Text Editor
Going Further

**F
I
V
E**

The UNIX system provides several different text editors as standard parts of the system. These editors differ greatly and are generally optimized for a subset of the text editing work that you do. None of them is a true word processor like you find in other small computer environments; word processing or document formatting is provided by a separate set of tools. In addition to the standard editors, many word processors and desktop publishing systems are available as add-on tools. You can buy an editor with just about any features that you wish. Here, however, we will discuss only the standard text editing tools.

Like many other subjects in the UNIX system, text editing introduces a great many new concepts and powerful ideas. Because text files are streams of characters, many of these ideas involve modifying or *filtering* character strings. The most powerful idea, the *regular expression*, reaches beyond text editing to influence the entire environment.

The text editing tools are designed for a terse, very fast user interface and operation that favors the skilled expert at the expense of the novice. The best way to learn editing under the UNIX system is to watch a skilled user, but short of hiring your own expert, you can continually review the editing documentation and slowly learn new features as you master earlier material. If you find that an editor can't do something that you might want it to do, it is usually because you don't know how to do it, not because the editor is unable to do it.

Basic Editing with ed

The original general-purpose text editor that has been a part of the UNIX system since the earliest days is the **ed** (for editor) program. Because **ed** is a line-oriented tool rather than a full-screen display like most modern editors, we will not discuss it extensively. The **ed** program introduces some of the key concepts of editing and text manipulation and is the basis for the other editors. It is unwise to become dependent on **ed**, however.

You invoke **ed** from the shell with an optional filename as the argument:

```
$ ed old.file
260
```

If the file already exists, **ed** will copy the file into its *buffer*, so that you are not changing the original file as you make changes. The size of the file in characters ("260" in this example) is returned to signal that **ed** has read the file. If the file does not exist, **ed** will create it. The filename given as the argument is called the *current file*. When you write the file back to the disk from the **ed** buffer, it will be written to that filename. If you give no argument, **ed** will work correctly, but because there is no current file, you will have to name an explicit file when you write the new file to disk.

If you named a new file when you started, then instead of displaying the count of characters in the file, **ed** will signal that its buffer is empty with the following:

```
$ ed new.file
?new.file
```

At this point you are in the **ed** program and have a complete set of editing commands available.

Modes in ed

The **ed** program has two different *modes* of operation. Command mode is used to enter commands to **ed**, such as writing a file, searching for text strings, and so on, while *input mode* is used to enter text that is added to the file you are editing. You cannot enter commands while in input mode, because the command will become part of the text file. Similarly, you cannot enter text while in command mode, because **ed** will interpret all your keystrokes as commands. By default, **ed** does not tell you which mode you are in, though it begins in command mode when you enter the program.

Turning on Prompts and Help

You can enter the **P** (for prompt) command to tell **ed** to display a prompt character when you are in command mode.

```
$ ed new.file
?new.file
P
*
```

Now **ed** will prompt you with "*" whenever you are in command mode. You can turn off the prompt by pressing P again.

Similarly, when you make a mistake in a command, by default **ed** will only display a terse "?", as shown here.

```
$ ed new.file
?new.file
XXX
?
```

"XXX" is not a valid command. You can turn on a more verbose error message display with the **H** (for help) command.

```
$ ed new.file
?new.file
XXX
?
H
XXX
?
illegal suffix
```

This may not be much better, but at least it provides some information. You can toggle the help off again by pressing H.

Write and Quit

While you are in **ed**, the changes that you make to the file are kept in a buffer. The **ed** program does not change the original file until you explicitly *write* the file with the **w** command.

```
$ ed old.file
260
P
*w
260
*
```

The number of characters written out is displayed. After you write the file, you have permanently changed it and cannot recover the original version.

When you are through editing, you can quit **ed** with the **q** command.

```
$ ed old.file
260
q
$
```

The **ed** program ends and you are back to the shell. If you try to quit after you make changes to a file but before you write it, **ed** will prompt for confirmation. If you press **q** again, **ed** will obediently exit without writing the file.

Working with Lines

Most operations in command mode work on lines of the text file. You move around in the file by jumping from line to line, and most commands act on the *current line*. In command mode the current line is called . (dot), and the last line of the file is called $ (dollar). Line numbers are rarely used in text editing in the UNIX system, but **ed** always keeps track of which line you are currently working with, and you can use line numbers with **ed** commands if you wish.

The **p** (for print) command is used to display the current line. This is a lowercase *p*, while the prompt command is the uppercase *P*. By default, the **p** command will print only the current line.

```
$ ed old.file
260
p
see you later          .... steve
```

When you first read a file into **ed**, the current line is the last line of the file.

```
$ ed old.file
260
p
see you later          .... steve
.=
6
$=
6
```

The = (equal sign) operator tells you the line number: .= reports the number of the current line, while $= reports the number of the last line in the file. In this example the file has six lines.

Most commands in **ed** can take a line or a range of lines preceding the command. If you don't give this line range, **ed** usually assumes that you mean only the current line, dot. The preceding **p** command could also have been written **.p**, **$p**, or **6p**. Because dot and dollar are the same in this example, line 6, all these versions of the **p** command are the same. To specify a range of lines, give the first line number, followed by a comma, and then the last line number.

```
$ ed old.file
260
1,2p
hi jim, how was your vacation?  I've been learning
the UNIX operating system recently, and it's a lot of
```

The first line number must be smaller than the second one. You could also use dot and dollar in these line number addresses.

```
$ ed old.file
260
3,$p
fun.   The UNIX operating system seems to be much more
powerful than any other small computer os, and I'm sure
it will help us a lot.
see you later          .... steve
```

Similarly, you can use simple arithmetic expressions in line addresses.

```
$-2,$p
powerful than any other small computer os, and I'm sure
it will help us a lot.
see you later          .... steve
```

To display the entire file, you can use the short form **,p**.

You can also change the current line while in command mode. Simply entering a NEWLINE will move forward one line, displaying the contents of the current line. The command –

(minus) followed by a NEWLINE will move back one line. You can also name a line number directly, and **ed** will make that the current line.

```
.=
6
2
the UNIX operating system recently, and its a lot of
.=
2
```

The current line was changed to line 2, and **ed** displayed the line. Simple arithmetic expressions are also allowed. You could have used **$-4** in this example instead of 2.

Input Mode

When you enter input mode from command mode, you always start on a new line either before or after the current line. Use the **i** (for input) command to enter input mode just before the current line and the **a** (for append) command to enter input mode just after the current line. When you are in input mode, there will be no prompt, and all the characters you enter at the keyboard will go into the file. To return to command mode after you are through entering text, use . (dot) on a line by itself.

```
$ ed new.file
?new.file
a
hello world
another line
a third line
.
,p
hello world
another line
a third line
```

When you are in input mode, you stay there until you enter . (dot) on a line by itself, so you can enter as many lines as you wish. To correct a line that contains an error, you must return to command mode and make changes, as discussed in the following paragraphs. The **i** and **a** commands can also take line addresses preceding them: **14a** tells **ed** to append following line 14 of the file.

Deleting Lines

The **d** (for delete) command will delete lines from the file. By default, **d** deletes the current line.

```
,p
hello world
another line
a third line
2
another line
d
,p
hello world
a third line
```

This deleted line 2 from the buffer. The **d** command can also take a line number or range of line numbers if you want to delete more than one line.

Undoing Mistakes

The **ed** program remembers the last command you enter, so you can *undo* the last change you made to a file. Only the last change can be recovered in this way. The **u** (for undo) command restores the buffer, as shown in this example:

```
,p
hello world
a third line
u
,p
hello world
another line
a third line
```

If you press **u** again, the restored line will again be deleted, because restoring it with **u** was the last change you made.

```
,p
hello world
another line
a third line
u
,p
hello world
a third line
```

The undo feature will successfully undo even very large changes, but only the last operation can be recovered.

Searching for Strings

The **ed** program can find any sequence of characters on a line. Use the / (slash) operator to instruct **ed** to search for a string.

```
/string
```

The **ed** program will start at the current line and search forward in the file until it finds a line that contains the string. When it finds the string, it will stop searching and display the line, making it the current line. If there are no instances of the string before the end of the file, **ed** will start again at the beginning of the file and continue until it reaches the current line. If no instances of the string were found in the entire file, **ed** will display the "?" error indication. You can also search backwords in the file from the current line with the **?** (question mark) character.

```
?string
```

The program will start at the current line and search toward the beginning of the file, stopping when it finds the string. If none are found, it will wrap around to the end of the file, searching backward until it hits the current line. Since **ed** remembers the search string, you can repeat the search for the same string simply by entering / or ?, followed by NEWLINE.

Substituting Sections of Text

The **ed** program provides the s (for substitute) command to substitute one string for another. Following the s, enter the delimiter / (slash), then the string you want to delete, then another slash, then the new string you want to substitute.

```
p
powerful than any other small computer os, and I'm sure
s/powerful/flexible
flexible than any other small computer os, and I'm sure
```

The changed line is echoed to verify that the change has been made. The **s** command can take a line number or range of line numbers if you wish to make the substitution on more than one line. This command

```
2,5s/the/another
```

will make the substitution on the first occurrence of the string **the** on each of the lines 2 through 5. To delete a string with this mechanism, just name an empty string for the target.

```
2,5s/the//
```

In this case you add a closing / (slash) to complete the substitution command. The closing / is also needed if there is a trailing **g**. In general **ed** will print the changed line if the closing / (slash) is omitted and will not print the line if it is included.

Use the special operator ^ (caret) to designate the beginning of a line and $ (dollar) to designate the end of a line. So, to add a string to the end of a line, you might give the following command:

```
s/$/new text at end
```

To add a string at the beginning of a line, you would use this command:

```
s/^/new text at beginning
```

Making Global Changes

Normally the **s** command will change only the first occurrence of a string on a line. You can add a **g** to the end of the substitute command to force the **s** command to make the substitution *globally* on every occurrence of the string on the line (or sequence of lines if you give an address range).

```
s/old text to delete/new text to add/g
```

This will change every occurrence of the string on the current line. To change every occurrence of a string in the whole file, use the following:

```
1,$s/old/new/g
```

You can use a *context address* instead of a line number if you wish. Actually the "$" shown above is an example of a context address, but any search string can be given as a line address.

```
/hello/,/goodbye/s/old/new/
```

The **ed** will search from the current line until it finds the matching string **hello**, then will make the substitution until it finds a line containing **goodbye**. This usage is more difficult to control than using line numbers, but it leads to the often-stated fact that all editing under the UNIX system can be done without line numbers. In fact **ed** is often called a *context editor* because of this property.

The rules for searching and substituting are actually much more powerful than just described, as you will see when we discuss *regular expressions*.

Moving and Copying Lines

The **m** (for move) command lets you move a line or sequence of lines from one location in the file to another. For example, to move the current line to the end of the file, enter the following:

```
.m$
```

The **m** command also can take a line address or range of lines like the other commands. This command

```
3,5m1
```

moves lines 3, 4, and 5 to immediately follow line 1.

To copy a line from one place to another without deleting the original, use the **t** command.

```
2,4t$
```

This will copy lines 2 through 4 to the end of the file.

Reading in Another File

You can read another file into the buffer at the current line with the **r** (for read) command. This command

```
r old.file
```

will insert the file **old.file** after the current line. You can use a line address if you wish. This command

```
0r old.file
```

will read the file at the beginning of your buffer, at line zero.

Shell Escapes — The Bang Operator

Finally, you can jump out of **ed** to execute any command from the shell by entering ! (bang), followed by the command you wish to execute.

```
!cat old.file
```

This is called *escaping to the shell*.

When the command is completed, **ed** echoes ! for you and then returns to action. To temporarily suspend your **ed** session and create an interactive shell, you can enter the following:

```
!sh
```

This is called a *subshell*, because your editing session is still present, waiting for your return. When you are through with whatever you are doing in the subshell, you can kill that shell by pressing CTRL-D or **exit** to return to the **ed** session.

These are only a few of the capabilities of **ed**.

Regular Expressions

The **s** command of **ed** is much more powerful and flexible than we have described so far. Instead of only simple character strings as targets for searching, **ed** provides a syntax that allows you to specify many different strings to find or match. This syntax is called the *regular expression*. Regular expressions provide some of the most powerful text operations in the UNIX system. Whenever you can use the operation /**string**/ in **ed** to search for a matching string, you can use a regular expression instead of a simple string. In fact a character string is just the least complex form of the regular expression.

A regular expression consists of operators that describe single characters to search for. For example, the string **abc** consists of three characters. For each character, you could have substituted a complex expression to describe the character you were looking for in that position in the string. The . (dot) character is one of the regular expression operators and stands for "any single character."

You could use the string **a.c** to refer to any string beginning with *a* and ending with *c*, with any character between them. The string **adc** would match, as would **a#c** or **aSc**, but **abdc** would not match because there are two characters between the *a* and the *c*. You could match **abdc** with the regular expression **a..c**, with the regular expression **a...**, or with **.....**

Similarly, you can use other operators to build up a regular expression. The operators **[** and **]** (brackets) denote a set of characters, any one of which will match. The expression

[abc]

will match any of the single characters **a**, **b**, or **c**. The expression

[aA]

will match either an uppercase or lowercase *a*. This expression, a set of characters enclosed within square brackets, matches only one character in the file you are searching.

You can make sequences of these expressions to search for more than one character. For example, this expression

```
[aA][bB]
```

will match any of the strings **ab**, **aB**, **Ab**, or **AB**. Because each sequence surrounded with square brackets matches a single character, the construction above matches a two-character string. In a substitution command to **ed**, you might use

```
s/[aA][bB]/new string
```

to replace the first occurrence, on the current line, of any of the matching patterns with **new string**. To replace all occurrences of **ab**, **aB**, **Ab**, or **AB** in the file with **new string**, you could use the following command:

```
1,$s/[aA][bB]/new string/g
```

You can build up these regular expressions to any level of complexity, but each sequence enclosed in square brackets can only match a single character.

The square bracket operator can also match on single characters in a *range* of characters in the alphabetic **sort** sequence. For example, to find all occurrences of numbers in the file, you could use the following:

```
[0123456789]
```

However, a shorter form is as follows:

```
[0-9]
```

The – (dash) works within the bracket operator to denote a range of characters. To find any alphabetic character, you would use the following:

```
[A-Za-z]
```

This will find any single alphabetic character, either upper-case or lowercase.

To search for the special operator **[** directly, without having **ed** interpret it as the beginning of a regular expression, you must precede it with a \ (backslash). This command

```
s/\[/{/g
```

will replace every occurrence of the bracket on the current line with the { (curly brace) character. You can *escape* the special meaning of any regular expression operator in this way.

You can combine single-character regular expressions to match longer strings, as shown here:

```
s/[0-9][0-9][0-9]/WW
```

This will replace the first three-digit sequence of numbers on the current line with **WW**. You can add the * (star) operator to denote *zero or more* occurrences of the preceding single-character regular expression. For example, to replace a sequence of digits of any length, you could use the following:

```
s/[0-9][0-9]*/WW
```

Why can't you just use this

```
s/[0-9]*/WW
```

as your substitute command? Because * denotes zero or more occurrences of the string, this command will always add **WW** at the beginning of the current line, which is not what you intended. The initial **[0-9]** forces at least one digit to appear in the pattern before the optional digits.

You can substitute the entire line of the file with the following:

```
s/^.*$/WW
```

This will make the entire contents of the current line **WW**. You can read this as: start at the beginning of the line (^), take any character (.) any number of times (*), until the end of the line ($). You can build up very complex and clever regular expressions with these building blocks.

One important rule is that regular expressions match the longest matching string. If you have the string

```
abc1234def
```

and use the command

```
s/[0-9][0-9]*/WW
```

the result will be

```
abcWWdef
```

because the **[0-9]*** section will try to find all the digits in the string and substitute them all.

Sometimes you wish to name a string in the search section of the **s** command but do not wish to substitute it all. For example, you might want to add a word following a string of digits. You cannot use

```
/s/[0-9][0-9]*/new string
```

because this will delete the sequence of digits and replace it with **new string**. The special operator **&** (ampersand), when used in the substitution section, allows you to name *whatever you matched in the search section*. For example, with the string

```
abc1234def
```

and the command

```
s/[0-9][0-9]*/&newstring
```

the result will be

```
abc1234newstringdef
```

The **&** operator substituted the matching string back into the output line. As usual, you can get a literal **&** character into the output by escaping it with \ (backslash).

These regular expressions are the key to editing under the UNIX system. They occur not only in **ed** but also in all the other standard editors, and even in the shell. You might recognize the shell wild-card operators as a simplified form of the regular expressions discussed here. Unfortunately, the syntax for regular expressions in the shell command line is not identical to the form used in **ed**, so confusion is possible even for expert users.

The grep Command

The UNIX system provides a filter that lets you search for strings in files, using regular expressions to specify the match string. The **grep** (for global regular expression and print) command reads its standard input or a list of files given as arguments and writes to its standard output any lines that contain the match string. The first argument to the **grep** command is the pattern to search for. Use

```
$ grep any_pattern files
```

to search the list of files. The search string (**any—pattern**) can be any regular expression. In its simplest form the regular expression can be a simple sequence of characters.

```
$ grep world old.file
hello world
$
```

Each line that matches the pattern will go to the standard output of **grep**.

You can use any regular expression as the match pattern:

```
$ cat another.file | grep "^[a-z]12"
```

will find any line that begins with a lowercase letter followed by the digits 1 and 2 from the output of the pipeline. Quote the regular expression you are searching for to prevent the shell from interpreting the bracket characters before **grep** sees them.

The **grep** command also allows you to select every line that does not contain the pattern. The −**v** option is used. Here,

```
$ grep -v world old.file
another line
a third line
$
```

every line that does not contain the string **world** will be displayed.

The **grep** command also provides many other options. The −**c** (for count) option produces only a count of matching lines, like piping the output of **grep** to **wc** −**l**. The −**n** (for number) option adds the source file line number to the matching output. The −**i** (for ignore) option ignores case distinctions in finding matches.

In addition, two other flavors of the **grep** command optimize the search for some special cases. The **fgrep** (for fixed grep) command takes only a fixed string to search for, rather than a regular expression. The **egrep** (for extended grep) allows a richer set of regular expression operators than does **grep** and is optimized for more complex searches. In most situations the original **grep** is a good compromise between these features.

The **egrep** command provides some additional regular expression operators that differ slightly from the **grep** operators. In addition to the * operator to designate zero or more occurrences of the single-character pattern, **egrep** also provides the + (plus) operator, which denotes one or more occurrences of the character. For example, in **grep** you write

```
[0-9][0-9]*
```

for any sequence of digits of any length. This will work with **egrep**, but you could also write

```
[0-9]+
```

to mean the same thing. Similarly, the operator ? (question mark) denotes *zero or one occurrence* of the pattern. For example, this expression

```
^[0-9]?a|b
```

will match a line that begins with an optional digit and then either the letter *a* or *b*.

In **egrep**, the operator | (pipe) denotes *either* of a pair of regular expressions. For example,

```
^a|b
```

will match a line that begins with either a or b. The **egrep** command also allows a parenthesis operator to group multi-character regular expressions. The command

```
$ egrep "([0-9][0-9]*ab)*1234" file
```

will find any strings that begin with a sequence of one or more digits, followed by ab, followed by a sequence of one or more digits, followed by ab, and so on, for any number of these patterns.

In **egrep**, you can use the −**f file.name** (for file) command-line option, which takes the regular expression from the file specified after the −**f** flag, rather than from the command line. In **fgrep**, the file contains the list of strings to search for.

The **grep** command is widely used and provides a very quick and powerful mechanism for finding arbitrary character strings in text files. When using it, try to specify the smallest regular expression that meets the needs, because the output from a large **grep** command can be verbose if the match is more general than you want.

The sed Stream Editor

Some of the features of both **ed** and **grep** are combined into the **sed** (for stream editor) command. The **sed** command is a filter like **grep**, but it lets you make changes to files. On the other hand, it is not interactive like **ed**. The **sed** command reads its input line by line and writes the lines one by one to its standard output. For each line read in, **sed** applies a substitute operation of the form used with **ed**. If the match succeeds, the substitution is made and the line is written out; if there is no match, the line is written unchanged.

A major advantage of **sed** over **ed** or other editors is that lines are read, modified, and written one by one. Therefore, there is no in-memory buffer of the entire file, which means that files of any size can be changed with **sed**, even ones that are too big for **ed** or other text editors. The **sed** command is often used to edit files that are larger than one megabyte. Most normal text editors cannot handle such large files.

The **sed** command is invoked with a command line like **grep**, except that you can use a full substitution operator. This command

```
$ sed "s/hello/goodbye/" in.file
```

will substitute the first instance of **hello** on each line of the file **in.file** with the string **goodbye**, and write the line to the standard output.

```
$ echo "1234hello5678" | sed "s/hello/goodbye/"
1234goodbye5678
$
```

Quote the substitution command to protect it from interpretation by the shell. As usual, the match string can be any regular expression.

The **sed** command also allows many other operators. You can delete all the lines that contain the string **hello** with the following command:

```
$ sed "/hello/d" in.file
```

In this example the command means: "search for the string **hello**, and if you find it, then delete the line." This **sed** command has the same result as the following:

```
$ grep -v hello in.file
```

To delete only the string **hello** from the line, without deleting the line as a whole from the output, you would use this form instead:

```
$ sed "s/hello//" in.file
```

Like **ed**, the **sed** operators can also take a line address or range of addresses if you wish to restrict your changes to a part of the file. This command

```
sed "3,7s/hello//" in.file
```

will delete the first **hello** from lines 3 through 7 of the file and leave the rest of the lines unchanged. Furthermore, you can use a context address instead of a line number if desired.

```
sed "/hello/,/goodbye/s/bad/good/g" in.file
```

This command will find the first instance of the string **hello**, change all instances of the string **bad** to **good** until the string **goodbye** is found or the file ends. In this example, if there is another instance of **hello** after the **goodbye** is found, then the substitution will begin again until the next instance of **goodbye**.

Actually **sed** is even more powerful than we have described so far. If you put the command in a file instead of on the command line, you can use the **−f** (for file) option to **sed**.

```
$ sed -f command.file in.file
```

In this command the regular expression operators are in the file **command.file**. Otherwise, **sed** acts as expected. With only a single command, as in the preceding examples, there is little use for the command file, though complex regular expressions can sometimes be more easily debugged if you can keep them in a relatively permanent place. However, the command file has a more important function: you can write multiline scripts for **sed** so that a series of operations can be performed on each input line before **sed** writes it to the output. For example, you can create a file named **command.file** with the following command list:

```
s/hello/goodbye/
s/good/bad/
```

Now, if you execute

```
$ echo "1234hello5678" | sed -f command.file
```

the output will be

```
$ echo "1234hello5678" | sed -f command.file
1234badbye5678
$
```

The operations specified in the file are executed sequentially on each line of the input until the line is either deleted or end of the file is reached. When the command set is completed, the line is written to the standard output; then the next line of the input is read, and the process is repeated.

There are many other options in the **sed** command set. Using **sed**, and regular expressions in general, is a skill that is best learned through experience and careful reading of the relevant pages in the *UNIX User's Manual*.

The vi Text Editor

Having completed this (long!) introduction, we can now discuss the most widely used text editing tool, the full-screen editor **vi** (for visual). All modern UNIX systems include the **vi** editor, so most people learn it soon after **ed**, and many become experts with it. However, it is not to the taste of some people, and the **emacs** (for editor from Project MAC at MIT) editor is also widely used. The **emacs** editor is not a standard part of the UNIX system like **vi**, so you may have to purchase it separately.

The **vi** editor is a subset of a larger editor called **ex**, and some of the documentation refers to **ex** commands. The **ex** editor is a line-oriented tool much like **ed**, except that it includes many more commands and functions. Actually **ex** itself is rarely used, and so we will not discuss **ex** independently of **vi**.

The **vi** editor is a full-screen text editor that displays a screenful of text on the screen. As you move to a new part of the file you are editing, **vi** redraws the screen so that the current line is always on screen. However, **vi** is not a word processor or a publishing system; it does not format text or allow integrated graphics. On the other hand, **vi** is terminal independent, so that you can use it equally well on the system console or from a remote terminal. To use **vi** on different terminals, you just have to tell the program what kind of terminal you are using. The *TERM* (for terminal) environment variable handles this chore. The **vi** editor reads this environment variable when it starts up and changes its output to display the file efficiently for your terminal. Most systems do not automatically define *TERM* when you log in unless you are on the system console. However, much software uses *TERM*, so you should be sure it is defined. You can set the variable directly from the shell.

```
$ TERM=ansi
$ export TERM
```

This is correct if the terminal is a standard ANSI terminal or similar. Most popular terminals are supported. The second command in this example, **export TERM**, allows all your subshells as well as the log-in shell to use the *TERM* variable. You can include these two commands in your **.profile** so that *TERM* is always set when you log into the system. The **.profile**, including a procedure to set the *TERM* variable, is discussed in Chapter 7.

vi and other full-screen programs, such as the **help** command, read the *TERM* variable and then look in a database to find a symbolic description of the terminal specified. On SVR3 systems this database is located in the directory tree under **/usr/lib/terminfo**. This directory contains subdirectories for each letter or number that can begin a terminal type understood by full-screen programs. For example, the directory **/usr/lib/terminfo/a** contains a list of terminals whose name begins with the letter *a*, such as the ansi. The directory **/usr/lib/terminfo/2** contains a list of terminals whose name begins with 2, such as the HP2626. You can check to see if your terminal is included in the database by browsing this *terminfo database*. System releases before SVR3 may use a different database scheme for the terminals. If so, all the terminal descriptions will be in the file **/etc/termcap**. If the **/usr/lib/terminfo** directory tree is present on a machine, it will be used instead of the **/etc/termcap** database for **vi** and most other full-screen applications.

The 80386 systems use the line **TERM=AT386** for logins on the console. On a remote terminal, **TERM=ansi** (for ANSI-standard) will work on many terminals. If ANSI does not work on your terminal, browse through **/etc/termcap** or the directories in **/usr/lib/terminfo** to find the name used for your terminal. Most popular terminals are included in the database, but you may have to search to find the correct name of your terminal. If your *TERM* variable is incorrect, or if you have not set and exported the *TERM=*... variable, **vi** and other full-screen applications will not work correctly.

Basic Principles of the vi Editor

The **vi** editor is a large superset of the **ed** editor, and most of your experience with **ed** will apply to **vi**. However, **vi** has many more functions than **ed**, especially the full-screen commands.

The **vi** editor can be invoked from the shell with an optional filename list as argument.

```
$ vi old.file
$ vi new.file
$ vi new.file old.file
$ vi
```

These are all acceptable commands. If you give more than one filename as arguments, **vi** will edit them one by one, loading them into the text buffer when you start **vi** or switch files. The *current filename* is accessible with a **vi** command. If you execute **vi** with no filename as argument, you will have to name a file before you write the text buffer.

With these commands, **vi** will start with the first line of the file as its current line. This differs from **ed**, which begins with the last line of the file as the current line. While **vi** is in operation, the line that the screen *cursor* is on is the current line. When you change the current line with a **vi** command, the cursor will move, redrawing the screen if necessary.

The **vi** editor allows several other command line arguments. You can use the + option with a following line number to make the given line number the current line. This command

```
$ vi +45 old.file
```

will make line 45 of the file **old.file** the initial current line. This command

```
$ vi +$ old.file
```

is used to start **vi** at the end of the file. You can also use

```
$ vi +/string old.file
```

to make **vi** search for **string** and make the first occurrence the current line. In fact you can use any **vi** command following the +, and it will be interpreted before **vi** first draws the screen for you.

The **vi** display fills the entire screen with the text file, leaving only one line at the bottom for special information. However, if the file is short or you load it at the end of the file, **vi** will fill the unused portion of the screen with empty lines that begin with ~ (tilde). The ~ just marks an unused line in the **vi** text display. When you load **vi** with a new filename or no filename, the entire screen will have the ~ at the left side because no text is in the buffer.

In operation **vi** has three different modes, two of which are similar to the **ed** command mode and input modes. You must switch between text entry into the file and commands to change the current line, write the file, and so on. When you are in input mode, you can jump to command mode by pressing the ESCAPE key, which is marked ESC on many keyboards. Enter input mode from command mode by using one of the text commands discussed below.

Each mode acts differently and has its own command set. Consult Table 5-1 for a summary of the major commands for **vi**.

Last Line Mode

In addition, **vi** has a third mode called *last line* mode. You invoke this mode from command mode by entering a : (colon). The cursor will jump to the last line of the screen and **vi** will wait for your command. You can enter any command acceptable to **ed** after the :, and it will be executed by **vi** as you expect.

Enter Input Mode		Move Cursor	
i	before cursor	l	one space right
a	after cursor	h	one space left
I	at start of line	j	one line down
A	at end of line	k	one line up
O	open line above	$	end of line
o	open line below	^	start of line
		w	next word
		e	end of word

Delete		Change	
dw	delete word	cw	change word
dd	delete line	cc	change line
D	to end of line	C	to end of line
x	char at cursor	r	char at cursor

Other Functions		Screen Control	
u	undo	CTRL-d	scroll forward
/	search forward	CTRL-u	scroll back
?	search backward	CTRL-f	next screen
n	next occurrence	CTRL-b	previous screen
.	repeat last action	CTRL-l	redraw screen
Y	yank line		
p	put below		
P	put above		
ZZ	write and quit		
ESC	cancel command		

Last Line Mode		When in Input Mode	
:w	write file	BACKSPACE	delete char
:q	quit	CTRL-w	delete word
:wq	write and quit	ESC	command mode
:n	next file		
:r	read file		
:e	edit file		
:f	file name		
:set	change options		
:!	shell escape		
:n	line n		

Table 5-1.   Major Commands for the **vi** Text Editor

This mode is used to *write* the file, with the **w** operator (enter **:w** from command mode), *quit* the editor with the **q** (or **:q**) operator, and so on. Even search and substitute operations in the **ed** format are allowed from last line mode, so you could use only **ed** commands to modify the file if you wished. For example, this is a legitimate command from **vi** command mode.

```
:/hello/,45s/1234/678/g
```

This command searches for the string **hello** from the current line. If there is a match, all occurrences of the string **1234** from there until line 45 will be changed to **678**.

Jumping to last line mode with : does not change the current line, so operations such as

```
:r another.file
```

will read **another.file** into the current buffer after the current line. You can write a portion of the file with the following:

```
:5,30w another.file
```

As usual, context addresses and filename arguments are allowed with these read and write operations from last line mode.

When you use a command like

```
:w another.file
```

the file **another.file** may already exist. If it does, **vi** will not overwrite it so easily. It will respond with the following message:

```
File exists - use "w! another.file" to overwrite
```

This is to prevent you from overwriting a file by mistake.

These messages will appear at the bottom of the screen, replacing the : command. You can add the ! (bang) operator after the **w** to force **vi** to perform the operation anyway. No spaces are allowed between the **w** and the !, but a space is required after the ! before the filename. Similarly, if you execute the command

```
:q
```

after you have made changes to the file but before you have written the file back to disk, **vi** will object, responding with the following:

```
No write since last change (:quit! overrides)
```

Again, you can use the ! if you want to abandon your changes to the file:

```
:q!
```

This will return you immediately to the shell, though normally you will wish to write out your changes before you leave the editor. You can also concatenate **w** and **q** into a single command.

```
:wq
```

Finally, you can use the command **ZZ** (two capital **z** characters) as a synonym for **:wq** to write your file and exit back to the shell.

The ! also has other uses within last line mode. You can use

```
:!command or pipeline
```

to temporarily suspend **vi** and execute a command in a sub-shell. When the shell command is completed, **vi** returns. For example, this command

```
:!ls
```

will run **ls** on the current directory. To get a full shell, you can use the special case

```
:sh
```

The **vi** will be suspended, and you will see your PS1 prompt. When you are through with the shell, end it with **exit** or by pressing CTRL-D, and **vi** will go back into action.

You can add the standard output of any command to your current buffer with the following:

```
:r !command
```

This will read the standard output of **command** into your file at the current line. Similarly, this command

```
:w !command
```

will write the file into the standard input of **command**.

In addition, you can filter a portion of the current file through a pipeline with the following:

```
:3,56 !command
```

This will write lines 3 through 56 into the standard input of **command**, delete the lines from the buffer, and read in the standard output of **command** in its place. As usual, context addresses can precede any of these commands to restrict the operation to a subset of the file.

The **vi** has several more functions available from last line mode. If you enter / (slash) instead of a colon, you can enter a regular expression for searching. The **vi** will search forward to the next occurrence of the regular expression and position the cursor at its beginning. You can also enter **?** instead of /, followed by a regular expression, and **vi** will search backward in the file until it finds the expression. As usual, if the expression does not appear, **vi** will loop back to the beginning of the file and search until the current line is reached.

If you have entered **vi** with a list of filenames, the command **:n** (for next) will close the current file and switch to the next file in the argument list. However, **vi** will not let you edit more than one file at once; there is always only one current file. Both **:n!** and **:q!** are allowed, to force **vi** to execute the function even if you have not written one of the files or completed editing all the files in the argument list.

Finally, you can instruct **vi** to display an on-screen indicator when you are in input mode that disappears when you enter command mode. The command

```
:set showmode
```

enables this function. The **:set** command also has several other options, as we will see.

Command Mode

When **vi** starts, it loads the file, redraws the screen to display the current line near the middle, and then waits for your input. At this point **vi** is in *command mode*. This command mode differs from that of **ed**, because the **ed** commands are accessible in last line mode. The **vi** command mode includes new commands and operators that are designed for the full-screen operation of the editor. These commands are used to enter input mode, change the contents of the file, move the cursor, and *mark* regions of text for some action. There are a great many operators in **vi** command mode, and we will discuss only the major ones. The first set of operators discussed below perform the described action and leave you in input mode to enter text.

The **o** (for open) command will open a new line of text after the current line and position the cursor at the beginning of the newly created line. The uppercase operator **O** (letter *O*) will open a line above the current line. Use **a** (for append) to enter input mode on the next character after the cursor. Material to the right of the cursor will be pushed to the right as you enter text into the line. The uppercase operator **A** will enter text mode at the end of the current line. Similarly, the **i** (for input) operator will enter input mode just before the current cursor location, and **I** (uppercase letter *I*) will enter input mode at the beginning of the current line. When you are in input mode, you can enter as much text as you wish, including new lines. The ESC key is used to return to command mode.

All the above commands enter input mode without changing any of the text already present. Several operators will enter text mode and allow you to change existing text. The **r** (for replace) command followed by a single character will change the character at the current cursor position with the character you type. This command leaves you in command mode, because it changes only a single character. The **R** operator allows you to replace as many characters as you wish, starting at the current cursor position. This command leaves you in input mode, but you can replace only to the end of the current line. Any new lines will be added to the file right after the current line. When you return to command mode with the ESC key after the **R** operation, any characters left on the current line that you did not overtype will remain as they were. The **C** (for change) command acts similarly to **R**, but the whole line is changed even if you changed only one character before returning to command mode. The **J** (for join) operator merges two lines of text by deleting the NEWLINE separating the current line and the following line. To split a single line into two lines, just enter input mode with the cursor where you want to split the lines and press the NEWLINE key.

Another batch of commands are used to change the current cursor location. These can be used instead of the last line commands introduced earlier. The **w** (for word) operator jumps the cursor ahead to the beginning of the next word. The **b** (for back) jumps the cursor backward to the beginning of the previous word. The SPACE key moves the cursor ahead a single character, and the BACKSPACE will move the cursor backward a single character. NEWLINE moves the cursor to the beginning of the next line, and − (minus) moves the cursor to the beginning of the previous line. The ^ (caret) moves the cursor to the beginning of the current line, and $ (dollar) moves the cursor to the end of the current line. All these motion operators can take a numeric argument, or *repeat count*, preceding the operator. For example, the command **5w** will move the cursor ahead five words, and **6−** will move the cursor back to the beginning of the sixth line previous to the current line. The **H** operator will move the cursor to the top line of the currently displayed screen, and **L** will move to the last line displayed on the screen. To move to the first line of the file, you can enter :**1**, and to move to the last line of the file, you use :**$**, as discussed under last line mode. Pressing CTRL-F will move you forward in the file by one complete screenful, redrawing the screen as it moves, while pressing CTRL-B will move you backward in the file by one screenful.

If the display gets confused for any reason, press CTRL-L to cause **vi** to redraw the screen, updating it to its current idea of what is in the file.

Many terminals include cursor control keys on the keyboard. Usually **vi** will honor these keys in addition to the motion operators defined above. Because these keys vary from keyboard to keyboard, you must experiment with the keys on your terminal and with your version of **vi** to see how they act.

Operators are also provided to delete sections of text. The **x** operator deletes the current character, and **6x** will delete the next six characters from the cursor position. The **dd** operator deletes the current line, and **6dd** will delete the current line and the next five lines. You can delete a single word with **dw** or five words with **5dw**. You can use the **c** (for change) operator with the repeat count and the **w** command to change sections of text. Use **cw** to change the current word and **6cw** to change the next six words. The **cc** operator will change the current line, and **6cc** will change the next six lines.

The . (dot) operator will apply the last change again to the current cursor position. This includes text addition and deletion operations and replacements.

There are many more command mode operators in **vi**, and as you learn the editor, you will find some of these more to your taste than others. One of the more important ones is the **u** (for undo) operator. Like **ed**, **vi** only retains a memory of the last change made to the file, and you can restore this last change at any time with **u**.

Input Mode

Most of the functions of the **vi** input mode are intuitive. When you are in input mode, all the text you enter goes into the file. NEWLINEs entered go into the file, and this is how you add additional lines to the file. If you make an error in typing, the BACKSPACE key lets you back up, deleting characters as you go, until the beginning of the line. However, **vi** will not let you backspace past the beginning of a line. To change a previous line, you must enter command mode, reposition the cursor to the error, and then make the change. You can press CTRL-W to delete the current word without leaving input mode.

A common error is to attempt to enter commands while in input mode without first pressing ESC. Even **vi** experts make this mistake, or make the opposite error, trying to enter text while in command mode. This second error is more devious because you can make multiple changes to the file as you type, and they usually cannot be "unwound" correctly with **u**, because the **undo** command can repair only the *last* change. To prevent problems associated with these *mode errors*, frequently write the file back to disk with the **:w** command when you are sure it is correct.

Going Further

There is a great deal more to editing under the UNIX system. Here we will mention a few more **vi** and **ed** features and then quickly discuss **emacs**, the other major editor.

Configuring vi Options

The **vi** editor has many options that change its behavior, which are accessed in one of two ways. First, the **:set** command discussed earlier with **:set showmode** is an example, and nearly 50 options in addition to **showmode** can be set this way. The command

```
:set all
```

will display them all. When you change an option, use the option name after the **:set** command to turn the option on, and enter **no** in front of the option name to turn it off. This command

```
:set showmode
:set noshowmode
```

will turn **showmode** on and then off.

Some of the options take an argument. This command

```
:set window=10
```

will make the logical window size ten rows high. You can experiment with the **vi** options to customize the editor for your taste and terminal environment. Some of the more widely used options are **terse** for a shorter message display, **autoindent** to start a new line at the same column as the beginning of the previous line, and **number** to display line numbers of the file on the screen. The **tabstop** option changes the number of character positions that the cursor moves after a TAB key is pressed. The **ignorecase** option allows both uppercase and lowercase characters to match in regular expression searches.

The options that you set with **:set** are only active for the current editing session with **vi**. When you exit the editor with **:q**, the options are lost, and you must reset them the next time you run **vi**. However, **vi** allows two mechanisms to set options permanently, so that when **vi** starts up, it configures itself according to your instructions. First, the environment variable *EXINIT* can contain a **set** command that is executed when **vi** begins. For example, this command

```
$ EXINIT='set number tabstop=4 ignorecase' ; export EXINIT
```

will configure **vi** with **number, ignorecase**, and tabs set to four spaces. Normally you set this environment variable in your **.profile** so that it is active each time you log into the system. Second, you can put these commands into a file called **.exrc** (for **ex** run commands) in your home directory. When **vi** loads, it will read the file and take the actions specified.

Another powerful use of the *EXINIT* variable and the **.exrc** file is the **map** command. You can use this command to map any keystroke to any **vi** function or sequence of functions. This allows you to configure **vi** to perform complex actions with only a few keystrokes. Unfortunately, this function uses an obscure and difficult programming language, and it is useful mainly to **vi** experts.

Buffers in vi

The **vi** editor can maintain several internal buffers for blocks of text that are not part of the file you are editing; these blocks can be pulled out of the file into a buffer and then read back into the file from the buffer. There is a single default buffer, or you can name a buffer with a one-character name. When you perform an operation on a buffer, you use the name of the buffer to refer to the buffer. These operations are known as **yank** and **put**, and they operate in **vi** command mode, not last line mode. You can read a section of text into a buffer with the **y** (for yank) command, which takes a number of lines to yank. For example, this command

```
7y
```

will yank seven lines into the default buffer. You can reposition the cursor and then use the **p** (for put) command to put the lines of text back into the file after the cursor. Uppercase **P** is used to put the lines into the file just above the cursor.

Because the default buffer is also used to store the last change for the **u** operation, the text will only remain in this buffer until you make another editing change. You can keep the text in the buffer longer by naming a buffer with a one-character name, preceded by " (double quote). This command

```
7"ay
```

will yank seven lines into the buffer named **a**. Many differently named buffers are allowed simultaneously. The named buffer can be put back into the text with the following:

```
"ap
```

This puts the contents of buffer **a** into the file after the current line.

ed Scripts

The **vi** editor executes with different terminal controls than most programs, so the concepts of standard input and output do not apply to **vi** as they do to other programs. The **vi** program is totally interactive and requires that its input and output be directed to a terminal. However, **ed** uses standard I/O, and you can take advantage of that property to create **ed** *scripts*, which are often used to automatically modify files when you know the contents of the file and can predict the sequence of **ed** commands that will be needed to make the desired changes. A simple **ed** script is the following file:

```
$ cat ed.script
/findme/
a
hello
goodbye
.
w
q
$
```

If these commands were entered interactively to **ed**, they would have this effect: set the current line to the first line containing the string **findme** (/**findme**/), append after that line (**a**), enter **hello** and **goodbye** in input mode, return to command mode (.), write the file (**w**), and, finally, quit (**q**) the editor. The command

```
$ ed old.file < ed.script
$
```

will execute the commands and change the file without input from the user. This form appears in several system *shell scripts* but is only useful if you know the exact changes you wish to make on the file before you create the **ed** script.

You can suppress the various information output produced by **ed** during its processing of a script with the —s (for silent) command line option.

The emacs Editor

The **emacs** is another full-screen text editor that is nearly as popular as **vi** but is not part of the standard UNIX system. However, **emacs** is widely available for any version of the UNIX system running on any machine; **emacs** is usually the first or second piece of software ported to new machines as they are designed. Several versions of **emacs** are available for SVR3 running on the 80386 machines.

The **emacs** is very different in its philosophy from **vi**, but like **vi**, it is not a word processor in the modern sense. Neither editor will format text or allow embedded graphics. Like **vi**, **emacs** allows you to use nearly any terminal, as specified by the *TERM* environment variable. However, some versions of **emacs** do not use the **/usr/lib/terminfo** terminal database; instead, they have their own terminal description file in **/usr/lib/emacs/terminals**. Other library material related to **emacs**, such as the text of available *macros*, may also be in the directory **/usr/lib/emacs**. These directory locations may vary in different versions of **emacs**.

In operation **emacs** is fundamentally different than **vi**. There is no input or command mode, and all normal characters typed at the keyboard go into the text file at the cursor position. That is, **emacs** is always in input mode. In fact the term *mode* has a different use in **emacs**, referring not to the editor's command state but rather to the options that are currently set. For example, when the editor displays line numbers for the file being edited, it is said to be in *line number mode*.

Commands to move the cursor, read and write files, open additional lines, and so on, are special keystroke sequences beginning with the ESC key or the CTRL key. For example, to exit from **emacs** back to the shell, use the keystroke sequence CTRL-X followed by CTRL-C. In **emacs** terminology these CTRL keys are denoted ^**X**^**C**, where the ^ (caret) preceding the other characters means to hold down the CTRL key while pressing the X and C keys. Other commands are invoked with the ESC key preceding the command, such as the sequence ESC-M (ESC key followed by the M key), which displays the current **emacs** options in effect. In **emacs** terminology these escape sequences are denoted with the letter **M** (for meta) preceding the letter, such as M—m for the **escape m** command. Remember, any character sequences that do not begin with either **escape** or a CTRL character are treated as text to be entered into the file. The **emacs** uses nearly all the CTRL keys for various functions, and the $^\wedge$**X** combination introduces longer sequences that have specific meanings, such as $^\wedge$**X**$^\wedge$**M**$^\wedge$**M**. We will discuss some of these operators shortly.

Many users prefer the "modeless" operation of **emacs** over the three different modes in **vi**, though the command set used by **emacs** is even less mnemonic than the **vi** commands, and some users find the advanced features of **emacs** more difficult to learn than **vi**.

The **emacs** is invoked with an optional filename.

```
$ emacs old.file
```

It will not accept multiple filenames given as arguments. The file, if any, is read into the *main* buffer of **emacs**. The optional argument **+n**, where *n* is a number, will cause **emacs** to position the cursor on line *n* as it starts. After loading, it is possible to read additional files into additional **emacs** buffers, and up to 12 files can be edited simultaneously. The $^\wedge$**X**$^\wedge$**F** (for file) command is used to read a new file into a new buffer. This differs from the $^\wedge$**X**$^\wedge$**R** (for read) command, which reads a file into the current buffer after discarding the current contents of the buffer (if any). The $^\wedge$**U**$^\wedge$**X**$^\wedge$**R** command will read a file into the buffer at the current cursor position without deleting the current contents of the buffer. Both of these commands will prompt for the name of the file to read.

Figure 5-1 shows a typical **emacs** display after the program is loaded with **/etc/profile**. This display may differ slightly on other releases of **emacs**. The top section of the display shows the current line and surrounding lines of the file you are editing, with line numbers in this case. You can change the size of the display and whether or not the line numbers are displayed with **emacs** commands by using the $^\wedge X{}^\wedge M$ (for change mode) command sequence as discussed below. The bottom of the screen contains the **emacs** version number, followed by the current buffer number **(0)** and current buffer name (Main). The = (equal sign) signifies that the file has not been changed since you started editing it, and this will change to the > character as soon as you have changed the contents of the buffer. The name of the file that you are editing appears last on the line. The last two lines of the display are **emacs** information lines, reserved for special messages from **emacs**. Here it is telling you that electronic mail is waiting for you. The **emacs** usually includes special commands to read your mail into a text buffer or to send the contents of a buffer as mail.

```
1    #
2    #  FILE:  /etc/profile
3    #  Initialization script for all logins.
4    #
5
6    trap '' 1 2 3
7
8    set `who -r`
9    if [ "$3" = "S" ]
10   then
11           sync;sync;sync
12           /etc/killall
13
14           ##  Any shutdown procedures (such as slancard reset) can be
15           ##  put in /etc/shutdaemon, and will be executed without
16           ##  changing /etc/profile.
17
18           if [ -d /etc/shutdaemon ]
19           then
20                   for i in /etc/shutdaemon/*

EMACS 4.9b     (0) Main = /etc/profile
 You have mail
```

Figure 5-1.   Typical **emacs** screen display

```
1    root:We34lKw/4Wpmg:0:0:Root:/:
2    daemon:NONE:1:1:Admin:/:
3    bin:NONE:2:2:Admin:/bin:
4    sys:NONE:3:3:Admin:/:
5    adm:NONE:4:4:Admin:/usr/adm:
6    uucp::5:6:uucp:/usr/spool/uucppublic:/usr/lib/uucp/uucico
7    nuucp::5:6:uucp:/usr/spool/uucppublic:/usr/lib/uucp/uucico
8    uucpadm:NONE:5:6:Uucp Administration:/usr/lib/uucp:
9    lp:NONE:71:1:Lp Administrator:/bin:
```

```
1    #
2    #    FILE:   /etc/profile
3    #    Initialization script for all logins.
4    #
5
6    trap '' 1 2 3
7
8    set `who -r`
9    if [ "$3" = "S" ]
10   then
```

```
EMACS 4.9b    (0) Main = /etc/profile
 You have mail
```

Figure 5-2.   Typical two-window **emacs** screen display

The **emacs** can split its display screen so that any two of the buffers can be displayed and edited simultaneously. If you read another file into a second buffer with $^\wedge$**X**$^\wedge$**F**, then you can split the screen with $^\wedge$**X2** (for two windows). The **emacs** will prompt you to select the name or number of the new buffer to add to the screen. Though **emacs** can edit up to 12 different buffers simultaneously, only 2 can be displayed at once. You can return to a single-window display with $^\wedge$**X1**. Again, **emacs** will prompt you to select the buffer to retain on the screen. When you display or hide a buffer, it still remains in the internal **emacs** memory, so you have not closed the file or deleted any changes to it. Before you return to the shell, **emacs** will prompt you to write each buffer or discard the changes.

Figure 5-2 shows a typical two-window display. In this example the bottom window is the active one, where all your changes to the text will go. The information line at the bottom of the screen displays the name and buffer number of the active window. You can make the other window the active buffer with the ^X^O command, or you can change the displayed buffers completely with ^X^B.

After you make changes to the buffer, you can write it with ^X^W (for write). The **emacs** will prompt you at the bottom of the screen with the following:

```
Write file?
```

You can press Y to write the current file or n to abort the write operation. If you type in a new filename instead, then that file will be written instead of the default filename. To write the currently active buffer to its current filename, use the ^X^S (for save) command. To quit from **emacs** back to the shell, use ^X^C (for close). The **emacs** will prompt for confirmation if you try to quit back to the shell before you have written the file.

At any time you can enter **M−?** followed by a command, and **emacs** will provide a short explanatory message for the command. Although this help is terse, it sometimes provides the information that you need.

Changing the Cursor Position

A rich set of operators is provided for changing the current cursor position, where all text entry takes place. The ^F (for forward) command moves the cursor ahead one character, while ^B (for backward) moves the cursor back one character. The ^N (for next) operator moves the cursor to the next line, and ^P (for previous) moves the cursor back one line. The ^A moves the cursor to the beginning of the current line, while ^E (for end) moves the cursor to the end of the current line. The **M−<** command moves the cursor to the beginning of the buffer, and **M−>** moves the cursor to the end of the buffer. The **M−f** option moves the cursor ahead one word, while **M−b** moves the cursor back one word. The ^V command moves the cursor ahead one screenful, redrawing the screen to display the new block of text; and **M—v** moves the cursor back one screen-ful. Most of these commands can take a numeric argument to multiply the action. These arguments are entered beginning with the ESC key, then the number, and then the argument given above. For example, to move forward by eight words, press ESC, then 8, then ESC, and then f. You can jump to a specific line of the buffer with **M—nM—g** by giving the line number in place of the n.

Deleting Text

Because any normal characters that you type go into the text buffer at the cursor position, there is no difficulty inserting text with **emacs**. However, more special commands are needed to delete text. The BACKSPACE key will delete the character just to the left of the cursor, and $^\wedge$**D** (for delete) will delete the character directly under the cursor. The $^\wedge$**K** (for kill) command will delete the rest of the current line after the cursor position or join the current line with the next line if the cursor is at the end of the line. If an argument of **0** is given, all the text from the beginning of the line to the cursor position is deleted, but if an argument greater than 0 is given, that number of lines forward from the cursor is deleted. If the argument is less than 0, that number of lines is deleted backward from the cursor.

More complex deletion and text movement commands involve *marks*, and **emacs** allows up to 12 marks. One mark is normally associated with each text buffer allowed, and this is the usage when you use marks without specifically naming one. However, when you name a specific mark in a command, that mark becomes associated with that location, no matter what buffer it is in. You name marks by giving the mark number just as you name buffers. Place a mark at the current cursor position with **M—space** (the SPACE BAR, not the string **space**). To name a mark, use ESC followed by the mark number, followed by ESC, and then the SPACE BAR. The mark will not be displayed on the screen in most versions of **emacs**. The ^**W** command will delete all the text between the current cursor position and the mark. The ^**W** command can take an argument to specify which mark to use in the deletion operation.

Moving Text from One Buffer to Another

When material is deleted from a text buffer, **emacs** maintains the material in a *kill stack*. The last eight deletions are maintained in the kill stack. You usually move text by marking the beginning of the block, moving the cursor to the end of the block, and then deleting the block with ^**W**. The text is not really lost, so you can move the cursor to the location where you want the text to go and issue the ^**Y** command to insert the last killed block of text at the cursor position. The ^**Y** command is also useful to *undo* errors in deleting text, because the text is retained on the kill stack after a deletion.

The **M—p** (for pick up) command will grab the text from the mark to the current cursor position and place it on the kill stack. However, this command does not change the current buffer, so it is used with ^**Y** to *copy* blocks of text from one region of the buffer to another or from one buffer to another.

Searching and Replacing Text Strings

The **emacs** has powerful search operators to locate text strings or regular expressions in the current buffer. The **M—^S** (for search) command starts the action, and **emacs** will prompt for the regular expression to search for. Regular expression syntax as used in **ed** is accepted. This command also takes an argument, a positive number for forward search or a negative number for backward search from the cursor position. If the argument is **1** or **—1**, the search will wrap around the end of the file, stopping after a complete search of the buffer. With other arguments, the search will stop at either the end or the beginning of the file. After the search string is found, you can continue to search for the next instance of the same string with $^\wedge$**S** (for search) or $^\wedge$**R** (for reverse) in the forward or backward direction, respectively.

A similar procedure is provided to substitute strings from regular expressions matched. The **M—**$^\wedge$**R** (for replace) command is used, and **emacs** will prompt for the match string and the substitute string. Syntax is the same as for regular expressions in **ed**, though **emacs** allows an interactive substitution mechanism. The **emacs** will find the match string and then pause for a command. Press **y** if you want the substitution to be made on that occurrence of the match; press **n** to skip that one. In either case **emacs** will go on to the next occurrence of the match string, if any. You can also press **r** to instruct **emacs** to silently replace all the rest of the occurrences of the pattern in the file, or you can enter $^\wedge$**G** to abort the operation and return to normal **emacs** behavior.

Escaping to the Shell

Like many other commands, **emacs** allows you to temporarily suspend its operation while you do other work from the shell. Enter **M—!** and **emacs** will prompt for a command line to execute. The **emacs** will wait until the command is completed; then it will redraw the screen and resume its actions. If you give an argument to **M-!**, such as $^\wedge$**UM—!**, then the current buffer is given to the command line as its standard input. Similarly, the command **M—$** executes a command line, but **M—$** saves the standard output from the command line in an **emacs** buffer called **.exec**. This allows you to bring the standard output of the command line into your editing session.

Modes and Macros in emacs

The $^\wedge$**X**$^\wedge$**M** command is used to display and set the many internal *modes*, or configurable elements, within **emacs**. After $^\wedge$**X**$^\wedge$**M**, **emacs** will prompt you for the specific mode you wish to set. If you enter an additional $^\wedge$**M**, **emacs** will display the setting of all the modes. You can change the setting of a mode by entering its name after the $^\wedge$**X**$^\wedge$**M**. This will set the mode to its default state. If you give an additional argument after the mode name, then the mode will be set to that value. Some of the more important **emacs** modes are *save*, which tells **emacs** to automatically save your buffer to disk after you enter a number of characters specified by the *savetype* mode. You should keep this mode off while you are learning to use the editor so that you don't overwrite an important system file. The *fill* mode is turned on when you want an *autowrap* feature so that **emacs** will add a newline whenever you type more than *fillcol* characters on a single line. The **emacs** breaks up the line intelligently at word boundaries. The *lnumb* mode is used to toggle the line number display, and *overwrite* mode will make **emacs** overwrite characters under the cursor rather than insert your keystrokes at the cursor. The *height* and *width* modes give the dimensions of the screen display, which is useful if you have a windowing user interface on your machine. Many other modes are also available, although they vary somewhat among **emacs** versions. Experiment with these modes with your own **emacs** editor.

When **emacs** starts, it reads the file **.emacs_init** in your home directory. This file contains a set of **emacs** keystrokes that you could enter directly to the editor from the keyboard. The **emacs** executes these commands before it draws the screen and turns control over to the user. The **.emacs_init** file is used to customize the modes and environment to your personal tastes.

The **emacs** also provides excellent extension and customization tools. These *macros* are composed of a series of normal **emacs** commands, and they can contain calls to other macros that have been defined. Most commercial versions of **emacs** include many macros, ranging from automated spelling checkers to tools that remap the keyboard for specific terminals. The macro definition commands are somewhat easier to use than the **vi** map functions but are still not very usable. However, nearly unlimited extensions of the **emacs** system are possible, such that some **emacs** gurus run their entire sessions from within the editor, with so many customized tools that the normal shell and commands are barely visible.

More Useful
General-Purpose Commands

S I X

By now we have introduced the basic style of the UNIX system shell and user interface, as well as some of the more commonly used commands. The UNIX system as a whole includes more than 400 different executable commands, and we will discuss this rich set of tools by topic in the remaining chapters. Here, we will discuss commands that you will need almost daily to effectively use the UNIX system.

Unlike the other chapters, this chapter concerns tools that have very little in common with each other. They are generally useful commands that can make your life with the UNIX system a pleasure rather than a chore. These commands are also the fundamental building blocks for *shell scripts*, which are used to automate your common tasks. In Chapter 7, we will discuss shell scripts in detail.

The Environment Revisited

Recall that when a command is executed, the system establishes an execution *environment* for the command and passes some of your environment variables to that environment. Commands frequently use this environment. For example, the full-screen editors described in Chapter 5 use the *TERM* environment variable.

Not all of the environment variables are available to the commands you execute. When a command is executed, the shell gives it a starting environment that can be passed on to subprograms executed from that program. Only those environment variables that are *exported* are available to subprograms through this mechanism. This is a subset of the full list of environment variables. If you give the command

```
$ export
```

with no arguments, a list of the exported environment variables will be displayed. You can add a new environment variable to this list by naming it as an argument to the **export** command.

```
$ export TERM
$
```

This will export the *TERM* environment variable to your commands and subprograms.

Using the PATH Variable

One of the most important environment variables is the *PATH* variable. When you execute a command by naming the full pathname of the command, such as

```
$ /usr/bin/vi
```

the shell can find the command to execute by searching from the root of the directory hierarchy. However, if you do not give a full pathname, such as

```
$ xxx
xxx:   not found
$
```

the shell does not know where to look for the executable program. The *PATH* variable provides a list of directories that the shell will search to find the commands you name without requiring the full pathname. Here is a typical *PATH* variable:

```
$ echo $PATH
:/usr/steve/bin:/bin:/usr/bin:/usr/lbin
$
```

Your *PATH* may differ, but the syntax is common to all UNIX systems. The *PATH* is a short database, with individual entries separated by a : (colon). When you give a command without a full pathname, the shell will search each directory specified in the *PATH*, trying them in turn from left to right, until it finds a command with that name. If no such command resides in any of the specified directories, the shell will complain. If the command is found in one of the directories, it will be executed as you expect.

You may have more than one command with the same name on a machine, if the commands are in different directories. Because the directories in the *PATH* are searched in order, the one you will execute is determined by the order of directories in the *PATH*. In the example above the directory **/usr/steve/bin** appears before **/usr/bin**, and different commands with the same name can appear in each directory. Some other user may not have **/usr/steve/bin** in the *PATH* but probably does have **/usr/bin**. That user would execute the version of **vi** in **/usr/bin**, while you would get the version in **/usr/steve/**

bin. Thus individual users can control the set of commands available to them just by changing their *PATH*.

Most of the normal executable commands are located in one of the directories **/bin**, **/usr/bin**, or **/usr/lbin**. These will almost always be included in your *PATH*. You can add other directories as you wish, either to customize the execution of commands or to hold your personal commands. Sometimes the directory **/etc** will be included in the *PATH*, but usually only the *superuser* really needs the commands kept there. The superuser is an administrative login id that has complete power to make any changes whatsoever in the system. The **root** login id has these superuser privileges.

If you have installed some add-on application software such as a word processor or database management system, the directory location of these applications might also be included in your *PATH*.

Individual entries of the *PATH* are separated by a :. If there is an extra : in the *PATH*, as at the beginning of the previous example, then the current directory is used at that point. The difference between

```
$ PATH=/bin:/usr/bin:/usr/lbin
```

and

```
$ PATH=:/bin:/usr/bin:/usr/lbin
```

is that the current directory, whatever it is, will be searched first in the latter but not in the former. In the former example the current directory will not be searched. You can instruct the shell to search the current directory *after* all the other directories with the following command:

```
$ PATH=/bin:/usr/bin:/usr/lbin:
```

The extra : was added at the end of the *PATH*. The *PATH* variable is usually set and exported for you when you log into the system, and you need to change it only if you want a setup different from the default.

The banner Command

The system provides many general-purpose commands, and though some of them are more fun than useful, each has its place in the system. One of the simplest is the **banner** command, which blows its arguments up to large size and writes them to standard output.

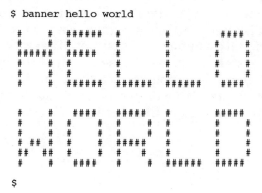

```
$ banner hello world
```

The **banner** command will make separate lines for its output intelligently on individual word boundaries to keep the screen display relatively sane. It is often used in such output functions as print spoolers to display various kinds of information.

The date Command

The UNIX system's excellent time-keeping facilities control time in the system at all resolutions from milliseconds through years. Nearly all systems have built-in clock/calendar chips, and time is usually set correctly by the kernel when it boots. All files have an associated modification time stamp, as we have seen. In addition, there is a general-purpose command to display the current date and time.

```
$ date
Wed May 27 18:12:56 EDT 1987
$
```

By default, the date is displayed according to your local time and time zone, and the system can determine the start and end of Daylight Savings Time. If the Daylight Savings Time laws change, however, the system may become confused. The **date** command is often used to time-stamp your work.

In addition, **date** can format its output differently and is used to set the system time. Because so much of the internal system activity depends on the correct time, the date should always be set correctly. We will discuss these additional features of the **date** command in Chapter 18.

The cal Command

The **cal** (for calendar) command falls into the category of useful "fun" commands. Given without arguments, it produces a calendar of the current month on its standard output.

```
$ cal
   May 1987
 S  M Tu  W Th  F  S
                1  2
 3  4  5  6  7  8  9
10 11 12 13 14 15 16
17 18 19 20 21 22 23
24 25 26 27 28 29 30
31
$
```

If a year is given as an argument, **cal** will print a full calendar for that year. Any year from 1 through 9999 can be displayed. Notice that the year 89 is early in the Christian era, not 1989. In addition, **cal** can take a second argument before the year, specifying a month during that year. The command

```
$ cal 9 1752
```

will display a calendar for September 1752. What is interesting about this month? The **cal** command is not buggy.

The calendar Command

The **calendar** command provides a rudimentary reminder service that you can use to record your coming appointments. This is a simple-minded calendar compared to other timing features in the UNIX system, but it can be useful for beginning users. If a file named **calendar** is present in the current directory, the **calendar** command will effectively **grep** through the file searching for lines that contain either today's or tomorrow's date anywhere on the line. In practice, you can edit your file **calendar** to add new appointments as they come up, one per line. You can run the **calendar** program at least once a day to show the current events.

```
$ calendar
Doctor's appointment on May 28 for checkup
$
```

The **calendar** command can handle several different date formats, including that shown in the previous example and also 5/28, though European date format such as 28/5 is not processed correctly. You might set things up so that **calendar** is run whenever you log into the system, so you can see your activities for the day. The **calendar** file is usually in your home directory.

The pg and tail Programs

We have met the **pg** program, which presents output to your display one screenful at a time, waiting for you to press newline before going on to the next screenful. Usually **pg** is used at the end of a pipeline or with a list of filenames as arguments.

```
$ pg /etc/profile /etc/inittab
```

The command will pause after each screenful of output, prompting with ":" (colon) at the bottom of the screen. To go on to the next screenful, you can simply enter a carriage return. If a number is entered before newline is pressed, **pg** will skip forward that number of screenfuls before displaying another. If the number is negative, **pg** will skip backward that number of screenfuls. The l (the letter *l*, for lines) command causes **pg** to move forward line by line instead of by screenfuls. It can also take a positive or negative argument to specify how many lines to scroll.

In addition, **pg** can accept many other commands at the ":" prompt. You can enter a regular expression following the : in the syntax of **ed**, beginning with / or ?, and **pg** will search forward or backward, respectively, for that expression. It will then display the segment of text surrounding the matched expression. A number *n* preceding the / will cause **pg** to search for the *n*-th occurrence of the expression.

```
:6/[fe]grep/
```

This example will search for the sixth occurrence of the string **fgrep** or **egrep** following the current line. The . (dot) operator causes the current screen to be redisplayed, and $ causes the last screenful of the file to be displayed.

If there is more than one file in the argument list to **pg**, then **n** (for next) will skip to the beginning of the next file, and **p** (for previous) will skip back to the beginning of the previous file. Both **n** and **p** can take a number before the letter to specify the *n*-th previous file.

```
:3p
```

Naturally, the **n** and **p** commands will not work if **pg** is invoked at the end of a pipeline. The **h** (for help) command will display a list of **pg** commands, and **q** (for quit) or the DEL key will exit from **pg** back to the shell.

The **pg** command uses the *TERM* environment variable to

format output for most full-screen terminals, so this variable must be correct or **pg** will get confused.

The **pg** command starts its display at the beginning of the file. To see the end of a file with **pg**, you must step through the entire file or use the $ operator. Use the **tail** command to look at the end (or tail) of the file given as argument. You can also use **tail** at the end or even in the middle of a pipeline if you wish. It writes the last 10 lines of the file to its standard output.

```
$ tail /etc/profile
EDITOR=/usr/bin/vi
FCEDIT=/usr/bin/vi
EXINIT='set ai'
ENV="\${-:+$HOME/.ksh.aliases\${-##*i*}}"
export HISTFILE EDITOR FCEDIT EXINIT ENV
>$HISTFILE

stty brkint echoe ixon ixany erase

trap 1 2 3
$
```

In addition, **tail** can take a number following the — argument flag, to specify the number of lines instead of 10 to display.

```
$ tail -1 /etc/profile
trap 1 2 3
$
```

A character can follow the number, to count in units other than lines. The commands **c** (for characters) and **b** (for blocks) will cause **tail** to count in characters or blocks, respectively.

```
$ tail -50c /etc/profile
stty brkint echoe ixon ixany erase

trap 1 2 3
$
```

This displays the last 50 characters of the file, starting in the middle of a line if necessary.

The **tail** command usually exits back to the shell when it reads the end of the file. Often some program is writing to a file and you wish to watch the end of the file continuously as it grows. You could accomplish this by repeatedly executing **tail** —3. However, the —**f** (for follow) option to **tail** causes it to continue to execute, displaying each new line of the file as it gets written.

```
$ tail -f growing.file
```

Because **tail** **−f** does not end on its own, you must kill it by pressing the DEL key when you are through viewing the tail of the file.

The cmp and diff Commands

It is often desirable to compare two files to see if they are the same. The **cmp** (for compare) command will compare any two files, including binary files. It takes two filenames as arguments.

```
$ cmp /bin/sh /bin/ksh
/bin/sh /bin/ksh differ: char 5, line 1
$
```

This somewhat limited output tells only the first byte number, if any, at which the files differ. The −l (letter *l*) option causes **cmp** to list the byte number and the differing values for each of the differences in the two files. This is often more useful, though it can produce substantial output if many differences exist.

The **cmp** command can take an argument of − instead of the first filename, in which case the standard input is used instead of a filename.

```
$ cat /bin/sh | cmp -l - /bin/sh
$
```

If there are no differences, **cmp** is silent.

A much more powerful tool, the **diff** (for differences) command, is available for text files. This command produces a complete index of all lines that differ between two files, along with their line numbers and what must be changed to make the files the same.

```
$ cat file1
this is a simple file
with only a few lines,
all very straightforward.
This file will show how "diff" works.
$ cat file2
this is a simple file
with only a few lines,
all very easy.
This file will show how "diff" works.
$ diff file1 file2
3c3
< all very straightforward.
---
> all very easy.
$
```

The first part of the **diff** output will be the line numbers that differ in the two files, separated by **c** (for changed). The next line displays the line in the first file, marked with <, and then the line in the second file, marked with >. The output will be correspondingly larger with larger files and more differences, but **diff** can easily handle large files with many differences and lines that are missing on one or the other of the files. It will almost always successfully find the smallest set of differences in two files.

If one of the filenames is replaced with − (minus), the standard input will be used in that position instead of a named file.

Extra blanks or tab characters in the files usually cause **diff** to mark the lines as different. But the −**b** (for blanks) option causes **diff** to ignore lines that differ only in their white space so that tabs or spaces in a file can be treated as the same.

```
$ cat file3 | diff -b - file2
$
```

As usual, if the files are the same, **diff** will say nothing.

The output from **diff** resembles **ed** commands that convert the first file into the second. In fact the −**e** (for **ed**) option produces a script that **ed** can use directly to convert the files.

```
$ diff -e file1 file2
3c
all very easy.
.
$
```

The following output can be used to actually convert **file1** to **file2**.

```
$ diff -e file1 file2 > ed.script
$ ( cat ed.script ; echo w ) | ed file1
109
98
$ diff file1 file2
$
```

This example contains several ideas. Because **ed** reads your commands from standard input, you can use a pipeline to send commands to **ed** instead of typing them directly at the terminal. When **ed** sees an end-of-file from the pipeline, it will exit and return to the shell. So if you **cat** the output from **diff** −**e** into **ed**, **ed** will respond to those commands and then exit when the file **ed.script** finishes. This is why no **q** is needed to end the **ed** session. However, the script from **diff** −**e** has no **w** command for **ed** to write the file, so by default **ed** will make the changes and then exit without writing them back out. To get **ed** to write the file, you must add the **w**, which you do by using the **echo w** command.

The **cat** of **ed.script** is separated from **echo w** by the shell operator ; (semicolon), which separates multiple commands on the line. This is almost what you want. However, the end of **ed.script** will signal an end-of-file mark, and **ed** will then exit before it sees the **w** from the **echo** command. You can prevent this by enclosing within parentheses the entire sequence of commands that you want **ed** to see. This use of parentheses as a shell operator causes all the commands within them to be executed in a single subshell rather than as individual commands. This causes the output of all of them to be concatenated as input to the **ed** command, thus eliminating the undesirable end-of-file otherwise caused by the ;.

Another way to write the same command could be as follows:

```
$ echo w | cat ed.script - | ed file1
```

The two numbers 109 and 98, in the previous example, are the standard output from **ed** when it reads and writes the file, respectively. Experiment with these ideas on your own machine. What are the differences between the form with the parentheses and the example just shown?

The sort and uniq Commands

The UNIX system provides two more tools that are often used in pipelines to filter text files in useful ways. The **sort** command reorders a stream of text lines in alphabetical order. It can take a list of filenames as arguments or read its standard input. It writes the sorted lines to its standard output.

```
$ cat text.file
This is a short file.
Each line begins with a different letter.
each line starts with a four-letter word.
Most lines start with capital letters.
$ sort text.file
Each line begins with a different letter.
Most lines start with capital letters.
This is a short file.
each line starts with a four-letter word.
$
```

The **sort** command will sort all the lines of all the input files together, so it includes functions often called *merge* in sorting tools in other operating systems. It also can handle very large files, though its performance will seriously degrade when files of more than about one thousand lines are sorted. It is often faster to sort several large files separately and then merge them with the −m (for merge) option of the **sort** command.

By default, **sort** will use the ASCII *collating sequence* to determine the sorting order, starting at the beginning of the line. The ASCII collating sequence sorts white space first, then most punctuation marks, numbers, and uppercase letters, and finally lowercase letters. When the first characters of two lines are the same, **sort** will look at the next character, up to the NEWLINE if necessary, to find the correct order. When you are sorting alphabetical files, this is often the correct behavior, but when you sort numeric data, things may not be as you expect.

```
$ cat data.file
1
2
10
11
21
$ sort data.file
1
10
11
2
21
$
```

This occurs because 1 precedes 2 in the collating sequence, so all lines beginning with 1 will precede any line beginning with 2. The −**n** (for numeric) option to **sort** causes the output to appear in the correct order for numbers.

```
$ sort −n data.file
1
2
10
11
21
$
```

The **sort** command also allows you to ignore the difference between uppercase and lowercase characters in the sorting comparison. Use the −**f** (for fold) option.

```
$ sort −f text.file
Each line begins with a different letter.
each line starts with a four-letter word.
Most lines start with capital letters.
This is a short file.
$
```

In this case "Each" and "each" are treated as the same; the first difference in the lines appears in column position 11, where "begins" is sorted before "starts." Similarly, the −**d** (for dictionary) option suppresses sorting on embedded punctuation or other special characters; only letters, digits, and white space are significant. The −**M** (for month) option causes **sort** to consider the first three characters of the line as months, so that "Jan" will sort before "Feb" rather than after it, as you would otherwise expect.

So far the *sort key* has appeared at the beginning of the input line. The sort key is the section of the data that **sort** uses to consider whether the line is out of order. The **sort** command allows you to specify any section of the input line as the sort key if you wish, but **sort** always keeps each line together as a whole. That is, **sort** will not break up its input lines, which are considered as *records*. You can instruct **sort** to use some other part of the input line as the key with the +**n** and −**n** arguments, where *n* is a number specifying a *field* in the line. A field is a sequence of characters separated by a *delimiter*. By default, a white space character (blank or tab) is the field delimiter, and the beginning of the line starts field 0. That is, +**1** tells **sort** to use the next field rather than the beginning of the line as the sort key.

```
$ sort +1 text.file
This is a short file.
Each line begins with a different letter.
each line starts with a four-letter word.
Most lines start with capital letters.
$
```

This example is sorted beginning with "is" or "line."

Similarly, use the −**n** option to tell **sort** to stop its comparison just before field **n**.

```
$ sort +1 -3 text.file
```

This will use only the second and third fields as the sort key.

When data is sorted using fields and the lines differ only in fields that are not included in the sort key, you cannot predict in what order those lines will appear in the output. However, you can control sorting in all fields of the file by using more than one field in the **sort** command.

```
$ sort +3 -4 +0 -1 text.file
```

This will sort based on field 4 as the *primary key*. On lines in which this key compares as equal, the beginning of the line will be used as the *secondary key*.

```
$ sort +3 -4 +0 -1 text.file
This is a short file.
Each line begins with a different letter.
Most lines start with capital letters.
each line starts with a four-letter word.
$
```

Compare this output with the following:

```
$ sort +3 -4 +6 text.file
This is a short file.
Most lines start with capital letters.
Each line begins with a different letter.
each line starts with a four-letter word.
$
```

What accounts for the difference?

You can change the field separator from the default white space with the −t option, which takes a character as argument. For example, to use the : (colon) as a field separator, type the following:

```
$ sort -t: /etc/passwd
```

Of course all the different options and sort keys can be combined to produce sorted output in just about any sequence you desire. It usually takes some experimentation with **sort** to get exactly the output you want. In addition, **sort** allows the −b (for blanks) option to ignore blanks in the sort key and the −r (for reverse) option to reverse the sort order of output.

The **sort** command is often used with **uniq** (for unique) to produce a count of occurrences of a specified line or field in a file. The **uniq** command reports on repeated lines in a file, but its input must be sorted correctly before it can work.

The **uniq** command reads its standard input or a list of filenames and writes to its standard output. By default, **uniq** will write one instance of each input line that is different than other lines.

```
$ cat data2
abc
def
ghi
def
abc
$ sort data2 | uniq
abc
def
ghi
$
```

Only one copy of each differing line is written; **uniq** produces a list of the unique lines of the file. Again, the input to **uniq** must be in correct sort order or **uniq** will fail.

The −**c** (for count) option of **uniq** is often used. It produces a count of the number of occurrences of the unique lines preceding the line itself.

```
$ sort data2 | uniq -c
   2 abc
   2 def
   1 ghi
$
```

That is, there are two instances of the line "abc" in the input and only one of the line "ghi." The −**u** (for unique) option produces only the lines that are *not* repeated in the input, while the −**d** (for duplicate) option produces only the lines that are duplicated in the input.

The **uniq** command can also restrict its examination to specific fields of the input. The −**n** option, where *n* is a number, will ignore the first *n* fields of the line in its comparison. As with **sort**, fields are delimited by white space. The +**n** option, where *n* is a number, will ignore the first *n* characters of the line. When −**n** and +**n** are used together, fields are skipped before characters.

The cut and paste Commands

The **cut** command was discussed in Chapter 3. It is used to split up its input lines according to column positions or fields. Like **sort**, it operates on specific parts of the input line; unlike **sort**, however, it will usually not copy the entire line to its output. The **cut** command is used to eliminate sections of the line from the output. In addition, **cut** has a companion command that will join lines from two files into its output. The **paste** command takes two or more filenames as input, reads a line from each file, combines the lines into a single line, and writes the newly created line to its standard output. Each input file is assumed to provide a field in the output line, and by default a tab character is added as a delimiter between the contributions of each file. The −**d** option allows you to specify a different delimiter character if you wish.

```
$ cat new.d1
1111
2222
3333
$ cat new.d2
AAAA
BBBB
CCCC
DDDD
EEEE
$ paste -d: new.d1 new.d2
1111:AAAA
2222:BBBB
3333:CCCC
:DDDD
:EEEE
$
```

The **paste** command can take any number of filenames, and it pastes together lines in the output in left-to-right order from the input lines. If any of the files do not have the same number of lines, **paste** simply puts in the delimiters with nothing in the field. Any filename can be replaced by − (minus), and **paste** will read its standard input for that file.

In the previous example a : (colon) was used as the delimiter. In fact there can be more than one character following the −**d** option, and each delimiter in that list is used in turn to delimit one pair of fields in the output. When all the characters in the list have been used, **paste** circles around to start the list again. Occasionally this feature is useful to separate different fields with different delimiters. It is normally used when there are as many delimiters in the list as there are fields to separate.

```
$ paste -d123 file1 file2 file3 file4
```

This example will take the first line of **file1**, add the digit 1 after it, add the first line of **file2**, add the digit 2, add the first line of **file3**, add the digit 3, and add the first line of **file4**. The resulting line will be terminated with a NEWLINE and written to the standard output. The **paste** command will continue like this on each additional line until the last file is completed.

Database Operations for Text Files

The commands just discussed have great utility on their own to process text files, producing new permutations of their input. They are also frequently combined into pipelines, sometimes using temporary files for intermediate output. With these tools, you can accomplish very complex operations on your data, including cutting, sorting, and counting, to produce useful reports and new combinations of the data files. In fact these operators are the basic tools needed to perform relatively sophisticated database operations. Once you understand the basic commands and their major options, it becomes very easy to create complex databases. These databases are usually composed of simple text files consisting of individual lines that make records, with each field of the record separated by your chosen delimiter. The tab and : characters are most often used as delimiters.

In practice you can create several files containing data, either with your editor or as output from some application program. Single files usually contain related data, and different files usually contain unrelated data. If any one field of the files is the same or can be related through two fields of a third file, then you can write command lines to implement *relational databases*. By creating new combinations of commands and pipelines as you need them, you can create ad hoc queries on the data without using specially written software such as a database management system. Many large and complex databases have been developed under the UNIX system with just these commands, and the possibilities are nearly limitless.

In the next example we will try only to convey an appreciation of the possibilities. Try these ideas on your own data-related problems. Although these tools and filters may execute a little more slowly than a professional database management system, the files are usually in easy-to-read text format, and you can add and reformat data, generate queries, and produce complex reports very simply.

For example, you can easily determine the user id's of all the users allowed on your machine.

```
$ cut -f1 -d: /etc/passwd
root
daemon
bin
sys
adm
uucp
nuucp
slan
sync
lp
listen
sysadm
setup
```

```
powerdown
checkfsys
makefsys
mountfsys
umountfsys
jim
admin
msnet
pat
steve
$
```

Similarly, you can determine the shell that these users get when they log into the machine.

```
$ cut -f1,7 -d: /etc/passwd > temp.data
$ cat temp.data
root
daemon
bin
sys
adm
uucp
nuucp:/usr/lib/uucp/uucico
slan
sync:/bin/sync
lp
listen
sysadm:/bin/rsh
setup:/bin/rsh
powerdown:/bin/rsh
checkfsys:/bin/rsh
makefsys:/bin/rsh
mountfsys:/bin/rsh
umountfsys:/bin/rsh
jim
admin
msnet
pat
steve:/bin/ksh
$
```

The output was redirected for later use to the temporary file **temp.data**. This example is a bit tricky: if there are no contents in the last field of the input line to **cut**, then **cut** will not include the delimiter in the output. In the file **/etc/passwd**, the user "root" and others have no shell specified in field 7. Compare the output above with the corresponding line for user "steve." If you want to add the default shell /**bin/sh** to these lines that have no :, then you need an additional command.

```
$ grep -v : temp.data | sed 's/$/:\/bin\/sh/' > new.data
$ cat new.data
root:/bin/sh
daemon:/bin/sh
bin:/bin/sh
sys:/bin/sh
adm:/bin/sh
uucp:/bin/sh
slan:/bin/sh
lp:/bin/sh
listen:/bin/sh
jim:/bin/sh
admin:/bin/sh
msnet:/bin/sh
pat:/bin/sh
$
```

This command **greps** for all lines that do not contain a : in your temporary file, and then **sed** adds the string :/**bin**/**sh** to the end of each line. The **sed** command is a little different than you have seen before, because the substitution expression includes the / (slash) character as a normal character rather than as a delimiter. You must escape the special meaning of / by preceding it with a \ (backslash) when you mean it as a normal character.

At this point the contents of the file **new.data** contain only those users who had no shell specified in the /**etc**/**passwd** file. To include the other users, you can add the following command:

```
$ grep : temp.data >> new.data
```

This simply adds all the lines containing the : to the end of the file.

Now you can ask some questions about the use of shells by the users on your machine. What different shells are in use?

```
$ cut -f2 -d: new.data | sort | uniq
/bin/ksh
/bin/rsh
/bin/sh
/bin/sync
/usr/lib/uucp/uucico
$
```

How many users use each shell?

```
$ cut -f2 -d: new.data | sort | uniq -c | sort -nr
 13 /bin/sh
  7 /bin/rsh
```

```
    1 /usr/lib/uucp/uucico
    1 /bin/sync
    1 /bin/ksh
$
```

The last command, **sort −nr**, puts the results in descending numeric order. Many more questions can be asked and answered in this way. Further, there are several other ways to formulate this query from the original /**etc/passwd** file. What are some of them?

Writing complex pipelines like this usually requires experimentation. In practice you slowly build these commands up from the components, letting the output come to the terminal until you are sure that it is correct. Often it is wise to use a small test database instead of your real data, especially when the real data is voluminous and the commands are complex. It is usually helpful to keep the command line in a file, modifying it with your editor as you experiment rather than retyping it every time. The command form

```
$ sh cmdfile
```

will execute the command line in **cmdfile**, or you can make **cmdfile** executable with the following:

```
$ chmod +x cmdfile
```

Then you can execute the command directly.

```
$ cmdfile
```

This technique, which can shorten long and complex pipelines to easily typed commands, also forms the basis for *shell programming*, as you will soon see.

Going Further

There are a great many commands, and there are even more tricky ways to use them. As you experiment and watch other users work, you will soon learn procedures to solve your particular data-related problems. In later chapters we will discuss many of them.

The sleep Command

An interesting and useful command is **sleep**, which takes a numeric argument that is interpreted as a number of seconds. The **sleep** command will do nothing but delay that number of seconds and then exit back to the shell.

```
$ date "+%r" ; sleep 100 ; date "+%r"
11:18:23 AM
11:20:04 AM
$
```

The **sleep** command can err in its timing up to 1 second, so the command

```
$ sleep 1
```

may not produce exact results.

One of the simplest uses of **sleep** is to create an alarm clock. This command will ring the bell at your terminal and display a message 10 minutes after the command is entered.

```
$ sleep 600 ; echo "\007 Time for lunch! \007" &
```

This command will work only if you do not log off the machine until after the alarm goes off, but the command is executed in the background with **&** so that you can continue to do other work while it is running. The string \007 in the **echo** command is another form of specifying characters to echo: 007 is the octal ASCII code for the CTRL-G key combination, which sounds a beep at the terminal. The string \007 in this context is very different than \07, 007, 7, or \7. You tell **echo** that this is a single character rather than three digits by escaping it with the backslash.

Because the UNIX system is multitasking, you should relinquish control of the CPU when you want to delay for an interval. This allows another program, perhaps executed by another user on the machine, to work while your command is delaying. This differs from the common practice on single-tasking systems such as MS-DOS, where you can implement a delay by actively using the system. Counting iterations of some active loop is common, but this *busy wait* approach can be very wasteful under the UNIX system, where other programs may be demanding use of the system while your command is waiting. One principle of the multitasking system is that all users share the system resources. When you are idle, even if your command is active in the background, you must use commands that turn system resources over to other users. The **sleep** command does this for you, so that when a command is sleeping, you are not really using much of the system resources. An added benefit of **sleep** is that its timing depends on the internal clock and not on the system load or basic processer speed. Its timing is always exact to the nearest second.

The find Command

When you examine the contents of a directory with **ls** or copy files with wild-card expansion, as in

```
$ cp * $HOME/new.directory
```

you may notice that these commands only act on files in one specific directory. Often, however, you will want to copy or examine the contents of a complete directory subtree rather than work with each directory separately. The **find** command offers this capability. Though **find** is one of the most powerful of all the commands, it also has one of the most difficult command line structures. Still, **find** is so useful that generations of users have successfully wrestled with its syntax.

The **find** command descends a directory hierarchy and locates all the files that meet special criteria given on the command line. It can be made to take several different types of actions on the files that it finds. Its command line is basically

```
$ find path-name-list expressions
```

where *path-name-list* is the list of directories to search. It can be one or more directories, with either full or relative path-names. The *expressions* section contains the list of operators that describe both the selection criteria for the files that you wish to locate and the action you wish **find** to take when a file matches the selection criteria. For example,

```
$ find $HOME -print
```

is one of the smallest **find** command lines. This command will print the names of all the files and directories in your home directory.

Additional directories can also be specified in the *path-name-list* section of the command line. This command

```
$ find /usr/steve /usr/jim -print
```

will display the names of all the files and directories under **/usr/steve** and **/usr/jim**. Wild-card pathnames are also allowed.

```
$ find /usr/* -print
```

In the **find** command line, all the pathnames immediately follow the command name, and the operators follow at the end of the command. All the operators begin with the − (minus) flag, and none of the items in the *path-name-list* section can begin with −.

By default, **find** will not act on the files that it finds, so you must use −**print** if you want to list the files that **find** locates. The −**print** option instructs **find** to write the items that it finds to its standard output, one item per line. This property lets you use **find** to count all the files and directories on your machine.

```
$ find / -print | wc -l
2842
$
```

This machine has 2842 files and directories! Large-scale **find** operations like this one, which searches through the entire directory structure, can take a lot of real and CPU time, especially on large machines. You should limit your use of **find** to the minimum size *path-name-list* that meets your needs.

You can add other operators to restrict the search to some subset of the files encountered during the search. The —**name** argument specifies that only files with the given name are found.

```
$ find / -name profile -print
/etc/profile
$
```

The specified name can use the shell wild-card characters if they are quoted.

```
$ find / -name "*profile" -print
/etc/profile
/usr/jim/.profile
/usr/pat/.profile
/usr/steve/.profile
/.profile
$
```

When **find** searches through the directory hierarchy, the order in which it finds files depends on the internal organization of the file system, which you cannot control. Occasionally you may process the output with **sort** or some other tool to put the names into some specific order.

When multiple options are specified for **find**, they are executed in left-to-right order on each file that **find** encounters. The command

```
$ find / -print -name "*profile"
```

is not the same as

```
$ find / -name "*profile" -print
```

because the first example will print the filename and then select for the name. The second example will select the matching names first and then print the names.

As you add more options to **find**, you must keep this behavior in mind. The **find** command searches for each filename in its *path-name-list;* then it uses the *expressions* section to select or reject the filename until all expressions have been executed. If a filename is rejected on one of the expressions, then the rest of the expressions will not be executed. In **find** terminology the expression evaluates to *true* if the filename is selected and to *false* if the filename is rejected.

There are many other options for **find**. Several of them specify files with selected attributes: −**user pat** selects files owned by user "pat," and −**group sys** selects files belonging to group "sys." The command

```
$ find / -user $LOGNAME -print
```

will display the names of all the files in the machine owned by you.

The −**type c** option selects files of type *c*, where *c* can be any of the types in the leftmost column of the permissions from **ls** −**l** (*f*, for file, and *d*, for directory, are the most commonly used). The −**mtime n** option selects files that have been modified exactly *n* days ago. Use −**mtime** −**n** to select files modified within the last *n* days, and − **mtime** +**n** to select files modified more than *n* days ago. The −**size n** option selects files of exactly *n* blocks in size, −**size** −**n** selects files smaller than *n* blocks, and **size** +**n** selects files larger than *n* blocks. Usually 1000 blocks or 512,000 bytes is a relatively large file. Try this command

```
$ find / -size +1000 -print
```

to see all the large files on your machine.

All these operators can be negated. If the operator name (such as −**size**) is preceded by ! (bang) and a space, then the following operator is made false when it would normally be true and vice versa. For example, this command

```
$ find . ! -print
```

negates the printing of the list. But this is an expensive no-op! A more useful example might occur if you want to find all the files in your home directory that you do not own.

```
$ find $HOME ! -user $LOGNAME -print
```

The ! (bang) character must be surrounded by white space in the command line, and it will only negate the immediately following operator. To see a list of all files in your home directory that are both not owned by you and larger than 50 blocks, use the following:

```
$ find $HOME -size +50 ! -user $LOGNAME -print
```

In addition, you can specify one operator *or* another.

```
$ find $HOME -size +50 -o ! -user $LOGNAME -print
```

The **−o** (for or) operator connects the two expressions that it lies between, "−size +50" and "! −user $LOGNAME" in this case. This will select a file that has either attribute. By default, adjacent operators not separated by **−o** are logically connected by an **and** operation, which selects a file only if both the attributes are true.

Finally, **find** can execute any command for each file that it finds with its other operators. The **−exec** (for execute) operator takes a command line following it. The command can include the name of the current file that **find** is processing, using the special syntax { } (left and right curly braces). The command line ends with the special operator \; (backslash-semicolon). This might be used, for example, to change the permissions of all files in a directory subtree.

```
$ find . -exec chmod -rw {} \\;
```

This command will not print the filenames as they are changed, but the following command will.

```
$ find . -exec chmod -rw {} \\; -print
```

The **−exec** operator will be true if the command it executes returns a zero exit value, and false otherwise. Of course other **find** selectors and operators are also allowed with the **−exec** operation, and, as usual, the **find** command line is processed left to right until an expression evaluates to false.

The stty Command

The last command to discuss in this section is **stty** (for set tty), which is used to examine and change the communications parameters associated with your terminal in your current login session. The UNIX system provides considerable control over the way both keystrokes and output to the terminal are processed. The **stty** command allows you to set up your terminal options for a specific terminal or communication line.

To look at your current terminal settings, use the **−a** (for all) option to **stty**.

```
$ stty −a
speed 9600 baud; line = 0; intr = DEL; quit = ^|; erase = ^h; kill = @; eof = ^d
−parenb −parodd cs8 −cstopb −hupcl cread −clocal −loblk
−ignbrk brkint ignpar −parmrk −inpck istrip −inlcr −igncr icrnl −iuclc
ixon ixany −ixoff
isig icanon −xcase echo echoe echok −echonl −noflsh
opost −olcuc onlcr −ocrnl −onocr −onlret −ofill −ofdel tab3
$
```

The options are displayed in a form that could be used to reenter the options if needed. Each terminal option has a name, such as **ixon**, and most can be either *set* or *clear*. If the option name is preceded by − (minus), the option is clear; if there is no −, the option is set. For example, **ixon** refers to XON/XOFF flow control as controlled by the terminal. If this flow control is enabled, the option displays as **ixon**, as above; if it is disabled, the option will display as **−ixon**. Setting ixon allows you to use CTRL-s to stop output to your terminal and CTRL-9 to restart stopped output.

You can change the value of an option by giving it as a command line option to **stty**. Use the − when you want to turn the option off (clear it), and do not use the − when you want to turn the option on (set it). This command

```
$ stty ixon
$
```

turns on flow control, while this command

```
$ stty −ixon
$
```

turns it off. Multiple options are allowed on the command line, as shown here:

```
$ stty −ixon 1200
$
```

This command sets the terminal to 1200 baud and turns off flow control.

The list of options is long, and you must take care not to make changes that disrupt your session. Typically, when your terminal is not acting correctly, it is completely out of action. Most often no output is displayed or your keystrokes are not read correctly by the shell. Sometimes the NEWLINE may display as a linefeed with no carriage return, or your typed NEWLINE characters are not read correctly by the shell. The procedure to create a new login id will usually establish the **stty** options correctly, and you seldom need to make changes in normal use. However, if your TERM variable is not set correctly, or if you want to experiment with new terminals or communication channels such as local area networks, changes to the **stty** options may be required.

If you log into the machine and the terminal is acting normally but then gets deranged for unknown reasons, your best response is simply to log off and log into the system again. The system will then reset your terminal options to the "good" values they had. However, a less severe solution is the following command:

```
$ stty sane
$
```

The **sane** command is a collection of **stty** options that appear to work on most types of terminals most of the time. It does not change the speed of the communication channel, but is usually has a beneficial effect when the terminal is pretty deranged. The **sane** command will probably not allow full-screen applications like **vi** to work correctly, and if you cannot immediately fix any problems after you set the **sane** option, just log off and log in again. If the terminal is not working correctly at login, your login will probably not succeed.

If the terminal becomes deranged so that your NEWLINE key is not understood to end your command lines, you can usually press CTRL-J as a substitute NEWLINE until you execute **stty sane**. In this case you can terminate the **stty sane** command with CTRL-J to get the system to understand it.

The major options for the **stty** command are as follows: the **parenb** option enables parity, while −**parenb** disables it. The

parodd and **−parodd** options select odd and even parity, respectively (**parodd** is only used if **parenb** is set). The **cs5**, **cs6**, **cs7**, and **cs8** options set characters size of 5, 6, 7, and 8 bits, respectively. The **300, 600, 1200, 2400, 4800, 9600,** and **19200** options set the named baud rate, while the **cstopb** and **−cstopb** set two or one stop bit, respectively. The **tabs** option sets the system to use tabs instead of sequences of spaces when the amount of output would be reduced. The **−tabs** option uses only spaces and is used when the tab character is not processed correctly by the terminal.

In addition, **stty** is used to control the keys that you use for some specific control functions. You have used CTRL-D as the end-of-file character, though some users prefer CTRL-C for this function. You can change it with **stty**

```
$ stty eof c
```

where c in this example is replaced by the specific control character you want.

You can enter control characters directly by preceding the character with a \ (backslash) followed by a ^ (caret). This command

```
$ stty eof \^c
$
```

will set your end-of-file character to CTRL-C. This syntax is also used to change your **erase** character (usually BACKSPACE) and your **intr** (for interrupt) character (usually DEL). To change your **erase** character to BACKSPACE, use the following:

```
$ stty erase \^h
```

You can also set your session so that when you enter a BACKSPACE, the system responds with the sequence "backspace-space-backspace." This causes the character that you just backspaced over to be removed from the display. Use this command

```
$ stty echoe
```

to turn on this feature.

The full list of options for **stty** is presented in the *UNIX User's Manual*, and you should consult the manual and your local communications guru before straying too far from the instructions given in this chapter. Terminal modes and their management, which are some of the most arcane and difficult topics in the UNIX system, should be treated with care.

# SEVEN

Shell Programming and More

**S
E
V
E
N**

Now that you have met many of the most general commands and understand most of the issues involved with command lines and their construction, we can address the most interesting features of the shell. The modern shell is a very functional and flexible environment for users; there are many tools that make working with the system much easier and quicker than you might suspect. Most users create some custom tools using the shell. In fact the shell is really a full-scale programming language something like BASIC, and *shell programming* is widely used for capturing the individual commands and procedures that you perform frequently. The shell programming language is similar in concept to MS-DOS *batch* programs but much more complete and powerful.

Shell programs are often used in system administrative tools and commands. System designers normally write applications in the shell language when ease of understanding and ease of change for the procedure are more important than the run-time efficiency and speed of the application. However, the modern shell provides excellent performance for executing *shell scripts*, as shell programs are often called. In fact full-scale turnkey applications systems have been developed entirely in shell scripts.

In this section we will first discuss some additional shell features and then dive into shell programming. Finally, we will mention some more advanced shell features.

Multiline Commands

A command line entered at the shell may be longer than the width of the terminal. This is often true of complex pipelines with several commands and long filenames. As long as you do not enter a newline character, most terminals will wrap around to the left-hand side of the next display line, and you can continue to enter the command. When you enter the NEWLINE at the end of the command, the shell interprets that as the signal to begin processing the command line.

However, the shell allows commands to span more than one line, which is often useful to logically segment a command for readability or for other reasons. You can continue a command on a second line (or even more lines) by entering \ (backslash) as the last thing on the line before the NEWLINE character. This *escapes* the NEWLINE, and the shell will ignore it, allowing more input for the same command on the next terminal line. The command can also be extended after the end of a line if the shell determines that the command is not complete when it sees the NEWLINE character. This could happen if you quoted a command argument and pressed NEWLINE before closing the quotation marks. In either case the shell will store the part of the command that you have already entered and display another prompt instead of "$" to remind you that it expects more of the same command.

```
$ cat /etc/profile \
>
```

The new prompt is known as PS2 (for second-level prompt string), just as your normal "$" prompt is known as PS1. PS2 can be set and exported just like any other environment variable.

```
$ echo $PS2
>
$ PS2='more:'
$ echo $PS2
more:
$
```

In this case the PS2 was originally set to >. The PS2 signals that the command you have entered is incomplete for some reason and the shell is expecting more input. You can abort the command at the PS2 prompt by pressing the DEL key. The stored command text will be discarded, and the PS1 prompt (usually "$") will return, signaling that the shell is ready for another command.

here Documents

The shell treats any commands that are entered on multiple lines as a single command line. However, the PS2 prompt can appear under two different situations. First, if you escape the newline with \, or if a quoted argument is not closed before the newline, the shell will simply ignore the presence of the newline and use PS2 to signal that more input is expected. Second, some shell operators flow across multiple lines, and the embedded newlines provide syntactic information to segment the commands.

A good example of this property is the *here document*, so-called because the input data is here rather than stored in a file. The shell operator <<**name** introduces a here document. The *name* can be any string of characters, and the << acts similarly to the normal redirection operator from a file. No white space is allowed in this construction. Starting on the next line, following the <<**name** operator, is the actual data that the command will read. A line that contains only *name* ends the here document.

For example, the command

```
$ cat - <<MARKER
> hello
> goodbye
> MARKER
hello
goodbye
$
```

defines a two-line section of data as a here document, and the command **cat** – displays the here document as its standard input. As you type this command, press NEWLINE after **<<MARKER**. The shell determines that you have begun a here document and displays PS2 for more input. All lines that you type until the one that contains only "MARKER" are part of the here document, and the shell stores all the input until it sees the mark. After the shell sees the closing mark, it executes the command **cat** – using the here document as standard input. Then it returns to PS1 for the next command.

In this example the shell is interpreting your NEWLINE as a true end-of-line mark, so the output from **cat** – is on several different lines. However, it does not interpret the newline as the end of the command, because it is waiting for the end of the here document.

There are several other cases where multiline commands will be used. If PS2 appears when you are entering a single-line command, you know that you have made a mistake; when it appears in a multiline command, you know that the shell is responding correctly.

The use of here documents is preferred over redirection of standard input when you wish to use shell variables in the data. A redirected file will always be read directly by the target command, but a here document will be processed by the shell and then fed to the command. For example:

```
$ cat - <<HereDocument
My login id is $LOGNAME
HereDocument
My login id is steve
$
```

In addition to shell variable substitution, use of the ` (grave) operator to capture the standard output of a command line is also allowed in the here document. For example:

```
$ cat - <<XYZZY
> echo "There are `ls $HOME | wc -l` files in $HOME"
> XYZZY
```

This allows powerful combinations of shell variables and command output to be merged in a text stream.

Storing Shell Commands in Files

Recall that any commands, or sequence of commands, that can be typed directly at the terminal can also be stored in and executed from a file. The execution of commands stored in a file is identical to that of commands typed directly. In this case the shell arranges things so that the file is connected to its standard input, rather than the terminal. One way to execute commands in a file is to give the filename as an argument to **sh**, which will execute as a subshell.

```
$ cat cmd.file
echo $LOGNAME
pwd
$ sh cmd.file
steve
/usr/steve
$
```

Here the file **cmd.file** contains the two commands **echo $LOGNAME** and **pwd**. The commands are executed with **sh cmd.file**, and the output comes to **stdout**, as expected. The file **cmd.file** is an example of a short shell script. Another way to execute the command is as follows:

```
$ chmod u+x cmd.file
$ cmd.file
steve
/usr/steve
$
```

If the shell script has executable permissions, then you needn't give it as an argument to an explicit subshell. The login shell will figure out that it is a shell script and then execute its own subshell to carry out the command. Thus a shell script can be executed just like a binary program, and there is seldom a reason to distinguish between the two different kinds of commands.

In the script new commands begin on new lines of the file, but otherwise they are entered just as you would enter them at the terminal. All the functions that can be performed directly at the terminal can be included in shell scripts. For example, it is often useful to define shell variables that have a lifetime only for the duration of the shell script.

```
$ cat cmd2.file
DIR=`pwd`
echo $DIR
$ cmd2.file
/usr/steve
$
```

The *DIR* variable is set to the current directory; then **echo $DIR** echoes it. Shell variables set in this way are known only within the shell script in which they are defined; they do not remain in force when your login shell resumes after the script completes.

Similarly, other commands in shell scripts do not continue beyond the scripts in which they appear.

```
$ cat cmd3.file
pwd
echo Changing directory....
cd /usr/jim
pwd
$ cmd3.file
/usr/steve
Changing directory....
/usr/jim
$ pwd
/usr/steve
$
```

Changing directories within a shell script is allowed, but the **cd** operation affects only the script and not the rest of your session.

Because the system does not distinguish between binary executable programs and shell scripts, you can include shell scripts as commands within other scripts. Occasionally it is desirable to pass environment variables defined in a parent shell script to a *subscript*. When you define an environment variable with a command such as

```
$ VAR=`pwd`
```

the value of *VAR* is known only within the script in which it is defined.

To pass it along to the subshells, use the **export** command.

```
$ export VAR
```

As usual, this can be done directly from the terminal or in a shell script in a file. The **export** command allows subscripts (in fact all executed subprograms) to access the value of the exported variable. But a subshell or shell script can never change the value of a variable in the parent environment or script.

Commenting Shell Scripts

Shell programs saved in files, especially long and complex scripts, should usually have comments to remind readers of what they do. The # operator is used to introduce a comment in a shell script (or at the terminal). However, if your erase character is #, you must escape the # with \ (backslash) before using it to mark a comment. Everything on the same command line following the # character is ignored by the shell.

```
$ #cat /etc/passwd
$ echo hello  #this is a comment at the end of a line
hello
$
```

The comment will override the \ (backslash) operator that normally escapes the NEWLINE for shell commands and files, because all the material after the # is ignored. Comments can be very helpful in maintaining shell scripts, and they should be used liberally given that they cost nothing in performance.

The if Operator

The shell provides the tools to make many types of decisions based on the current execution environment for a command or shell script. One of these is the **if** operator, which introduces a conditional operation. The format of the **if** command is as follows:

```
$ if expression ; then commands ; fi
```

This command is shown on a single command line, but **if** introduces a multiline command sequence that is not closed until the characters **fi** (for inverse **if**) are interpreted. The *expression* is any logical expression or a command that returns a value. Recall that most commands return a numeric value that is available in the **$?** shell variable right after the command completes. This is the value of *expression*.

If the expression resolves to a zero return value, the commands following the **then** part are executed, up to the **fi** characters. For example:

```
$ if true ; then echo hello ; fi
hello
$ if false ; then echo hello ; fi
$
```

These commands have a ; (semicolon) separating the parts, but the commands are normally written on multiple lines, with the PS2 prompt reminding you when the command sequence is still incomplete.

```
$ if true
> then
>        echo hello
> fi
hello
$
```

If the NEWLINEs are not present, the semicolons are required; one or the other must delimit the parts of the commands.

The previous example shows a special logical operator available to shell scripts, **true**. This always returns a value of zero so that **if** will execute the commands following the **then**. Also available is **false**, which always returns a nonzero value.

```
$ false
$ echo $?
1
$
```

As many commands as needed, including other nested **if** commands, are allowed within the **then** part of the **if** construction.

```
$ if true
> then
>        echo hello
>        echo `pwd`
> fi
hello
/usr/steve
$
```

If a second leg of the **if** construction is needed, the **else** operator is provided. Commands following the **else** operator are executed when the expression part returns a nonzero value.

```
$ if false ; then
>       echo hello
> else
>       echo goodbye
> fi
goodbye
$
```

As usual, the command list following the **else** can include as many commands as needed.

Additional **if** constructions can follow the **else** if needed and are introduced with the short form **elif** (for else if).

```
$ if false ; then
>       echo hello
> elif true ; then
>       echo goodbye
> fi
goodbye
$
```

The **then** section after **elif** is required. Again, the whole construction is closed with **fi**.

The test Command

So far we have used only a very simple expression for **if**, so simple that the examples given are probably not very useful. In practice you would like the expression to encompass nearly any kind of logical operation. For example, it would be nice to have an operation that compares two numbers and then executes the **then** section if they are the same. Or, if a specific file exists, then the commands following **then** are executed.

These and many other capabilities are provided by the **test** command, which is designed to follow **if** and provide truth values (or return codes) that are interpreted by **if**. The **test** command has two different forms, which are synonyms for each other. Both forms are often used in shell scripts, so you should use the one you prefer, though your shell scripts will be more readable if you use the same form throughout. First is the command name **test** itself, followed by arguments that are resolved according to rules that we will discuss now.

```
$ if test $VAR
> then
>        echo hello
> fi
$
```

If the environment variable *VAR* is not defined, then the operation **test $VAR** will fail and the **if** will treat the result as false. If the environment variable is defined, then the test will succeed.

```
$ if test $HOME
> then
>        echo hello
> fi
hello
$
```

The other form of **test** uses the special operators **[** and **]** (square brackets). The **test** arguments are enclosed within the brackets, and the word *test* does not appear.

```
$ if [ $HOME ]
> then
>        echo hello
> fi
hello
$
```

The brackets must be surrounded by white space, or the shell will not interpret the command line correctly. Notice that this use of the square brackets differs from their use as a wild-card or regular expression operator for filename expansion. When they are used after the **if** operator, the shell can understand the difference.

Many different tests are possible, depending on the arguments within the brackets. The **test** command provides operations for files, for comparing numbers, and for comparing strings of characters and the values of environment variables. In all cases white space must surround the brackets and each of the operators.

The form **−f file** (for file) returns true if the file exists and is a normal file.

```
$ if [ -f /etc/passwd ] ; then echo file exists ; fi
file exists
$
```

Similarly, **−r file** (for readable) returns true if the file exists and is readable, **−w file** (for writable) returns true if the file exists and is writable, **−x file** (for executable) returns true if the file exists and is executable, and **−d file** (for directory) returns true if the file exists and is a directory. The form **−s file** returns true if the file exists and has a size larger than zero. Several other file-related operators are also possible but are seldom used.

String comparison operators test the presence and value of environment variables. This allows you to perform some operation, assign the value to an environment variable, and then test the value of the variable to decide whether to take more action. For example, you may wish to execute certain commands only if you are in a particular directory.

```
$ DIR=`pwd`
$ if [ $DIR = $HOME ]
> then
>         echo In home directory!
> fi
In home directory!
$
```

Note that the = (equal) operator tests whether two character strings are identical: true is returned if the strings are the same, false if they are not. The form != can be used to return true if the strings are not equal. All these operators must be separated by white space from the brackets and the other arguments within the brackets.

In addition, the string or an environment variable can appear alone to determine if the string has been defined.

```
$ if [ "$NOVALUE" ] ; then echo hello ; fi
$
```

If the environment variable *NOVALUE* has not been defined, **test** returns false and the **then** section is not executed.

The = operator is reserved for strings comparison and cannot be used to compare the equality of numbers. The **test** command can compare integer numeric values, but shell programming is not as good at numeric problems as most other programming tools. Numeric comparisons within **test** use the form

```
if [ n1 -eq n2 ]
```

where *n1* and *n2* are expressions that resolve to a number. The operator −**eq** (for equals) evaluates to true if the two numbers are equal.

```
$ echo $VAL
2
$ if [ $VAL -eq 2 ]
> then
>        echo equal
> fi
equal
$
```

Other numeric operators are **−ne** (for not equal), **−gt** (for greater than), **−lt** (for less than), and **−le** (for less than or equal). The operator **−lt** can be read as "if the first number is less than the second, then the expression is true." The other operators also follow this syntax.

These numeric operators are often used to test the return value of some command or pipeline and then take some action if the return value is a specific number. Most commands return zero if they complete successfully.

```
$ mkdir /tmp/SS
$ RET=$?
$ if [ $RET -eq 0 ]
> then
>        echo "mkdir succeeded"
> else
>        echo "Couldn't make directory"
> fi
mkdir succeeded
$
```

Of course these examples are more likely to appear in shell scripts than in commands that you enter directly at the "$" prompt, but they all can be entered directly if you wish.

The **test** command provides tools to combine operators to build up complex expressions. The ! (bang) operator negates another operator, as shown here:

```
$ if [ ! -f file ]
> then
```

```
>        touch file      # this creates the file
> fi
$
```

This command creates a file if it doesn't already exist. Other combination operators available to **test** are **−o** (for or) and **−a** (for and), which are used to separate other operators.

```
$ Fl=filel ; F2=file2
$ if [ ! -f $Fl -a -f $F2 ]
> then
>       echo "$Fl doesn't exist, but $F2 does exist"
> fi
$
```

You can combine these operators into very complex expressions, and you can group complex operations within parentheses if needed. In practice, however, you should try to keep **test** commands relatively simple.

The exit Command

You can use the **exit** command inside shell scripts to immediately end execution of the script. The **exit** command can take an argument that becomes the value that the script returns back to the calling shell.

```
$ if true
> then
>       exit 6
> fi
$ VAL=$?
$ echo $?
6
$
```

When you use return values from within shell scripts, you should follow the standard convention: commands that complete correctly should return zero. Nonzero return values are reserved for various failure conditions.

The expr Command

Although the shell programming language is not optimized for numeric calculations, commands are provided to do computation. The **expr** (for expression) command, the most useful of these, takes numbers and arithmetic operators as arguments and computes the result, returning the answer on its standard output.

```
$ expr 4 + 5
9
$
```

Longer commands are also allowed, but each piece of the expression must be surrounded by white space, because **expr** treats each argument as a part of the expression to be evaluated. Only integers are allowed. The operators + (plus), − (minus), * (multiplication), / (division), and % (for remainder) are allowed, though * and / must be escaped with a \ (backslash) to keep the shell from interpreting them before **expr** gets to them.

```
$ expr 3 \* 4 + 2 \/ 2
13
$
```

Normal arithmetic precedence is used, so here the 3 * 4 and the 2 / 2 are evaluated before the +. This precedence cannot be changed on the command line, so complex calculations may take several operations.

```
$ VAL=`expr 3 \* 4 + 2`
$ expr $VAL \/ 2
7
$
```

This example shows how **expr** is normally used within shell scripts. Environment variables are usually defined to store numbers, and you can use their value later in other **expr** commands or in **test** operations.

The for Operator

Other operators in the shell programming language provide *looping* constructs that repetitively execute a section of the shell program. The **for** operator is an example, and it uses the form

```
$ for var in item1 item2 item3 ; do commands ; done
```

where *var* is an environment variable that you name, and items make a list of character strings with each item separated by white space from the others. For example:

```
$ for VAL in 1 2 3 4 ; do commands ; done
```

When this command is read by the shell, it sets *VAL* equal to the first item in the list and then executes the commands given between the **do** and its matching **done**. The shell then sets *VAL* equal to the second item in the list and executes commands again, repeating this procedure until all members of the list have been processed. The value of *VAL* is available within the command list if needed.

```
$ for VAL in 1 2 3 4
> do
>         echo $VAL
> done
1
2
3
4
$
```

As usual, the commands within the **do-done** delimiters can be as complex as needed, including **if-fi** expressions or more **for** operations.

The **for** construction is often used with filenames to repeatedly perform some operation on each file. Because the **for** command is interpreted by the shell, wild-card expansion is performed.

```
$ for FILE in * ; do echo $FILE ; done
```

This command will echo the name of all the files in the current directory because * is replaced by the names of all the files before the **for** command is executed.

A particularly inefficient way to count the files in a directory might be as follows:

```
$ COUNT=0
$ for FILE in *
> do
>         COUNT=`expr $COUNT + 1`
> done
$ echo $COUNT
14
$
```

As you can see, there is no rule that makes you use the environment variable that follows the **for** command, but it must be present to tell **for** how many times to iterate the **do-done** section.

Standard output of a command can also create the list. This

```
$ for VAR in `ls`
> do
>         echo $VAR
> done
```

is an acceptable command because the shell executes the **ls** command, places its output into the **for** command, and then executes the entire construct.

The **for** command has many uses, both in shell scripts and directly at the terminal, because it allows you to iterate through a list of objects, executing a (possibly) large list of commands on each member of the list. The **for** command is one of the most frequently used of the shell operators.

The while Operator

The **while** operator combines some of the characteristics of both **for** and **if**; it takes a following **test** command and then a **do-done** section. If the test part resolves to true, then the **do-done** section is executed. If the test part resolves to false, the

do-done part is not executed, and the loop completes. After the **do-done** part is executed, the test section is executed again, and the loop continues until the test section resolves to false.

```
$ while [ ! -f file ]
> do
>         echo Trying to create file
>         touch file
> done
```

This example keeps trying to create a file until the creation succeeds.

You should include some commands to change the result of the test section within the **do-done** section, or the loop is likely to continue forever! This example creates ten files, named **file1**, **file2**, and so on through **file10**.

```
$ VAL=1
$ while [ $VAL -lt 11 ]
> do
>         touch file$VAL
>         VAL=`expr $VAL + 1`
> done
```

Another way this command could be written is as follows:

```
$ for VAL in 1 2 3 4 5 6 7 8 9 10
> do
>         touch file$VAL
> done
```

As usual, any commands, including other **while** operations, could have been included within the **do-done** section.

You can substitute **until** for the **while** keyword to reverse the sense of the test. That is, **while** executes the command list as long as the test is true; **until** executes the command list as long as the test is false.

When you write shell scripts, you should indent each new

sublevel of the commands an additional tab stop, as shown in the previous examples. This helps to organize the program, because commands at the same level line up vertically, and makes it easier to read than if all the commands started at the left margin or right after the PS2 prompt. Indenting the commands does not affect the way that the shell interprets the script, but it definitely improves the way that humans interpret it!

The case Operator

The shell provides one additional control operator, **case**, which acts like a large **if-elif-elif-...-elif-fi** command. Given a character string, **case** determines which one of several categories the string matches and then executes a list of commands associated with that category. The other, unmatched categories are ignored. The format of the **case** operator is as follows:

```
$ case $VAR in
>       pattern1 )
>               command-list
>               ;;
>       pattern2 )
>               command-list
>               ;;
>       pattern3 )
>               command-list
>               ;;
> esac
```

You can have as many patterns and command lists as you need, but the command list associated with each pattern must be terminated by the special operator ;;. Also, each pattern must be different from all others, and the whole construct must be terminated by **esac** (for case backward). Finally, the **)** (right parenthesis) operator is required after each pattern. *VAR* can be any environment variable or any expression that resolves to a character string. As usual, any other shell operators can be nested inside the command list for each **case**.

The following command will print a special greeting for each user on the machine.

```
$ case $LOGNAME in
>       jim)
>                   echo Hello Jim, welcome back
>                   echo from your vacation
>                   ;;
>       pat)
>                   echo Pat, do not forget to read your mail
>                   ;;
>       steve)
>                   echo Please delete some files, you are using
>                   echo too much disk space....  Thanks!
>                   ;;
> esac
```

Normally a script like this would be executed from a file, perhaps by users as they log into the machine. This could be implemented as part of the profile discussed in the next section.

The pattern section of the **case** operator allows the use of regular expressions in the shell wild-card format. In the previous example you could have used **ste***, ***te***, **?teve**, or another pattern to successfully match **steve**.

In addition, the | (pipe) character can be used to mean "or" in the pattern section, as shown here:

```
$ case $LOGNAME in
>       steve|jim)
>                   echo do not forget the meeting today
>                   ;;
>       *)
>                   echo Welcome to our UNIX system
>                   ;;
> esac
```

The first case is for steve or jim. The second case, *****, will match any other string and is used as a catchall default case.

Remember, only one section is executed each time the **case** construct as a whole is executed, and that will be the *first* pattern that matches the character string. If none of the patterns match, then none of the cases is executed.

The .profile and /etc/profile Scripts

One of the best examples of shell scripts, and one that each user normally creates and maintains individually, is a standard script that is executed by the system during login. This shell script is usually used to configure your login sessions according to your preferences and to create some of the environment variables that the commands expect to find. The *profile* is somewhat equivalent to AUTOEXEC.BAT in MS-DOS systems, except that it is specific to your login id, and other users can have their own.

Actually, two different scripts are executed when you log into the system. One is owned by the system and sets up your environment according to system-wide permissions. This script is located in **/etc/profile** and is usually readable by all users. The **/etc/profile** script is executed first, right after you successfully log into the system. We will not discuss it here, but you should browse it on your own machine. When the system administrator changes the environment for all users, for example, adding a new directory to the default *PATH*, the change is usually implemented by modifying **/etc/profile**.

The other profile is executed after **/etc/profile** but before the shell gives the first "$" prompt. This is called **.profile** and is located in your HOME directory. You normally do not see your **.profile** with **ls** in your home directory, because the leading **.** (dot) keeps **ls** from displaying it. The command

```
$ ls -a
```

(for all) will display it and other files beginning with . if it is executed from your home directory. You own your **.profile**, and you can use it to further configure your personal environment beyond what the system gives you with **/etc/profile**. You usually put personalized commands that are always executed on login in your .**profile**.

A Typical .profile

The system administrator for your machine will give you a simple **.profile** when your login id is created, but this is rarely sufficient. As you gain experience with the UNIX system, you will probably want to customize the environment to your preferences. Figure 7-1 shows a typical .**profile** to suggest the kinds of changes that are usually made in the environment. Though few of them are needed, they can make a session more pleasant because your preferences will be honored instead of the system defaults.

First, the *PATH* variable is redefined to pick up the current directory and a private bin ahead of the system commands. This allows you to override some of the normal commands with your private, customized commands. However, this can be a security risk if the directories are writeable by other users, because someone could put a corrupt version of a command into your directory, which you would then use instead of the system default. The current directory is usually also included in the *PATH*, either at the beginning or at the end. Next, the **stty** command resets the terminal configuration to enable XON/XOFF flow control, to send tabs instead of spaces when possible, and to make BACKSPACE the erase character. The **echoe** option makes the system send a BACKSPACE-SPACE-BACKSPACE sequence when you press a BACKSPACE. This erases your typed characters from the screen as you backspace over them. Next, the script changes the PS1 and PS2 to more preferred prompts.

The largest part of this sample **.profile** handles different terminals that you might use. First, the local environment variable *PORT* is used as a target of the **test** command to determine if you are on the system console or a remote terminal. On the console /etc/**profile** will correctly set the *TERM* variable, so this long **if-fi** section is not executed. If you are not logged into the console, the **.profile** will prompt you for the terminal you are using.

This command

```
read TERM
```

```
#   typical .profile
#   edit yours to meet your own needs...

# Change PATH to put private directories ahead of system bins
# Note: this can be a security risk
PATH=:$HOME:$HOME/bin:/bin:/usr/bin:/usr/lbin

# reconfigure the terminal for tabs, XON/XOFF,
# and "backspace-space-backspace" for erase
stty tabs echoe erase ixon ixoff ixany

# change the prompts....
PS1='[!] F> '
PS2=' >> '

# Now special processing for each of the different
# terminals we might use....  If we're on the console,
# we can skip this part....
PORT=`tty`
PORT=`basename $PORT`
if [ $PORT != console ] ; then

        # prompt for the terminal this session,
        # and read it into an environment variable
        echo "\\nTERM=\\c"
        read TERM
        case $TERM in
                s*)     # AT&T UNIX PC
                        if [ $TERM = ss ] ; then stty cr2 nl1 ; fi
                        TERM=ansi
                        stty -tabs
                        ;;
```

Figure 7-1. A typical **.profile**

```
              pc|2621)          # HP 2621 or terminal emulator
                      TERM=2621
                      tabs -Thp
                      ;;

              ansi|v*)          # DEC VT100, VT102, or VT200
                      TERM=vt100
                      tabs
                      ;;

              *)        # all others are treated as very dumb terminals
                        TERM=dumb
                        stty -tabs
                        ;;
        esac
fi

# repeat what terminal is really being used
echo "TERM=$TERM"

# this is for the "vi" editor
EXINIT='set ai'

# some software likes to know the name of my preferred editor
EDITOR=/usr/bin/vi
EDIT=/usr/bin/vi

# For "cd" commands

CDPATH=:$HOME:$HOME/bin

# and make sure they are all exported
export PATH TERM PS1 PS2 EXINIT EDITOR CDPATH EDIT

# display the date and time
date

# display any news that we haven't seen yet
news

# prompt if any old mail saved in "$HOME/mbox"
if [ -f mbox ] ; then echo "You have oldmail!" ; fi

# setup for use with the Korn Shell
FCEDIT=/usr/bin/vi
MAILCHECK=60
ENV="\\${-:+$HOME/.ksh.aliases\\${-##*i*}}"
HISTFILE=$HOME/.ksh.history
export ENV HISTFILE FCEDIT

# last, we switch shells from the default to the ksh
exec /bin/ksh
```

Figure 7-1.   A typical **.profile** (*continued*)

```
# setup for use with the Korn Shell
FCEDIT=/usr/bin/vi
MAILCHECK=60
ENV="\${-:+$HOME/.ksh.aliases\${-##*i*}}"
HISTFILE=$HOME/.ksh.history
export ENV HISTFILE FCEDIT

# last, we switch shells from the default to the ksh
exec /bin/ksh
```

Figure 7-1.   A typical **.profile** (*continued*)

waits for you to enter a line from the keyboard and then stores
that line in the environment variable *TERM*. Next, **case** is used
to perform different processing depending on what is entered,
usually just to set the *TERM* variable correctly for each different terminal. The **tabs** command sends out the proper escape
sequences to set the tab stops at the terminal, in case the
terminal cannot remember the tab settings when its power is
shut off. The **tabs** command works with **stty tabs** to reduce the
amount of output sent to the terminal by replacing a number of
spaces with tabs, when appropriate.

Because the *TERM* variable might have changed as a
result of the **case-esac** block, the *TERM* value is echoed back.
Then a few more environment variables are set. *EXINIT* is
used by the **vi** editor, and the *EDITOR* and *EDIT* variables tell
some software what the preferred editor is. The help facility
(and other software) uses these environment variables.
CDPATH is an advanced shell feature that allows a short and
intelligent form of the **cd** command. Next, the script makes
sure that all of your subshells have access to these environment
variables, by exporting them.

Following these operations, a little administrative work is
done. The **date** command just displays the current date and
time, and **news** will automatically display any news that you

haven't read yet. The short **if-fi** block that follows reminds you that some saved mail exists. Mail should be deleted when you are through with it, so if the **mbox** file exists, there is probably some unfinished business that needs attention.

Finally, some more environment variables are set up. These are associated with another shell that is often used instead of the default shell. Last of all, the script actually switches to that shell with **exec /bin/ksh**.

Your **.profile** will probably differ from the one shown here, but most customization of the individual user environment and login processing belongs in the personal **.profile**.

The . Operator

Normally **.profile** is executed for your benefit when you log into the system. However, when you are editing and testing your **.profile**, it is tedious to repeatedly log off and log into the machine to test it. Because **.profile** is a normal, executable shell script, why can't you just execute it like any other shell script? The answer is a little tricky. Recall that shell scripts are executed in their own subshells, and changes to environment variables within subshells do not propagate back to the parent shells. Therefore, any effects that your **.profile** might have, such as changing your *TERM* variable, will not make permanent changes to your environment if it is just executed directly with the following:

```
$ sh .profile
```

However, the shell provides another operator that effectively tells the shell to "execute a script by the current shell rather than create a subshell to execute it." This is the . (dot) command, and it takes an argument naming the script you wish to execute.

```
$ . .profile
```

Any shell script is an acceptable argument, but the dot command is usually used with **.profile** for testing or for loading a profile during execution of another shell script in a subshell. Changes made to the environment with the . operator permanently change the current environment (and possibly subshells that might be created later) but still do not change parent or higher-level shells that may exist.

Command Line Arguments

Several more issues related to shell programming remain to be discussed, including *command line arguments*. You can create shell programs that process command line arguments in exactly the same format as other commands. In fact you should usually try to duplicate the normal argument syntax as much as possible, so that your commands will work the way that users expect. Because of this intention, operators are provided in shell scripts to process command line arguments that are constructed in a familiar way.

The $#, $*, and Positional Parameters

You have already met the $# and $* shell variables, which are interpreted by the shell as the *number* of command line parameters to a shell script and the *values* of all the parameters, respectively. In this shell script

```
echo $#
for VAR in $*
do
        echo $VAR
done
```

the shell expands the $* variable to be all the command line arguments to the script.

For example, if the above shell script were called ECHO.ARGS, you might execute it with a command such as the following:

```
$ echo.args first second third
```

The arguments **first, second,** and **third** are passed to the script.

```
$ echo.args first second third
3
first
second
third
$
```

The 3 in the output results from the **echo $#** command in the script, and the remaining output results from the **for-do-done** loop.

In addition, each command line argument to the script is available individually, with the names **$1, $2, $3,** and so forth for as many as nine command line arguments. For example, the previous script could have been written as

```
echo $#
echo $1
echo $2
echo $3
```

with exactly the same results as shown above. Each of these command line arguments can be used to pass filenames or other information into a shell script from its command line.

These command line arguments are usually only useful in shell scripts that are executed as commands, because the login shell has no arguments associated with it. That is,

```
$ echo $#
0
$
```

No command line arguments are defined to your login shell, with one exception; **$0** is a legitimate argument just like **$2**, and it returns the command name itself.

```
$ echo $0
sh
$
```

The first command line argument after the name is **$1**.

In addition, the shell provides an operator to set these command line arguments if needed.

```
$ echo $#
0
$ echo $2

$ set hello goodbye third
$ echo $#
3
$ echo $2
goodbye
$
```

The **set** operator assigns its arguments to the *positional parameters* so that scripts can use the names **$2** and so on even if no command line arguments are given. For example, you might write a script that does something with its command line parameters, but if none exist, then the script itself can set them to default values. The **set** operator is often used within shell scripts.

Errors and Error Messages in Using Shell Scripts

Shell scripts usually require some experimentation and testing before you get them right. The shell provides some diagnostic error messages when it cannot execute a script that is incorrect, but this normal output is often terse.

```
$ for VAR in `ls` do
> hello
syntax error: `hello' unexpected
$
```

The error here was to omit the ; or the NEWLINE before the **do** keyword, but the shell's error output did not provide much information. More information is available if you execute a script from a file with **sh -x**, as shown in Figure 7-2. This *trace* displays each command with a leading + as it is executed, though after the shell carries out its substitutions and processes **test** and other operators. When an error occurs, it is much easier to follow the train of execution leading to the error when the trace command is operating. Another aid is the −**v** (for verbose) flag, which displays much more about each command in the script as it is executed.

```
$ sh -v shell.script first second third
echo $#
3
for VAR in $* ; do
        echo $VAR
```

```
done
first
second
third
$
```

Going Further

There is much more to writing and using shell scripts than we have reviewed here. You will learn shell programming by practicing, by constantly experimenting with short scripts entered directly at the terminal, and by reading and changing the scripts of others.

There are many examples of shell scripts in the commands, and usually you cannot easily tell if a command is a binary compiled program or a shell script with executable permissions. In most systems the commands **/usr/bin/calendar**, **/usr/bin/spell**, **/bin/basename**, and **/usr/bin/uuto** are shell scripts, among many others. Examine these on your own system and try to follow what they do. Can you understand their logic?

```
$ cat shell.script
echo $#
for VAR in $*  ; do
        echo $VAR
done
$ sh -x shell.script first second third
+ echo 3
3
+ echo first
first
+ echo second
second
+ echo third
third
$
```

Figure 7-2.   Trace (−x) output from executing a shell script

The shar Command — An Instructive Shell Script

Figure 7-3 gives another example of a moderately complex shell script, one that actually produces another shell script as its output. This is an implementation of the **shar** (for shell archive) command, whose job is to produce a single file that contains several other files within it. One file is usually easier to move between machines via electronic mail or **uucp** than several files.

The **shar** command is limited compared to some other file-packing tools because it only handles text files and not binary or compiled files, but it is widely used to exchange data between UNIX systems. In practice users often create **shar** archives of several short source files and then send the files to someone else, who will unpack or **unshar** the file to recover the originals. Like all good data communication tools, the **shar** program includes some tests to detect whether anything was lost during the **shar-move-unshar** procedure.

The **shar** program is executed as follows:

```
$ shar filename-list > /tmp/out.file
```

The script reads the files in the list and writes the archived material to its standard output. You would usually redirect this to some other file, probably in a different directory than the one you are bundling with the **shar** command.

The **shar** archive produced by this shell script is itself an executable shell script, and the original files can be unpacked from the **shar** archive with

```
$ sh /tmp/out.file
```

or with

```
$ chmod +x /tmp/out.file
$ /tmp/out.file
```

This simple **shar** mechanism provides a way to pack files into a shell script, and the program shown in Figure 7-3 rewards extensive study. We will describe it briefly.

The first few lines are comments. Remember, you should use comments extensively in all programming, but especially if others are expected to understand the program. The next few lines just determine whether any filenames are given as arguments to the **shar** command; if not, it prints an error message and exits.

The real work begins with the **echo** commands. This script is actually executing some commands, and writing some other commands to its output with the **echo** statements. After echoing a few messages, the main loop begins. **$*** is a shell operator that evaluates to the list of command line arguments for the script. The number of arguments that are produced by **$*** is the same as the number given by **$#**. However, **$*** evaluates to the actual arguments, separated by white space, while **$#** is only the number of arguments. Within the loop, **shar** tests whether each file is actually present. The **test** section resolves to true if the file is not readable or if it does not exist. The parentheses are used to group the **test** operators, but the parentheses must be escaped with backslash to prevent the shell from misinterpreting them. If the file is not found by these tests, **shar** echoes an error message, but to prevent the error message from going into the archive it is building, the output from **echo** is redirected directly to the terminal with > **/dev/tty**.

The next several lines are tricky, since they are building some executable commands into the output script. In fact, **shar** is creating a here document in the output, and enclosing the actual file inside it. The **sed** commands just add **X** to the beginning of each line of the here document. The line **echo +SHAR+MARK+** ends the here document.

The next few lines embed the results of **ls −l** in the output, from the original file. The line **echo ls −l $file** near the end of

```
# shar:  shell archive shell script
# Runs in  /bin/sh
# shar:  group files into distribution package in "shar" format
#        suitable for extraction with sh, not csh.

# stash the total number of command line args
XX=$#
export XX

# but there must be at least one arg
if [ $XX -lt 1 ] ; then
        echo "usage: shar file1 file2 file3 ... fileN"
        exit 1
fi

# now we begin building the output file.
# first is a general header....
echo ': To unbundle, "sh" this file -- DO NOT use csh'
echo ': SHAR archive format.  Archive created '`date`

# each file is processed in turn:  "$*" is the list of args
for file in $* ; do

        # if the file doesn't exist, complain, but don't quit
        if [ ! \( -r $file -a -f $file \) ] ; then
                echo shar:  "Cannot archive '$file'" > /dev/tty
                continue
        fi

        # the file is found, so we put out its name"
        echo "echo x - $file"

        # Make a here document out of the file,
        # and write the here document intact to the output

        # count the matching quotes... this is tricky!
        # we're echoing a "sed" command line, not executing "sed"
        echo "sed 's/^X//' > $file <<'+SHAR+MARK+'"

        # Here we execute the "sed" to prefix 'X' to each line.
        # write it to stdout
        sed 's/^/X/' $file

        # now we close the here document
        echo "+SHAR+MARK+"

        # we "ls" the file, then stash the results inside an "echo"
        echo "echo '`ls -l $file`    (as sent)'"

        # this one processes the permissions in the "ls -l",
        # creates a "chmod" # command, then write the
        # "chmod" command to the output
        ls -l $file | sed \
                -e 's/^.\(...\)\(...\)\(...\).*/u=\1,g=\2,o=\3/' \
                -e 's/-//g' \
                -e 's/.*/chmod & '"$file/"

        # now a direct "ls" for the output script
```

Figure 7-3.   **shar** shell script

```
      echo "ls -l $file"

done    # and the end of the per-file loop

echo "exit 0"   # and an exit command for the output
```

Figure 7-3.   **shar** shell script (*continued*)

the script causes the **ls** command to be executed on the receiving side. It's up to the recipient to check whether the two files are the same size. The complex **sed** command transforms the **ls** −l output into a **chmod** command to set the permissions correctly on the receiving file. Can you understand what it is doing? Finally, an **exit** command goes into the output.

When this command executes, it embeds the files in the **shar** argument list into a new executable shell script. Try this script on your machine. How does it work? This version of **shar** will not handle files in subdirectories well. Can you improve it?

The getopts Command

So far we have discussed arguments to shell scripts that might be names of files or other input arguments. However, the normal command line syntax allows flags that begin with − (minus) to modify the operation of the command. Shell scripts can also have flags as part of the argument list. The **getopts** (for get options) command is designed to facilitate the job of parsing command line flags, when these flags may be in any order on the command line and may in turn have associated arguments. The **getopts** operator replaces an older form named **getopt**; in SVR3 systems you should use the **getopts** function, but in older versions you must use **getopt**.

The **getopts** command allows you to create shell scripts that can process command line arguments like other executable commands. It uses the **set** function internally to pull the options and flags out of the command line arguments, leaving the nonflag arguments as **$1**, **$2**, **$3**, and so on.

Figure 7-4 gives a sample shell script that shows how to use the **getopts** function. The line

```
while getopts yz:x VAR
```

defines a loop using **getopts**. The **getopts** function takes two arguments of its own. The first is a list of acceptable command letters with no embedded white space. In this list each letter that requires a following argument has a : (colon) after it. The second argument, *VAR* in the example, is a temporary environment variable containing the value of the current command line option, which is set each time through the **while** loop. The **while** loop is executed once for each command line argument given; when all the arguments have been processed, **getopts** returns false and the **while** loop ends.

The command line flags −**x**, −**y**, and −**z** are allowed, and the −**z** option must have a following argument. Assuming that the script is named **script**, then the following command lines, among others, are allowed.

```
$ script
$ script -x
$ script -y -x
$ script -z hello
$ script -x -z hello
$ script -z hello -y
```

The shell variable *USAGE* is defined by the **getopts** function and reports which options were allowed in the **getopts** command embedded in the **while** loop. The shell variable *OPTARG*, also defined by the **getopts** function, is set to the value of the argument following the current flag option. In this example *OPTARG* can be defined only for the −**z** option, because the control string for **getopts** only included the : after the **z** option.

Within the **while** loop, you can process each of the allowed command line arguments, setting some variables or processing as needed when an argument is given. For flags that take their

```
# first we parse the command options, assigning shell
# variables to mark which of the legal flags have been set.
while getopts yz:x c
do
        case $c in
            x)
                        XFLAG=true
                        ;;
            y)
                        YFLAG=true
                        ;;
            z)
                        ZFLAG=true
                        ZOPT=$OPTARG   # OPTARG is the "current" value
                        ;;
            *)
                        echo $USAGE
                        exit 2
                        ;;
        esac
done

# now we've parsed all the flags and options, we just reset
# the argument list to be only what's left after these are
# taken from the input line
shift `expr $OPTIND -1`

# now XFLAG, YFLAG, or ZFLAG may be set, depending
# on what args were on the command line.
# ZOPT is set to "str" if option "-z str" was given
# We can go on now to the rest of the shell script, as needed
```

Figure 7-4.   Use of the **getopts** operator

own arguments, such as the −z option in the example, you must use another environment variable to store the value of the argument because **getopts** will only define *OPTARG* while a specific command line option is current in the **while** loop.

After all the command line arguments have been processed using this **while** loop, the **shift** command will change the $* variable to remove the flags already processed so that a new $1 is defined to be the first command line argument that has not yet been processed. Once all the flags have been processed, the script can continue to do the work for which it was intended.

Shell Layers and the shl Command

The SVR2 and SVR3 systems provide a tool that allows more than one shell to be active on a single terminal. This is not a windowing system such as found in Microsoft Windows or the Apple Macintosh, but each shell takes the full screen. Tools are provided that allow you to create additional shells, switch between them, and kill shells when you are done with them. With this *shell layers* procedure, the system treats each separate shell as an independent session; so it appears to the system that you have logged into the machine multiple times on separate, distinct terminals. Each session is treated as a *virtual terminal* called a *layer*, and the different layers do not interact. Because each layer occupies the full screen, special tools are provided that allow you to switch to another layer when you wish. With this scheme, you can run several programs simultaneously, and all of them will have full-screen access to your terminal. The shell layers system has many uses but is limited to the **tty** devices, so it cannot be used over some local area networks.

The **shl** (for shell layers) command will start the *layer manager*, which controls access to the different layers that can be created. After executing the **shl** program, it displays a new prompt to signal that you are not in a normal session but rather under the auspices of **shl**.

```
$ shl
>>>
```

At this point **shl** is waiting for a command. You can create a new layer, kill an existing layer, or close the layer manager entirely.

To create a new layer, enter **create** after the ">>>" prompt.

```
$ shl
>>> create
(1)
```

The new layer is created and is given a name, which is usually the number of the layer, from 1 through 7, the maximum number of layers allowed. The PS1 prompt for the layer is changed to the layer name to help distinguish which layer is currently active on the screen. After the commands given in the example, the login shell is *suspended* and the layer (1) shell is listening to commands. You can use this layer just like any normal shell, and you can kill it with the **exit** command or CTRL-D. When you kill a layer, you return to the layer manager with the ">>>" prompt and can then instruct **shl** what to do next.

Once the **shl** program is running, no matter which layer is active, you can return to the ">>>" prompt at any time. The key combination CTRL-Z tells **shl** to wake up and listen to your input. When CTRL-Z is pressed, **shl** immediately displays the ">>>" prompt and waits for a command. You can create a new layer if you wish, as shown here:

```
$ shl
>>> create
(1) CNTRL-z
>>> create
(2)
```

Now you have two layers, and the currently active one is layer (2).

You can create a layer, start an application there that produces output, and then create a second layer. In this situation output from the first layer (and all active layers!) will come directly to the terminal, overwriting output from the current layer. That is, applications in layers continue to execute, writing their output to the terminal, no matter how many layers are active. However, only one layer, the current one, can listen for your keystrokes. The other layers are *nonblocking* because they continue to run even when they are not active.

You can use the **stty** command to change this behavior, and when a layer is active, you can change it to *blocking* so that output from a layer stops until that layer is made the current one. Use

```
(2) stty loblk
(2)
```

to make layer (2) blocking and

```
(2) stty -loblk
(2)
```

to make the layer nonblocking.

You can return to the **shl** program at any time with the CTRL-Z key combination, and several other commands are available in addition to **create**. Most of them take an argument specifying the name of the layer to which the command is to refer. For example, the **block** command acts the same as the **stty loblk**, except that it is given to **shl** rather than directly within the active layer. The **block** command takes the layer you want to block as an argument. This command

```
>>> block 2
```

will cause layer (2) to be blocked. The **unblock** command acts the same as **stty -loblk**. Again a layer number is given as argument.

To switch from one active layer to another, press CTRL-Z, wait for the ">>>" prompt, and enter the command **resume** with the layer number you wish to become active.

```
(1) CNTRL-z
>>> resume 2
resuming 2
```

Now layer (2) is active. It did not display any prompt, however, because it took over control just where it was in the processing of whatever task was executing in that layer. In this case layer (2) was waiting for your next command. If a program was producing output, then that output would begin to appear at the screen. If it was waiting at the PS1 prompt, then pressing NEWLINE would produce a new prompt. In no case will switching layers cause the program to redraw the screen. That is your responsibility after you resume a layer.

You can switch freely between layers by using the **resume** command or, more simply, just by entering the name of the layer to make current, without the **resume** keyword.

```
(2) CNTRL-z
>>> 1
(1)
```

To kill a layer, press CTRL-D in the layer itself or use the **delete** command to the ">>>" prompt, with a layer number as argument.

```
(2) CNTRL-z
>>> delete 2
>>>
```

Finally, **quit** will kill the layer manager and return you to the original log in shell. All active programs in any layer will be killed.

The CTRL-Z key combination to wake the **shl** program is called the *switch* character, and you can change it to suit your personal preference with the **stty** command

```
$ stty swtch c
```

where *c* is the new character to use instead of CTRL-Z.

Virtual Consoles

An important adaptation of the **shl** concept is the *virtual console*. Some releases of SVR2 and SVR3 allow the use of PF keys on the system console to directly switch between layers, bypassing the **shl** command and its CTRL-Z procedure. The virtual console feature is limited to the system console, but **shl** can run on remote terminals as well as on the console.

In some releases, pressing a PF key clears the screen and causes a login: prompt to appear, which allows you to log into the machine again. In other releases, the current login is preserved and pressing the PF key starts a new shell. Once a session is established, you can immediately switch to it by pressing the associated PF key.

Usually, the screen will be redrawn when you switch sessions, which solves one of the major drawbacks of the original **shl** command. In addition, the virtual console is always available and you need not start it with a command such as **shl**.

The virtual console feature is limited to the system console, but **shl** can run on remote terminals as well as on the console. Consult the documentation for your release of SVR3 to see whether it supports this feature and how many sessions it allows simultaneously.

Shell Functions

The SVR2 and SVR3 shells provide an additional mechanism for creating scripts that is slightly more efficient than the script file approach discussed previously. However, these *shell functions* are more difficult to control than normal shell scripts because they are defined directly to the shell and do not have permanent life in a file. When you define a shell function, the current shell reads the definition, and the function is stored inside the currently active shell. You can execute a shell function just like any other command or shell script, but when you log off, the function will be lost. Of course you can put definitions of shell functions in a file and execute the file with the **.** **filename** mechanism, which allows the filename to be read and interpreted by the current shell rather than by a newly created subshell. Shell functions are *not* exportable or automatically available to subshells; they must be reread by subshells if needed.

Shell functions are defined by the form

```
$ name () {
>        command-list
> }
```

where *name* can be any name you choose for the function. The ( ) (left and right parentheses) are required, and the { (left curly brace) begins the command list. Any normal executable commands or shell operators are allowed in the command list, as you have come to expect. In addition, the **$#**, **$***, and **$1** through **$9** positional parameters are available within the function. For example:

```
$ show () {
>        echo $1
>        echo $2
>        exit 2
> }
$ show hello goodbye
hello
goodbye
$
```

This example defines a shell function named **show** that echoes its first two arguments and then returns the exit value 2 to the calling shell.

Shell functions can be as complex as you wish, and you can make frequently used shell scripts into shell functions with potential savings of system CPU resources. However, if you routinely use a set of shell functions, you must take care to install them in your **.profile** or use some other mechanism to assure that they will always be available when you want them.

The Korn and C Shells

The shell is a user-level process like any other command. It has no special relationship with the kernel nor any special privileges not enjoyed by other commands. Thus it can be changed at the user's discretion, and many alternative shells are available that look different or are optimized for different functions.

The standard shell, the one that we have discussed so far, is known as the *Bourne shell* after its developer, Steve Bourne of AT&T Bell Laboratories. This small shell was designed for general-purpose use and is relatively efficient. Over the years (the Bourne shell was introduced in about 1978), more features and improvements, such as shell functions, have been added to keep it current with the rest of the UNIX system. However, it has several disadvantages for expert users. First, there is no *command history*—no way to repeat a command line without completely retyping the command. Further, the standard shell lacks *aliasing*—the ability for users to customize the command names that they frequently use. You can solve both of these problems with the Bourne shell by creating new commands as shell programs, saving them in a file, and giving the file the name you wish. But this solution is inefficient because a sub-shell is required to read the shell program and execute its contents. Finally, there is no quick and easy way to edit commands on the fly because the shell program is relatively permanent in the file.

These considerations motivated the development of two popular enhanced shells, the *C shell* and the *Korn shell*. Both shells replace the Bourne shell for interactive user-level sessions and act identically to the Bourne shell in those areas discussed so far. The C shell was originally developed as part of the BSD version, and the Korn shell was developed by David Korn of AT&T Bell Laboratories in response to the C shell. Though neither shell is a standard part of the SVR3 system, both are widely available as add-on software packages.

The C shell was designed solely for interactive use. That is, it cannot be named /**bin**/**sh** and thus cannot be used for all the things that the system does with the shell behind the back of the user. The C shell is also relatively inefficient compared to either the Bourne or Korn shell. Nevertheless, it has many devotees, especially among fans of BSD UNIX systems. The Korn shell has features for interactive use and can also completely replace the Bourne shell as /**bin**/**sh**. It is larger than the Bourne shell, but it is noticeably more efficient because it has more built-in functions that can be performed directly by the shell and do not require a separate subshell.

Both newer shells provide many enhancements beyond /**bin**/**sh**, including more shell programming operators, built-in arithmetic operators to replace the **expr** command, and better string-handling features. But the most important advantages of the Korn and C shells are *command editing, command history,* and *aliases.*

Command editing refers to the ability to use normal **vi** or **emacs** editing commands to modify command lines while they are entered. Environment variables allow you to set which editing command set you prefer. Then you can use these familiar editing commands to break out of the normal command line entry behavior and into editing mode. For example, if you type a long command line that includes an error with **vi** editing mode set, you can press ESC to enter editing mode and then move around in the command line with normal **vi** cursor movement commands such as **b**, **3w**, **x**, and so on. Regular expression searching and substitution is allowed. When the command line is correct, press NEWLINE and the shell will execute the resulting command.

Command history refers to the shell's ability to keep a log of all the commands that you enter during your session. The history is used with command editing to recall a previous command that you have executed and execute it again either without retyping or after you have edited it. These tools are very beneficial when you are debugging complex pipelines or shell scripts, because you can quickly make changes in relatively long commands without calling up a normal editor or retyping the command completely.

The other major feature of both the Korn and C shells is command aliasing. An alias is a command name defined to the shell with a special **alias** operator, which defines the name you wish to use and includes a definition of a real command to substitute when the alias is seen at the beginning of the command line. For example, you can define the following:

```
$ alias ls="ls -FC"
$
```

This defines an alias for the **ls** command, so that whenever you enter

```
$ ls
```

the command that is actually executed is

```
$ ls -FC
```

This *alias expansion* happens on all uses of **ls** that are made without specifying the full pathname, so that

```
$ /bin/ls
```

is interpreted exactly as typed, but

```
$ ls -l
```

will be interpreted as

```
$ ls -FC -l
```

when executed. Because this alias expansion is handled directly by the shell without requiring the execution of a subshell, it is very quick. Aliases let you customize your session and commands to your taste without expensive system overhead.

Many other shells have been developed for special purposes. One of the most common types provides a full-screen or window-oriented user interface that offers menus for common command execution, function selection with a mouse, online help, and other user-friendly functions. Special shells are often used to ease system administration tasks or as front ends for turnkey application packages. Such shells are frequently called *user agents*, and the functions that they provide vary widely from one implementation to another. They are often provided by a software vendor and are not officially a part of the UNIX system. When your system has a user agent, there are usually ways to gain access to the standard shell. Often a menu selection is provided to create a window attached to a shell.

# EIGHT

Understanding UNIX System Documentation

Most UNIX systems include a copy of the *UNIX User's Manual*, which is usually called simply the *User's Manual* or the *UNIX Manual*. In addition, many implementations of SVR3 contain an online help facility that can help you determine the correct command for an application and select the right option for a command. In this chapter we will discuss both of these documentation tools.

The UNIX User's Manual

The *User's Manual* is the official documentation for the UNIX system and has had as much development and modification over the years as the system software itself. All the commands, arguments to commands, subroutine libraries, file formats, utilities, and tools are documented completely in the *User's Manual*, and it is the next-to-final authority on all issues under the UNIX system. The final authority, of course, is empirical testing of a system attribute directly on your own machine.

Unfortunately, while the *User's Manual* is a complete reference document, it is not as accessible as you might desire. It is not uncommon for several users or developers to pore over a single sentence of the manual, discussing (even arguing about) the meaning or implication of a word or phrase. Invariably the *User's Manual* is correct, but it sometimes is difficult to understand what it means.

The *User's Manual* is a reference document. It is designed to be as concise as possible, to bring the great scope of the UNIX system into a form that experts and near experts can use to find out any of the many specific details of the system. It is very difficult, if not impossible, to learn to use the system from the *User's Manual*, but it is just as difficult to become an expert user without the manual.

If you do not have a *User's Manual* readily available, ask your vendor for a copy of the manual provided specifically for your release of the system and your computer hardware. Although the *User's Manual* does not differ between versions by very much, at some point you will probably be led astray if you use the wrong version.

Layout of the User's Manual

The *User's Manual* was first published as a single small volume that contained all the information that was available for the operating system at that time. The original document contained eight major sections, which are still preserved today:

1. Commands and Application Programs

2. System Calls

3. Subroutines

4. File Formats

5. Miscellaneous

6. Games

7. Special Files

8. System Maintenance Procedures

These *User's Manual* sections are often referred to by their number: Section 1 is the Commands section, Section 3 is the Subroutine section, and so on.

Most of the commands discussed in this book are documented in Section 1, though some related issues are dealt with in Sections 4, 5, 7, and 8. User commands such as **cat** and **uux** are documented in Section 1 of the manual.

Sections 2 and 3 are primarily of interest to software developers because they describe subroutines that a developer would use in a C or FORTRAN language program. Because some of the function names in Sections 2 and 3 are similar to the names of Section 1 commands, you must be certain that you have the correct section when you use the *User's Manual*. While both Sections 2 and 3 contain information on subroutines that developers can use, the sections differ from one another. The *system calls* in Section 2 are entry points into the kernel, similar in function to MS-DOS interrupts, while the Section 3 items are real subroutines or *functions* that are provided with the system. Many, but not all, of the subroutines use system calls internally. Although system calls and functions usually look the same, the distinction can be important for system designers and developers.

Section 4, File Formats, documents the way that data is stored in the files that the system uses. You can find a section describing the file **/etc/passwd** or your profile, as well as sections on the format of an executable file and the format of the terminal description files used by the **terminfo** system.

Section 5, Miscellaneous, contains useful information that would be inappropriate in other sections. For example, there is a table of ASCII character codes, comments on the shell environment variables, descriptions of the **troff** text editing macro packages, discussion of terminal tab settings, and much more.

Games and toys are described in Section 6. Some systems do not include this section if the implementation does not include games, but add-on software for games will usually include documentation that should be filed under Section 6.

Section 7 includes the formats of the *special files* that live in the directory /**dev**. This material is of most interest to software developers who wish to use these special device files in their programs. Section 7 includes discussions of disk and tape formats, synchronous and asynchronous terminal interfaces, and local area network interfaces.

Section 8, Maintenance Procedures, includes procedures for booting the system, diagnosing hardware failures, and doing other low-level administration tasks. This material is somewhat outdated and is usually of minimal use for a microcomputer-based SVR3 system.

While the basic format of the document has stayed the same, the rapid growth of the UNIX system has made the single manual unwieldly, and it is now published in three separate parts: the *User's Manual*, the *Programmer's Manual*, and the *Administrator's Manual*. Because each part includes some of the material in each of the eight sections, a Section 1 command might not appear in the *User's Manual* but might be in the *Administrator's Manual*. Unfortunately, it is not always easy to understand which manual a particular command occurs in, so you often must search for a command that you wish to read about.

Except for the Permuted Index and some of the introductory material, the *User's Manual* as a whole is organized according to topic—each command or subroutine is documented separately. Each item is called a *manual page* or *man page*. A topic is called a *page* even if it spans several printed pages in the document. This organization is excellent for a reference document, because each man page is independent of the others. As the system has grown and developed, the modular nature of the *User's Manual* has made it very easy to update. You can replace outdated man pages with new ones as you modify your system. Further, most of the material about a specific topic is collected into a small space, making it very easy to find if you know what to look for.

Developers creating new software or new tools usually write man pages for their applications. Documentation writers then use these man pages to produce glossy user documentation or online help. Because the original developer of an application usually writes the man page, the man page often describes the application's behavior more accurately than other documentation.

Referring to the Manual Section of a Command

When you name a command or other item in the UNIX system, you may wish to indicate the manual section that the command comes from. It is usually included in parentheses following the name. For example, **uname(1)** refers to the user command **uname** that is documented in Section 1 of the manual, while **uname(2)** refers to the developers' subroutine documented in Section 2. Sometimes an additional letter will follow the section number, as **df(1M)**. This letter identifies the subsection of the manual that the command is categorized with. So **1M** is a Section 1 command associated with the *System Administrator's Manual*, **3C** is a C language subroutine, and **3F** is a Fortran subroutine.

Each command, subroutine, or file type that has its own man page is filed alphabetically within its section, with the exception that some man pages may be in the *User's Manual* while others may be in the *Administrator's* or *Programmer's Manual*. In addition there is an excellent indexing system, which we will discuss shortly.

A Typical Man Page

Figure 8-1 shows a short but complete man page for the **df(1M)** command. This page is taken from the *User's Manual* because **df** is a general user command that appears in Section 1. However, this command is of most interest to system administrators, as indicated by the **1M** identifier.

The command name appears at the top of the page, both on the left and right sides. This name is used to alphabetize the man page in the manual as a whole.

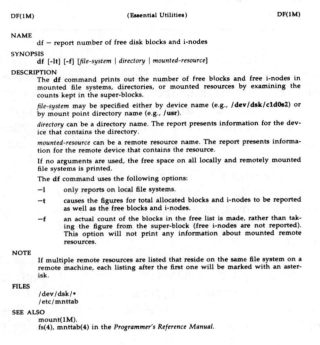

DF(1M)   (Essential Utilities)   DF(1M)

NAME
      df — report number of free disk blocks and i-nodes
SYNOPSIS
      df [-lt] [-f] [*file-system* | *directory* | *mounted-resource*]
DESCRIPTION
      The **df** command prints out the number of free blocks and free i-nodes in
      mounted file systems, directories, or mounted resources by examining the
      counts kept in the super-blocks.

      file-system may be specified either by device name (e.g., **/dev/dsk/c1d0s2**) or
      by mount point directory name (e.g., **/usr**).

      directory can be a directory name. The report presents information for the dev-
      ice that contains the directory.

      mounted-resource can be a remote resource name. The report presents informa-
      tion for the remote device that contains the resource.

      If no arguments are used, the free space on all locally and remotely mounted
      file systems is printed.

      The **df** command uses the following options:
      −l   only reports on local file systems.
      −t   causes the figures for total allocated blocks and i-nodes to be reported
              as well as the free blocks and i-nodes.
      −f   an actual count of the blocks in the free list is made, rather than tak-
              ing the figure from the super-block (free i-nodes are not reported).
              This option will not print any information about mounted remote
              resources.
NOTE
      If multiple remote resources are listed that reside on the same file system on a
      remote machine, each listing after the first one will be marked with an aster-
      isk.
FILES
      /dev/dsk/•
      /etc/mnttab
SEE ALSO
      mount(1M).
      fs(4), mnttab(4) in the *Programmer's Reference Manual*.

Figure 8-1.   A typical *User's Manual* page

Some special additional release information will usually
appear in the middle of the page heading, such as Essential
Utilities in this example. The SVR3 version of the system is
divided into several different software *sets*, or separately loada-

ble units. These sets can sometimes be purchased separately and can be installed separately on a machine. If a particular command is unavailable on your machine, the software set that includes it was probably not loaded. In the example **df(1M)**, the command is included in the Essential Utilities Set. Other examples of software sets are the Software Development Set and Documenter's Workbench.

The man page sometimes includes a date at the bottom that gives the last date that the page was changed or the date that it was printed. The page number relates to the beginning of that man page, not the document as a whole. You can remove an outdated man page and replace it with a newer version without discarding the whole manual.

Within the body of the man page, the material is divided into several subject *headings*. The *name* of the command is first, along with a short summary of the command's function. This is the *primary* command that is given at the top of the man page. *Secondary* commands are sometimes documented with the primary command. They are usually closely related to the primary command and do not rate their own page. These commands will not appear on the page heading, so you may not find a command if you simply look at the alphabetical page headings. Even common commands may not have their own man page; for example, **mv(1)** and **ln(1)** are given as secondary commands under the man page for **cp(1)**. Look up the command in the index to avoid this problem. The command name(s) and the summary line are indexed word by word in the manual's Permuted Index.

Synopsis

The *synopsis* gives a short summary of how you invoke the command from the command line. It is expressed in a condensed format in which each character is significant, though you seldom enter the command in the form given in the synopsis. Once you understand this format, you can determine how to enter the command according to your needs. Items given in boldface type, such as **df** and −**f** in the **df(1M)** example, are typed in the command line just as they appear in the synopsis, or they are not included in the command line at all. Italicized items represent argument prototypes that can be substituted as needed in your command line. The string **file-system** in the example is not entered as printed, but you use the name of the file system you are interested in.

An element enclosed in square brackets, as [−**f**], is optional, and you only include it in your command line if you need it. For example, use the −**t** option only if you want the total listing. When several elements are separated by | (pipe), your command line can contain any one of the elements separated by the | character. In the case of **df(1M)** you can omit the directory name argument because it is enclosed with square brackets. However, if you include it in your command line, then you can give only one file system name, directory name, or some other mounted resource. You do not enter the square brackets or the | character (unless you mean for the shell to create a pipeline for you).

The entry . . . (ellipsis) signifies that the synopsis element just preceding the ellipsis can be repeated as often as desired. For example,

```
cat [ -u ] [ -s ] [ -v [ -t ] [ -e ] ] file ...
```

means that you can have one or more files. This example also shows another feature: these synopsis elements can be nested. The −**v**, −**t**, and −**e** arguments are optional. However, −**t** and −**e** are embedded within the square brackets for −**v**. This means that −**v** is optional, but if you give −**t** or −**e**, you must also give the −**v** option. The −**u** and −**s** arguments are independent and can be used either with or without the −**v** argument. This nesting of arguments is common in the UNIX system, and in the man page synopsis.

Finally, you can include the modifier arguments given with command line flags in the same scheme.

```
ed [ - ] [ -p string ] [ -x ] [ file ]
```

All the arguments are optional here, but if you give the —**p** argument, you must also include a prompt string.

Description

Use the synopsis as a quick reference when you mostly understand the command usage but wish to check on a specific component for your command line. When you need a slightly more verbose description of the command, its arguments, and its intention, read the *description* section that follows the synopsis. It explains the use of the command and all the options. This section differs widely from page to page, but it provides a complete if terse description of the command. You may need to read and reread the description to fully understand all the details and implications of the command and its arguments. Each sentence in the description is usually *exactly* correct, but you may also need to examine the command output along with the man page to really understand the material.

The Other Parts of the Man Page

Several other man page sections usually follow the description. These are not as well defined or as standardized as the name, synopsis, and description sections, and one or more may not be present if they are not needed.

The *note* section provides footnote information that is considered important but does not fit well within the description for some reason. Similar to the note section is the *warnings* section, which discusses potential pitfalls to observe when using the command. You should understand the warnings, if any, before using the command.

The *see also* section gives related commands or relevant material in other manual sections. You can use this section to find another command that might be better suited to your needs than the one documented or that has related functions. In Figure 8-1 **mount(1M)** is a command whose operation changes the output from **df(1M)**.

The *files* section gives the pathnames of databases and other files that are used or changed by the command. The connection between the command and the listed files is not always discussed in the description section. It would be useful if these files were indexed so that when you run into a file in browsing the file system, you could look up the file's purpose, but this has not been done.

The *diagnostics* section gives a short description of the possible error messages or return values for the command. This is rarely a complete list of the diagnostic messages that a command can produce, but it does provide some clues when the command does not act as you expect.

The *bugs* section gives a few of the conditions under which the command does not act as expected. This does not discuss the real bugs in the command, which would be fixed if developers knew about them. The items included as bugs are more like limitations, where you might wish the command did more than it actually can do.

Some manual pages, especially those produced for add-on software or application packages, may include other sections, such as *author* or *limitations*. These are usually easy to understand.

The Permuted Index

The *Permuted Index* is the most effective way to enter the *User's Manual* when you have a specific question or problem. You cannot assume that a command or function is listed under its own man page, and in any case the key concepts associated with commands are not usually given in the name. Luckily, the Permuted Index is arranged in an excellent format that almost always provides the information needed.

The Permuted Index alphabetically lists each word of the name section of each man page. Because the short summary given with the command name consists mainly of conceptual *keywords*, this index is quite effective. The index is called KWIC (for keyword in context) in some computer settings. Each of the three parts of the manual has its own Permuted Index, so you must sometimes consult more than one index to find what you need. The Permuted Index appears at the front of the bound manual, in keeping with its importance, rather than at the end, like most indexes.

Figure 8-2 gives an example of a page from the Permuted Index of the *User's Manual*. The alphabetical listings run down the middle of the page, and the man page containing that alphabetical item appears at the far right of the page. You look up a word by finding it in the middle of the page and then turning to the command given at the right edge of the page.

The Permuted Index takes each word of the name section of each man page and places it in the center of the page. The following words in the name are printed at the right of the particular word in question, and words preceding it in the name appear to the left. The end of the summary is marked with the / (slash) character. Sometimes the material to the right of the current keyword is too long to fit on the line, so it is rotated around to the beginning of the line, as in the **paste(1)** example in Figure 8-2. Similarly, sometimes there are too many words to the left of the current command, so they are rotated to the right part of the line.

For example, you cannot find the command **ln** by looking for a man page headed **ln(1)** in the body of Section 1 of the manual. However, you can find it in the Permuted Index by looking for **ln** in the center of the correct page. You can see that it is described under the man page for the **cp(1)** command in Section 1. Similarly, if you want to link two files together, you

Permuted Index

uustat(1C) uucp status inquiry and	job control	uustat(1C)
operator	join(1) relational database	join(1)
terminal	jterm(1) reset layer of windowing	jterm(1)
	jwin(1) print size of layer	jwin(1)
makekey(1) generate encryption	key	makekey(1)
a UNIX system command using	keywords locate(1) identify	locate(1)
	kill(1) terminate a process	kill(1)
	label(1G) - label the axis of a GPS file	stat(1G)
pattern scanning and processing	language awk(1)	awk(1)
bc(1) arbitrary-precision arithmetic	language	bc(1)
command programming	language /the standard/restricted	sh(1)
batch(1) execute commands at a	later time at(1)	at(1)
jwin(1) print size of	layer	jwin(1)
shl(1) shell	layer manager	shl(1)
terminals layers(1)	layer multiplexor for windowing	layers(1)
jterm(1) reset	layer of windowing terminal	jterm(1)
rename login entry to show current	layer relogin(1M)	relogin(1M)
windowing terminals	layers(1) layer multiplexor for	layers(1)
archives ar(1) archive and	library maintainer for portable	ar(1)
line(1) read one	line	line(1)
nl(1)	line numbering filter	nl(1)
cut out selected fields of each	line of a file cut(1)	cut(1)
send/cancel requests to an LP	line printer lp(1) cancel(1)	lp(1)
	line(1) read one line	line(1)
col(1) filter reverse	line-feeds	col(1)
comm(1) select or reject	lines common to two sorted files	comm(1)
uniq(1) report repeated	lines in a file	uniq(1)
of several files or subsequent	lines of one file /merge same lines	paste(1)
subsequent/ paste(1) merge same	lines of several files or	paste(1)
cp(1) ln(1) mv(1) copy,	link or move files	cp(1)
ls(1)	list contents of directory	ls(1)
	list(1G) - list vector elements	stat(1G)
xargs(1) construct argument	list(s) and execute command	xargs(1)
files cp(1)	ln(1) mv(1) copy, link or move	cp(1)
command using keywords	locate(1) identify a UNIX system	locate(1)
newgrp(1M)	log in to a new group	newgrp(1M)
	log(1G) - logarithm	stat(1G)
relogin(1M) rename	login entry to show current layer	elogin(1M)
logname(1) get	login name	logname(1)
passwd(1) change	login password	passwd(1)
	login(1) sign on	login(1)
	logname(1) get login name	logname(1)
nice(1) run a command at	low priority	nice(1)
send/cancel requests to an	LP line printer lp(1) cancel(1)	lp(1)
enable(1) disable(1) enable/disable	LP printers	enable(1)
lpstat(1) print	LP status information	lpstat(1)
requests to an LP line printer	lp(1) cancel(1) send/cancel	lp(1)
information	lpstat(1) print LP status	lpstat(1)
	lreg(1G) - linear regression	stat(1G)

8   USER'S REFERENCE MANUAL

Figure 8-2.   A typical Permuted Index page

can look up the keyword **link**. By reading the rest of the summary, paying attention to the / that marks where the summary begins, you see that the line

```
cp, ln, mv: copy,    link or move files . . . . . . . cp(1)
```

is what you want. Again, you look at the **cp(1)** man page.

Once you understand the format of the index and have some feel for the jargon used in the name section of the man pages, the Permuted Index becomes a very useful tool. However, when you do not hit the correct keyword exactly and cannot find the exact command that you need, you should look at the man page for a similar command and consult the *see also* section. The command you want is often listed there.

Online help Command

In addition to the indispensable *User's Manual*, SVR3 provides an online *help* facility that can often substitute for the manual in a pinch. This facility takes a lot of disk space, so it may not be present on all small machines. However, it is often worth the disk space for novice users, and its use is recommended if it is available.

The name "help" was first used as a small part of the **sccs** (for Source Code Control System) software development tool. UNIX system releases prior to SVR3 have this usage, and the facility discussed here is a completely new package that shares very little with the older version.

Enter the help subsystem with the command **help**, which displays a menu to prompt you for your next action.

```
$ help

 help:  UNIX System On-Line Help

            choices              description
               s                 starter:  general information
               l                 locate:   find a command with keywords
               u                 usage:    information about commands
               g                 glossary:  definitions of terms

               r                 Redirect to a file or a command
               q                 Quit

 Enter choice >
```

You are still in the help subsystem and can take further action according to the prompts. To exit back to the shell, enter **q** at the "Enter choice >" prompt. You can also copy the contents of the screen to a file or use it as the standard input to a command if you enter **r** at the prompt.

```
Enter choice > r
Enter > file, | cmd(s), or RETURN to continue >
```

At this point you can enter > followed by a filename or | followed by a pipeline to redirect the current screen to a file or command, respectively.

```
Enter choice > r
Enter > file, | cmd(s), or RETURN to continue > >/usr/steve/help.menu
Enter choice >
```

In this example the output was redirected to the file **/usr/steve/help.menu**. The action is taken and the help system returns to the current level for another menu selection. Only the current topic is saved, usually a single screenful. Each help submenu allows this redirection, so it is easy to grab data for later use.

This top-level menu provides access to all the other help capabilities. Enter **s** here to see starter information, and the system will prompt with another menu, as shown in Figure 8-3. The starter section is an excellent way for new users to become familiar with the UNIX system. The simplest commands and features of the system are available under the **c** menu selection. The **d** selection provides a bibliography of useful documents, although the sources listed in this output may be difficult to locate. The **l** selection provides information about capabilities and features local to this specific machine; your system administrator can add this section by using the **helpadm** command, discussed shortly. The **t** option lists other teaching aids available online. This usually includes only the *Instructional Workbench* package, which may not be available with all SVR3 implementations. The Instructional Workbench is a full-fledged computer-aided instruction system that provides powerful tools for development of online training for many topics, not only for the UNIX system. You can return to the top-level menu

```
Enter choice > s

starter:  General UNIX System User Information

    starter provides general information for  system  users.  Enter
    one of the choices below to proceed.

            choices              description

                c                Commands and terms to learn first
                d                Documents for system users
                e                Education centers for UNIX System training
                l                Local UNIX System information
                t                Teaching aids available on-line

                r                Redirect to a file or a command
                q                Quit
                h                Restart help
```

Figure 8-3.   Screen display for help **starter** menu selection

at any time by entering **h** from any menu within the help system.

If you select **l** from the top-level menu, the help system helps you locate commands by entering keywords that describe the action you wish to perform, as shown in Figure 8-4. Select **k** from this submenu if you want the system to search for some keywords that you enter. In this example **print** was typed as a keyword and the help system located several commands associated with printing files. The help system and the manual use different keywords, so you may see some commands here that differ from what you see in the manual. However, not all of the system capabilities are included in this help facility. For example, the test with the keyword **print** did not reveal anything about the **lp** printer subsystem. While useful, the help system cannot substitute for the *User's Manual*.

If you select **u** from the top-level menu, you get specific information about how to use a command, including help on the

```
Enter choice > l

 locate: Find UNIX System Commands with Keywords

      Give locate one or more keywords related  to  the  work
      you want  to  do.  It  will print a list of UNIX system commands
      whose actions are related  to  the  keywords.

      For example, you enter the keywords print file

    locate could produce the list:   The cat (concatenate) command
                                      The ls (list) command
                                      The pr (print) command

      Enter a k to use locate.

                  choices           description

                     k              Enter a list of keywords

                     r              Redirect to a file or a command
                     q              Quit
                     h              Restart help

Enter choice > k
Enter keywords separated by blanks > print

Commands found using print:

The cat (concatenate) command
The echo command
The line command
The ls (list) command
The pcat (concatenate packed file) command
The pr (print) command
The pwd (print working directory) command
The tail command
```

```
Choices:   UNIX_command ,  k (new keywords),  r (redirect),  h (restart help),
 q (quit)
```

```
Enter choice >
```

Figure 8-4.   Screen display for help **locate** command

available arguments and how they are used, as shown in Figure
8-5. Enter the name of a command if you know it, and the
system will prompt you to select the kind of information you are
interested in. Select **d** for a description of the command, **e** for

```
Enter choice > u

 usage:  Information about Commands

      usage provides information about specific UNIX System commands.

           Within usage, double quotes " " mark options or literals,
      and angle brackets < > mark argument variables.

           You should see starter for basic UNIX system commands and
      terms before going on to anything else.

      Enter one of the choices below to proceed.

             choices              description

           UNIX_command          Obtain usage information for a command

                p                 Print a list of commands

                r                 Redirect to a file or a command
                q                 Quit
                h                 Restart help

 Enter choice > cat
 Enter  d (description),  e (examples), or  o (options) >
```

Figure 8-5.   Screen display for help **usage** command

some examples, or **o** for a list of the command options. If you select **d**, the result might look like Figure 8-6. This material is not identical to the contents of the *User's Manual,* so you can often get additional ideas about how to use the command or its options. The **o** (options) and **e** (examples) menu selections provide additional information that can be helpful.

Frequently the material in these sections extends over more than one screenful, and you can select **n** (for next page) when you see "MORE" at the bottom of the display. As usual, you can redirect the material to a file or command for later examination.

The **g** selection from the top-level menu provides a glossary of terms and special characters. Enter the term or character and the help system will return a short but useful definition that is not available in the *User's Manual.*

```
Enter  d (description),  e (examples), or  o (options) > d
cat:  Description

Syntax Summary:  cat [ -u ] [ -s ] [ -v [ -e ] [ -t ] ] [ file_name ... ]

       where:  file_name  is the name of a file.

Description:
     cat is  shorthand  for "concatenate".  Use cat to send the
     contents of a file to standard output.  If more than one file name is used,
     cat prints each file in sequence on the standard output.  cat
     echos standard input if you do not list a file name or if you use "-" as an
     argument. See also:  cp(1), pg(1) and pr(1) for commands with functions
     similar to cat.

Choices:   o (options),  e (examples),  UNIX_command ,  p (print list),
 r (redirect),  h (restart help),  q (quit)

Enter choice >
```

Figure 8-6.   Screen display for help **description** command

Use of Help from the Command Line

Instead of selecting an option from the top-level menu of the
help system, you can enter a command directly from the shell to
enter one of the help subsystems. Use

```
$ locate
```

or

```
$ locate [ keyword ]
```

to enter the *locate* subsystem directly. If you give the command
with no arguments, the locate menu is presented so that you can
enter a keyword. If you give the keyword as an argument for
the **locate** command, the help system will give the results only
for that keyword.

Similarly, you can use

```
$ glossary
```

or

```
$ glossary [ term ]
```

to enter the *glossary* subsystem directly, and

```
$ starter
```

or

```
$ usage [ -d ] [ -e ] [ -o ] [ command name ]
```

for the other top-level options. The additional arguments for the **usage** command start the help system at the submenu for **description**, **examples**, and **options**, respectively.

Going Further

The help subsystem is a flexible tool that can be adapted or expanded. In the next sections we discuss tools by which a system administrator, logged into the machine as *root*, can change the database. In addition, we will describe a few more SVR3 tools at the end.

Help Directory Structure

Most help system commands reside in the directory **/usr/bin**. The help data files are kept in the directory **/usr/lib/help** and its subdirectories.

```
$ cd /usr/lib/help
$ ls -FC
HELPLOG*     checklen*    default      ge           lib/         un
ad           cm           defnlen*     glossary*    list*        ut
admgloss*    cmds         delete*      he           locking*     vc
admstart*    co           editcmd*     helpclean*   prs
bd           db/          extract*     interact*    rc
cb           de           fetch*       keysrch*     replace*
$
```

The files with short names, such as **cm**, **he**, and **un**, belong to
the older part of the help system associated with the **sccs**
system. The executable commands are the basic executable
components that constitute the new part of the help system.
The **HELPLOG** file is associated with a help activity logging feature discussed shortly. The directory **lib** contains
more executable parts of the help system, while **db** is the
major directory that contains the displayable help text
materials.

```
$ ls -FC db
descriptions.a    glossary.a        screens.a
examples.a        options.a         tables/
$
```

The files ending in **.a** are the actual text of the parts. The
subdirectory **tables** contains more information for the help
displays, in a more compact form than the *.a files. Because
these files are read by software, you should not edit them
directly.

Changing the Help Database

The online help facility provides its own tools to customize the
output and to add information on new commands and keywords. You must be superuser to access these materials. The
command /etc/helpadm (for help administration) is used to
administer the help database; it will prompt you through all the
changes needed to install a complete entry. As you respond to

the **helpadm** prompts, the system will often execute an editor
on your behalf. To get your favorite editor, be sure that you have
the *EDITOR* environment variable correctly set.

```
$ echo $EDITOR
/usr/bin/vi
$
```

If this variable is not set, then the default editor is **ed**.

The **/etc/helpadm** command will prompt you for the
information that it needs to update the help database, as shown
in Figure 8-7. The menu format is similar to that used in the
normal help displays. You can select either **starter**, **glossary**,

---

```
# /etc/helpadm
        helpadm:  UNIX System On-Line help Administrative Utilities

These software tools will enable the administrator to change
information in the help facility's database, and to monitor use of
the help facility.
        choice              description
          1                 starter
          2                 glossary
          3                 commands
          4                 prevent recording use of help facility
          5                 record use of the help facility
          q                 quit


Enter choice>
```

Figure 8-7.   Help administration menu

or **commands** to update that section of the help system. In addition, you can turn the help usage log on or off and use **q** to exit back to your shell. When you go down to the next menu level, you are prompted for the specific materials that the help system needs, as shown in Figure 8-8. When you make a selection at this point, **helpadm** executes your *$EDITOR* with the text material as its content. You can change the material as you choose.

Each of the other menu selections of the **helpadm** system allows you to add or change the materials. Its use is mostly self-evident, though only the superuser may change the help database.

```
Enter choice> 1
        helpadm:   starter
Which screens of starter do you want to make changes to?

        choice            description

          c               commands screen

          d               documents screen

          e               education screen

          l               local screen

          t               teach screen

          q               quit

Enter choice>
```

Figure 8-8.   Help administration submenu

The Other Sections of the Manual

The man page format in the manual sections other than Section 1 differs slightly from the Section 1 standards that we have discussed so far. The differences occur primarily in the Synopsis section. Most users will have little reason to refer to these manual sections, but you should understand the layout if you do need them.

In Sections 2 and 3 the synopsis gives the C language programming conventions and the subroutine arguments needed to call the functions documented. These pages also include a *return value* section that is useful for developers. In Sections 4 and 5 the synopsis (if present) usually gives the programmer information about how to include the material in software under development. Section 6 man pages are similar to those in Section 1 because these are commands available to the user. The man pages in Sections 7 and 8 seldom include a synopsis because there is no concise way to represent the contents of these sections.

Online man Command

Many larger-sized machines include the entire contents of the manual online, usually including man pages for locally installed software as well as the standard *User's Manual*. The text is usually 2 to 3 megabytes in size, so most smaller machines do not include the online manual.

You can display these online manual pages with the **man** (for manual) command, which writes the requested man page to its standard output. It is called with an argument that gives the man page you wish to display. This command

```
$ man diff
```

will display the man page for **diff(1)**. If an entry under the name occurs in more than one section of the manual, all of the man pages will be displayed, one after the other. You can redirect the output to a file for later examination if you wish. Because the man pages are often formatted with **nroff** before they are displayed, the man command may take a relatively long time to produce output, often up to a minute or two on a heavily loaded machine.

The **man** command may take several options. To restrict the output to a man page in a single manual section, you can enter a section number before the name of the page. This command

```
$ man 1 man
```

will produce the man page for the **man(1)** command only.

To format the output for a specific terminal, enter −**T** (for terminal) and then the terminal type. This command

```
$ man −Tvt100 1 man
```

produces **man(1)** formatted for the DEC vt100 terminal or its clone. If you don't give the −**T** option, your *$TERM* environment variable is used for the terminal type.

There are several other options: −**d** (for directory) will change the default search path to the current directory rather than the system standard; −**c** (for col) will produce a form of the output without reverse linefeeds, suitable for most simple printers.

When present, the man pages are located in the directory **/usr/man** and subdirectories. Usually there are several immediate subdirectories of **/usr/man**, the major ones being **u_man** (for user's manual), **p_man** (for programmer's manual), and **a_man** (for administrator's manual). Each of these directories includes subdirectories for each manual section included in that part of the manual: **man1** (for the Section 1 commands), **man2** (for the Section 2 commands), and so forth through **man8** (for the Section 8 commands). The man pages are usually stored in their original **troff** source format and must be formatted with the **troff −man** or **nroff −man** text preparation tools before they look like the printed manual. They are kept in source form so that they can be formatted for any printer or terminal as needed.

In addition, some systems will maintain a set of the man pages in preformatted files, so that they can be accessed online without the delay and CPU usage involved in formatting the pages on demand. If so, the directories are usually named **cat1** through **cat8** in the **u_man**, **p_man**, and **a_man** directories. Response time for the **man** command is much quicker when the man pages are preformatted, but of course the preformatted pages are usually prepared by the system administrator for the least powerful printer or terminal on the system.

Assist

A few SVR3 systems have a new front end for command execution called **assist**. This tool is not well known, but it provides all the features of the help system, including keyword search, command syntax summaries, and a menu orientation. It can also execute commands from a form- and menu-oriented user interface; this helps to generate commands with arguments that are syntactically correct by providing extensive prompts and error checking before accepting your command. The **assist** feature is not a shell but an application program that sits in front of the shell, reading your input and passing the correct commands to the login shell for execution. The **assist** system is designed to be self-training, so you can probably use it successfully with little documentation or training. It includes its own online help. There are, however, many gaps in its coverage of the Section 1 commands.

Execute the command **assist** to enter the **assist** subsystem. It displays a top-level menu of key phrases that describe common functions that you use, such as "Compare Files," or "Find

Files." You can select a menu item to see a list of related commands with a short summary of their action. When you select a command, **assist** presents a form that prompts you for any filenames, lists the optional flags for that command, and allows you to enter a file for redirecting the output. As you enter the information on the command form, **assist** checks your input for errors and prompts you to correct them. When the command is entered correctly, you can execute it.

Finally, **assist** has a walkthrough mode that can show you how to use a command.

# NINE

Computation and Number Processing

An important area that most people use regularly is *computation*. Number processing is one of the original reasons for the development of computers, and though word and character processing has overtaken number processing in small computers, computers can ease your work with numbers.

The UNIX system provides many tools for computation. At the simplest level, the **expr** command, discussed in Chapter 7, can make simple arithmetic computations, but its powers are definitely limited. At the most sophisticated level, the C programming language allows just about any computation that you can imagine. In between, several tools are available to make computation easier.

The computation tools available in SVR3 are line-oriented tools that are more like programming languages than the full-screen pocket calculator simulations seen in other personal computer systems. Full-screen calculators are available as add-on software for many versions of the UNIX system that use a bit-mapped system console, and some vendors include one with their system. In this chapter we will focus on the tools provided in the standard system, which can be used on a remote ASCII terminal as well as the system console.

A Comment on Electronic Spreadsheets

The SVR3 system does not include an *electronic spreadsheet* such as Lotus 1-2-3 or Microsoft Multiplan. Though several spreadsheets have been developed for the UNIX system, none has attained enough popularity to be included in the standard release. However, add-on spreadsheets are available from several sources, including most popular spreadsheets from the Apple or MS-DOS worlds. Notable exceptions are Lotus 1-2-3 and Symphony, which have never been ported to the UNIX system. If you have learned a spreadsheet other than Lotus in the past, you can probably get the same product in a version for the UNIX system.

Shell Reprise

You have seen that the shell's filter and pipeline orientation is very useful in processing large blocks of characters, either text files or databases. With the shell programming tools and the **expr** command, you can perform quite clever computations. However, these tools are inefficient for numeric operations, and without some assistance from executable programs, they can be tedious. Several programs designed for use in shell pipelines have been developed for numeric computing, but few of these have survived. One example is the **stat** package, oriented toward statistical computations; it is not included in many SVR3 implementations, but you can probably purchase it as part of the Graphics Utilities Set if it is needed.

The dc and bc Calculators

Two powerful line-oriented *calculators* come with the standard system: the **dc** (for desk calculator) and **bc** tools. The **bc** calculator is actually a preprocessor for **dc**, but these two tools implement the two different user interface models for modern calculators. The **dc** calculator uses *postfix notation*, the so-called *reverse polish* notation, in which you enter computations by typing in two numbers and then the operator.

```
$ dc
2
3
+
p
5
```

Here you would enter **2** and **3**, then the arithmetic operator +, and then **p** to display the result. The **dc** calculator prints the answer: 5. The **bc** command, on the other hand, uses *infix notation*, which is similar to the normal arithmetic operations taught in elementary school.

```
$ bc
2+3
5
```

Here you enter **2+3** and **bc** prints the result. You can use either command, but the features of the two calculators differ slightly, and one may be more convenient for some operations than the other. Both allow any *precision* and can compute in any number base or *radix* in addition to normal decimal. The **dc** calculator is stack oriented, where all operations take place on a single variable stack, while **bc** is procedure oriented, and you can define local subroutines and assign values to variables as part of the computation. The **bc** calculator includes logical operators and statements, making it more of a programming tool than **dc**.

The dc Command

After the **dc** command is executed, it reads instructions in its internal command language from standard input. Alternatively, you can name a single file on the command line, in which case that file is read until it ends, and then **dc** will switch to reading its standard input for more commands. Input from a file is treated identically to instructions from standard input, except that an end-of-file instruction (CTRL-D) from the keyboard ends execution of **dc**, while the end of the input file does not. The **q** (for quit) command also ends **dc** from either input source.

An instruction to **dc** may be a number, which is immediately pushed onto the **dc** stack. Numbers may contain decimal points, and negative numbers are preceded not by − but by the __ (underscore) character. For example, the following commands are acceptable numbers for **dc**.

```
123
123.5
123.45678901234455
_23.4
```

The **dc** calculator recognizes the arithmetic operators **+** (addition), **−** (subtraction), **/** (division), **∗** (multiplication), **%** (remainder), and **^** (exponentiation), which cause the appropriate action for the top two numbers on the stack. The result of the operation is placed on the stack, replacing the two numbers.

A large number of special commands allow you to further control operations. The **p** (for print) command, for example, causes the top value on the stack to be displayed but does not change the stack.

```
$ dc
3
4
*
p
12
q
$
```

In these examples each command is shown on a separate line of input, but **dc** can accept several commands on a single line if needed. Numbers are delimited by white space, but other commands can run together. The previous operation could also have been written as follows:

```
$ dc
3 4*pq
12
$
```

In addition, **dc** can perform several operations in a row when several numbers are on the stack. Because the result of an operation is put onto the stack in place of the numbers used in the operation, the next operation will use that value and the next number below it on the stack. For example:

```
$ dc
3
4
7
+ - p
-8
```

Here the + operator adds the top two numbers, 7 and 4, producing 11, which is then put onto the stack. Then the − operator subtracts 11 from 3, producing −8.

By default, computations retain as many decimal digits as needed. The **dc** man page suggests that all computations are performed on integers unless you change the *scale factor* with the **k** command, but this is not completely correct. The addition and subtraction operators work on all digits included in the input numbers; only the multiplication and division operations return results that depend on the scale factor.

Other stack-oriented commands are **c** to clear the stack, **d** to duplicate the top element of the stack, and **f** to print all elements of the stack in order.

Variables in dc

No operation is provided to simply pop the top stack element and discard it. However, **dc** allows *register* variables — named variables that can contain a value. Stack elements can be popped into registers, and register variables can be pushed onto the stack. Register names are single lowercase characters, so 26 register variables are allowed at any time. The **s** (for save) command takes a following register name and pops the top of the stack into the named register. The **l** (the letter *l*) command is the inverse. It pops the value out of the named register and pushes it back onto the stack.

```
2.34
4.56
p
4.56
st
p
2.34
lt
p
4.56
```

To discard a value from the top of the stack, just use **s** to put it into an unused register. This intermediate register procedure is also used to *reverse* the order of elements on the stack, if needed.

The **s** and **l** commands can also work with auxiliary stacks. If the register name is an uppercase character, then it is treated as a stack. If the command is **s**, the top value on the main stack is pushed onto the auxiliary stack.

```
2.34
sT
p
empty stack
5.44
sT
p
empty stack
lT
p
5.44
lT
p
2.34
```

If a stack is empty or does not contain enough numbers to complete an operation, the "empty stack" message is printed.

A character string surrounded by [and] (square brackets) is treated as an ASCII string and pushed onto the stack.

```
[hello world]
p
hello world
```

This ability to store ASCII strings is an unusual feature for a calculator. You cannot use these strings for numeric operations, but the **x** (for execute) command takes a string from the top of the stack and executes it as a **dc** command. You must explicitly remove the string from the stack after the command is executed, if desired. In addition, the **!** (bang) command is a shell escape that causes **dc** to execute the rest of the line in a subshell. When the command is finished, **dc** resumes operation.

The **dc** calculator allows many other commands, including **v** to replace the top element of the stack with its square root and several commands to change the number base or *radix* for further computations. The **i** (for input) command causes **dc** to use the number at the top of the stack as the radix for input numbers, while **o** (for output) causes **dc** to use the named radix for output. This allows base conversion and computations in bases other than the default base 10.

```
2
i
1001
p
9
2
o
p
1001
```

Of course, if the input radix is changed, all numbers entered after that point must be consistent with the new radix.

Users familiar with HP pocket calculators or the FORTH programming language will recognize that this relatively small command set is more than sufficient for any computation that computers normally do, even iterative solutions to integrals and transcendental functions. However, if you are not familiar with postfix notation, **dc** can be confusing. The **bc** program may provide a friendlier environment.

The bc Calculator

Although **bc** is really a preprocessor for **dc** and uses **dc** to do its work, it contains many more functions than **dc** does, including named functions, logical operators, and mathematical functions such as **sqrt** (square root). The overall command language looks something like the C language, but it is much simplified. The **bc** command is executed simply, and its interactions with **dc** are not visible to the user.

```
$ bc
```

The **bc** calculator starts silently and waits for your input. To exit from **bc**, use the **quit** command, or enter CTRL-D to signal end of file. The **bc** calculator reads its standard input and writes to its standard output, so redirection from a file is allowed. When the file ends, **bc** exits.

```
$ cat cmd.file
/* comments begin with slash-star, and end with star-slash as here */
6+5
$ bc < cmd.file
11
$
```

In addition, **bc** can take a filename as an argument.

```
$ bc cmd.file
```

This differs from redirecting a file to the standard input of **bc**. When a filename is given as argument, **bc** reads the file, processes its commands, and then switches to the terminal for its input. This allows you to store complex commands and functions in a file and then possibly use them directly from the keyboard.

bc Notation

The **bc** calculator uses an *infix* notation, and the end of the input line signals that the command should be evaluated.

Numbers in **bc** can be as long as is necessary and may contain a decimal point and an optional — (minus) sign to mark a negative number.

```
-3.45667
```

The normal arithmetic operators are allowed for computations.

```
$ bc
3.45 + 2
5.45
```

Variables are allowed, and they can have lowercase names of a single character. Values are assigned to variables with the = (equal) operator, as shown here.

```
w = value
```

The **w** can be any lowercase letter. Variables are used to temporarily store numbers for later use and can be referenced like numbers.

```
$ bc
y=4
3+y
7
```

Variables retain their values until they are reused in another assignment statement.

In addition, **bc** understands arrays of numbers if the array operators **[** and **]** surround the array index.

```
s[2]=3.3
```

Array indexes start at 0, so this example sets the third element of the array named **s** to 3.3. The array index can be any expression that **bc** can resolve to a number.

By default, **bc** performs many calculations as if the numbers were integers, but you can change the scale factor by assigning a number to the *scale* variable. The number is the number of digits to the right of the decimal point that you wish **bc** to retain in its calculations.

```
$ bc
6.456/5.678
1
scale = 3
6.456/5.678
1.137
```

In addition, you can use the *ibase* and *obase* variables as in **dc** to set the input number radix and output number radix, respectively.

```
$ bc
ibase=2
1001
9
obase=8
1001
11
```

You can use these features to perform base conversions or to do arithmetic in number systems other than decimal.

The **bc** calculator allows many other operators in addition to the normal arithmetic operators understood by **dc**. The ++ (plus-plus) and −− (minus-minus) operators increment and decrement the value of a variable, respectively.

```
s=4
s
4
--s
3
s
3
```

They change the value of the variable and return the value that was set, so this operation will work:

```
s=4
t[--s]=3.3
t[3]
3.3
```

Here, **t[4]** is undefined, and **s** is 3 after the operation. The ++ and −− operators can be used before or after the variable name. When used before the name, the value is changed before it is returned; when used after the name, the value is changed after the value is returned.

```
s=4
t[s--]=3.3
t[4]
3.3
```

In both cases the final value of **s** is 3, but the array **t** differs.

bc Statements and Operators

These additional *assignment* operators are also allowed, and they act by directly changing the named variable.

```
=-
=+
=-
=*
=/
=%
=^
```

That is,

```
s =- 3
```

is the same as

```
s = s - 3
```

You may group sequences of operations inside the { and } (curly braces). All commands bracketed in this way are treated as a single object by **bc** and can be used as a single statement.

```
{ s=3 ; y=4 }
```

The statement will return whatever values each of the component parts return.

```
{ s = 3 ; s }
3
```

This grouping operation is useful when you wish to take advantage of the *logical operators*, which evaluate the material within the braces if some test operation is true.

The **bc** calculator supports the logical operators **if, for,**

and **while**. These have the same meaning as the similar operators in the shell programming language, but they differ in how
they are used. For example, the test part of an **if** statement is
included within **(** and **)** (parentheses), and if the test is true,
then the statements within curly braces are evaluated.

```
s=3
if ( s == 3 ) {
        s =+ 2
}
s
5
```

This example contains a lot. First, **bc** constructs can span
multiple lines if a grouping operator such as **(** or **{** is opened but
not closed. The **bc** calculator will not prompt for continuation
like the shell does with its PS2, but if the command is entered
incorrectly, **bc** will complain with the terse message.

```
syntax error on line 4, teletype
```

The source of the input is named along with the line number. In
this case the input is from the terminal, known to **bc** as the
"teletype."

Second, the logical operators == (for is equal), <= (for is
less than or equal to), >= (for is greater than or equal to), !=
(for is not equal to), > (for is greater than), and < (for is less
than) can be used within the test part of the **if** to specify a test to
perform. If the answer to the test is true, then the material
within the curly braces is executed; if the test is not true, then
the material within the curly braces is not executed. Note that
the **if** command has no **else** part, so you must repeat the test
with the sense reversed if you want to take some other action
after the first test fails. The test is executed only once, and the
material within the braces can be executed only once, if the test
succeeds. When writing constructions like this, you should
indent each line within a block, as in these examples, to make it
easier to understand the logical relationship of the commands.

The format of the **while** operator is similar except that it begins a *loop* in which the material within the braces is executed repeatedly until the test fails. The material within the curly braces must include commands to change the values of the test variable.

```
s=4
while ( s > 0 ) {
        s
        s =- 1
}
4
3
2
1
```

If the test variable is not modified by the operation of the **while** loop, then the loop will continue forever!

The **for** operation is like a more complete version of **while**. Three different parts are included within the parentheses, and they are separated by a ; (semicolon). The first part sets the value of some test variable, and the third part modifies it. The middle part is the test operation as used in the **while** command. For example, the previous command could also have been written as follows:

```
for ( s = 4 ; s > 0 ; --s ) {
        s
}
```

The result is the same, but the logical grouping of the index-related operations within the **for** statement makes this command easier to understand than the **while** command. The **for** operator is usually used when the index variable is relatively self-contained, and **while** is used when some complex or external factor causes the test variable to change. You can include as many commands or nested **for** and **while** constructs within the { and } as you need.

To exit from a loop before the condition part tests false, use the **break** statement. For example:

```
for ( s = 4 ; s > 0 ; --s ) {
        if ( s <= 2 ) break
        s
}
4
3
```

Here **break** simply causes the loop to end, and the command following the end of the loop is executed. Actually, if there are multiple nested loops, **break** just exits from the innermost one. No single operator breaks out of all the nested loops. The **quit** command is executed immediately when it is read from the input, so it cannot be used inside **bc** programs.

bc Functions

Finally, **bc** allows the construction of *functions*. A function is a procedure that has a name, can take arguments, and returns a value when it is used. A function is defined by the **define** command, a following name, named arguments enclosed in parentheses, and then the body of the function enclosed in curly braces.

```
define x ( a, b ) {
        for( s=a; s<b; ++s ) {
                s
        }
        return( 22 )
}
```

Functions have single-character names, just as variables do. The *arguments* in the function definition are formal names that can be used as variables inside the function. As many arguments as needed are allowed, though you should keep their number small. You can also use other external variables inside the function. In the previous example, *s* is such an external variable that will have changed its value after the function is executed. Local variables, known only within the function, are also allowed if you *declare* them as such within the function by using the **auto** statement. This example uses a local *s* variable.

```
define x ( a, b ) {
        auto s
        for( s=a; s<b; ++s ) {
                s
        }
        return( 22 )
}
```

Any externally defined variable named s will not have changed its value after the function is executed.

To execute a function, you name it with the correct number of variables enclosed in parentheses and separated by a comma. The actual values of the arguments as given when the function is called will be used in place of the formal arguments specified when the function is defined. For example, the function in the previous example might be called with

```
x( 3, 6 )
```

and the result would be

```
x( 3, 6 )
3
4
5
22
```

The numbers 3 through 5 come from the evaluation of the expression s each time through the **for** loop, and the 22 is the return value from the function.

You can assign the return value to another variable if you want to save its value.

```
w = x( 3, 6 )
3
4
5
```

Now the variable w contains the value 22. This is how functions are normally used, to hide a complex or repeatedly used section of the program into a simple name that can be called when needed. Functions are normally defined as part of longer programs stored in files and then read into **bc** when they are needed.

Some mathematical functions are predefined for **bc** and can be included when **bc** is loaded. The −l (for library) command line option loads the math library.

```
$ bc -l
```

The following functions are included in the math library: **s(x)** returns the sine of x, **c(x)** returns the cosine of x, **e(x)** returns the exponential of x, **l(x)** returns the log of x, **a(x)** returns the arctangent of x, and **j(n,x)** returns the Bessel function of x. When the math library is loaded, you must take care not to redefine these function names.

The **bc** calculator can be extremely useful both for creation of simple sums and products and for more complex computations, limited only by your imagination. Because **bc** can calculate at an arbitrary level of precision, it has a great many uses. Because it reads its standard input for expressions, it can be used in shell programs and with the ` (grave) operator in assignments to shell variables. However, neither **bc** nor **dc** is much good at reading data from files, although they can readily read in programs that have been saved in files. Input to **bc** and **dc** is intended to come from the terminal or be given at run-time as arguments to function calls. The UNIX system provides the **awk** tool, which is better at reading input data from files.

The awk Command

One tool is very useful both for computation and for *pattern processing* tasks. This is the **awk** command and its associated control language. The name **awk** is an acronym comprising the last initials of its three developers (Aho, Weinberger, and Kernighan), though some users have complained that it is awkward to use. However, **awk** is really a very powerful and elegant programming language that has never lived down its extremely terse and arcane documentation. The **awk** command can do things that no other tool can handle without extreme contortions. Though quite inefficient in operation, it is extremely useful.

The **awk** command scans a list of input files for lines that match a set of specified *patterns*. For each pattern matched, a specified set of actions is performed. These *actions* can involve field manipulations within the line or arithmetic operations on the values of the fields. The **awk** tool is a programming language with features of the shell programming, **bc** and C programming languages. It is completely interpreted like **bc**, contains field variables from each input line named like the shell **$1**, **$2**, and **$3** arguments, and contains printing and control operators similar to those of the C language.

To use **awk**, you must create a program that specifies a list of pattern and action sections. The **awk** command reads the input files and, for each input line matched to a pattern, executes the associated action. Execute **awk** with this command line.

```
$ awk -f prog filename-list
```

In the **awk** format the set of patterns and actions is given in a file named after the −**f** (for file) option. Any additional filenames are the text files that **awk** reads to perform its actions. If no filename list is given, **awk** reads its standard input.

You can also insert standard input in the middle of a filename list with the special − (minus) argument. For example:

```
$ awk -f prog file1 - file2
```

Here **awk** will read the program from the file **prog**, process **file1**, read its standard input until it reaches an end-of-file mark, and then process **file2**.

The **awk** command also allows the program to be included directly in the command line, if the −**f** option is not used. In this case the program appears literally, following the **awk** name but before the filename list. However, even **awk** experts will take several tries before debugging an **awk** program, so the inline form is rarely used except in carefully prepared shell scripts. Inline use can save an additional file in an application, but be sure that the program is working correctly before removing the −**f file** form.

How awk Reads Input Lines

Each line read from the files or from standard input is treated by **awk** as containing fields separated by white space. You can change the field delimiter to any other character if you give the −**F** (for field) option on the **awk** command line, with a new delimiter given as argument. For example, to make **awk** use the : (colon) as delimiter, you might use the following command line:

```
$ awk -F: -f prog files
```

You can refer to each field in the input line with the special names **$1**, **$2**, **$3**, and so forth. The first field on the line is **$1**. The special variable **$0** refers to the input line as a whole, without being divided into fields.

awk Patterns and Actions

The pattern-action pairs define the operations that **awk** performs on the lines and fields that it reads. The format of these pattern-action pairs is as follows:

```
pattern { action }
```

You separate the action portion from the pattern by enclosing it in { and } (curly braces). A missing action part causes the line to be printed. A missing pattern part always matches the line; that is, if the pattern is missing, the action applies to every line. The action may include a complex series of operators, including variables and logical operators, much like **bc**, with the field variables **$1**, **$2**, and so on used as the input data.

A common operator is **print**, which writes its arguments to the standard output. The action

```
{ print $2, $1 }
```

will reverse the first two input fields and write them out. If the input data is

```
$ cat in.file
hello goodbye again
111 222
thirty forty
$
```

and the **awk** program is

```
$ cat awk.prog1
{ print $2, $1 }
$
```

the output will be

```
$ awk -f awk.prog1 in.file
goodbye hello
222 111
forty thirty
$
```

The arguments to **print** in this example are separated by a , (comma), which causes **print** to insert the current field delimiter between the output data. If the comma were omitted, **$1** and **$2** would be run together in the output.

Remember, when the pattern matches the input line, the action is taken. In the previous example there was no pattern section, so the action was taken on each input line.

A pattern is a regular expression or sequence of regular expressions separated by the operators **!** (not), **‖** (logical or), **&&**

(logical and), or parentheses for grouping. You must enclose each regular expression in / (slash) as used in **ed**. For example, the **awk** program

```
/hello/ { print $2, $1 }
```

will process the **in.file** given above.

```
$ awk -f awk.prog2 in.file
goodbye hello
$
```

Only one line of the input file matched the pattern /**hello**/, so only one line was printed with the action part. Because no action was specified for the other lines, no action was taken and nothing appeared in the output. However, multiple pattern-action statements are allowed to handle different cases.

```
/hello/ { print $2, $1 }
/thirty/ { print $1, $2, "and more" }
```

This program gives different results.

```
$ awk -f awk.prog3 in.file
goodbye hello
thirty forty and more
$
```

The entire **awk** program, including all the different pattern-action pairs, will be processed for each input line. This example illustrates another feature of the **print** command: literal strings surrounded by quotation marks can appear in the arguments to **print**, and the string will appear in the output as expected.

You can join the patterns with logical operators to broaden the range of possible tests. For example, the program

```
/hello/||/111/ { print "hit", $1, $2 }
```

will produce

```
$ awk -f awk.prog4 in.file
hit hello goodbye
hit 111 222
$
```

The ‖ operator tells **awk** to perform the action if either of the regular expressions matches the input line, the **&&** operator tells **awk** to perform the action only if both of the regular expressions match the input line, and the ! operator tells **awk** to perform the action only if the regular expression does not match the input line. The ! operator precedes a regular expression and does not separate two expressions.

```
!/hello/ {
       print "not hello"
}
```

Of course more complex regular expressions are allowed. This command

```
/^[Hh1]/ { print "hit", $0 }
```

will produce

```
$ awk -f awk.prog5 in.file
hit hello goodbye again
hit 111 222
$
```

Note the use of **$0** to display the original input line in its entirety.

The action part can span as many typed lines as needed, with each additional statement in the action on a separate line.

The entire action is enclosed within the curly braces. For example:

```
$ cat awk.prog6
/hello/ {
       print $2
       print "another"
       print $1
}
$ awk -f awk.prog6 in.file
goodbye
another
hello
$
```

Each **print** statement causes a new line of output, but all the output is produced by the one line in the input file that matches the pattern /**hello**/.

Numeric Operations with awk

As these simple examples show, **awk** has excellent facilities for matching and juggling strings. In fact a principal use of **awk** is to reformat text data according to rules specified in the program, because **awk** allows reformatting operations that are too complex for **sed** or other tools. However, the real power of **awk** is in the logical and arithmetic operators that you can use in the action portion. The **awk** command is very intelligent in its use of numeric variables and has tools for conversion between character strings and numbers. The use of **awk** for arithmetic differs from the use of **bc** in that **awk** can use the pattern section to pick up a subset of the lines in an input file. This allows some fields that contain key information and other fields that contain the data to be processed by **awk**. Also, **awk** can readily convert input between character and numeric formats, and it includes better tools for formatting output than **bc**. On the other hand, **bc** is more efficient, has greater precision, and is somewhat easier to learn. Each tool has its place in the UNIX system.

One of the friendliest features of **awk** is that it automatically interprets character string input fields as either strings or numbers as appropriate to the context. For example, the built-in **awk** function **length** returns the length of an input field taken as a character string, while numeric variables can be assigned the value of the field taken as a number. For example:

```
$ cat awk.prog7
{
        s += $2
        print $2, "length=" length($2), "s=" s
}
$
```

This example adds up the numeric values in the second field of each input line. The *type conversion* is done automatically by **awk**, and you neither have to declare the variable *s* in advance nor worry about its type. When this program is executed, here are the results.

```
$ awk -f awk.prog7 in.file
goodbye length=7 s=0
222 length=3 s=222
forty length=5 s=222
$
```

Strings that cannot be converted to numbers take the value of zero so that things work as expected. The string **thirty** is of this form and cannot be converted, but the string **222** can be converted correctly by **awk**. By default, a form such as **222** is treated as a number, though you can force **awk** to treat it as a string if you enclose it in quotes.

The **awk** command allows you to assign values to variables, as in **s=0**. Variables in **awk** are treated much like variables in **bc**, except that **awk** variable names can be more than one character long. In fact, they can be any length as long as they begin with an alphabetic character. Array variables are allowed, with the array index enclosed in square brackets like the **bc** usage. These are legal **awk** variables.

```
s
S
SS
S1
qwerty[42]
```

You need not declare or initialize variables before using them. The **awk** command initializes a variable to an empty string, but you can use a variable to store a string or a number as desired, with no difficulty. In fact a single variable can change its type as it is used in an action. For example,

```
/hello/ {
        SSS = 34
        print "SSS is", SSS
        SSS = hello
        print "SSS is", SSS
  }
```

might produce the following output:

```
$ awk -f awk.prog8 in.file
SSS is 34
SSS is hello
```

This automatic variable typing makes **awk** variables easy to use, and **awk** will complain if you try to use this power inappropriately.

Special Patterns for the Beginning and End of Processing

In addition to the regular expression patterns that **awk** uses to decide whether to apply the action to an input line, two special patterns are always executed: These are the **BEGIN** and **END** patterns. **BEGIN** is executed at the beginning of an **awk** program, before any input lines are read; while **END** is executed at the end of the program, after the last input line. **BEGIN** is usually used for the initialization of variables and so on, and **END** is used to make final calculations and produce summary output. Neither **BEGIN** nor **END** is required in the **awk** program, but they can be included if needed. For example, this program will produce the mean or average of a list of numbers.

```
BEGIN {
        print "Beginning to process the input data...."
      }
      {
        s += $1
        n++
      }
END   {
        print "mean of these", n, "data items is", s/n
      }
```

The action associated with **BEGIN** is executed at the beginning of the program, printing the message. Then each input line is read. Because no pattern is associated with the action, the action is executed for each input line. This action adds the first field of the input line to variable *s* and increments the count by one. Finally, the action given after the **END** pattern is executed after all the input has been read. It prints out the results of the computations.

awk Statements

The **awk** command provides a great variety of actions, allowing you to write complex programs that can combine numeric and string actions. The basic form is the *statement*, which is a single operation defined by **awk**. A statement is terminated by a NEWLINE or a semicolon. For example, these are **awk** statements.

```
s += $1
print $2 $1
```

In addition, **awk** treats any sequence of statements enclosed in curly braces as a single statement. All the action parts of the pattern-action pairs shown previously are statements because they are all enclosed in curly braces.

Many logical constructs are also statements. For example, **if** is used in **awk** much like it is used in **bc**.

```
if ( conditional ) statement
```

This statement translates to "if the value of the conditional part is true (nonzero), then execute the statement." Of course, you can include many **awk** statements in the statement part if you enclose the entire construct in curly braces. For example:

```
{
        if ( s < 2 ) {
                ++s
                print s
        }
}
```

This entire example is a single **awk** statement composed of several other statements.

Many simpler forms of a statement are also allowed. *Assignments* of arithmetic expressions to variables are the most common. The format is the same as in **bc**; the common mathematical operators are allowed. For example,

```
x = 3
n += 3
n++
w = 14 / 4 + 32 - ( 14 * 6 ) / 5.2
```

are all valid assignment statements. The **awk** command converts all numbers to floating point before doing its computations, so integers and floating-point numbers may be freely mixed in **awk** statements.

Looping operators are also supported. The **while** operator takes the form

```
while ( conditional ) statement
```

where the *conditional* is any expression that resolves to a zero (false) or nonzero (true) value. If the conditional is true, then the statement is executed. For example:

```
{
        while ( s < 10 ) {
                s = $1 / 32.3
                ++m
        }
}
```

The two statements within the curly braces are executed if *s* is less than 10.

The **for** command is similar except that it takes three parts.

```
{
        for ( s = 0 ; s < 10 ; ++s ) {
                s = $1 /32.3
                ++m
        }
}
```

Each part within the parentheses is separated from the other parts by a ; (semicolon). The first part can be used to initialize any local variables. The second is the conditional, and the statement following the **for** is executed if the middle part resolves to true. The third part is executed after the statement has been executed but before the conditional is tested again for another pass through the loop. It is usually used to change some variable that appears in the conditional part. The statement is executed as often as needed until the conditional resolves to false. Of course any of these operators may be further embedded inside the statement part of the action, if necessary. For example, this is a complete action.

```
{    for ( s = 2; s < 10; ++s ) {
        print "begin loop:  s is now", s
        if ( s > 3 && s < 6 ) {
            print "inside 'if':  s is now", s
        }
    }
}
```

You can use the **break** statement inside a **for** or **while** loop to cause an early exit from the loop, even though the conditional part may still be true. After the **break** statement is processed, execution begins at the first statement after the end of the **for** or **while** loop. For example:

```
{    for ( s = 2; s < 10; ++s ) {
        print "In loop:  s is now", s
        if ( s == 4 ) break
    }
    print "loop finished, s is", s
}
```

This causes the **for** loop to end when s is equal to 4, even though the **for** conditional ($s < 10$) is still true. The **break** statement causes the immediately executing loop to end. If there are nested loops, **break** will end only the innermost loop, and the outer loops will continue.

Similarly, the **continue** operator starts the next iteration of a loop at the top, even though all the statements in the loop have not been executed. For example, the **awk** program

```
$ cat awk.prog9
BEGIN { for ( s = 2; s < 6; ++s ) {
            if ( s == 4 ) continue
            print "s is now", s
        }
      }
```

will cause this output.

```
$ awk -f awk.prog9
s is now 2
s is now 3
s is now 5
$
```

In the conditional

```
if ( s == 4. )
```

the == operator is a logical "if equal" test that returns true or false. The form

```
if ( s = 4. )
```

is an assignment within a conditional that will return the value 4., which is evaluated as nonzero (true). In addition, the second form assigns 4. to the variable s, while the former does not changes s. Misuse of the = and == operators within conditional expressions is a very common and hard-to-detect error. Take care when you use the conditionals.

Two other operators that control **awk** program flow are **next** and **exit**. The **next** operator causes the current action to end; **awk** will then immediately read the next input line and restart with it. Similarly, **exit** causes **awk** to stop processing the current action and then discard all remaining input lines and proceed to an **END** section, if one exists. If there is no **END** section, **awk** will exit back to the shell when it sees the **exit** command.

Formatting Output with awk

The **print** command in **awk** can be very useful for producing simple output, as shown in the previous examples. However, for more complex printing, the **printf** (for print function) command is available. This command differs from **print** in that it allows complete control over how output is produced. In fact **printf** implements the complete set of functions available in the **printf** function in the C language.

This is a powerful and complex list of output formatting commands, so here we will cover only the major forms. The **printf** command takes two kinds of arguments. The first is a *formatting specification* that is a character string. This specifies the general form of the output and may include special holes in which real data will be inserted. The second type of argument to **printf** is a list of variables. There will be as many of these variables as there are holes in the formatting specification. The holes are called *conversion specifications*, and they define how the variables will be printed. For example,

```
printf "this is a number %d and a string %s\n", 333, "333"
```

produces

```
this is a number 333 and a string 333
```

The first argument after the **printf** command is the formatting specification, which includes several words that are printed as they appear and two conversion specifications. The conversion specifications begin with the % (percent) character, and the specification is made with the characters immediately following the %. The **d** (for decimal), **s** (for string), **c** (for a single character), **o** (for octal), **x** (for hexadecimal), and **f** (for float) are the major formats allowed. In the previous example **%d** means "display the variable as a decimal integer," and **%s** means "display the variable as a character string." Variables given after the conversion specification are displayed according to the format specification, with type conversions made as needed to the correct format.

By default, **printf** selects an appropriate length for the conversion, acting intelligently where possible. Use as many digits as necessary to make the conversion and do not worry about the length. However, you can force the conversion to a specific length if you give a number, with the desired number of digits, after the % and before the conversion type. For example,

```
printf "one= >%1d<, two= >%2d<, three= >%3d<\n", sss, sss, sss
```

will use *at least* one, two, or three digits to format the variable *sss*. However, **printf** will use more digits if needed. That is, if *sss* has the value 42, the **printf** statement in this example gives the following result:

```
one= >42<, two= >42<, three= > 42<
```

When more digits are specified in the conversion specification than are needed in the conversion, **printf** will pad the format with white space on the left, making digits *right-justified* in the field. If a — (minus) follows the % and precedes the field width, the output will be *left-justified* within the field. For example,

```
printf "one= >%1d<, two= >%2d<, three= >%-3d<\n", sss, sss, sss
```

will cause this output

```
one= >42<, two= >42<, three= >42 <
```

These field size specifications allow columnizing output under your control, but remember that **printf** will not truncate a number if the field specification is too small for the value to be printed. Instead, it will expand the field specification as needed.

For floating-point numbers, which will contain a decimal point on output, a more complex length specification is recognized. The length is given as two numbers separated by a . (dot). The number to the left of the decimal point is the total field width desired, and the number to the right of the dot is the number of digits after the decimal point in the output. For example,

```
printf "short= >%6.1f<, longer= >%6.4f<\n", 6.345678, 6.345678
```

will produce this result.

```
short= >   6.3<, longer= >6.3457<
```

The results are rounded correctly to fill the field. This kind of truncation of the output occurs with **printf** only to the right of the decimal point. The **printf** command will use as many digits as needed to correctly represent the part of the number to the left of the decimal point. The — can also be used after the % with floating-point output to left-justify the number within the field. However, the precision will dominate, and the right will be padded with white space. This command

```
printf "short= >%-6.1f<, longer= >%-6.4f<\n", 6.345678, 6.345678
```

will produce this output.

```
short= >6.3   <, longer= >6.3457<
```

In addition, **printf** recognizes these special control characters: \n means "output a NEWLINE," and \t means "output a tab character." This command

```
printf "hello 12\t%c%c\ngoodbye", 3, 4
```

will produce this output.

```
hello 12        34
goodbye
```

The **printf** command supports several more operators and conversion specifications. However, the ones we have described will be sufficient for the great majority of your work with **awk**.

Going Further

There are many more tools for computation. These are the several programming languages that developers can use to write programs, and they usually must be purchased as part of the Software Development Set. Serious programs are almost always written with one of these programming languages, but ·here we will just mention some of the important software development tools available with the UNIX system, after a bit of news about **awk**.

The New awk Program

A new version of the **awk** programming language is included in some releases of SVR3. It is called **nawk** (for new **awk**), and it may replace the older **awk** in the future. In most cases it is compatible with the original **awk** and is noticeably faster. In addition, it has more built-in functions than the original and is useful in a wider variety of situations. However, some **awk** programs will not work with **nawk**, and many **nawk** programs are not compatible with **awk**. All the examples we have discussed will work with both **awk** and **nawk**.

The major difference in **nawk** programming is the presence of a larger set of built-in functions and variables. You have access to the command line arguments, the name of the current input file (or **stdin**), the number of fields in the current line, the sequence count of the current line, and other variables. Further, a large number of built-in functions allow various substring and character indexing operations on the input records and **getline** operations that read the next input record. Together these new operators merge many of the features of

awk and **sed**. Consult the **nawk** man page for more information on its features.

The C Language and UNIX System Development Tools

By far the most important tool is the C programming language. Nearly all the tools, as well as most of the kernel, are written in C. Recently C has taken hold in other environments besides the UNIX system, and C compilers and tools are now available for nearly all operating systems. C is regarded as one of the best systems programming languages in use, allowing the developer a great deal of flexibility in spanning the range from assembly-level code to very high level, abstract programming concepts.

In addition, you can use the **make** program to reduce the compilation time required for development of large projects. The **make** program uses a predetermined list of *dependencies* between source files and the target application to determine the minimum recompilation needed to regenerate the application after any part has changed. The file system modification date is used to determine which files are newer than their dependents. The **make** program then efficiently rebuilds these modules and reconstructs the application. In large software projects that consist of many source files in several directories developed by several people, **make** can significantly reduce the development effort.

The **make** program has many applications outside software development as well. It can be useful in any application where output depends on several input files or has several different recipes for creating it. Often used in documentation projects, it can serve small as well as large projects.

The **sccs** (for Source Code Control System) provides library services for source code so that all changes to software can be indefinitely maintained. That is, **sccs** keeps a library file that contains all versions of a source module. Tools are provided to extract, administer, and update the library file as the source code changes over the development cycle. Together these tools, along with the rest of the editors and text-handling utilities, make the UNIX system the environment of choice for most modern software development.

The lex and yacc Tools

Finally, the Software Development Set includes two tools for *lexical analysis* and development of programs from linguistic descriptions of the *effects* that the programs should have. The **lex** (for lexical analysis) and **yacc** (for yet another compiler-compiler) are fourth-generation development tools. They allow development of lexical state machines and compilers by describing how the applications should act rather than making the programmer specify what they should do. However, these are sophisticated tools designed for experts, and you need considerable experience to use them successfully.

FORTRAN and Other Compilers

A FORTRAN compiler and run-time libraries can be provided as part of the Software Development Set under the name **f77**. Other FORTRAN compilers and other languages and development systems are available for the UNIX system from several sources. Nearly any development tool that you might desire is available for UNIX systems, including full-scale statistics and graphics packages, BASIC interpreters and compilers, and many full-screen calculators for different terminals and displays.

The Process

The multitasking aspects of the UNIX system are generically understood under the topic of the *process*. A process or *task* is an instance of an executing program. Your login shell is a process while you are logged in because it is always present until you log off. If you execute a command from the "$" prompt, that command is a process while it is executing. Processes have many properties, and there are many commands to manipulate processes and their properties. In this section we will discuss the issues associated with multitasking and consider how to control the execution environment to your advantage.

For example,

```
$ cat /etc/passwd
```

will generate one process that lives until the **cat** operation is completed. If you create a shell pipeline with the | operator, each command component is a separate process. The command line

```
$ cat /etc/passwd | wc
```

289

will generate two processes, one for each command. These processes communicate with each other through the pipe.

How many processes are created by the following command?

```
$ SIZE=`cat /etc/passwd | wc -l`
```

The answer is two, one for the **cat** and one for the **wc**. The assignment to the environment variable *SIZE* is handled internally by the shell, and no additional process is created for that operation. Similarly, some commands are executed directly by the shell rather than creating a new process. The **cd** command and, usually, **echo** are *built-in* shell commands and do not involve a separate process. But most of your commands, and many others created by the UNIX system for its own purposes, are processes.

Time-Sharing in the UNIX System

Because UNIX systems usually have only a single *central processing unit* (CPU) that executes programs, only one program can really be executing at any time. A major purpose of the *kernel*—the portion of the UNIX system that manages the system as a whole—is to provide control and support for the many programs that might wish to use the CPU at any time. If you share the machine with others, each user's shell is a process, along with any applications or commands that they are working with. Several programs may request access to the single CPU at once, and the kernel must grant access to only one of these applications (or keep control for itself) at any time. A process executes for a short time, and then control passes to another process. Because these changes of task, or *process switches*, occur at least once every second, and usually more often, individual users have the impression that they own the whole machine. This is why multitasking operating systems are called *time-sharing systems*: the single CPU is a resource that is shared by all users and processes. The kernel also provides each individual process with the impression that it has the whole machine, though it may only really control the machine for less than a second at a time. Because a process need only wait for a short while before regaining control, the user at a terminal seldom notices that the system is being used by other programs and users.

Of course the system can become more heavily loaded than was intended when it was configured; when this happens, noticeable delays may appear for the user running commands and applications. In fact once you know how fast a specific UNIX system usually tends to work, you can use extreme delays in *response time* to detect problems and errors in the system. You cannot think of any specific delay as being a system error, however, because different commands will naturally take more or less time to complete, depending on how much processing is required. It is the system's deviation from normal behavior that tells you something may be wrong.

Again, a process is an instance of an executing program. A command as stored on disk may be executable, and you may invoke it with a command name, but unless it is running or waiting for access to the CPU, it is not a process. Processes describe the *current* status of the machine.

Controlling Process Priority

Most processes have equal *priority*, that is, equal share of the CPU. However, the UNIX system provides tools for modifying the priority of a process that you create. Increasing priority usually causes the process to complete more quickly, at the cost of other processes in the machine, which will not get as much CPU time and thus will complete more slowly. Lowering process priority, on the other hand, will make a process demand less CPU time during each interval, so it will take longer to complete. Other processes in the machine will benefit because they will get a bigger share of the system's resources.

Unless you are the superuser, you cannot increase the priority of a process; it could be viewed as unfriendly if you set your process to such a high priority that other processes get little or no access to the CPU. However, you can easily lower a command's priority with the **nice** (for nice and friendly) command. To use it, begin your normal command line with **nice**, as shown here:

```
$ nice cat /etc/passwd
```

The command line that you really wish to execute is the argument(s) to the **nice** command. The above command will reduce the priority of the command **cat /etc/passwd** by 10, the default value. The number is an arbitrary scheduling value that can range from 0 to 19.

More or less priority reduction is also allowed; you simply give an argument to **nice** that contains the numeric increment you wish to make.

```
$ nice -14 cat /etc/passwd
```

This will reduce the priority of the **cat** command line by 14 priority units. If your application consumes a large amount of CPU time, you can usually run the command at a low priority so that it *soaks* idle CPU time but really does not interfere with the normal, higher-priority work going on in the machine.

The superuser may increase process priority but should use this privilege with discretion. Give the **nice** command with a negative priority argument to increase priority of a command. This command

```
# nice --14 cat /etc/passwd
```

will increase the priority of the **cat** command by 14 priority units.

Background Processes

You will usually use the **nice** command in association with commands that you run from the shell but that run in the *background*. This means that the program is executing for you, but your shell is still available and you can run other commands at the same time. The shell provides the **&** (ampersand) operator to let you run commands in the background. Just add it to the end of your command line.

```
$ cat /etc/passwd &
```

In this example the **cat** command is executed in the background, but its output will still come to your terminal because you did not redirect it. When you run a command with **&**, the shell will return immediately for you to enter another command, even though the process that you created is still executing in the system. The shell returns a *process number* or *pid* (for process id), so you can refer to the job, and then returns to your prompt for another command.

```
$ cat /etc/passwd &
1536
$
```

We will discuss the meaning of this number shortly.
    You will usually redirect the input and output of commands that execute in the background so that your terminal session is not interrupted by the output.

```
$ cat /etc/passwd > file.copy &
1540
$
```

    You may wish to redirect the standard error output as well, or it will come to your terminal even though the standard output is redirected.

```
$ cat /etc/passwd > file.copy 2>error.out &
1544
$
```

You may want the standard error to come to the terminal to alert you to errors in your background processes.
    The UNIX system lets you create as many background

jobs as you wish, up to some maximum number specified in the kernel. System performance will usually begin to suffer well before you reach this limit. When a background process completes, the system will not notify you, but you can monitor the status of background processes with the **ps** command. If you have redirected output to a file, you can examine the output at your convenience.

Logging Off While Background Processes Are Running

If you create background processes during your session, they will be killed when you log off because they are associated with your login shell. The UNIX system provides a tool to allow background processes to continue to run after you log off, which can be very useful for jobs that might run all night (or all week!). The **nohup** (for no hangup) command does this for you. Use **nohup** like **nice**; put it at the beginning of your command line.

```
$ nohup cat /etc/passwd &
```

This tells the **cat** command to ignore your logging off the system and to continue to run until completion. Usually **nohup** is used with background commands because you can't tell the shell to log you off if you don't have a prompt.

When you use **nohup** with a pipeline, you must use the **nohup** command to begin each element of the pipeline.

```
$ nohup cat /etc/passwd | nohup wc > out.file &
```

If you don't do this correctly, the member of the pipeline without the **nohup** command will be killed when you log off, and the pipeline as a whole will collapse.

If you do not redirect your output, **nohup** will create an output file for you, because if you log off the machine, there will be no terminal for output to go to.

```
$ nohup cat /etc/passwd &
1565
Sending output to nohup.out
$
```

Here you get the identifying number from the shell because you used the **&** operator, and the "Sending output..." message comes from **nohup** as it creates a redirection for output. The **nohup.out** file in the current directory will contain the results of the command executed under control of **nohup**. You should take care to handle standard error output separately if you don't want it in the **nohup.out** file.

Parents and Children

When you log into the system, the operating system creates a shell process for your use, and this process disappears, or *dies*, when you log off. You always have at least one, and frequently more than one, process associated with your session.

Processes are said to be *born* when they start and *die* when they end. Many processes come and go this way in the system, depending on how the system is being used. Some start when the system is turned on and live until it is powered down. More often, though, a process has a relatively short lifespan that corresponds to the duration of the command that you enter at the terminal.

A new process can be born only if another process starts it. The older process is known as the *parent process*; the created one, the *child process*. A parent may *spawn* multiple children, but a process may have only one parent. Similarly, a process may spawn a child, which in turn may spawn another child, and so on. Though you don't speak of the grandparent of a process, you can actually trace the parentage of any given process, through its intermediate parent processes, all the way back to when the system was turned on. The intermediate processes may or may not exist, but each process has a definite parent. If a process spawns a child and that child spawns its own child process, the intermediate process may die. When a parent dies, all its children usually die, but you can arrange things so that the child does not die. When this occurs, the original parent *inherits* the children of the process that died. Thus every process always has a parent.

When you use **nohup** to execute a command, **nohup** listens for you to log off. If you do, **nohup** reassigns the parent of your process to be process 1, so it has no more association with your login. Normally, processes that you create from your shell are children of the shell and will die when the shell dies.

All users on the machine have processes associated with their current login, and there are also system-wide processes created by the system. Some system-wide processes are created by the system for a specific purpose and then die. For example, a process is created to send your electronic mail to another machine, and then it dies. Other processes, such as the *spooler* for the **lp** printer subsystem, are likely to stay around for the entire time the machine is running.

The ps Command

You can examine the processes currently alive in the machine with the **ps** (for process status) command, which displays information about processes that are alive when you run the command. If you run the command more than once, the output will probably be different each time; **ps** produces a snapshot of machine activity. If you execute the program with no arguments, it shows you information about processes associated with your login session.

```
$ ps
   PID TTY       TIME COMMAND
  6756 tty00     0:01 -sh
  6760 tty00     0:02 ps
$
```

You have two processes running now. One is for the shell, which is born when you log into the system and dies when you log out.

The other process is executing the **ps** command. Each process has an execution time associated with it, 2 seconds for the **ps** command in this example. This time is not elapsed or clock time; it is the total amount of CPU time that the process has used since it was born.

A process may have an associated terminal that it reads from and writes to, and this is given in a column of the output. A process associated with your login is usually, though not always, attached to your terminal. Some processes are attached to no terminal, in which case the TTY column of the output contains **?** (question mark). Finally, each process has a unique pid that identifies it within the system. These pids start at 0 when the system is turned on, and each process gets the next one until the maximum number, usually 32767, is reached. In this example the **ps** process was the 6760th process to execute since the system was turned on. When the maximum number is reached, the count starts again from 0, except that a new process will not use a pid that is being used by another process that is still alive. Children usually have a higher pid than their parents, but if the parent pid is near the maximum, a child may have recycled back to a low number.

Actually there is much more information associated with each process, some of which is available with the −**f** (for full) option of **ps**.

```
$ ps −f
     UID    PID  PPID  C    STIME TTY       TIME COMMAND
   steve   6756     1  6 13:04:57 tty00     0:01 −sh
   steve   6761  6756 23 13:05:19 tty00     0:01 ps −f
$
```

The command name, time of execution, tty, and pid are displayed in this output, and some other information is also available. On the left is the user id; each process is owned by the login id that created it. The column PPID gives the pid for the parent of each process. Because the system created the shell for you when you logged into the machine, its parent pid is a very low number, the pid associated with part of the kernel. Pid 1 is usually the parent of most processes created by the system. When you executed the **ps** command, that process was created by the shell, so the parent pid of the **ps** process is the pid of your shell. You can trace chains of parents and children by looking at their pid and ppid.

The next column of the output, C, gives the amount of CPU resources that the process has used recently. The kernel uses this information when deciding which of several processes will next have access to the CPU. The kernel will let a process with a low C value have control of the CPU before one with a higher value. The **nice** command works by changing the internal algorithm by which this number is computed, but this column is seldom useful except to developers working on kernel improvements and drivers.

Finally, *STIME* gives the time of day when the process started. You can use this information to track old or rogue processes that have been in the system incorrectly for a long time.

Activity of Other Users

The **ps** command can also give information about what other users are doing on the machine at any time. If you know that a specific user is logged into the system, you can display the status of his or her processes with

```
$ ps -u user
```

where "user" is the login id of the individual you are interested in.

On a small system it is usually easier to see the activity of all users at once. Use the **-a** (for all) option of **ps**.

```
$ ps -af
    UID   PID  PPID  C    STIME TTY      TIME COMMAND
   root    82     1  0   Apr  9 console  0:05 -sh
  steve  6756     1  3 13:04:57 tty00    0:01 -sh
  steve  6762  6756 21 13:05:28 tty00    0:00 ps -af
$
```

Several items are of interest here. First, another user is currently logged into the machine. This login id, *root*, is reserved for system administration and can be logged in only from the main system console, as you see in the TTY column. Apparently the root user logged in soon after the machine was turned on because a relatively low pid is associated with that login. If you examine the STIME column, you can see something more: the start time of a process is expressed in hh:mm:ss format for *today's* times; however, for processes born on previous days, the time is given only as the month and day. This format simply reduces the size of the output; the UNIX system keeps all times exactly.

System Processes

We have examined the processes associated with each user, but there are also long-lived processes that support the activities of the system and transient processes that are born and then die as the system goes about its business independently of individual users. The **ps** option −**e** (for every) gives information about all the processes active in the machine. This **ps** −**e** output helps you examine what the machine is doing behind your back and is key to diagnosing problems. The exact output is very dependent on the software installed on the machine and on the hardware I/O devices attached to the system. The system processes are organized differently in different versions of the UNIX system. In moving to a new version on a new machine, try to understand which processes are normal; then you can identify problems or errors in the **ps** output when things go wrong. Try these commands frequently on your own system to get the feel for what is normal.

If you run the command

```
$ ps -ef
```

on a SVR3 system based on the Intel 80386, this output might be typical.

```
$ ps -ef
    UID    PID  PPID  C    STIME TTY       TIME COMMAND
    root     0     0  0    Apr 9  ?        0:00 sched
```

```
root       1     0   0  Apr  9  ?         3:03 /etc/init
root       2     0   0  Apr  9  ?         0:00 vhand
root       3     0   0  Apr  9  ?         2:46 bdflush
root       4     0   0  Apr  9  ?         0:16 bmapflus
root      82     1   0  Apr  9  console   0:05 -sh
root      78     1   0  Apr  9  ?         0:45 /etc/cron
steve   6756  6755   3  13:04:57 tty00    0:01 -sh
steve   6762  6756  21  13:05:28 tty00    0:00 ps -ef
$
```

The first process to execute when the machine boots is the *scheduler*. The key to the time-sharing features of the UNIX system, it is responsible for determining which of the processes that are ready to run actually gets access to the machine's resources. It is named **sched**, has pid 0, and in turn starts **init** (for initialization), which keeps standing system processes running. (We will discuss **init** more in Chapter 19.) The **init** process gets pid 1. Next is **vhand** (virtual handler), which manages the virtual memory of the machine and swaps active processes between disk and real memory as they get to run or get temporarily pushed aside. The **vhand** process is responsible for most of the administrative work that the system does to manage system memory in the multitasking environment. The **sched** and **vhand** processes work closely together and make up the core of the kernel; **vhand** gets pid 2.

Finally, **bdflush** (for buffer to disk flush) and **bmapflus** (for buffer map flush) manage the disk I/O for the system. Because the system contains many internal data buffers that act much like a RAM disk acts on other operating systems, there is a possibility that if the system fails unexpectedly, or *crashes*, the data in the buffers will not correctly match the disk. To prevent this, **bdflush** and **bmapflus** periodically write all the buffers to disk by causing a **sync** operation. The frequency of this operation is a system-dependent parameter, but on many small machines it happens once every 20 seconds. Only the things that have changed get written to disk each time. The **bdflush** process gets pid 3, and **bmapflus** gets pid 4.

Except for **init**, these system processes are stored on disk within the file /**unix** that represents the kernel, and no disk file contains the executable **sched**, **vhand**, **bdflush**, or **bmapflus**.

These processes are created when the system boots and

stay alive until the system is shut down. For this reason, the TIME column of the **ps —ef** output may show a great deal of apparent CPU time allocated to the process. This is not always accurate, however, because some implementations arbitrarily assign all idle CPU time to **sched** or another of the kernel processes. This is seldom a cause for worry; if these kernel processes are not working, the system probably will not even be sane enough to execute **ps**!

The remaining system processes can trace their parentage back to **init**. It is responsible for maintaining the system processes according to the contents of the file **/etc/inittab**. All terminal lines and other standing processes arise from **init**. As processes are born and die, the pid count keeps rising, but all processes with no living parent are ultimately inherited by **init**. Notice that the ppid of many processes in the system is 1.

The rest of the processes in the output from **ps —ef** belong either to users or to special applications that you are running. For example, if you have the **lp** print subsystem running on the machine, there will be a line in the **ps —ef** output for its *demon* (sometimes spelled *daemon*). A demon is a system process that acts without a user requesting it. This can be a standing system process, like **vhand**, an application process that is always running, like **lpsched** for the **lp** subsystem; or a process that executes under control of the timing subsystems, like **uuxqt**. These scheduled processes seldom live very long, but you might see some of them when you run **ps**, and of course they cause the pid count to continue to rise.

If you had installed a local area network application, the STARLAN network, for example, you would see its demons on the machine.

```
$ ps -ef
     UID   PID  PPID  C    STIME TTY        TIME COMMAND
    root     0     0  0   Apr  9 ?          0:00 sched
    root     1     0  0   Apr  9 ?          3:03 /etc/init
    root     2     0  0   Apr  9 ?          0:00 vhand
    root     3     0  0   Apr  9 ?          2:47 bdflush
    root     4     0  0   Apr  9 ?          0:16 bmapflus
    root    82     1  0   Apr  9 console    0:05 -sh
    root    83     1  0   Apr  9 ?          0:00 /usr/net/slan/lib/admdaemon
    root    78     1  0   Apr  9 ?          0:45 /etc/cron
  listen    86     1  0   Apr  9 ?          0:05 listen -n starlan -l 696E74656C2E
7365727665 -r 696E74656C
   steve  6756  6755  3 13:04:57 tty00      0:01 -sh
   steve  6767  6756 22 13:06:36 tty00      0:00 ps -ef
$
```

The STARLAN installation has added two demons, **admdaemon**, which administers the local STARLAN server, and **listen**, which listens for network activity directed to this machine. Other networks and some applications will have similar demons associated with their activity.

There are many more options for the **ps** command, but these are primarily designed for the use of system designers and application developers. Try **ps −l** for a cryptic example.

Diagnosing Problems with Processes

By frequently looking at the output from **ps −ef**, you can get an idea about what is normal on your machine. A small system will usually have relatively few processes active at any time, although this number will vary depending on the time of day. If any process seems to have accumulated an inordinate amount of time in the TIME column, if it is the parent of a large number of other processes, or if the response time of the machine suddenly gets very slow, then a process is probably not acting correctly.

You must understand what is normal in your machine before you can detect what is abnormal, and this varies widely from one machine to the next. Also, diagnosing the source of a problem may not help to repair the problem. Most problems are related to a specific command or application, and they are frequently related to missing files or directories or to incorrect permissions on existing files. Because the UNIX system is a multiuser and multitasking operating system, a single problem can affect the rest of the machine. This can cause the machine to slow down significantly and act very abnormally, though it rarely damages other programs, users, and files on the machine. In pathological failures, however, this may not be true, so you should back up data and files to floppy disk or tape regularly, especially if you are experimenting.

An application that is not acting correctly will usually show one of several failure modes:

1. *Its process will die prematurely*. If it is a command, the system will usually return to the shell unexpectedly. If it is a demon, **init** may repeatedly try to spawn the application. In the former case you will not find any process associated with the application in the output from **ps**, and the application will appear to execute much more quickly than it normally does. In the latter case the system will slow down dramatically, and it usually will take several minutes for any command to start, but the machine's disk will be working full time. Sometimes rebooting will repair this type of problem, but more often you will have to uninstall the application or even remove the entry in **/etc/inittab** that refers to the program.

2. *The process will spawn many children*. Occasionally a program will fail in such a way that it repeatedly spawns more and more child processes. You can detect this problem if the machine slows down dramatically or if there are many more processes listed in the output from **ps** than normal. These unexpected processes will usually all have the same parent pid, and this parent is the likely cause of the problem.

    Sometimes this failure results in a single stray process being created each time the offending application is run. When this happens, you will see several copies of the stray process; the parent is usually no longer active, however, so the parent pid of the stray process will not be meaningful. This case is difficult to diagnose, but you can try to execute the suspected culprit and see if a new stray process appears. The TTY or STIME column of the **ps** −**ef** output can sometimes help you determine when or where the stray process was born.

3. *The process will consume inordinate amounts of CPU time*. Occasionally a single process will go astray and take all the CPU resources that the machine can grant it. You can detect this problem if the machine appears to slow down noticeably and a single process in the **ps** −**ef** output has accumulated a lot— usually several minutes worth (or

more) — of CPU time. If you repeatedly execute **ps —ef**, you see that the offending process is getting almost all the CPU time in a system that might otherwise be almost idle. This is the most difficult problem to detect because you must be sure that a good application doesn't have legitimate use of all the CPU time. Processes that are running correctly will usually take longer to complete if they need a lot of CPU resources but will not noticeably slow the machine down.

Again, the key information for detecting process-related problems is a noticeable change in response time or unusual disk activity with no apparent cause. As you become more experienced with the machine, you can detect changes in its performance, and you can usually determine the source of the problem with **ps** .

Killing a Process

If a process has gone astray, or even if you have started some large job that you wish to stop before it completes, you may want to *kill* it. The UNIX system provides tools for killing processes, and you may kill any process that you own. The superuser may kill any processes in the system except for pids 0, 1, 2, 3, and 4, but normal users may only kill processes that they own.

Use the **kill** command with a pid as argument to kill a process.

```
$ kill 4314
$
```

If the kill succeeds, the process will disappear from the **ps** output, and the **kill** command will return silently. Unfortunately, **kill** can fail for various reasons, so always check the **ps** output after killing a process to make sure that it actually was killed. You should also check that the system did not immediately start the process again (with a new pid!). When you **kill** a process, **init** may inherit its children, and the children may not be killed. Therefore, when you kill a process that has children, you should kill all the children at the same time. You can give multiple pids as arguments to the **kill** command.

```
$ kill 4320 4326 4356
```

Killing processes, especially when you are logged in as **root**, can be dangerous because you may be interrupting an important function in the system. If you incorrectly kill a process, you must usually reboot the machine to straighten things out.

Signals

In killing a process you are actually instructing the system to send a *signal* to the process. Signals are used to communicate between processes, and many different signals can be sent — usually 22 in SVR3. Most signals refer to various error conditions within the system. For example, if a process tries to access system memory outside its authorized memory area, the UNIX system will send it signal number 11, a memory segmentation violation. The full list of signals is given in the signal (2) man page.

Signals are sent when you turn off power at the terminal, when you press the DEL key, when a child process dies, and when an internal alarm clock goes off. There are several other important signals. The application must respond appropriately to the signal, either by dying or by rectifying the condition that led to the signal.

When you execute the **kill** command, by default the system sends a signal 15 to the pid(s) you specify. This is a software termination signal that usually causes the process to die. However, the process need not honor this signal, so an unconditional kill signal (number 9) is provided, which will always work immediately. You can give the signal number to the **kill** command as a flag.

```
$ kill -9 4367
```

Again, you must take care not to kill any processes unnecessarily.

Going Further

Processes and their management can be a confusing part of the UNIX system, but careful observations of the **ps —ef** output can help you determine the cause of a problem. In addition, there are several more issues to discuss with respect to processes.

Processes That Respawn

The UNIX system provides the facility for processes to restart if they die. Occasionally a wayward process will automatically restart after you kill it. If this happens, you must tell the system not to restart the application in question. The information about which processes to restart is kept in the file /**etc/inittab**. This file contains a great deal of information, so when you change it, you must take care not to make any mistakes. Only superusers can change /**etc/inittab**.

A typical /**etc/inittab** file is shown in Figure 19-5. The /**etc/inittab** file is one of the key files that support system operation, and we will discuss it further in Chapters 19 and 21. Here we will only review the issues associated with changing the file to control wayward processes that respawn under control of **init**.

The /**etc/inittab** file is a simple database in which each record is a line, each line has four fields, and each field within a record is separated by the : (colon) character. The **init** program uses each line to control one process that may respawn according to rules established for the file. If field 2 of the record contains the digit 2 or 3 (for example, 1245 contains 2 but 145 does not), and field 3 contains the string **respawn**, **init** will automatically restart the process whenever it dies. The last field of the line contains the command and arguments that are executed.

If you diagnose a problem with a specific process from the behavior of your machine and from the output of **ps** −**ef**, and you note that the program immediately restarts when you kill it, look for the program name in the last field of a line in **/etc/inittab**. If it is there, and if field 2 of the record contains 2 or 3, and if field 3 contains **respawn**, then you can turn off the offending process while you determine why it is going astray. You may lose the use of the application while it is shut off, but the rest of the system should be available.

To turn off such an application, you can edit the file **/etc/inittab** if you are logged in as **root**. Change the contents of field 3 of the line of the file you are interested in from **respawn** to **off**; then write the file and leave your editor. Now you must signal to the **init** process that you have changed its instructions and that it should reread the file **/etc/inittab** for the new information. Use the command **telinit** (for tell **init** what to do), with the argument **q** (lowercase *Q*):

```
# telinit q
#
```

The program associated with the line in **/etc/inittab** will no longer restart automatically. However, if an instance of the program is still running, you may have to kill it manually by finding it in the **ps** −**ef** output and then using **kill** with its pid as argument. The **telinit** procedure will not kill an existing process but will stop it from respawning.

You can reverse the process simply. Change the contents of field 3 of the line in **/etc/inittab** from **off** to **respawn** and run **telinit q** again. Of course, you should be sure that the problem does not start up again with the new process.

First ps Takes Longer

To do its work, the **ps** command needs information about the in-memory executing kernel. It then reads the internal process tables to build its output for each process. This time-consuming task may take 7 to 10 seconds of CPU time for a small system and much longer for a large system with hundreds of processes. To relieve you from this delay for each use of the **ps** command, the SVR3 **ps** command retains a table of some of this data in the file **/etc/ps_data**. It is a binary file that is kept in a data format suitable for **ps**. The presence of this intermediate data noticeably speeds up the execution of **ps**.

However, the kernel information in the table may differ after a reboot of the system, so the **ps** command may automatically rebuild the table when **ps** is first run after a reboot or whenever the file **/etc/ps_data** is not present. Consequently, the speed of **ps** depends greatly on whether it has been recently executed and thus can seem very slow or quite quick. You can test this by deleting the file **/etc/ps_data** and executing **ps**. Does the file reappear?

Waiting and Defunct Processes

When a process spawns a child, it will usually wait for the child to complete before resuming its activities. The login shell normally acts like this when you execute a command at the terminal. When the child completes, the kernel recognizes the fact and sends signal 18—death of a child process—to the parent. The parent acknowledges the death, and the system goes about its business. The scenario differs slightly when you run a process in the background with the **&** operator; in this case the shell does not wait for the child to complete and may not even be the parent of the background process.

If the parent of the dying child is busy doing something else, it may not acknowledge the death. In that case the system refuses to let the child die a normal death. It puts the process into a *zombie* or *defunct* state, in which the process is not really dead but is also not executing or using any CPU time. As soon as the parent acknowledges the death of the child, the defunct process disappears from the system.

When you run **ps**, you may occasionally see a defunct process in the output, marked by *<defunct>*. This is only a problem when the defunct process stays around for an hour or more or when the number of zombie processes seems to grow as time passes. Because the parent of the zombie must acknowledge its death, the presence of defunct processes usually points to some problem with the parent. The parent is probably blocked for some reason and cannot acknowledge the death of its children. You can usually kill this wayward parent process to restore the system to sanity.

Process Groups

In the creation of processes in the UNIX system you have seen that process number 1, **init**, is responsible for spawning most of the major processes in the system. These major processes in turn spawn most of the children that do the real work. Your login shell is an example of these superparents, as are many other processes whose parent is process 1. These processes can (and often do) produce whole families of related subprocesses. These families are known as *process groups*, and the superparent process is the *process group leader*. Not every parent is a process group leader because these processes have a special status. A process group leader is usually a child of process 1, but this is not required because a program can change its own process group without changing its ppid.

The **ps** command will not display only process group leaders but can display only processes that are not group leaders. Try **ps −df** to see all these processes. What distinguishes the process group leader?

You can use **kill** to send a signal to all the processes in a process group instead of to just a single process. This command

```
$ kill 0
```

will send a signal 15 to all the processes in your terminal process group. Of course you cannot kill any other process groups in this way unless you are superuser.

Your login shell is usually set to ignore signal 15 (the software termination signal), so **kill 0** might not have much effect unless you had some background processes running. But what if you execute **kill −9 0**, which sends the unconditional kill signal to all processes in your process group? When you log off the system, the system effectively uses **kill −1 0** to send the hangup signal to all the processes in your process group. This kills all your processes unless you have made special arrangements by invoking some programs with the **nohup** command.

# ELEVEN

UNIX System Administration

System administration is the routine maintenance that the system requires as it grows and changes. That is, adding and deleting user login id's, installing new software, cleaning up log files, formatting floppy disks, and backing up all fall into the category of system administration. One user of a UNIX machine is usually designated as system administrator, whose job is to keep the system up and running, in the service of the other users. These are important functions even in a single-user UNIX machine.

Though administration chores are significantly more complex on a multiuser system than on MS-DOS, recent releases of the UNIX system have provided greatly improved tools that can ease these chores. Most SVR2 and SVR3 systems include a *user agent* for administration, which is usually a menu-oriented tool that prompts the administrator through the functions and does complicated work without much detailed attention by the user. Most user agents include full-screen menus and forms for data entry, with good error-checking facilities.

These tools can make running a UNIX system much easier than ever before, and even experts tend to use them instead of the manual methods. However, the manual methods still exist, and in many situations the simplified tools are not adequate. In this chapter we will discuss the basics of system administration, including some discussion of the different user agents that are present in different implementations. We will give a more detailed analysis of the individual topics in later chapters.

The Superuser

The system administrator is usually an individual user who is responsibile for keeping the system running correctly. Experience has shown that a single person can maintain system consistency much better than several users. In a small personal UNIX machine the owner is probably the system administrator, and he or she gives access to other users, backs up the disk files, and so on. In a multiuser system the administrator must also act as a policeman and fireman, keeping the machine sane for the benefit of users.

The UNIX system provides a special login id, **root**, for the system administrator. The **root** id has its own password and has special privileges, including full access to all system files and resources. Thus the **root** login is called the superuser. This login id should *always* have a password, which should be known only by the system administrator and possibly a backup person. The **root** user can cause great damage to the system software and files, and the login should be used with care. Even if you are the system administrator, you should reserve the **root** login id for system administration tasks and use a normal login id for your routine work. This will provide some measure of protection because the system will usually complain if a normal user tries to make changes reserved for the administrator.

The Superuser Environment

The shell provides a special PSI prompt, the # (pound), to remind you that you are the superuser and that you have extra access to the system.

The rest of the system environment for the **root** login id is also very different than that for the normal user. The HOME directory is the / (slash or root) directory, and the default PATH will probably differ as well. Some commands will also act differently when the superuser uses them. They almost always provide expanded capabilities, so all the command lines that you might use as a normal user will also work when you are **root**. The **root** login id gets **.profile** services just like a normal user, and you can create or change the file /.**profile** to change the superuser environment.

On modern UNIX machines use of the **root** login id is limited to the system console; you cannot use it from a remote terminal. From the console, you should log out from your normal login id and login again as **root** when you want to do administration tasks. Go back to your normal login id when the administrative work is complete.

The su Command

The UNIX system also provides a tool that lets you *switch* your login id temporarily, without logging out. This is the **su** (for superuser) command. It is accessible from a remote terminal, so in an emergency you can log into the machine remotely using your normal login id and then switch to **root** privileges with the **su** command. When finished, you should exit from the **su** privileges as soon as possible.

You can use **su** to change to any other login id in addition to **root**, but **root** is the default. Execute the following command:

```
$ su
Password:
#
```

After you enter the correct password for the **root** login id, the prompt will switch to the root PS1. As usual, the password is not echoed as you enter it. If you do not have the correct password, the **su** command will fail.

```
$ su
Password:
Sorry
$
```

On some systems the **su** command requires a full pathname.

```
$ /bin/su
```

Not using the full pathname can be a security risk, for reasons discussed in Chapter 20. It is good practice to use the full pathname whenever you execute **su**.

While the **su** command is running, you will have full system administration privileges. When you wish to exit back to your normal login id, just press CTRL-D or use the **exit** command.

```
$ /bin/su
Password:
# exit
$
```

Actually the **su** command provides a subshell on top of your normal login, and when you finish with **su**, you are returned to your normal environment.

The su Environment

This invocation of **su** provides a shell environment that is like your normal environment, except that **root** privileges are added. That is, your normal *PATH* is active, your HOME directory is the same, and so forth. To switch completely to the root environment and abandon your normal environment temporarily, execute the **su** command with the — (minus) option.

```
$ /bin/su
Password:
# echo $HOME
/usr/steve
# exit
$ /bin/su -
Password:
# echo $HOME
/
# exit
$
```

In fact **su** provides **.profile** services for the **root** user when the — argument is given but does not when the — is not given, so be sure to use the — when you want a full **root** environment.

Switching to Another Login

You can also use **su** to change to another user instead of **root**. Just give the user id as the last command line argument.

```
$ /bin/su - jim
Password:
$
```

As usual, you will be prompted to enter the correct password for the user you wish to change to. The − argument acts as expected to create that user's login environment. The new PS1 will be for the named user, not "#", which is reserved for **root**.

Finally, you can use **su** to execute a single command as if you were the named user. When the command completes, the superuser privilege will be revoked and you will immediately be returned to your normal environment.

```
$ /bin/su - root -c "chgrp bin /unix"
Password:
$
```

With this form, you must give the user id and then give the command to execute in quotes. Use the − argument to get the user's environment. The −**c** (for command) argument is required before the command you wish to execute. It tells **su** to use a subshell for the command. You can use −**r** (for restricted) instead of −**c** if you want the command to execute in a *restricted shell* rather than a full shell. (We will discuss the restricted shell in Chapter 20.)

When you are logged into the system as **root** and then run **su** to change to another user, **su** will not prompt for the password because the **root** user already has full privileges. In addition, if the user has not specified a password, **su** will not prompt for it. In all other cases you must know the correct password before you can change to another user.

Use of **su** with an associated command to execute is often used in shell scripts when special privileges are required.

Using Color Monitors

Many terminals and system consoles in today's machines support *color displays*. No standard command in the UNIX system is provided to manage the color of material displayed on the screen, but many releases provide special commands to change the background color and color of the ASCII characters as displayed. In addition, experts can often use the **terminfo** (for terminal information) feature (discussed briefly at the end of this chapter) to highlight specific displays, such as the PS1 and command lines, or messages from shell scripts, in specific colors. You can usually change the default background/foreground colors on the console but not on a remote terminal. However, you can usually set up a **terminfo** description file that allows some use of color on a remote terminal.

Many SVR3 releases include the **setcolor** command for setting the default background and foreground colors on the console. The **setcolor** command usually takes two arguments that specify the background and foreground colors, respectively. These arguments are color names or numbers; consult the man page for your release of the UNIX system for details. For example, this command

```
$ setcolor blue white
$
```

produces white characters on a blue field. In some releases **setcolor** can take additional flags to specify a light or dark shade or may use coded numbers instead of color names to specify the color. You can experiment to get a pleasant display and then add the command to your **.profile** to make it permanent.

Creating News and the Message of the Day

One of the system administrator's responsibilities is to create most of the system's news. If other users are on the machine, it is polite to announce scheduled downtime, new software, and other information as it becomes current. The **news** command is often used because users usually get news announcements when they log into the machine.

For higher-priority news, the **motd** (for message of the day) is automatically displayed for each user when he or she logs into the machine. The system administrator can edit the file **/etc/motd** to create the message, and that is all that is needed. Because the **motd** cannot be avoided when a user logs into the machine, it is best to use this feature sparingly and to delete out-of-date messages as soon as possible.

For very high priority announcements, use the **/etc/wall** (for write all) command, which reads its standard input for a message and then immediately writes the message directly to the terminals of all users currently logged into the machine. Use it only for messages of immediate value, such as imminent system shutdowns. (These features are discussed in more detail in Chapter 13.)

System Administration User Agents

Most routine system administration chores can be handled through the user agent provided by the software vendor for that purpose. Consult the specific documentation for your machine to determine the command name to get you into the administration subsystem. Only the superuser should use these tools, though some releases of UNIX allow you to *delegate* system administration privileges to other users. When you establish a new user id, you can usually choose whether the user has the privilege. However, security is best maintained when only one or two users on the machine have the privilege.

On older releases the system administration tool is called **sysadm** (for system administration). If you have this command, you must always execute it from the **/usr/admin** directory—the HOME directory for the system administrator. If you are not logged into the machine as **root**, or your current directory is not /**usr/admin**, **sysadm** will not work.

```
# cd /usr/admin
# sysadm
```

The Microport Systems release includes the **sysviz** (for visual system administration) command, and on newer AT&T SVR3 releases it is called **adm** (for administration). The **adm** command is strictly for administration, but the **sysviz** menus include such user functions as displaying files and directories, sending mail, and executing installed applications.

These user agents are generally large menu systems that have many prompts and have several different subsystems for the different administration chores. They differ substantially in appearance and in details, but all include similar functions because all UNIX systems require the same basic administration tasks. We will review the functions, but remember that the specific prompts and menu selections on your system may differ slightly from those shown in these examples. You can match the functions with the menu items available on your machine. Explore the features of your user agent; it can substantially simplify most use of the UNIX system!

Table 11-1 gives a list of functions usually available within the user agent. We will discuss them one by one.

Main Operation	Subfunctions
Backup to Removable Media	Backup History
	Personal Backup
	System Backup
Change Password	
Date and Time	Date
	Time
	AM/PM
	Time Zone
	Daylight Savings Time
Disk Operations	Floppy-to-Floppy Copy
	Format 1.2 MB UNIX Floppy Disk
	Format 360 KB UNIX Floppy Disk
File System Operations	Create File System
	Mount File System
	Unmount File System
Mail Setup	This System
	Other Systems
Peripherals Setup	Printer Setup
	Second Hard-Disk Setup
	Serial Ports Setup
	Second Serial Port Setup
Printer Operations	Printer Queue
	Printer Restart
	Printer Status
Restore from Removable Media	Personal Restore
	System Restore
Shutdown	
Software Management	Install
	Remove
	Display
System Information	System Name
	Disk Free Space
	Serial Port Status
	Last Backup

Table 11-1.   Administration Functions in Most SVR3 User Agents

Main Operation	Subfunctions
	Parallel Port
	Users Logged in
User Logins	Add
	Change
	Delete
	Display

Table 11-1.   Administration Functions in Most SVR3 User Agents (*continued*)

Handling Floppy Diskettes

The **Disk Operations** or **diskmgmt** menu is intended for *media management*—for formatting and copying floppy disks.

Usually you *format* a floppy disk, create a *file system* on the floppy, and then *mount* the disk at a location in the file system. After all these steps have been accomplished, you can use the floppy disk just like a normal directory. You can **mv** or **cp** files to the disk, change the modes of the files, or use the directory pathname in your commands and shell scripts. When you are through with the disk, you can *unmount* it and remove it from the floppy drive. A second mode of accessing disks is available with the **cpio** (for copy in/out) command, which is used for the **backup** and **restore** functions. (Media are discussed in detail in Chapter 16.)

Formatting Floppy Disks

Select the appropriate option from the **Disk Operations** menu to format a floppy disk. You can usually format both 360-kilobyte (KB), double-sided, double-density diskettes and

1.2-megabyte (MB) high-density disks if your machine uses 5.25-inch disks. If your machine uses 3.5-inch plastic-coated disks, then you can format these instead. Because the physical diskettes differ in the different formats, you must have the correct disk in order to complete the formatting operation. You will be prompted to insert the floppy and close the drive door before the procedure starts. You cannot format *write-protected* disks, so be sure that the tab is removed from the notch in the diskette before you insert it in the drive. In most cases you must use drive 0 or drive A for formatting through the administration user agent.

The system will usually provide some error messages if the format operation fails. If it does, try the format again, but discard the diskette if the format fails after two tries. Diskettes are always cheaper than the data you put onto them. Don't take chances with bad floppies!

To erase a disk, just reformat it.

Making a File System on a Formatted Diskette

After formatting a diskette, you must create a file system on the floppy before it can be mounted. If you are using a floppy for backup, you do not need a file system; the format step alone is sufficient. However, if you wish to use the floppy like a normal directory within the file system, you must use the administrative tool to create a file system on the disk. This procedure is handled in the **File System Operations** or **diskmgmt** menu.

Insert the formatted disk and select the **Create File System** option from the user agent. You will be prompted to enter the file system name. This is the place in the file system where the diskette will appear when it is mounted. This means that you can **cd** to that directory to access the contents of the floppy. Mounted diskettes are treated just like normal directories, but when they are unmounted, they will disappear from the file system. Usually the floppy disk will be at the directory location **/mnt**, and any files or subdirectories of

/**mnt** will be on the floppy. Enter the name without the lead-ing /, as **mnt**. You don't need to use **mnt**. You can use any directory location you wish within the / directory, but you must create it if it doesn't already exist.

You can *label* a diskette, which provides some identifica-tion for the floppy but is not required. The label can be up to six characters long. Some releases require you to choose the maximum number of files and directories allowed on the disk. The default is usually sufficient.

After you start the **Create File System** option, do not remove the diskette from the drive until the system prompts you to do so.

Mounting a Diskette

You can *mount* a diskette whenever you wish to use it. The *mount* option is usually found in the **File System Operations** or **diskmgmt** menu. The disk must be formatted and have a file system before it can be mounted. After mounting the disk, you can exit the user agent, use normal commands to refer to the disk under its directory location (usually /**mnt**), and use it as any normal directory. Reenter the system administration tool to *unmount* the disk before removing it from the drive. You can seriously damage the contents of the disk if you remove it without first unmounting it.

When you mount a disk, you must specify the file system location where the contents of the disk will appear. This will usually be the file system name that you specified when you created the file system on the floppy, but you can mount a disk at a different *mount point* if you wish.

Also, you can usually choose to mount the disk as *read-only* or both readable and writable. If you mount the disk as read-only, you cannot change any of its files, but you can use write-protected disks. On the other hand, the diskette must be write-enabled if you mount it with read and write access.

When you first mount a disk after creating the file sys-tem, it will be empty. Files or subdirectories that you create in the directory at the mount point will be on the disk, and they will reappear there the next time that you mount the diskette. If you change the mount point for a subsequent mount, the files will appear under the new mount point, not the old one. To copy a file to the floppy from the hard disk, you may use the **cp** or **mv** command but not the **ln** command.

Often the user agent will allow you to mount only one disk at a time, even if you have more than one disk drive. Thus, when you unmount the disk, you will not be prompted for the file system to unmount because the system knows where you have mounted the disk. Before unmounting, you must release any files on the disk that you may be using and **cd** out of any directory at or below the mount point. That is, the disk must be completely idle before you can unmount it.

Copying a Floppy Disk

You can copy a floppy disk from the **Disk Operations** or **diskmgmt** menu. Before copying, you must have a formatted disk of the same format as the source disk. Be sure to format the new disk first. You needn't make a file system on the disk that you are copying to because the tool will copy the file system from the source disk.

The disk-copying tool will prompt you to insert the original disk. It will read the disk and prompt you to remove it. Then it will prompt you to insert the new disk, and it will complete the copy. Copying is usually limited to drive A, so you cannot copy diskettes directly from one drive to another, but the system makes a temporary file on the machine's hard disk.

You can usually make multiple copies of the same source disk. The user agent will prompt you to insert another formatted blank disk after a copy is completed.

The copy will be a complete and exact copy of the source disk, with all file systems, directories, and time stamps preserved. You can copy mountable, backup, or bootable disk formats without trouble.

Disk Backup and Restoral

Use the **backup** and **restoral** options for backing up the system files and directories from the machine's hard disk to a removable disk or tape. This can save your valuable data if the hard disk ever fails or you mistakenly delete some important file. Normally you should keep your backed-up files current with your use of the system. The risk of losing your valuable data as a result of a system failure is *always* unacceptable. Failures may be rare, but they always seem to occur at the most inconvenient times. *Back up your data early and often.*

Three different procedures for backup are usually supported. First is a *full backup*, which you can perform soon after you install the system software. Then you can do regular, *incremental backups* to save only the files that have changed since the last backup. You must do a full backup before an incremental backup is allowed. Third, you can usually do a *personal backup* to save all the files within a specific HOME directory. In addition, you can sometimes get a display of the *backup history* for the machine. This will tell you when the last backups were performed and what was included.

Backups are usually made onto a floppy disk or a series of disks, though you can use magnetic tape if your machine has a tape unit. You must have enough formatted disks or tapes on hand to complete the backup because the backup procedure will prompt you to change disks when one is full.

Format a large number of disks before beginning the procedure; you will soon learn how many diskettes you need to back up the files that you select.

Carefully mark each disk with its sequence number immediately after removing it from the drive; you must insert them in the same order when you restore them onto the machine's hard disk.

You must usually select the individual file system to back up from a list of available file systems. This list will vary depending on your configuration and on how many hard disks are installed in the machine. Back up each file system separately—the fewer diskettes that you use in a backup, the less the chance of a floppy going bad and destroying your data. Backups are written to a sequence of floppy disks that can only be read in the order in which they are created, so if one of the first disks in a backup set is bad, the data on following disks will be lost.

The first time, you must do a full backup. Subsequently you can do incremental backups, but do not reuse your original set of disks from the full backup. A full backup copies all the system files in addition to your files, and can use as many as 20 1.2-MB floppies in a typical system. Finally, you must select the device to use, which must match your floppy disks.

Should it become necessary to restore the backed up data, select the **Restore from Removable Media** option. You will be prompted to load the disks in the order in which they were created. Be sure to select the same device that you used when the backups were created.

In case of a catastrophic system failure, you can recover an exact image of your system at the time of the last backup. Reload the system software from the original floppy disks, restore your full backup, and then restore each incremental backup in the order in which they were created. This is a time-consuming procedure, but it can guarantee the integrity of your system. Most experienced system administrators manually back up their data directory by directory, which is less prone to error and requires considerably fewer floppy disks. However, the manual procedures are more difficult to work with than the user agent.

On some implementations you can back up a specific list of files and directories. After selecting the appropriate menu item, usually marked **store**, you can enter a list of files and directories to store in the backup. You can edit, add to, or display the list at any time. When you give a directory name, all its files and subdirectories will be included in the list. When you are satisfied with the list, you can back up the files. The backup can overflow onto additional disks, so be sure that you have enough formatted disks on hand before you begin.

Displaying Hard-Disk Usage

Most user agents provide a tool to display the amount of disk space used on the system's hard disk and any file systems that are mounted when the command is executed. Usually this is part of a "system information" prompt or is found in the **diskmgmt** subsystem.

The disk space is usually listed as megabytes of free space and the total amount available. Often the numbers are also expressed as percentages. In some systems, however, the space is listed in 512-byte physical blocks within the file system.

The disk usage data is very important. Normal UNIX system operations require some temporary files that can demand disk space without warning and then free it soon after. If you have less than 10 percent free space, your disk can fill up unexpectedly and the system can fail.

Disks always tend to fill up over time, so you should examine the disk usage data regularly and back up and delete unneeded files when the filled space approaches 90 percent.

The System Information Display

In addition to the disk space usage, the **System Information** option collects several other data items in its display. It reports on the users currently logged into the system, gives the machine **uname** and system software release, often displays the current date and time, and also reports how the serial and parallel ports are currently configured.

Setting the Date and Time

The user agent will also provide a tool for setting the system's clock/calendar hardware. This is usually called **Date and Time** or **datetime** in the menu. The UNIX system uses the current time in many ways, and you should keep the system time correctly set. Many small computers do not keep good time, even with built-in clock hardware, so you should regularly examine the system time and reset it if it is more than a few minutes off. Be sure that the "time zone" and the "daylight savings time" prompts are answered correctly.

Shutting Down the Machine

The user agent often includes an option for shutting down the machine. The UNIX system differs from MS-DOS and other single-tasking operating systems in this area. You should *never* simply turn off the power to the machine while it is running because damage to the files on the hard disk can result. *Always* use the shutdown procedure in the administrative user agent or execute the **shutdown** command while logged into the machine as **root**.

Before starting the shutdown procedure, check to be sure that no critical operation is in progress. After it starts, the shutdown procedure will warn other users that the machine is about to be shut off, and it will give them time to log out. Then it will bring the machine down cleanly to a point where you can turn off the power. When you see

```
Reboot the system now.
```

    or

```
Reset the CPU to reboot.
```

you can turn off power, but *not before* this message is displayed. (Boot and shutdown are discussed in detail in Chapter 19.)

Adding and Removing User Login Id's

The **User Logins** or **usermgmt** menu is used to add or delete user login id's from the system. All system users should have their own login id and should not share login id's. This is important both for system security and for preventing users from damaging each other's files by mistake. However, all users can be in the same group if you wish, or they can be members of different groups. Recall that groups are used in the middle set of permissions for file access, as shown in the output from **ls** −**l**.

When you create a new login id, you should give the user a starting password, which the user can change when he or she logs into the system. In addition, when users leave the machine permanently, you should immediately remove or disable their login id's to prevent security problems later.

The **User Logins** menu may include many options, though only a few are used regularly. **Display** or **lsuser** will display information associated with the users known to the system. You can add a new user with **Add** or **adduser** and delete a user id with **Delete** or **deluser**.

In order to add a new user to the system, you must enter the login id and the user's name. The login id must be unique on the machine, and the user agent will test whether your entry is unique. Most users wish to select their own login id, so you should consult them before adding it. Enter the user's name correctly; it may be used by some software that can read it from the /**etc**/**passwd** file where it is stored.

On some systems you must select the user's *id number* and *group name*. These representations of the user and group id's are used by much system software. Let the system choose these to guarantee that there will be no errors. On many systems you are not asked to select these id's and cannot change the defaults. The default group puts all normal users into the same group, which is usually fine for small systems. Only if you have more than one distinct interest group among your users should you explicitly select a group. If so, you must create a new group by using an **addgroup** option if you have it or by manually editing /**etc**/**group**. (Groups are discussed in Chapter 20.)

Next, you must select the pathname for the user's HOME directory. Unless there is some special need, you should let the system select and create the HOME directory.

Finally, on some systems you can grant system administration privileges to the new user. If granted, the user will be able to access the administrative user agent, add or change new login id's, and grant system administration privileges to others. Because this is a security risk, only a few trusted users should have system administration privileges.

After all this material has been entered, the system will echo the information and give you the option to install the user or cancel the operation. Do not install the entry if there are any errors because this can introduce security risks into the system.

After the login is installed, you can create a starting password for the user. You should *always* create a password when adding users because they might not create their own, and an unprotected login id is a dangerous security risk.

The other options on the **User Logins** menu act similarly. To remove a login id, select **Delete** or **deluser**. The **Change** or **moduser** option allows you to change the attributes of a current login without removing and re-creating the login id. You can change the user's login id and often the password from this menu. You might wish to change the password to lock a user out of the system temporarily, without removing all his or her files and directories. Later you might change the password again, allowing the user to login again.

Installing Software Packages

Tools are usually provided that allow you to install and remove application software packages. If you have the **sysadm** menu, these will be available under **softwaremgmt**. If you have the **adm** command on your machine, software installation is supported differently: there are three non-menu commands for installing and removing packaged software—**installpkg**, **removepkg**, and **displaypkg**.

Not all add-on software is supported by these tools because the application developer must make the application fit within the scheme. However, if an add-on software package is compatible, you can install, remove, and list its name.

Follow the instructions with the application software to install it with **installpkg**. You can remove previously installed software with **removepkg** if you used **installpkg** to install it. The **displaypkg** command displays the list of installed applications.

Sometimes you can execute a conforming application from its floppy disk if you have the **runpkg** menu item. This will not always work, even if your user agent has the option, because some software must be installed on the hard disk. However, it can often let you execute infrequently used software without permanently taking the space on your hard disk. Beware that the application will be tediously slow to start and use when it is run from a floppy disk.

Setting the Machine Name

You can change the *node name* or **uname** (for UNIX name) of the machine from the **Mail Setup** or **machinemgmt** menu. The **uname** is the unique identifying name for the machine. This value must be unique, at least within the domain of machines that you communicate with via **mail**. Once chosen, the name will not be easy to change because the remote machines that send you mail will all have to change as well. When you first install the system, select a node name and stick with it. Do not allow your machine to keep its default node name, which is definitely *not* unique.

If your user agent includes a **Mail Setup** option, the entry for **Mail Name of This System** changes the **uname**.

Otherwise, the option will be in the **machinemgmt** menu.

The machine name should be no longer than eight characters and should begin with a lowercase letter (*a* through *z*). You can use numbers after the first character, but avoid special characters.

Along with the **uname** of the machine, you can specify the login id that other machines will use when they send you electronic mail. The default login id is **nuucp** (for new **uucp**), and you should not change it without a very specific need.

Finally, you can specify whether the **nuucp** login id will have a password. Because the data communication tools contain excellent security internally, you rarely need a password here and should not specify one. If you do, any machine that sends you mail must know the password. Thus you are effectively putting a password on the login id and immediately distributing it to all your friends (and usually their friends). Don't put a password on the **nuucp** login id unless you must restrict mail to a short list of machines.

Electronic Mail Names of Other Systems

Just as a remote machine needs information about your machine before it can send you electronic mail, your system must have information about other systems before you can send mail to them. The **Electronic Mail Names of Other Systems** or **uucpmgmt** menu is used to establish this information. To contact another machine, you need a data communications *modem*, a direct connection to another machine, or a *local area network* (*LAN*) connecting the machines. Then you must tell the UNIX system the unique name of each remote machine that you wish to contact. You must give the login id and password for data communications access, which you must get from the system administrator of each machine. Finally, you must tell your machine how to call the other machine, including the device and the communications speed to use. You can also restrict calling to some hours of the day or days of the week. You cannot send mail to another system if you have not set this data correctly, though other systems can sometimes call you even if you cannot call them. (More information on setting up this data is provided in Chapter 14).

Like the **User Logins** menu, **Other Systems** usually allows you to add, change, delete, and display the data. The **Add System** menu usually prompts you for the unique **uname** of the other system, its login (usually **nuucp**), and the password associated with that login id, if it has one.

If the connection will be made via a modem and dial-up telephone line, you must know the telephone number that connects to the dial-up modem on the other machine.

Some user agents only support adding systems that can be called via a telephone line, and you cannot add systems accessible over a LAN or direct connection. Other user agents support the selection of several different connection methods. The connection control tools in the data communications subsystems are very powerful and can quickly become confusing. Review Chapter 14 before adding systems that use any connection method other than dial-up calls.

Next, you must select the data communications speed for the link. Your modem must be capable of the same speed as the one at the other machine, or you will not be able to communicate with it. Most dial-up modems can be set for 300, 1200, or 2400 baud, but you should consult with the system administrator at the remote machine and agree on the communications speed.

You can usually restrict calls to specific days and/or times of day; that is, the data communications software will call the other machine only when permitted. This feature forces electronic mail to be sent when the remote machine is available or during late-night hours when both the workload on the machine and the telephone rates are low. You can also specify **Never** to force the other machine to call you to pick up mail queued for that machine. If you want quick delivery of your electronic mail to the machine, do not restrict calling times.

The Peripherals Setup Menu

Finally, the most difficult topic in the administrative user agent is **Peripherals Setup**. This task may be distributed within several menu items or collected into one. The major tasks are **Serial Port Setup** (or **ttymgmt**) and **Printer Setup** (or **machinemgmt**). Some systems include options for setting up other peripheral devices such as a second hard disk or tape drives. Usually this menu item will change when you add new hardware devices to your machine so that you can administer them.

Setting up a device differs from managing the device after it is installed, so there will usually be separate menus for these different functions. We will discuss printers first.

Printer Management

The UNIX system includes a powerful *print spooler* that manages the printers installed on the system. You can send output to any installed printer by giving the *name* of the printer when you want to print a job. To install a printer, you must give it a name, assign it to a parallel or serial port, and specify the printer type.

Once the printer is installed, you can manage the queue of jobs waiting to be printed. You can delete jobs from the queue before they are printed, change the printer on which a job is destined to print, or remove a printer from service.

Installing a Printer

The **Peripherals Setup** menu allows you to install a new printer on either a *parallel* (that is, LPT1 or LPT2) or *serial* (that is, COM1 or COM2) port. A specific printer can only attach to one or the other type of port. (Printing is discussed in detail in Chapter 12, and you should examine that chapter before installing a new printer.) The device files associated with these physical ports are given in Table 12-1.

You must also give the printer type. A large list of known printers is usually included in the user agent menu, and you can select your printer from the list. If your printer is not on the list, try the entry for **Dumb**. If none work, you will have to set up the printer manually.

Serial printers include a communications speed. Usually 9600 baud is a good choice if your printer is capable of that speed. You may need to set switches on the printer to configure its speed. Parallel printers do not use a communications speed selection.

Finally, you must name one printer as the *system default*, and jobs with no printer specified will be printed there. Only one printer can be the system default.

Managing an Existing Printer

Once a printer is installed and running, you can send output to it with the **lp** command. Several jobs may be queued before they are printed, and the **lp** system will manage the *spool* correctly.

The **Printer Operations** menu includes options for looking at the current spool of unprinted jobs, and you can usually delete an unwanted job from the spool with the **Printer Queue** option.

The **Printer Status** menu lists the printers configured into the **lp** system and reports on whether they are currently accepting requests for printing. This means that you can add new jobs to the print queue, even though the printer might not be actually printing them. If the printer runs out of paper or its power is turned off and then on again, it will no longer print but will be listed as accepting requests. There may be several jobs on the print spool, but the printer will be idle. When this happens, you must *restart* or *enable* the printer with the **Printer Restart** option in the **Printer Operations** menu. When you restart the printer, it should immediately begin printing if any jobs are queued. If a printer is listed as not accepting requests, you may need to remove and then reinstall the printer in the **Peripherals Setup** menu to get it working.

Serial Port and Terminal Management

The **Serial Ports Setup** or **ttymgmt** menu is used to modify the system configuration for supporting remote terminals. It sets the communications parameters that are used when remote terminals are to be connected to the machine, either directly or through dial-up modems. Unlike the configuration parameters set by the **uucpmgmt** menu, which control *outgoing* calls for data movement, **ttymgmt** sets parameters for *incoming* calls, primarily used for users connecting to the machine with terminals. However, the settings in the **uucpmgmt** and **ttymgmt** menus definitely interact, and you can make changes in either that will affect the other.

An RS232 port can be set to listen for incoming calls

through an attached modem, terminal, or local area network. When a call is received, the /etc/**getty** program answers it at a given communications speed (baud rate) and prints "login:" for the user. In addition to the communications speed, a full set of default **stty** parameters is established on the line. If the incoming call is not at the preset speed, the system can *cycle* through several other settings until the incoming call matches a speed or the caller hangs up. This allows the system to respond to incoming calls at any of several communications speeds. When the user finishes the session and hangs up, the system resets the line to some default **stty** parameters and then waits for the next call. The **Serial Ports Setup** menu hides much of this complexity, but if you have the **sysadm** command, you can set all these parameters, including the initial speed setting, the way that the speeds cycle when they don't match the call, and the **stty** parameters used on both login and logout.

To set up a serial port, you must at least specify the port to use, the kind of device that you are attaching to the port, and the device speed. Table 12-1 lists the serial devices that might be available. Usually COM1 and COM2 are installed on small machines, but you can use more serial ports if you have them.

You can attach a modem, terminal, computer, or other type of device to these RS232 ports. Modems usually connect to a telephone line; terminals connect directly to the machine; and other computers can also be connected. These devices differ in that modems and computers allow both incoming and outgoing calls, while terminals allow only incoming calls. If you have a local area network that runs on a serial port, select **other** for the device type.

You must also specify the communications speed for the device. The device speed may be called the *line setting* in some releases. Most modems communicate at 1200 or 2400 baud; terminals and computers can run up to 19,200 baud, though 9600 baud is common. In all cases you must match the speed you give in the **user agent** menu with the speed as set on the device you are attaching. If you have attached a serial printer to the port or the port is idle, set its device type to **none**.

If you select **modem**, you must select the type of modem because the communications software acts differently depending on the modem in use. This selection might be found under a *device type* menu. If your modem is not included and is not Hayes-compatible, you will have to install the entry manually after reading Chapter 14. Alternatively, you can restrict use of the port to incoming calls by selecting **Dumb** or **Non-Autodialing** as the device type.

If you selected **modem** or **computer**, you can specify that the system allow incoming calls, outgoing calls, or both. If you select **incoming**, you cannot use the port to call another machine, and if you select **outgoing**, other machines or users with terminals cannot call your machine. Select **both** unless you have some reason to restrict calls to one direction only. Of course your modem or other computer must be set up to allow two-way communications, or **both** will not work as expected.

Going Further

UNIX system administration is complex, and in the remaining chapters we will address it in one way or another. As your understanding of the UNIX system grows, you will find the administrative user agent quite helpful for most situations, and you will only need the manual procedures occasionally. Stick with the automated tools where possible; they are less prone to error than manual methods. In the rest of this chapter we will further discuss terminal devices and mention some other issues that have no other home.

The uname Command

The user agent and the system configuration tools provide tools for setting the machine's unique identifying name, or *uname*. In addition, a normal UNIX system command called **uname** is available for reporting or setting the uname from the shell:

```
$ uname
mysys
$
```

By default, *uname* displays the system name only. Use the −**a** (for all) option to display other information about the machine:

```
$ uname −a
mysys mysys 3.1 1 i386
$
```

The five items displayed are the system name first, then a nodename which may differ from the system name if the machine is a server on some types of network. Third is the operating system release number (3.1), then the version number of that release. Finally there is the type of hardware the machine uses (i386). **uname** has options to display any one of these items only, and it is often used in shell scripts whose behavior depends on some of this data.

The superuser can also use uname to set the system's name, though you should use the user agent rather than the uname command when possible. Use the −**S** (for set) option to set the machine name, followed by the new name you wish to use:

```
# uname -a
mysys mysys 3.1 1 i386
# uname -S steve
# uname -a
steve steve 3.1 1 i386
#
```

Remember that other machines may be using your uname to send you electronic mail, so you should take care to inform them when you change your machine's name.

More on Terminal Modes

Like all the tools in the administrative user agent, the **Peripherals Setup** or **ttymgmt** menus have analogues in manual procedures. Whenever a communications port is enabled to accept incoming calls, a demon process is listening to the port. This process, called /etc/**getty** (for get **tty**), waits for the carrier detect signal on the RS232 port. When the signal is asserted, **getty** sets the line to the initial line settings and then prints "login:" for the user. When the user finishes the session and logs out, **getty** restarts and waits for another login. A similar program called /**usr**/**lib**/**uucp**/**uugetty** is used when two-way communications are specified.

The line settings, which **getty** reads to determine how to set up the RS232 port, are stored in the file /etc/**gettydefs** (for getty definitions). This file consists of a series of lines, each with one line setting, separated from the others by a blank line. Here are two sample lines from the **gettydefs** file.

```
9600# B9600 OPOST ONLCR TAB3 BRKINT IGNPAR ISTRIP IXON IXANY ECHO ECHOE
ECHOK ICANON ISIG CS8 CREAD # B9600 OPOST ONLCR TAB3 BRKINT IGNPAR ISTRIP
IXON IXANY ECHO ECHOE ECHOK ICANON ISIG CS8 CREAD #login: #4800

4800# B4800 OPOST ONLCR TAB3 BRKINT IGNPAR ISTRIP IXON IXANY ECHO ECHOE
ECHOK ICANON ISIG CS8 CREAD # B4800 OPOST ONLCR TAB3 BRKINT IGNPAR ISTRIP
IXON IXANY ECHO ECHOE ECHOK ICANON ISIG CS8 CREAD #login: #2400
```

These are actually just two very long lines from a **gettydefs** file, even though each takes more than 80 characters and prints on multiple lines.

Each line contains five separate fields, delimited by the **#** (pound) operator. The first field is the name of the line setting. These two lines are called 9600 and 4800, respectively. The next field contains all the initial **stty** values for that setting, and the third field contains the final **stty** values. Each **stty** parameter has a name, and these names are separated by white space within the field. The fourth field is the string printed when **getty** detects an incoming call. This string is usually **login:**, but you can change it to whatever you wish. However, incoming **uucp** calls usually expect it to end with **login:**.

The last field is the name of another **gettydefs** line setting. If **getty** detects a break signal on the line before the user responds to the "login:" prompt, it will *cycle* to the line setting in the last field and try again. This cycling can continue as long as breaks are received. This feature allows a single incoming **tty** port to receive calls at several different speeds or **stty** values without constant manipulation by the administrator. If you don't want the port to cycle to a new line setting, you can use the name in the first field again in the fifth, causing **getty** to reuse the same setting on break.

Starting a getty

The **getty** demon is executed from the system scheduler as a result of placing an entry in the file **/etc/inittab**, which describes the **getty** parameters. A sample **/etc/inittab** file is given in Figure 19-4. The lines beginning 00 and 01 in that figure specify **getty** demons. We discuss the **inittab** fully in Chapter 19, but each line consists of fields delimited by a : (colon).

You can start a **getty** process on a port by changing the third field, **off**, to **respawn**, as in the line beginning 00. The fourth field gives the **getty** command line. First is the **getty** command itself, with the full pathname specified. The first argument is the **tty** device that the **getty** will listen to: **tty00** and **tty01** are the most common, referring to the COM1 and COM2 ports, respectively. The second command line argument for **getty** is the name of the line setting in **gettydefs**. Finally, a descriptive comment follows after the # delimiter.

The line beginning "co" in Figure 19-4 gives the **getty** entry for the system console. The console has both a device file named **/dev/console** and a **gettydefs** line setting called *console*.

The **getty** demon only allows incoming calls, so when a **getty** is running, the port cannot be used by the **uucp** subsystem for outgoing mail. Use the program **/usr/lib/ uucp/uugetty** instead of **/etc/getty** in your **inittab** lines if you want to use the port for two-way traffic. For example:

```
00:23:respawn:/usr/lib/uucp/uugetty -r tty00 9600 # the COM1 port
```

If you want two-way calling on COM2 (if it is installed in your machine), change the 01 line to the following:

```
01:23:respawn:/usr/lib/uucp/uugetty -r tty01 9600 # the COM2 port
```

The −**r** instructs **uugetty** to wait for a NEWLINE on the incoming call before it prints "login:". Therefore, if you have **uugetty** on a port and then call into it, you must press NEW-LINE before you can login. This small feature allows a hard-wired connection between two computers to support two-way communication, because neither machine prints "login:" until the other requests it by sending a NEWLINE.

The 9600 in these lines is the communications speed for the device. If you are attaching a hard-wired terminal to the port, you probably want 9600 baud. If you are attaching an external modem, you will probably use 1200 or 2400, depending on whether the modem is a 1200-baud or 2400-baud device.

Be sure that these changes are correct; then write the file and execute **quit** from your editor. Execute the following command to make the change take effect.

```
# telinit q
```

Remember, you must be logged into the machine as **root** to perform this procedure.

In newer SVR3 releases, changes that are made manually to **inittab** will disappear after you install a new hardware/software package that includes a device driver. If you change **inittab**, back it up to a safe place before installing such an add-on package.

Installing New Terminal Descriptions

When a program such as **vi** uses your *TERM* environment variable, the application looks up a *terminal description* based on the variable's value. These terminal descriptions are kept in the directory **/usr/lib/terminfo** and its subdirectories. The terminal capabilities are kept in a compiled form in this directory tree and are not directly readable by humans. In older releases the terminal descriptions were kept in text form in the file **/etc/termcap**. In addition, the format of the descriptions has changed between the **termcap** and **terminfo** versions. To support these changes, three new tools are provided in SVR3 systems.

The **tic** (for **terminfo** compiler) program takes a filename as argument.

```
$ tic desc.ti
```

The file contains a terminal description in source form. The

tic program compiles the description and puts the result into the **terminfo** database.

The **infocmp** (for **terminfo** compare) program can compare compiled **terminfo** descriptions or display the source form from the compiled form. Used without an argument, it displays the source form for the terminal currently set in the *TERM* variable. This powerful tool has many options and features. It can produce a source form that you can edit and then run through **tic** to produce a modified entry.

Finally, the **captoinfo** program helps convert terminal descriptions written in **termcap** form into **terminfo** form.

You cannot use these sophisticated tools correctly without some experience with terminals and the **curses** software package. Examine the manual pages for these commands before experimenting with them.

Using Escape Sequences for Color

In releases of the UNIX system that support color displays, the **terminfo** database contains descriptions for *escape sequences* that can change the color of the display. That is, the terminal or console responds to special sequences of characters that begin with the ESC character and contain codes for the different colors. You can use this feature to display character strings in color. The codes vary in different implementations (and on different monitors), but try this sequence if you have a color monitor.

```
$ echo "\033[34mHello world\033[0m"
```

What is the result? You can use the **terminfo** database to change the color composition of full-screen applications that use **terminfo** services, such as **vi**.

Printing

The UNIX system provides good tools for controlling printers and for spooling output to hard-copy devices. The software can be configured to allow attachment of a single simple printer that you can use for all paper output, or it can be configured so that a UNIX machine can act as a central print server driving dozens of hard-copy devices of different types. Many users can direct output to a printer simultaneously; the software will queue the output correctly and add banner pages to the printout so that individual users can find their own output.

Printer support is especially powerful under the UNIX because of the multitasking nature of the system. Unlike many small operating systems, the printer software in the UNIX system runs as a user-level application, with no exotic device drivers or RAM disks visible to the user. The print tools do an excellent job of hiding hardware dependencies.

In this chapter we will discuss the user-level commands that allow you to print your files and command output, and we also consider the configuration of the printer software as you add and change printers. We will review some of the problems that can occur with printers and the software that controls them. Finally, we will discuss issues associated with using a UNIX machine as a print server and how to set up a system for sending output from one UNIX machine to another for printing.

The printing tools are generically called the *lp* (for line printer) subsystem. They are so general and so powerful that no other printing software is usually provided in UNIX systems. Because of the philosophy of making tools that do only a specific job, such functions as pagination of output and hardware-specific formatting are done by special-purpose applications and filters rather than by **lp**. This allows the **lp** subsystem to specialize in print queue management and efficient driving of the hardware.

Using the lp Command

Primary user-level access to the **lp** system is with the **lp** command. You will frequently use **lp** as the termination of a shell pipeline,

```
$ cat /usr/spool/lp/model/dumb | lp
```

but it can also take a pathname as argument.

```
$ lp /usr/spool/lp/model/dumb
```

The **lp** command specializes in printing; if you want paginated output with special headers on each page, use an additional tool as appropriate in the command line.

```
$ pr /usr/spool/lp/model/serial | lp
```

By default, **lp** will place the named file or its standard input onto the print queue for the default printer. The **lp** command returns to the shell after the job has been queued, not when the printing has been completed.

The **lp** command allows several options that can modify the printing process. The −**m** (for mail) flag will provide notification by electronic mail after the file has been printed. Because the print queue is unlimited in size and the printing may take a considerable amount of time, this option can be useful. The −**n** (for number) option allows you to print more than one copy with one **lp** command. To print six copies of a file, with notification by mail when the job is complete, use the following command:

```
$ lp -m -n6 /usr/spool/lp/model/1640
```

The **lp** command will print a *banner* page at the beginning of each output job. You can control the contents of this banner with the −**t** (for title) option.

```
$ lp -t"This file belongs to $LOGNAME" /usr/spool/lp/model/prx
```

This title appears only on the **lp** banner page, not on each page of the output. Use the −**h** option of **pr** to put a header on each page.

The Request Id

When the **lp** command queues a print job, it returns a *request id* to its standard output.

```
$ lp /usr/spool/lp/model/prx
Request id is ATT470-78
$
```

Note this job number because you can use it to track or cancel the job. Some versions of **lp** on some machines do not return the request id, but you can still track your job with the **lpstat** command, which we will discuss shortly.

If you have several printers attached to the machine, you can direct **lp** to use one specific printer by using the −**d** (for destination) option. The −**d** option takes the name of a specific printer as argument.

```
$ lp -d ATT470 /usr/spool/lp/model/dumb
```

The **lp** command has several other options that allow you to copy files before printing (−**c**), write a message directly to your terminal when the printing is completed (−**w**), and pass printer-specific options directly to the actual program that controls the printer (−**o**).

Canceling a Job

You can cancel a print job before it has been printed with the **cancel** command. The **cancel** command takes a printer request id, or list of request id's, and removes the named jobs from the print queue.

```
$ cancel ATT470-78
request "ATT470-78" canceled
$
```

This will cancel a job even if it has started printing, allowing you to stop large but mistaken jobs without tying up the printer.

The **cancel** command can also take a printer name as argument, in which case it will cancel the job currently printing on the device.

```
$ cancel ATT470
request "ATT470-78" canceled
$
```

This will not affect jobs on the queue that have not started printing.

Determining Printer Status

The **lpstat** (for **lp** status) command provides information about the overall state of your **lp** system. If you execute it without arguments, **lpstat** gives information about your own spooled jobs.

```
$ lp /etc/profile
Request id is ATT470-79
$ lpstat
ATT470-79              lp            4290    Apr 27 19:07
$
```

The request id is first, followed by the hardware device that will process the request, the output size in bytes, and finally the date and time of the request. You can use **lpstat** in this way to determine the request id of your jobs if you forget them.

Similarly, you can use the −**u** option with a user id to see spooled requests for other users.

```
$ lpstat -u steve
ATT470-79              lp            4290    Apr 27 19:07
$
```

If you specify another user id, you may see a different picture of the spool.

When a job is printing, that information is also included in the output of **lpstat**.

```
$ lpstat -u steve
ATT470-79              lp            4290    Apr 27 19:07    on ATT470
$
```

When the job has finished printing, it is removed from the queue, and there is no longer any way to track it. However, if you know that the job was spooled, then its disappearance from the spool indicates that the job has been printed.

Command Line Options for lpstat

The **lpstat** command provides many other options that can tell you much about how the printer is configured. The **−d** (for default printer) option will report which printer is the default.

```
$ lpstat −d
system default destination: ATT470
$
```

The **−r** (for request) option tells you whether the printer system is in operation.

```
$ lpstat −r
scheduler is running
$
```

If the **lp** system is not available, **lpstat −r** will report that fact.

```
$ lpstat −r
scheduler is not running
$
```

You must take administrative action to turn on the **lp** system, as we will discuss soon.

The **−t** (for total) option for **lpstat** tells you everything about the printer system.

```
$ lpstat −t
scheduler is running
system default destination: ATT470
members of class Parallel:
        ATT470
device for ATT470: /dev/lp
ATT470 accepting requests since Aug 19 18:58
Parallel accepting requests since Aug 19 18:58
printer ATT470 now printing ATT470-85. enabled since Apr 27 21:03
ATT470-85              lp                  4290    Apr 27 21:01 on ATT470
ATT470-86              lp                  526     Apr 27 19:11
$
```

You can see the system default printer (ATT470 here), the hardware device pathname (**/dev/lp**) for that printer, whether or not the printer is accepting print jobs, whether the printer is enabled, and the spool of current jobs.

The printers can be grouped into *classes* so that several of the same type can be grouped together but be distinguished from those of another type. This allows more than one output device to share the workload while allowing you to force output to one type or another as your needs dictate. The **lpstat −t** command displays class membership of printers and tells you whether the class as a whole is accepting requests. We will discuss printer classes in more detail shortly. The −t option is one of the most useful of the **lpstat** options for a small system because all the output can usually fit easily on a single display screen. When there are many printers of several classes and many users requesting print output, one of the more limited **lpstat** options may be more desirable.

lpsched — The lp Demon

The **lp** system is controlled by a demon process called **lpsched** (for **lp** scheduler), which runs all the time that the **lp** system is up. When you execute the **lp** command to spool a file to the printer, **lp** communicates with this demon to tell it that a new job is ready for printing. The **lpsched** command also handles queue management, to prevent multiple jobs created at the same time from competing for the printer resources, and drives the printer devices, sensing when the printer is idle or nonfunctional.

You can see the **lpsched** program with the **ps −ef** command.

```
$ ps -ef
     UID   PID  PPID  C    STIME TTY       TIME COMMAND
    root     0     0  0   Apr  9 ?         0:00 sched
    root     1     0  0   Apr  9 ?         3:03 /etc/init
    root     2     0  0   Apr  9 ?         0:00 vhand
    root     3     0  0   Apr  9 ?         2:46 bdflush
    root     4     0  0   Apr  9 ?         0:16 bmapflus
    root    82     1  0   Apr  9 console   0:05 -sh
    root    78     1  0   Apr  9 ?         0:45 /etc/cron
      lp    69     1  3   Jan  1 ?         1:20 lpsched
   steve  6756  6755  3  13:04:57 tty00    0:01 -sh
   steve  6762  6756 21  13:05:28 tty00    0:00 ps -ef
$
```

The parent of the **lpsched** process is **init**, and it has no **tty**. It is owned by the user **lp**. In most systems a special user id is associated with the **lp** system, and you can use the **lp** login as a target for print jobs spooled from remote machines. Usually you won't try to log in as **lp**, and it is desirable to disable the password for the **lp** login in **/etc/passwd** for security reasons.

Starting and Stopping the Scheduler

You can determine if **lpsched** is running on your machine with **lpstat −r** as just discussed, or with **ps −ef**. If it is not running, you cannot queue jobs to the printer. The command

```
# /usr/lib/lpsched
```

will start the scheduler if it is not running, but this is usually done at boot time. The **lpsched** command and other **lp** administrative commands are reserved for the superuser. If **lpsched** is not running, that is usually a sign that something is wrong with your **lp** system.

You can turn off **lpsched** with

```
# /usr/lib/lpshut
```

This is usually safer than simply killing the **lpsched** process because it stops printing in an orderly way.

The lp Directory Structure

The **lp** tools are distributed within the file system. Some of the simpler user commands, such as **lp** and **lpstat**, are located in the directory **/usr/bin**, and the rest of the administrative commands are located in /**usr**/**lib**. You will usually need to give the complete pathname when you execute these commands because users rarely have /**usr**/**lib** in their *PATH*. You can easily examine the available commands because they usually begin with **lp**.

```
$ ls /usr/bin/lp*
/usr/bin/lp
/usr/bin/lpinfo
/usr/bin/lpsetup
/usr/bin/lpstat
$ ls /usr/lib/lp*
/usr/lib/lpadmin
/usr/lib/lpfx
/usr/lib/lpmove
/usr/lib/lpqueue
/usr/lib/lpsched
/usr/lib/lpshut
$
```

In addition, the commands /**usr**/**bin**/**enable**, /**usr**/**bin**/**disable**, /**usr**/**lib**/**accept**, and /**usr**/**lib**/**reject** are part of the **lp** system.

Most of the **lp** system is contained in the /**usr**/**spool**/**lp** directory and its subdirectories. The actual spool list, the files to be printed, an **lp** log, and the printer *interface scripts* are kept here. Become familiar with that directory because you will use it to add new printers or diagnose printer problems.

The contents of the directory may vary slightly on different systems and according to how the **lp** system is currently configured. The following results are common.

```
$ ls -FC /usr/spool/lp
FIFO          class/        log           oldlog        qstatus
SCHEDLOCK     default       member/       outputq       request/
baudrates     interface/    model/        pstatus       seqfile
$
```

The file **FIFO** is a communication path between the user command **lp** and the **lpsched** demon. **SCHEDLOCK** is a *lock file* that is used by **lpsched** to prevent multiple **lpsched** demons from running simultaneously. When **lpsched** is turned off, neither of these files should be present. Occasionally **lpsched** will not be running, but one or both of these files may be present. If so, **lpsched** cannot be started. Executing **lpsched** when these files are present causes it to return silently, but the demon will not be present in the output from **ps −ef**. If this happens, simply delete these two files and restart **lpsched**. Be careful, though, not to delete these files when **lpsched** is running.

The files **log** and **oldlog** contain records of the jobs that have been printed. When you stop and then restart the **lpsched** demon, **lpsched** moves the file **log** to **oldlog** and then starts a new **log**. The **outputq**, **qstatus**, and **pstatus** files are used in the internal operations of **lpsched**; they are in a binary format that is not too useful for people. The file **seqfile** contains a listing of the current request id number so that **lpsched** can assign a unique job id to each print request, even across system reboots. The file **default** contains the printer id for the printer established as the default device for **lp**. It is sometimes useful to examine these files if your output seems to get lost; perhaps you can pick up a clue as to the source of the problem.

The directory **request** contains subdirectories for each printer established on the machine. The **lp** command will put the text of files that are spooled for printing into one of these directories. After the job is printed, the file will be deleted from this queue.

The **models** directory contains some standard printer *filter* shell scripts that interface between the user-level **lp** command and the physical device that represents the printer. The other directories in **/usr/spool/lp** contain information about the different printers that you have established on the machine. We will discuss the contents of these directories next.

Printer Types

There are basically two types of printers: *serial* and *parallel*. These terms refer to the way that data is transmitted through the cable between the computer and the printer. Serial printers usually attach to the computer through an RS232 port, or possibly a serial modem, while parallel printers can attach to the computer through a unique parallel interface connector, or sometimes with a DB-25 connector like an RS232. You cannot attach a parallel printer to a serial port or vice versa, so it is important to discuss printer cabling with the printer manufacturer or with your hardware vendor. Printer cabling is usually specific to an individual printer, and attaching "unknown" printers to a computer, even if you know whether the printer is serial or parallel, can be difficult and tedious. It is best to purchase the correct cable for the connection when you acquire your printers.

Similarly, most printers include a large number of switches to configure the printer behavior. This area can also be very frustrating, so consult the printer manufacturer or your printer retailer for advice.

Configuring Printers

You can use both serial and parallel printers with the **lp** system without difficulty. Serial printers usually attach to a serial port that could otherwise be used to attach a modem or a terminal, while parallel printers usually attach to a special parallel port on the machine. Table 12-1 lists ports and their associated device files for 80386 UNIX systems. Many small machines are configured with only one parallel port, but if you have more than one, you might see the device files **/dev/lp1** or **/dev/lp2**, depending on how many parallel ports are available. Because you can easily add additional serial ports to most machines, you are likely to configure multiple printer systems with serial printers, using device files **/dev/tty02**, **/dev/tty03**, and so on.

You must know quite a bit about the printer you are attaching to a system because the **lp** system works by passing the output file through a filter program that is usually a shell script. This filter prepares the banner page, configures the I/O port (using **stty**), and writes the data to the correct device file. You must know what type of printer you are adding to the system so that you can use the correct filtering script. Occasionally you may wish to modify an existing script, or even write your own, to handle special printer configurations. Finally, a printer manufacturer will sometimes supply an **lp** filter for their device if it has special needs, but the **lp** system has several *model* scripts that you can use in most cases.

PC Name	Device File	Type
LPT1	/dev/lp	Parallel
	/dev/lp1	
LPT2	/dev/lp2	Parallel
LPT3	/dev/lp3	Parallel
LPT4	/dev/lp4	Parallel
COM1	/dev/tty00	Serial
COM2	/dev/tty01	Serial
COM3	/dev/tty02	Serial
COM4	/dev/tty03	Serial

Table 12-1. Printer Devices for 80386 Systems

Installing a Printer into the lp System

There are several steps involved in adding a new printer. First, you must verify that the printer is correctly attached to the machine and is working as you expect. Second, you must examine the printer script that you intend to use, verifying that it does what you expect. You may need to modify the script to make it fit your requirements; however, this usually involves only changing the baud rate or another **stty** option to match the printer. Third, you must inform the **lp** system that the printer is available. Finally, you must *enable* the printer so that the **lp** software will begin spooling your print jobs to it. We will discuss each of these steps in turn.

Testing Your Printer Configuration

You can usually test your assumptions about the printer hook-up by redirecting some output to the device file to which you think the printer is attached. You can write directly to the device file.

```
$ cat /usr/spool/lp/model/serial > /dev/lp
```

If the output does not appear at all, either the cabling or printer configuration switches are set incorrectly or the printer itself is nonfunctional. If the output appears but is garbled, the printer configuration switches are set incorrectly.

Set the communications speed between the computer and the printer to the highest value that the printer can actually print. For example, many printers designed for PCs can run at 9600 baud, but the printer itself can only print at a speed of less than 1200 baud. In this case you should set the communications speed to 1200 baud because this lower speed is slightly more efficient for the system. In any case the printer should provide flow control to the system so that printer overruns do not occur. You can set very high speed printers, such as some laser printers, to such a high speed that they cause the system response time to slow down, but this is rare. If it does occur, you can usually reduce the printer speed without harm. Set the printer communications speed with the printer switches, and set the speed at the UNIX system side in the printer interface script, discussed next. If there is a speed mismatch, the printer will usually produce some garbled output when you **cat** a file directly to the device.

Printer Interface Models

The directory **/usr/spool/lp/model** contains a number of shell scripts that interface between the **lp** user command and the device file that actually drives the printer. These scripts are responsible for setting the printer device attributes such as data communications rate and flow control. They are also responsible for formatting and printing the banner message that separates the different output jobs, for preparing multiple copies of the output, and so on. Generally, when you add a new printer, you must select one of these models to use with the printer. A typical default set of models in an SVR3 system might be the following:

```
$ ls -FC /usr/spool/lp/model
1640*     dqp10*    f450*     lqp40*    pprx*     serial*
5310*     dumb*     hp*       ph.daps*  prx*
$
```

These are all executable shell scripts. The **lpsched** command causes one of them to be executed with the name of the file that you wish to print as an argument. Each is specialized for a specific printer type, given in the name of the model: **1640** is for the Diablo 1640 printer, **hp** is for the Hewlett-Packard 1631A device, **prx** is for the Printronix P600, and so on. The specific models provided with your system may differ. Most simple dot-matrix or letter-quality printers designed for PCs can use the *dumb* model if they are parallel or the *serial* model if they are serial printers.

These models are shell scripts, and you can read them to

```
$ cat /usr/spool/lp/model/serial
#ident "@(#)serial     1.2"
# lp interface for serial line printer
#
# This script is identical to the "dumb" model, except that it does
# an stty that sets appropriate serial port characteristics:
#
#         8-bits, no parity, 9600 baud
#         XON/XOFF
#         pass tabs through to printer
#
# AND it does a dummy stty at the end of the script to force waiting
# for the output to drain.  This depends upon the fact that stty(1)
# does a TCSETAW ioctl().  If you do not wait for output to drain,
# the line discipline close will resume output even though the printer
# has done an XOFF, overflowing the printer's buffer.
#

stty -parenb -parodd cs8 9600 -hupcl -cstopb cread clocal -loblk \
 ignbrk -brkint ignpar -parmrk -inpck istrip -inlcr -igncr icrnl -iuclc \
 ixon -ixany -ixoff \
 -isig icanon -xcase -echo -echoe -echok -echonl noflsh \
 opost -olcuc onlcr -ocrnl -onocr -onlret -ofill -ofdel tab0 \
 line 0 \
 0<&1

x="XXXXXXXXXXXXXXXXXXXXXXXXXXXXXXXXXXXXXXXXXXXXXXXXXXXXXXXXXXXXXXXXXXXXXXXXXX\
XXXXXXXXXXXXXXXXXXXXXXXXXXXXXXXXXXXXXXXXXX"
echo "\014\c"
echo "$x\n$x\n$x\n$x\n"
banner "$2"
echo "\n"
user=`grep "^$2:" /etc/passwd | line | cut -d: -f5`
if [ -n "$user" ]
then
        echo "User: $user\n"
else
        echo "\n"
fi
echo "Request id: $1     Printer: `basename $0`\n"
date
echo "\n"
if [ -n "$3" ]
then
        banner $3
fi
copies=$4
echo "\014\c"
shift; shift; shift; shift; shift
files="$*"
i=1
while [ $i -le $copies ]
do
        for file in $files
        do
                cat "$file" 2>&1
                echo "\014\c"
        done
        i=`expr $i + 1`
done
```

Figure 12-1.   Serial printer model script

```
echo "$x\n$x\n$x\n$x\n\n\n\n\n\n\n\n\n\n\n\n\n\n\n\n\n\n\n\n\n\n\n\n\n\n\n"
echo "\n\n\n\n\n\n\n\n\n\n\n\n\n\n\n\n\n\n\n\n\n\n\n\n\n\n$x\n$x\n$x\n$x"
echo "$x\n$x\n$x\n$x\n\n\n\n\n\n\n\n\n\n\n\n\n\n\n\n\n\n\n\n\n\n\n\n"
echo "\n\n\n\n\n\n\n\n\n\n\n\n\n\n\n\n\n\n\n\n\n\n\n\n\n\n\n"
echo "$x\n$x\n$x\n$x\n$x\n$x\n$x\n$x\n"

# do a dummy stty to wait for output to drain.
stty erase '^h'

exit 0
```

Figure 12-1.   Serial printer model script (*continued*)

understand how they interface between the **lpsched** demon and the printer hardware. Figure 12-1 gives an example of a common serial model script, which is an executable program that takes a number of command line arguments and produces output on its standard output. For testing, you can execute the script from the terminal if you give the proper arguments, and you can watch the output or redirect it to a file. In operation the **lpsched** program will execute the script with its output redirected to the appropriate device file.

You can execute the script directly from your login shell.

```
$ serial 1234 steve "Banner Here" 1 /etc/passwd
```

The command line arguments are the request id (**1234**), the user id of the request originator (**steve**), the banner that will appear on the first page of the output (**Banner Here**), the number of copies you wish to print (**1**), and the list of files to print. The banner is included in quotes because it is a single argument, though it may contain white space. If you wish to skip the banner, you still must provide a null string for that argument position.

```
$ serial 1234 steve "" 1 /etc/passwd
```

The model scripts do not print their standard input because **lpsched** creates a temporary file for the output in case the printer is busy; the file may wait for a long time before it is actually printed. You can redirect the output to the print device for further testing.

```
$ serial 1234 steve "" 1 /etc/passwd >/dev/tty02
```

Of course the device file will differ if you have a parallel printer or if you have attached the printer to a different I/O port.

The script in Figure 12-1 shows most of the features of **lp** models. After the beginning comments, the first part of the script sets the I/O port parameters with the **stty** command. This particular **stty** sets the device for 9600 baud data transmission, 8-bit characters, and XON/XOFF flow control, among many other options. Consult the **stty(1)** page in the *User's Manual* for more details. Most of these options are simply the normally established defaults and needn't be included in the model. However, the speed, character size, and flow control options will differ depending on the printer type and on its internal switch settings.

The last part of the **stty** line, "0<&1", is included because the **stty** command will not directly write to a device when it is in a shell script. You can fool **stty** by telling the shell to read from the device, by redirecting **stdout** to **stdin**. This trick is generally useful only with the **stty** command and rarely appears outside of **lp** interface scripts. Anyway, the result is that the I/O port is set according to the options that you give the **stty** command. You can often get a nonfunctional printer to begin working if you change the options for the **stty** command here.

The next few lines format the banner page. Shell variable *$2* is the user id, *$3* is the banner that you passed in from the command line, and *$4* is the number of copies to print. The actual printing of the output is done in the **while**

...**do**...**done** loop, once through the loop for each copy. This script is simply a fancy way to **cat** a file. Finally, the script prints a trailing page with the last few **echo** commands and then waits for the last of the file to be printed before the script exits. Flow control was established in the initial **stty** command, so there is probably a short backlog of characters to be printed when the last **cat** command completes. The reason for this is discussed briefly in the comments at the beginning of the model script.

When you attach a new printer to a UNIX system, you usually must go through these tests to assure that the model script and the configuration are correct before you inform the **lp** software that the printer is present. If you need to create a new model script or modify an existing script, copy it into a new file in a directory different from the models and edit the copy. You must keep new model scripts in a different directory than **/usr/spool/lp/model** because the **lp** administrative tools have a glitch that requires you to distinguish between standard models and your own scripts. When you create a new interface script, make sure that it has executable permissions. Set the permissions of new scripts to be the same as those for the other models that came with the system software.

Configuring the lp Software

Use the command **/usr/lib/lpadmin** to set up and change the printer configuration. With this command you can add printers, define the printer type to the **lp** system, assign printers to classes, and logically enable or disable the printers. You can use it after making sure that the printer is correctly configured and that the model script is also correct. Administration of the **lp** software is reserved for the superuser.

You must be sure that the **lpsched** program is not running when you use **lpadmin**. First turn off **lpadmin** with the following command:

```
# /usr/lib/lpshut
```

Then you can administer your printers.

The **lpadmin** program is a sophisticated program that can take many options. Its major function is to take a printer *destination*—a name that refers to a printer or a class of printers—and pair that name with a model and a device file. You can name a printer anything you wish, but because this is the public name used in your commands, you should give it a name that bears some relationship to the printer type. In these examples the new printer will be called MYPRINT; there is already a printer in the system called ATT470. You can refer to a printer with **lpadmin** following the **−p** (for printer) option.

```
# /usr/lib/lpadmin −p MYPRINT ....
```

Other options for **lpadmin** give instructions on how to administer that printer.

In adding a new printer, **lpadmin** takes options that define the model script and the device, in addition to the printer name.

```
# /usr/lib/lpadmin −p MYPRINT −m dumb −v /dev/lp
```

The **−m** (for model) option takes the name of the model script, and the **−v** option takes the full pathname of the device file that you wish to use. This command will add a printer named MYPRINT to the system. Unfortunately, the **−m** option works only with predefined models that are delivered with the system. If you change a model for a new printer type, you must use the **−i** (for interface) option instead, giving it the full pathname of your edited interface script.

```
# /usr/lib/lpadmin −pMYPRINT −i/usr/steve/lpscript −v/dev/tty02
```

This is the simplest way to add a printer: simply give it a name and then specify an interface and a device.

If you are adding the first printer to the machine, you probably will want to make it the *system default* destination so that you can use the **lp** command with no printer as argument. If you have more than one printer, you want only one default printer. The lowest-quality printer is usually the default, but this is specific to a system. You can inform the **lp** system that a printer is to be the system default when you install it. Use the **lpadmin −d** (for default) option with the printer name after you have installed the printer as just described.

```
# /usr/lib/lpadmin -dMYPRINT
```

This makes MYPRINT the default destination. If you do not select a default destination, you will have to explicitly name a printer for your output each time you use the **lp** command.

You can execute **lpstat** to verify that the printer was added to the system.

```
$ lpstat -t
scheduler is not running
system default destination: MYPRINT
members of class Parallel:
        ATT470
device for ATT470: /dev/lp
device for MYPRINT: /dev/tty02
ATT470 accepting requests since Aug 19 18:58
Parallel accepting requests since Aug 19 18:58
MYPRINT not accepting requests since Apr 30 19:00 -
        new destination
printer ATT470 is idle.  enabled since Apr 30 17:56
printer MYPRINT disabled since Apr 30 19:00 -
        new printer
$
```

The printer was added, and several other items appear in the output. First, the printer is not accepting requests, and it is disabled. If the output does not look something like this after you add a printer, the command has failed and you should try again.

While **lpsched** is off, you can remove a printer from the system with the **−x** (for exterminate) option:

```
# lpadmin -x MYPRINT
```

Accepting Print Requests

When you add a new printer, it is installed but not activated. There are two more features of the **lp** system of interest here. You can configure a printer to *accept* or *reject* requests for printing without removing it from the system. The visible result is that the **lp** command will refuse to spool a job when the device is not accepting print requests. Use the command **/usr/lib/accept** to allow a printer destination to accept requests.

```
# /usr/lib/accept MYPRINT
destination "MYPRINT" now accepting requests
# lpstat -t
scheduler is not running
system default destination: ATT470
members of class Parallel:
        ATT470
device for ATT470: /dev/lp
device for MYPRINT: /dev/tty02
ATT470 accepting requests since Aug 19 18:58
Parallel accepting requests since Aug 19 18:58
MYPRINT accepting requests since May  1 18:33
printer ATT470 is idle.  enabled since Apr 30 17:56
printer MYPRINT disabled since Apr 30 19:00 -
        new printer
#
```

MYPRINT will now accept requests for printing.

You can use **/usr/lib/reject** to tell a printer to reject requests. You normally use this command when a printer is out of service for a relatively long time but you don't want to permanently eliminate it from the system with **lpstat −x**. The **/usr/lib/reject** command takes a printer destination as argument and, optionally, a reason for disabling it, following the **−r** (for reason) option.

```
# /usr/lib/reject -r"Down until Fri. for Repairs" MYPRINT
destination "MYPRINT" is no longer accepting requests
#
```

The reason will be displayed in the **lpstat −t** output and will also appear if a user tries to spool to the device with the **lp** command.

Enabling the Printer

A printer that is accepting requests may still not be completely functional. The jobs are just placed on the spool for that printer. You can see from the **lpstat** −**t** output that the printer is still *disabled*. You must *enable* it before it can actually print your jobs. Unlike the accept/reject condition, the **lp** software will automatically disable a printer if it tries to print to it unsuccessfully. If a printer runs out of paper or if power to the printer is turned off, the device will be automatically disabled. You can enable the printer with the **enable** command.

```
# enable MYPRINT
# lpstat -t
scheduler is not running
system default destination: ATT470
members of class Parallel:
        ATT470
device for ATT470: /dev/lp
device for MYPRINT: /dev/tty02
ATT470 accepting requests since Aug 19 18:58
Parallel accepting requests since Aug 19 18:58
MYPRINT accepting requests since May  1 18:35
printer ATT470 is idle.  enabled since Apr 30 17:56
printer MYPRINT is idle.  enabled since May  1 18:45
#
```

The printer is now fully functional.

The **lp** command will automatically disable a printer when it thinks that the printer is malfunctioning, but you must enable it manually when you have fixed the problem. A printer may seem to be incorrectly configured, when it is only disabled. Check the output from **lpstat** −**t** to assess the state of a printer that is not working.

You can disable a printer manually with the **disable** command.

```
# disable MYPRINT
```

The **disable** command can take two optional arguments. Use −**c** (for cancel) to cancel any jobs that are currently printing before the device is disabled. Use −**r** (for reason) to give a reason for disabling the device.

```
# disable -c -r"Out of Paper" MYPRINT
```

Usually **disable** is used to temporarily stop output to a printer while you add paper or turn off the power. Because **lp** is still accepting requests for that printer, you must get the printer back online relatively quickly or the spool of jobs may get large.

Moving Jobs from One Printer to Another

When a printer malfunctions or a spool to a single device gets too large, you may wish to distribute the jobs among several printers. The **/usr/lib/lpmove** command gives you this ability; it takes as arguments a list of request id's followed by a destination id. The requests are moved to the new destination.

```
# /usr/lib/lpmove ATT470-87 ATT470-88 MYPRINT
```

This command will move requests ATT470-87 and ATT470-88 to MYPRINT. You must be sure that **lpsched** is not running before you move jobs between devices. A second form of the **/usr/lib/lpmove** command moves all the jobs on one device to another printer.

```
# /usr/lib/lpmove ATT470 MYPRINT
```

This will put all the jobs queued to ATT470 on the spool for MYPRINT.

After you finish administering the **lp** subsystem, remember to turn the scheduler back on with the following command:

```
# /usr/lib/lpsched
#
```

You cannot use these **lp** administration commands while the scheduler is running.

Going Further

The material you have learned so far is sufficient for administering printers on smaller systems. However, a UNIX machine can also make an excellent *print server*, which can be dedicated to controlling many printers of different types. Such a print server can be attached to a local area network (LAN) to efficiently serve a large organization. This approach to printing can substantially reduce the costs associated with hard-copy output because many users can share the highest quality (and most expensive) devices. The **lp** tools, in combination with the communications commands, can readily provide software support for networked print servers.

Printer Classes

We have not yet discussed one feature of the **lp** system: a printer can be assigned to a *printer class*—a group of printers that share a single spool queue. That is, when a printer becomes idle, its next job comes off the shared queue. When another printer in the class becomes idle, it will take the next job off the same queue. The **lp** software manages the queue correctly, passing jobs one by one to individual printers as they become idle.

In practice printers of the same or similar type are assigned to one class and printers of a different type make up another. For example, several laser printers may all be in one class, while dot-matrix printers are in another. If you don't really care which device produces the output, you can usually put the devices in the same class.

You can refer to an entire printer class with a single destination id. With the printer configuration as in the previous examples, this command

```
$ lp -d ATT470 /usr/spool/lp/model/serial
```

will produce the same results as

```
$ lp -d Parallel /usr/spool/lp/model/serial
```

because the printer ATT470 belongs to the class **parallel**. Printer classes are displayed in the output from **lpstat −t**. Wherever you use a printer destination in the **lp** system commands, you can use a printer class instead.

Use the **−c** (for class) option with **lpadmin** to assign a device to a printer class.

```
# /usr/lib/lpshut
scheduler stopped
# /usr/lib/lpadmin -pMYPRINT -cdraft -i/usr/steve/lpscript -v/dev/tty02
# /usr/lib/accept MYPRINT
destination "MYPRINT" now accepting requests
# enable MYPRINT
printer "MYPRINT" now accepting requests
#
```

This example will assign MYPRINT to class **draft**. You must use the **−c** option when you initially install the printer with **lpadmin**. To change the class of an existing printer, completely remove it from the system with **lpstat −x** and reinstall it with the new class. The class name you assign can be either an existing printer class or a new class. If it is a new class name, **lp** will create a new class consisting of only that device.

After the command in the previous example has been executed, the **lpstat** −t results have changed:

```
# lpstat -t
scheduler is not running
system default destination: ATT470
members of class Parallel:
        ATT470
members of class draft:
        MYPRINT
device for ATT470: /dev/lp
device for MYPRINT: /dev/tty02
ATT470 accepting requests since Aug 19 18:58
Parallel accepting requests since Aug 19 18:58
MYPRINT accepting requests since May  2 11:03
draft not accepting requests since May  2 11:03 -
        new destination
printer ATT470 is idle.  enabled since Apr 30 17:56
printer MYPRINT is idle.  enabled since May  2 11:03
#
```

A new class has been established, of which the printer MYPRINT is a member. Previously, **/usr/lib/accept** was used to allow MYPRINT to accept requests for printing, but the new class, **draft**, is still rejecting requests. With the current configuration, you could spool jobs to MYPRINT but not directly to the class **draft**. You must also use **accept** for the class name if you wish it to be a destination.

```
# /usr/lib/accept draft
destination "draft" now accepting requests
#
```

Finally, you must turn the scheduler back on with **/usr/lib/lpsched** to restore everything to full operation.

Server Machines

A UNIX system with the **lp** software makes an excellent print server. Because printer support is a relatively low user of CPU resources, a single machine can easily support many printers. Machines configured primarily as print servers can usually also support some other activities simultaneously, such as user logins or data communications. You should test a specific configuration to see how much load printers put on the system; generally, three or four active printers will use about as much CPU resources as a normal user. This estimate will vary considerably, however, if the server is configured to do most of the processing of a print job, such as formatting output via **troff** or doing mailmerge operations on the file before printing.

One issue that you must carefully consider when configuring a print server is the disk space used. Queued files take space on the machine's disk, and you should weigh the rate of new jobs coming into the queue(s) against the maximum print speed of the attached devices. Naturally, you will need as many printers as are required by the print requests from the users. If a printer fails, the queue can grow quickly. There is seldom any intrinsic control over disk usage for spooled jobs, so a disk can fill without the knowledge of a system administrator. You must be vigilant when working with print servers, careful that the printers are always enabled and that the spool of waiting jobs does not overflow the available disk resources.

Remote Access to Printing via uucp

When you wish to spool jobs to a printer on another machine, you can easily create a new shell script to replace the **lp** command on the sending machines. Rather than overwriting the **lp** command, you will usually create a new name for your new tool, maybe **rlp** (for remote **lp**).

The key element of the new command will be the communication of the file from the local machine to the remote machine for printing. Several different methods are possible, but most systems support the **uucp** communications package (discussed in detail in Chapter 14). You can write a simple command with **uux** to invoke **lp** remotely. For example:

```
$ cat /usr/spool/lp/model/serial | uux - "lpserve!lp -t$LOGNAME -s"
```

This command will **cat** the file to the **lp** command on the remote machine **lpserve**, suppress the request id with the −**s** option, and place your login id on the banner that **lp** produces. You must administer the **uucp** system on your machine so that it can send files to the server, and you must also administer the server so that it allows **uux** jobs to be executed there.

In a real remote printer script there will usually be additional error checking of the input file, perhaps the ability to pass a destination id from the local **rlp** command line into the **uux** command and the remote **lp** command, and possibly the inclusion of the local machine **uname** on the banner line. You might also allow the local script to accept filenames for printing as well as (or instead of) the standard input and send electronic mail back to the user when the print job is complete.

Printer Drivers

The device file associated with a parallel printer is usually **/dev/lp**. The device driver that processes the data written to this file often adds additional page ejects and sometimes even banners to the output. Even if you **cat** a file directly to the device file, you may see extra material in the output. A second device file, **/dev/rlp** (for raw **lp** device), which does not process the output, is often present. If you want to change the output produced by **/dev/lp**, you can usually edit your interface script and assign the output to **/dev/rlp** rather than to **/dev/lp**. You may need to experiment because the behavior of **/dev/lp** and **/dev/rlp** often differs between systems. Notice also that both **/dev/lp** and **/dev/rlp** refer to the same physical I/O port on the machine, so you cannot use both of them at once without corrupting the output. Serial printers that usually use a tty port such as **/dev/tty02** do not have a raw device associated with them, so all manipulation of the output must be done in the interface script.

When you attach a high-performance print device to your machine, it may include an interface board with its own plug and cable for attaching a printer. Some laser printers or plotters and other graphics devices may require a plug-in board. These devices will use neither the parallel nor the serial model that we have discussed; nor will they use /**dev/lp** or /**dev/tty??** device files. A device driver associated with this special hardware will be supplied by the board manufacturer, along with instructions for installing the hardware and software. If it is intended for the **lp** subsystem, a model interface script is usually included, and a new device file is created in the /**dev** directory. By using the special interface script and the new device file, you can easily install the device into the **lp** system with **lpadmin**. You may need to create or modify the interface script, but there will not be any major conceptual differences from normal printers. You can readily attach nearly all types of hard-copy devices to a UNIX machine with the **lp** tools.

The Print Screen Function

Unfortunately, most versions of the UNIX system do not include a facility for dumping the contents of the console or terminal screen directly to the printer. Usually you will need to redirect the standard output of a command to a file, and then print that file. Consult the documentation for your specific release of the UNIX system to see if a print screen function is included.

Communications I

The news Command
The Message of the Day
The write Command
The mail Command Revisited
Terminal Emulation with the cu Command
Going Further

Some of the richest commands in the UNIX system involve *communications* between users who share a machine or who reside on different machines. It is generally agreed that the UNIX system provides some of the most robust and error-free tools for data communications of any popular operating system. Reliable, secure, and error-free communications across inherently noisy and unreliable communication channels such as telephone lines create definite complexities and potential problems. The UNIX system has tools that allow you to enter this complex topic at any level from the simple **mail** command to the sophisticated administration of queuing and security that arise in the **uucp** subsystem.

The communications tools in the UNIX system have a reputation for complex and arcane features, which, in a sense, is deserved. However, compared to communications software offered by most other computer operating environments, the UNIX tools are a model of clarity and trouble-free operation. Indeed, many other applications have borrowed liberally from the rich set of communications tools in the UNIX system, though with less success. Over the years the tools have been steadily improved in reliability, in features available to users, and in security. Today, many designers with communications-related problems will choose the UNIX system to solve them. This is especially true as local area networks grow in popularity, making communications even more important than ever.

In this chapter we will discuss the basic communications tools, primarily oriented toward ASCII files and messages, and also discuss terminal emulation. We will discuss the administrative issues associated with communications and the **uucp** file transfer subsystem in Chapter 14. As appropriate, we will look at some of the new features related to communications that were introduced in SVR3.

The news Command

We have previously introduced the most basic communications tools. First is the **news** command, which allows a user to read messages published by the system administrator. You can execute **news** to display all news items created since the last time you executed the command, but not old news items that you have already seen.

```
$ news

meeting (pat) Mon Jun 22 08:26:47 1987

    9:00 AM on Monday is the marketing review.  Expect everyone
    to be there with their comments on the proposal.   thanks!  -pat
$
```

After the messages have been displayed once, they will not be redisplayed if you execute **news** again.

```
$ news
No news.
$
```

Though news items are usually short, you can break out of a news item if you wish. Press the DEL key and **news** will stop display of the current news item and begin display of the next item, if any. A second DEL within 1 second after the first causes **news** to exit, returning you to the shell.

The **news** command includes several options to change this default behavior. The −**n** (for names) option causes **news** to list only the names of news items that have not yet been displayed.

```
$ news -n
news: meeting lunch welcome
$
```

The −**s** (for show) option provides a count of unread news items, without listing their names.

```
$ news -s
3 news items.
$
```

Both of these options are often used in the .**profile** so that a display of unread news is given each time you log into the machine.

The −**a** (for all) option causes **news** to display all the available news items, whether or not they have been read previously. This option can produce a lot of output on a large installation. You can display either old or unread news items with −**a**.

Any other options to the **news** command are assumed to be the names of specific items that **news** is to display.

```
$ news lunch

lunch (jim) Mon Jun 22 08:25:31 1987

   Don't forget, today is the big luncheon and party
   See you there...                              =jim

$
```

The **news** command works by maintaining a zero-length file named **.news—time** in the HOME directory. The modification time (displayed by **ls —l**) of **.news—time** is set to the time that the news command is executed. When **news** is run again, only files newer than this file are displayed, except when the **—a** option is used. If **.news—time** does not exist, it is created when **news** executes.

News items available to the **news** command are kept in the directory **/usr/news**. Each news item is a separate file in this directory, and the filename is the name of the news item.

```
$ ls -l /usr/news
total 3
-rw-r--r--    1 jim      other          74 Jun 22 08:25 lunch
-rw-r--r--    1 steve    other         125 Jun 22 08:26 meeting
-rw-r--r--    1 pat      other          32 Jun 22 08:24 welcome
$
```

The system administrator usually maintains this directory, deleting out-of-date news items. In this case the news directory may only be writable by the superuser, but it should be readable and executable by all users. On some systems, however, the **/usr/news** directory is publicly writable, so any user can create a news item by leaving a **news** file in the directory. In any case files created in the directory should be publicly readable, or the **news** command will fail.

The Message of the Day

Another facility with a similar function to **news** is the *message of the day*. No command exists for this, but most systems include the facility. The message of the day is generally used for higher-priority messages than news, such as expected downtime or last-minute system changes. In practice the system **/etc/profile** includes the line

```
cat /etc/motd
```

(for message of the day). Because the system profile is executed whenever a user logs into the machine, the contents of the file are displayed. Unlike **news**, the **motd** is displayed each time a user logs in, so out-of-date messages in this file tend to get tedious very quickly when users login repeatedly. The **motd** file should be readable by all but maintained (and thus writable) only by the superuser.

```
$ ls -l /etc/motd
-rw-r--r--  1 root     sys          1 Jun  6  1987 /etc/motd
$
```

The write Command

The **write** command provides direct communications between two users by sending messages directly to their terminal devices. It is similar to

```
$ echo message > /dev/other-tty
```

where **other-tty** is the name of the device that the user you wish to communicate with is using. These messages will interrupt any display on the terminal of the recipient.

The **write** command is a little more sophisticated than shown in the previous example, and it provides several additional services. First, **write** takes the login id of the recipient as an argument, so you can write to another user without knowing the tty device he or she is using.

```
$ write jim < message
$
```

The **write** command will determine the user's **tty** device and send the message there. When the message has been written, **write** will exit back to the shell. The **write** command will return an error message if the specified user is not logged in.

```
$ write pat
pat is not logged in.
$
```

Users can disable this kind of direct communications to their terminal by setting

```
$ mesg n
$
```

(for no messages). You can turn messages on again with

```
$ mesg y
$
```

(for messages yes). The **mesg** command works by changing the permissions on the device file associated with a terminal. If a user has set messages off, **write** will return a different error message.

```
$ write jim
Permission denied.
$
```

Access to **write** is often disabled when high-quality output is directed to the terminal, such as in some printing tasks.

Using write Interactively

Because **write** reads its standard input for the message to send, it can be used in a more direct mode. If the command is simply

```
$ write pat
```

with no redirection of input, **write** will make the connection to the recipient and then return two beeps to signal that the connection is open. Then you can type your message directly at the keyboard, and **write** will send it line by line to the recipient.

Once a connection is established with **write**, it is held

open until you break it with CTRL-D, the end-of-file operator. Until then, everything typed at your terminal will appear at the recipient's terminal. However, it is a one-way communications channel; the recipient cannot send messages back. Instead, the recipient must also use the **write** command with your login id as argument. Then two **write** paths will be open, one from your terminal to the recipient, and the other from the recipient back to you. Each connection must be broken individually by its creator before things return to normal.

When someone uses **write** to call you, a banner is displayed on your terminal; then the caller's message is displayed line by line.

```
Message from pat on my_sys (console) [ Mon Jun 22 08:29:58 ] ...
hi steve, how are you today?
```

You must **write** back to pat to answer the message. There is often a noticeable delay between each line of the received messages, both because the other user must type in the line and because the system must handle the line before it is sent to you. In a heavily loaded machine, communication with **write** can be relatively slow. Additionally, communication can become confused because both users can send messages at once, so you might try to answer a comment before the other user has finished.

Consequently, generations of users have evolved a simple protocol for using **write**, which usually works like this: the original sender creates a connection to the recipient and perhaps includes a one-line greeting. Then the recipient "writes" back, signaling a readiness to communicate. Then the first user sends a multiline message, ending with **o** (for over) to signal that the message is complete. Then the recipient will answer, using as many lines as needed and adding the **o** to signal the end. Then the original caller has another chance, and so on. One person will end the conversation with **o-o** or **oo** (for over and out). The other person can continue until also entering **o-o**. Both users might then enter CTRL-D to exit from **write** back to the shell. Remember, both sides must break out of **write** with CTRL-D to break their part of the two-way connection. This CB-like protocol is not enforced by the **write** program; it is only a convention that most users follow. Thus it is possible to become quite confused during two-way writes, and most users prefer **mail** over **write** for most communications. Nevertheless, **write** is a fun command that has a definite place in interuser communications.

The wall Command

The **write** command allows communications with only a single user named as its command line argument. Occasionally you need to write a message to *all* the users logged into the machine. For example, system shutdowns should be announced to warn all users to secure their session before the system goes down. For such situations, the UNIX system provides the **wall** (for write all) command, located in **/etc/wall**. The command is usually executable by all users but is routinely used only by the system administrator.

Like **write**, **/etc/wall** reads its standard input for the message to send.

```
# /etc/wall < message.file
```

It then sends the message to all users currently logged in,

including the originator. The same header produced by
write precedes the message, and the recipient can refuse the
message with the **mesg n** command. There is no facility for
wall recipients to write back to you.

The mail Command Revisited

The most widely used tool for interuser communication is the
electronic mail facility, which we discussed briefly in Chapter 2. The **mail** command is used by nearly all users, and
several electronic mail programs are available with different
features and functions, from very simple programs to extremely feature-rich and complex ones. Because the UNIX
system is so good at communications, electronic mail has
always been a most fertile area of development, and different
versions of the UNIX system provide mail tools that sometimes differ in subtle ways.

Most mail programs can only accept text messages; that
is, only normal ASCII files that are acceptable to the standard editors. Executable programs, binary files from advanced word processors, and nontext data cannot usually be
sent with normal mail tools. Though some advanced *mailers*
allow attaching binary files to messages, many mail-reading
programs and tools for mailing messages between different
machines will not accept nontext messages. The UNIX system provides other tools for transferring nontext files, and
mail should be reserved for sending text messages. However,
the mail messages can be of any length, so you can transfer
long text files, documents, or **shar** archives by mail if you
wish.

In practice, all mail programs will process the *incoming
mail* and store it in a special *mailbox* owned by the recipient.

It remains there until the recipient reads the message and deletes it from the mailbox. In most systems incoming mail is stored in the directory **/usr/mail**, with one file per user. This mail file is generally called your *mailbox*, but you can create additional mailboxes as you read and save mail into them. The mail tools will concatenate multiple messages sent to a user into this single file but will display the individual messages separately when the mail is read.

The basic electronic mail command is called simply **mail**. Use it both to send electronic mail to other users and to retrieve mail sent to you. The **mail** command takes a list of user id's as command line arguments and then reads its standard input for the message. When you give multiple users as command line arguments, the same message is sent to all the named users.

```
$ mail jim pat < message.file
$
```

In addition, **mail** will accept its standard input from the terminal if redirection is not used. In that case the CTRL-D end-of-file character is used to end the message.

```
$ mail jim pat
here is a short test message.
see you at lunch....  =steve
CTRL-d
$
```

Older mail programs may also allow you to end the message by entering . (dot) on a line by itself, but this no longer works on SVR3 mail. It was removed to prevent **mail** from ending when a legitimate . was present on a line in the middle of the message.

Reading Your Mail

When new mail is delivered to your incoming mailbox, the shell will display an announcement to the terminal.

```
You have mail.
```

This message can appear just after a command exits but before the shell displays the PS1 prompt. You can ignore it, but it will not be redisplayed unless more new mail arrives.

When you execute **mail** with no arguments, your mailbox will open and display the first message.

```
$ mail
From jim Mon Jun 22 08:37 EDT 1987

don't forget to return my book....  thanks.    -jim

?
```

After a message is displayed, **mail** pauses and prompts with "?" for a command. It expects you to skip over the message, save it, delete it, or take some other action. You can see the complete list of possible actions by entering **?** (for help) at the prompt. (The full set of options is shown in Figure 2-1.) Respond with **d** (for delete) to delete the message, **+** (for next) to skip over the message without removing it, **q** (for quit) to exit from the **mail** program, or **s** (for save) to remove the message from the mailbox and save it in a file. There are many other options. If the response is to move to a new message, then that message will be displayed, and **mail** will pause and again prompt you with "?". When there are no more messages, **mail** will exit back to the shell.

The **s** operator can take a filename as argument, which is the name of a file to be used for the message. If you enter **s** with no argument, the default file will be **mbox**, in the

HOME directory. When you save mail into an existing file, it is appended so that several mail messages can reside in a **save** file.

The mail command can take the **−f** (for file) argument, with a filename, to specify another mailbox rather than the system's in-box, allowing you to reread mail that was saved in different files. This command

```
$ mail -f mbox
```

will open the file **mbox** rather than the incoming mailbox. If the named file is a proper mailbox, as created by the "s" option from reading your mail, then all the normal functions of the **mail** program will work as expected on the named file.

mail Message Structure

The first lines of each message are called the *postmark*. On messages sent from users on the same machine as the recipient, the postmark will contain only one line; however, if the message was forwarded from another user or from another machine, then the postmark will contain one line for each step that the message took on its way to delivery in your incoming mailbox. The postmark was not created by the sending user; it was added by the **mail** delivery software. The postmark can be valuable, as you will see shortly.

Other material appearing before the actual message is usually called the *message headers*. The headers will usually be of the form

```
name: value
```

where "name" is the name of a specific header, and "value" is the specific contents associated with that name keyword. Many **mail** programs may produce voluminous headers, including **To:**, **From:**, **Date:**, and up to 20 or 30 other lines. These are usually added by the **mail** program before the message is sent.

The standard SVR3 **mail** program can produce one optional header, the **To:** line, though this is not added by default. The −t command line option will add this **To:** header if it is given when the message is created.

```
$ mail -t steve jim
```

In addition to the postmark, this message will include a **To:** line naming the intended recipients. The **To:** line can be helpful if the message is sent to more than one recipient and you wish each to know who else received it.

Displaying a Summary of Mailbox Contents

Each **mail** message received will include some postmarks and headers. You can instruct the **mail** program to display these headers in a formatted list, allowing a user to peruse the mailbox contents without reading through each message. Then you can pick a specific message for reading, deletion, or other action. The −**h** (for headers) option for reading mail will display this header summary when **mail** begins.

```
$ mail -h
```

Alternatively, the **h** option is available from the "?" prompt within **mail**.

```
? h
2 letters found in steve, 0 scheduled for deletion, 0 newly arrived
>   2    250      pat        Tue Jun 23 14:37 EDT 1987
    1    556      jim        Mon Jun 22 08:37 EDT 1987
?
```

The messages are listed in inverse order, with the most recent message at the top of the list. The current message is marked with > in the left-hand column, and many of the available commands, such as **s** and **d**, operate on the current message by default.

Each message has a number, in the left column after the >, and you can use this number to refer to the message. If you give the message number following the "?" prompt, that message will be displayed. This command

```
? 2
```

will display message number 2. You can also give the message number after some other commands. For example, to delete message number 1, enter

```
? d 1
```

regardless of which is the current message. The sender is listed next and, finally, the time stamp from the message postmark. This information is usually helpful if a lot of mail is received.

Deleted messages are not truly eliminated from the mailbox until the **mail** program ends. In fact the message is only *marked* for deletion but is no longer displayed in the header list. You can read deleted messages until you exit from the **mail** program, when they are physically removed from the mailbox and discarded. The **h a** (for headers of all messages) command will display both deleted and current messages.

```
? h a
2 letters found in steve, 1 scheduled for deletion, 0 newly arrived
      2    250      pat          Tue Jun 23 14:37 EDT 1987
>     1  d 556      jim          Mon Jun 22 08:37 EDT 1987
?
```

Message number 1 has been marked for deletion, as the presence of the "d" signifies. It can be undeleted before you exit **mail** with

```
? u 1
```

(for undelete). The named message will be undeleted; however, if no message number is specified, the current message will be undeleted.

Replying to a Mail Message

When you receive a message, you often wish to answer it. The **mail** command provides an option after the "?" prompt to allow this. Use the **r** (for reply) command, which deduces the name and mailing address of the person who sent the message and then spawns a new **mail** program to accept your reply. When the reply operation has completed, the sending **mail** program will exit, returning you to the mail-reading program. However, the reply operation can be tricky and must be treated with care, especially if the message was sent from a remote machine. The process of interpreting the postmark is sometimes very difficult, and the reply option does not always work as expected. You may need to address the message manually, discussed next.

Addressing Mail to Other Users

In the previous examples, the *addressee* for the message was a login id on the same machine.

```
$ mail jim pat
```

Here, jim and pat must be login id's for users on your machine. However, the mail facility also allows you to send messages to users on other UNIX machines. This is usually called *remote mail* because the addressee is a user on a machine remote from yours. In fact you can send mail to a user on another machine *through* a third machine. This *multihop mail* is very common, especially in environments with local area networks. Several international networks of UNIX system users actually communicate worldwide with these multihop mail features.

Address mail to remote users on the **mail** command line by entering the unique name of their machine and then their unique user id on that machine. The ! (bang) character separates the two items, with no white space allowed.

```
$ mail other!user
```

You can also specify multiple recipients in this way.

```
$ mail other!user remote!friend
```

In this example, "other" and "remote" are the names of machines, and "user" and "friend" are the user id's of the people to whom you might send mail.

In fact more than one other machine can be in the path that the mail will take to reach the recipient.

```
$ mail other!remote!user
```

Here the message will first be sent to the machine "other"; the mail software there will receive it and forward it to the machine named "remote," where it will be delivered to the "user." Up to 20 hops are allowed with this kind of addressing.

The remote mail tools rest on the **uucp** data communications subsystem, which we will discuss in Chapter 14. However, note here that you cannot send mail to a remote machine unless it is known to your **uucp** system, though you may be able to receive mail from it. Thus, when remote or multihop mail fails to be sent from your system, the likely culprit is the **uucp** list of known remote machines. These comments are especially significant with multihop mail, because each intervening machine must know about the *next* machine in the path created when the message is addressed. You must be certain that the path is valid before sending the message, or it will not be delivered as expected. In fact an intermediate machine may discard a message without returning an error to the original sender if the next machine in the path is unknown to it.

Forwarding Mail

You can specify that mail addressed to you be *forwarded* to another addressee. In SVR3 systems the **mail** command can take a command line option to specify a forwarding address. To use this −**F** (for forward) option, delete or save all the mail in your incoming mailbox. An empty mailbox is required for mail forwarding.

The command

```
$ mail -F new.address
```

will establish forwarding to the **new.address** specified. All the rules given above for message addressing also apply to the new address. For example, both a local addressee

```
$ mail -F jim
```

and a remote address

```
$ mail -F other!steve
```

are allowed.

The first form is often used when you use more than one login id on a machine or when someone else is covering your incoming mail. The remote form is usually used when you have login id's on more than one machine, and one is preferred. Most users forward mail from the less used login id to the more often used id or machine.

Once established, forwarding will stay in force indefinitely, and all incoming mail will be *bounced* to the forwarding address. To remove forwarding, give a null argument with the **−F** argument.

```
$ mail -F ""
```

The empty quotation marks instruct the shell to reserve an empty command line argument after the **−F**. This turns off forwarding, and incoming mail will again be deposited in your incoming mailbox.

When mail is forwarded, attempts to read your mail will

fail, so that you can test whether or not mail is forwarded.

```
$ mail -F jim
Forwarding to jim
$ mail
Your mail is being forwarded to jim
$
```

In releases before SVR3 the **mail −F** command is not present, so you must use a different mechanism to establish forwarding. First, delete or save all your mail. Then send a dummy mail message to yourself. Next, edit the file **/usr/mail/login** with your favorite editor, where "login" is your user id. Once in the editor, delete the entire contents of the file and then add the line

```
Forward to address
```

at the beginning of the file. The capital *F* at the beginning is required, and "address" is the forwarding address just discussed. Finally, write the file and quit from the editor. Forwarding will be enabled until you edit the file again and remove the "Forward to..." line. Do not create the file manually; let **mail** do it by sending a message to yourself. This will ensure that the incoming mailbox has the correct ownership and permissions, so the **mail** program will treat it correctly.

The rmail Command

There is an additional executable program associated with the mail facility, but you should never execute it directly. The **rmail** (for remote mail) command is used internally in the operation of the mail facility for sending mail. It must be present in the **/bin** directory, or the mail system will not work correctly.

Terminal Emulation with the cu Command

The UNIX system provides a standard *terminal emulation* program called **cu** (for call up). Though it is often called "call UNIX" by users, its use is not limited to connecting to another UNIX system. The **cu** command allows you to connect to nearly any other machine that provides asynchronous ASCII communications, including remote access to MS-DOS machines, bulletin board systems, and most *protocol converters* that convert from IBM 3270-type terminals to asynchronous ASCII form. Of course some additional functions are available with **cu** if the remote machine is also running the UNIX system.

The **cu** command is actually a part of the **uucp** data transfer system, and it uses the **uucp** control files and any external or built-in modem attached to the machine. An autodialing modem is usually required if terminal emulation functions are necessary. In a small machine, however, you may be able to manually dial a telephone attached to an external modem if the **cu** program is executed first and then the call is dialed.

The **cu** command is executed with a machine name as argument.

```
$ cu remote
```

The **cu** command consults the **uucp** control files to determine how to set up a connection to the named machine and then calls that machine. The call can be made over dial-up telephone lines, through a hard-wired permanent data link, or across some type of local area network. Communications parameters such as transmission speed and calling scripts will be taken from the **uucp** databases, so if no communications path is specified there, **cu** will fail.

When the connection is made, **cu** returns a message.

```
$ cu remote
Connected
```

If the connection fails for some reason, **cu** will return an error message. The possible error messages are the same as for the **uucp** system. Once the connection is made, **cu** will wait for your keystrokes and then pass them unchanged to the remote machine. There you can login or take whatever action is appropriate. All characters sent by the remote machine to the local machine will be passed through **cu** to your terminal. Thus you use the same *TERM* variable on the remote machine that you use on the local machine, and full-screen functions on the remote machine will work as expected.

In addition, **cu** allows you to specify the remote connection as a telephone number, although this form will work only if an autodial modem is attached to the system. This command

```
$ cu 5559876
```

will call the given telephone number. The telephone number can be as long as necessary, but it should be all digits except for some additional characters that have special meaning. The − (minus) character signals a delay of about 4 seconds so that **cu** can dial through telephone networks with long-latency switches or connection delays. The = (equal) character causes **cu** to wait for a secondary dial tone at that point. For example, in a business office where you might dial 9 to get an outside line and then a dial tone; then dial 1 and a long-distance number, and then wait for an answer from a remote PBX and get another dial tone; and then dial an extension number, this command may be appropriate.

```
$ cu 9=12015559876=1234
```

You must test these complex telephone numbers to be sure that they work correctly because the sequence of dial tones and delays usually must be worked out on a case-by-case basis.

Disconnecting from a cu Session

After completing your terminal emulation session at the remote host, log out of the remote machine normally. Then you can signal **cu** to hang up the call and exit to the shell. The ~. (tilde-dot) command will tell **cu** to exit. You must enter it on a line by itself, directly after a NEWLINE. Further, a NEWLINE must follow it immediately.

```
$ cu remote
Connected

~[uname].
Disconnected
$
```

The **cu** command prints the name of the local machine within the square brackets, after you enter the command. This is an example of an *internal command*, which we will discuss shortly. You should correctly log off the remote machine before entering ~. because some remote machines will not respond correctly when the communications line is hung up abruptly. Short of unplugging the cable from the communications port, there is no other way to end a session with **cu** because it passes all other characters to the remote machine.

cu Command Line Options

By default, **cu** expects the connection to be *full-duplex*, with character echo provided by the remote system. The connection *baud rate* (or speed) is usually determined by the **uucp** data files or defaults to 1200 baud when a telephone number is specified. However, you can change these defaults with command line options to **cu**. The −s (for speed) option takes as its argument the desired speed, which can be 300, 1200, 2400, 4800, or 9600 baud. This command

```
$ cu -s 2400 2345678
```

calls the telephone number and sets the communications speed to 2400 baud. The −s option will also override the setting in the **uucp** data file if it is used. This command

```
$ cu -s 9600 sysname
```

will connect to machine **sysname** at 9600 baud. Of course you must match the speed with the capabilities of the modem and the remote system.

If the remote system does not echo characters sent to it, you may specify the −h (for half-duplex) option, which causes **cu** to immediately echo all characters typed at your terminal. This is not a true "half-duplex" communications channel, because characters typed at the keyboard will be immediately sent to the remote machine even if it is sending characters to your machine. You may also specify −o (for odd) or −e (for even) to appropriately set the communications parity for characters sent to the remote machine. By default, no parity is used.

Use the −l (for line) option to specify a specific **tty** port to use for the communications. This option is useful when you wish to override the **uucp** data for some reason or when a communications device is directly attached to a serial port. For example, if an intelligent modem with a stored database of telephone numbers is attached to the COM2 port, the following command will allow direct access to the modem through **cu**.

```
$ cu -l /dev/tty01
```

When the modem answers by setting its *carrier detect* signal, **cu** will return the "connected" message, and your keystrokes will be read by the modem. You can reprogram the modem or use its built-in command set to dial out from there. You can also use the −**l** option when one machine is hard-wired to another over a serial port.

The −**d** (for debug) option, which instructs **cu** to display a trace of its progress in making a connection, helps you both diagnose problems with the connections that **cu** tries to make and learn more about how **cu** works. We will discuss debugging **cu** connections in Chapter 14 because it is really a part of the **uucp** subsystem. Though **cu** can take several other options, these have more limited usefulness.

Going Further

The **cu** program is much more powerful than you have seen so far. Its real power comes from its internal commands and in its ability to read and write command output across the communications line to the remote system. We will discuss these features of **cu** next.

cu Internal Commands

The **cu** program includes several *internal commands* that provide more features. You signal these commands by beginning the command with ~ (tilde), at the beginning of a line (right after a NEWLINE). The tilde signals **cu** that a command is coming next, and **cu** reads the rest of the typed line rather than passing it to the remote machine. For example, to exit from **cu** back to the shell, use ~. (tilde followed by dot). When **cu** recognizes the tilde, it immediately echoes it to the terminal. Then, when it recognizes the ".", it displays the name of the system within the brackets (**uname**) and then echoes the dot. The system name is always displayed for all tilde commands, though not until the next character is recognized.

The **cu** program provides many more tilde commands. While keeping the **cu** connection active, you can escape temporarily to a local subshell with ~! (tilde-bang). You can execute any commands from this subshell without hanging up the connection to the remote machine. When you are finished with the local shell, kill it normally with CTRL-D or the **exit** command. Then cu will echo a ! to signal that it is back in control and will resume sending your typed characters to the remote machine.

```
~[my_sys]!
$ echo $HOME
/usr/steve
$ exit
!
```

The **cu** program will not redraw the display screen after it regains control, as it immediately begins passing characters through to the remote machine. Any screen-refresh operation that is desired must be handled at the remote machine.

You can execute a single command on the local machine

with ~**!cmd** (tilde-bang-**cmd**) where **cmd** is any command line or pipeline. The **cu** program will temporarily suspend communications to the remote system and execute the command line in a local subshell. When the command completes, **cu** will echo ! and return to action.

ASCII File Transfer with cu

For communication between two UNIX systems, **cu** has built-in tilde commands for passing data in either direction. These are ~**%put** (tilde-percent followed by *put*), and ~**%take** (tilde-percent followed by *take*). These commands will send a file from the local machine to a remote machine and from a remote machine to the local machine, respectively. Each takes a filename as an argument.

```
~[my_sys]%put my.file
```

The remote machine must be waiting at the PS1 prompt for these commands to succeed. This example will create a file named **my.file** on the remote machine and copy a local file named **my.file** to it.

   While the transfer is in progress, **cu** will display a digit on the local machine marking each 1000-character chunk transferred. When the copy is complete, **cu** will display a final byte count and a completion message.

```
~[my_sys]%put my.file
stty -echo; cat - > my.file; stty echo
1234+
247 lines/4257 characters
$
```

The first output shows how **cu** implements the **put** and **take** operations. This is a command that is sent to the remote UNIX system. The **echo** feature is turned off, and the standard input is redirected to the filename. When **cat** ends, **echo** is turned on. The **cu** on the local machine will send the file, echoing 1, 2, 3, and 4 as each chunk of data is sent. Finally, the total byte and line count is displayed, and **cu** returns to displaying the PS1 prompt at the remote machine. These actions are reversed for the **take** operation.

You can change the name of the transferred file between the local and the remote machine if you give the second filename as another argument of the **put** or **take** operation.

```
~[my_sys]%take from.file to.file
```

Here **from.file** is copied from the remote machine into **to.file** on the local machine. The **put** operation is similar.

```
~[my_sys]%put from.file to.file
```

In this case **from.file** is the local filename and **to.file** is the new file created on the remote machine.

Remember, no error checking is provided by **cu** during these file transfer operations, so you should always confirm that the target file is the same size as the source file. The **wc** command can provide this information, but **cu** will sometimes replace tab characters in the source file with the appropriate number of spaces in the target file, so usually only the line and word counts from **wc** are helpful; the character counts may differ.

Transferring Binary Files
with cu

The **cu** program is designed for ASCII terminal emulation only. It can transfer ASCII files from one machine to another, but it *cannot* directly transfer binary or other non-text files between machines. The **cu** includes no error-checking file transfer protocol such as KERMIT or XMODEM. Usually **uucp** is used to transfer binary files. However, **cu** allows execution of a program on both sides of the data link, with input and output redirected through the ASCII communications channel provided by **cu**. Thus you can add application software at both ends of the data connection that can convert binary data to ASCII form, transfer it to the other side, and then convert it back to binary form.

One **cu** internal command can support this function. This is ~**$cmd** (tilde-dollar), where **cmd** is any command line. The **cmd** is executed on the local machine, but its output is sent over the communications line to the remote system rather than coming to the local display. This allows you to create a script on the local machine that can drive the remote machine. A login script is one example of how this feature might be used. Also, a file transfer application might be developed in which you execute one side of the application on the remote system and then use the ~**$** command to execute a matching command on the local machine.

The scenario is as follows. The remote application reads its standard input, so it will see data crossing the communications channel. Then the ~**$** (tilde-dollar) command will cause the output of the local **cmd** to be sent, where it is read by the remote application. The remote application can send the string ~>**:filename** (tilde-caret-colon), where **filename** is the name of a file on the local machine. After this command, all data sent from the remote machine will be redirected to the file. When the remote system sends a line consisting only of ~> (tilde-caret), the filename is closed, and **cu** begins sending received data to the terminal. This provides a general-purpose mechanism for transferring data between machines. The application programs on each side would be responsible for converting the data to ASCII form and then reconstructing the original binary data after the transfer.

Other Internal cu Commands

Several other useful tilde commands are provided by **cu**. The ~**%cd** (tilde-percent-**cd**) command will change the current directory on the local machine to the argument given to the **cd** command: This command

```
~[my_sys]%cd /usr/src
```

will change the directory that **cu** thinks is current, but this command

```
~[my_sys]!cd /usr/src
```

will not work because it will be executed in a subshell rather than directly by **cu**. When the subshell completes, **cu** will have the same current directory that it had before the ~! (tilde-bang) command was executed.

Finally, the ~**%b** (tilde-percent-**b**) command will send a break signal to the remote machine. This is seldom needed because **cu** can detect the BREAK key on most machines and correctly send a break signal to the remote machine. Several other tilde commands are available to **cu**, but these are designed for debugging and are rarely used.

The mailx Command

One more mail program is available in the standard SVR3 system—**mailx** (for experimental mail). It is a front-end processor for mail that provides advanced user-interface features. Mail messages created by **mailx** are actually sent by the **rmail** program, and **mailx** reads incoming mail from the same **/usr/mail/login** file used by **mail**. In practice users normally prefer to use either **mail** or **mailx** (or some even more advanced package), but not both.

The **mailx** command is executed like **mail**, although there are many differences in the acceptable command line options. This command

```
$ mailx
```

is used to read mail, while

```
$ mailx addressee-list
```

is used to send mail. The **−H** (for headers) option will cause **mailx** to print only the message headers and then exit.

The **mailx** program operates like **mail**, though **mailx** has a great many enhancements and convenience features. In addition to sophisticated tools for listing message headers, **mailx** includes a profile facility. When **mailx** is executed, it starts by looking for two files: **/usr/lib/mailx/mailx.rc**—a system-wide profile for all users, and **$HOME/.mailrc** (for mail run control)—a user-specific control file. These two files can contain commands in a special format defined for **mailx** that effectively make it a mail-oriented programming language, allowing extensive customization of its operation. We will not describe the details of this control language here, but they can significantly change the appearance of the header display for incoming messages. In addition, the control language allows you to create a semipermanent set of message headers that you can add to each message you create without reentering the headers each time. A wild-card expansion facility, with substitutions controlled by variables, allows you to add information such as the current date or the current **To:** list to the message. In addition, a signature facility allows you to predefine a block of lines that is added to the end of each message as it is created. Many more capabilities are provided by the **mailx** control file. The **mailx** program is a powerful and modern electronic mail utility, though it can be quite slow in operation, especially on a heavily loaded machine.

# FOURTEEN

The uucp Data Communications Subsystem

The uuto Command
The uupick Command
A Note on uucp Security
The uucp Command
The uux Command
The uustat Command
Administration of the uucp Subsystem
Going Further

In addition to the many communications tools already discussed, the UNIX system includes a very powerful and sophisticated *background* data communications facility that allows movement of files between machines, without much attention from the user. The **uucp** (for UNIX to UNIX copy) subsystem is a complete data movement package that can transfer both ASCII and binary files between machines, as well as control command execution on a remote machine. It can queue jobs for later transfer and automatically retry when a transfer fails for some reason. The **uucp** subsystem includes many user commands and functions, as well as complete customization facilities for different communication networks. It also contains strong security features, complete logging and debugging tools, and several different data transfer protocols, with error checking matched to the network type.

Intermachine electronic mail uses this facility. The **mail** program handles these interactions, releasing the **mail** user from knowing much about the **uucp** subsystem itself. However, **mail** is limited to transfer of ASCII text, usually short messages between users. To move large files or non-ASCII data between machines, you will usually use one of the **uucp** tools. Despite its power and sophistication, the **uucp** subsystem can be quite difficult to correctly administer and set up. We will discuss **uucp** administration shortly, but for the first few sections, we will assume that a working **uucp** subsystem already exists on a machine.

The uuto Command

The easiest way to move files between machines is with **uuto** (for UNIX to UNIX to) to send files and **uupick** (for UNIX to UNIX pickup) to retrieve files sent from another machine. The **uuto** command takes a filename list and a remote address as arguments.

```
$ uuto data1 data2 remote!login
```

The address is the last argument, following all the file names. It is in the same form specified for **mail**: a remote machine name and login id separated by the ! (bang) character. Unlike **mail**, **uuto** allows only a single destination, so you cannot send the same file to several recipients with a single command line. As many filenames as necessary can follow the **uuto** command, but the address must be the last argument.

The **uuto** command will not actually transfer the files; rather, it will queue them for transfer by the **uucp** system. Because the **uucp** subsystem can delay transfer according to how it is administered, the files may not reach their destination for some time. If the transfer is queued correctly, **uuto** will return to the shell after 1 or 2 seconds, and you can continue with your session.

The **uuto** command can accept two command line options. The −**m** (for mail) option causes **uuto** to send electronic mail to the sending user as well as to the recipient when the data transfer is complete. The −**p** option causes **uuto** to copy the file during the queuing process. If the −**p** option is not used, **uuto** requires that the file retain the same name and not be deleted until after the transfer is complete. If you change the file between the time it is queued and the time it is sent, the newer version will be sent. If the −**p** option is used, the contents of the file at the time it is queued will be sent, and the original file can be moved, deleted, or changed. The −**p** option causes the file to be duplicated, thus using additional disk space, which may be a consideration if many large files are to be transferred.

Unlike the **mail** command, **uuto** does not usually allow multihop addressing. If no direct path exists between the source and destination machines, use **uuto** to move the files to a third machine that knows about both and have a friend there forward the files to the final destination.

The uupick Command

When the files have been transferred, the **uucp** system on the receiving machine will send electronic mail to the recipient, announcing that the files have arrived from the other machine. The recipient can then use the **uupick** command to copy the files from the directory where **uucp** left them into the recipient's current directory. The **uupick** command is usually used with no arguments. It will locate the files sent via **uuto** and then prompt for a disposition of each file.

```
$ uupick
from system uname: file datal ?
```

The remote machine **uname** and the filename **data1** are displayed and **uupick** then waits for a command.

The * (star) command will cause **uupick** to display a summary of its available commands. Most useful is **m** (for move), which causes the named file to be moved to another directory. The **m** command can take a directory name as argument, in which case the file is moved to that directory instead of the current directory.

```
$ uupick
from system uname: file data1 ? m /tmp
642 blocks
from system uname: file data2 ?
```

The file size is displayed. Then **uupick** will go on to any other files. If all have been transferred, **uupick** will exit back to the shell. Use **m** . (dot) to move a file to the current directory.

The **a** (for all) command, similar in function to **m**, causes all the files from that remote machine to be moved at once. This can work faster than **m** if many files have been transferred. The **d** (for delete) command causes the file to be deleted rather than moved. The **p** (for print) command causes the file to be displayed, but **p** must be used carefully because binary files can be transferred with **uuto**. The **q** (for quit) command causes **uupick** to end. Any files that were not moved or deleted remain in the spool directory until you execute **uupick** again. Finally, **!cmd** (bang-command) is a shell escape that will execute **cmd** in a subshell and then return to **uupick**. This is often used to create directories or change permissions before moving files.

The **uupick** command can take one command line option, −**s** (for system), followed by a specific system name. This restricts the search by **uupick** only to files transferred from the named machine. Both **uuto** and **uupick** are usually shell scripts, and you can browse them in **/usr/bin** for more information on how they work.

A Note on uucp Security

Security is an important consideration for the **uucp** subsystem. File transfer from one machine to another can be extremely dangerous to both the machines and the privacy of their files. The **mail** and **uuto** commands are preferred for most data transfers between machines because they allow transfers only *from* the local machine *to* the remote machine, and all files are moved into safe public directories owned by the appropriate subsystem. However, the **uucp** subsystem as a whole is much more powerful and includes remote execution of arbitrary commands. Consequently, extensive security protections exist within the **uucp** subsystem, and many of the command forms and actions discussed here will be prohibited on some machines but allowed on others. We will discuss administration of **uucp** security in detail in Chapter 20, but here you should be aware that many of the most powerful **uucp** features may be disabled in specific systems or networks for security reasons. Over the years **uucp** security has become increasingly restrictive as a result of bitter experience within the UNIX system community. Only in the friendliest machine environments, with no access to public telephone lines or dial-up modems, can the most powerful **uucp** features be trusted.

The uucp Command

Although the **uuto** command provides the easiest access to the **uucp** subsystem for most file transfers, the **uucp** command can provide more control over the data transfer in specific situations. Unlike **uuto**, **uucp** lets you request a file from a remote machine for copy to the local machine.

The **uucp** command format is

```
$ uucp source.files destination.file
```

The **uucp** command will copy the **source.files** argument list to the **destination.file**. These filenames are actually addresses in the familiar **machine!target** format, except that the **target** is not a user login id but rather a pathname of the file or directory to copy. In the syntax of **uucp** the **machine!** part can be omitted if it refers to the local machine. For example, this command

```
$ uucp /etc/profile uname!/usr/spool/uucppublic/profile
```

will copy the file /**etc**/**profile** on the local machine to the file /**usr**/**spool**/**uucppublic**/**profile** on the machine named **uname**. Multiple files are allowed if the target is a directory. This command

```
$ uucp $HOME/* uname!/usr/spool/uucppublic/xfer.dir
```

will transfer all files in your HOME directory to the **/usr/spool /uucppublic/xfer.dir** directory on the remote machine.

In addition, **uucp** can copy files from the remote machine to the local machine if the **machine!** part is included in the **source.file** list. This command

```
$ uucp "uname!/tmp/hello/*" /usr/spool/uucppublic/xfer
```

will move all the files in the directory **/tmp/hello** on the remote system to the directory **/usr/spool/uucppublic/xfer** on the local system. The source list is quoted to prevent the local shell from expanding the * character. It will be expanded on the remote system.

You can also include the **machine!** part on both source and destination file lists, in which case the **uucp** command will perform a third-party transfer from one machine to another.

```
$ uucp machine1!file machine2!file
```

Neither machine need be the local machine if **uucp** security is administered to allow this usage.

Logical Pathnames

Security for **uucp** is usually administered so that file copies are allowed only from some specific *public* directories on the machines. The **/usr/spool/uucppublic** directory is such a public directory. Thus the pathname mechanism just described will seldom work in full generality, so the **uucp** command allows some forms of logical path naming that get around these security limitations. If the filename portion is ~**user** (tilde-**user**), where **user** is a login id on the target machine, **uucp** will create the file in that user's HOME directory. For example, many systems allow each user to create a public directory called **rje** (for remote job entry) within their HOME. This command

```
$ uucp local.file my_sys!~steve/rje
```

will write the file **local.file** into the **rje** directory of user steve on the machine named **my__sys**. A filename beginning with ~/ (tilde-slash), such as ~/**destination**, will write the file into the directory destination in the standard **uucp** public directory on the remote machine. This public directory is usually /**usr**/**spool** /**uucppublic**, so the command

```
$ uucp local.file my_sys!~/steve
```

will copy **local.file** to /**usr**/**spool**/**uucppublic**/**steve** on the machine named **my__sys**. This will work for transferring single files, but if more than one file is to be transferred, the ~/**destination** should end with a final / (slash) to instruct **uucp** to create a directory with the given name and copy all the source files into that directory, retaining their original names.

```
$ uucp $HOME/* system!~/steve/
```

This command is actually very much like **uuto** except that **uuto** will use a more complex naming convention for the target directory, built up from the local machine name and the recipient's login id on the target system.

Command Line Options for the uucp Command

The **uucp** command allows many command line options that modify its function. Many of these are used principally by **uucp** experts to fine tune the operation of **uucp** data transfer, but some are of general utility. The −**m** (for mail) option instructs **uucp** to send mail to the requester when the transfer is completed. The −**n** (for notify) option takes a login id on the remote machine as argument and sends mail to that user on the remote machine when the copy is complete. The −**C** (for copy) option causes the file to be copied into the **uucp** public directory before the transfer, allowing you to delete or change the original file. If you do not use this option, you cannot delete or rename the file before the transfer is complete.

By default, **uucp** is silent if the job is successfully queued for transfer. However, the −**j** (for job) option causes **uucp** to display a unique job identification number as it queues the job. This identification number helps you track the success or failure of the transfer, as discussed shortly. The −**x** option takes a digit between 1 and 9 as an argument and causes debugging information to be displayed at the terminal. The larger the number, the more debugging output will appear.

Finally, **uucp** will immediately try to send the job after it has been successfully queued. If you do not wish the connection to the remote machine to start immediately, use the −**r** option, which causes the job to be queued but delays the transfer. The **uucp** command will try to send the file during its next regularly scheduled cycle, usually about once an hour. You might use the −**r** option when you know that the target machine is not running or the connection is inoperable for some reason.

The uux Command

The most powerful command available within the **uucp** subsystem is **uux** (for UNIX to UNIX execute). The **uux** command lets you generate command lines that will be executed on a remote machine. This command can collect files named in the command line from various machines, assemble the command on the target machine, and execute it there. Because of these outstanding capabilities, **uux** is a very dangerous security risk, so its use is severely crippled on most systems. When allowed, it can be very useful in network environments in which movement of files between machines is quick and efficient.

The **uux** command takes a normal command line as argument, except that the command name and any filenames given as arguments can be preceded with the **machine!** form. This instructs **uux** to execute the command on that machine or to collect the named files from the machine given. For example, this command

```
$ uux "sys1!cat sys2!/etc/profile sys3!/etc/rc2 > !/tmp/output"
```

will collect the file **/etc/profile** from machine **sys2** and the file **/etc/rc2** from machine **sys3**, and move them to machine **sys1**, where the **cat** command will be executed. Output is redirected to the file **/tmp/output** on the local machine. Any part of the command line with only **!** (bang), without a named machine, is interpreted as the local system. The entire command line is quoted to prevent the local shell from interpreting the redirection character **>** before **uux** sees it.

In multicommand pipelines no command following the first can have the **machine!** part because **uux** requires that all parts of the pipeline be executed on the same machine.

```
$ uux "sys1!cat !/etc/profile | grep HOME > !/tmp/out"
```

The **uux** command will take the file **/etc/profile** from the local system and move it to machine **sys1**, where the pipeline **cat | grep** will be executed. The output is redirected to the file **/tmp/out** on the local machine. You can use the − (minus) character within the **uux** command as a filename part, in which case **uux** will read its standard input for that file. The previous command could also have been written as follows:

```
$ cat /etc/profile | uux "sys1!cat - | grep HOME > !/tmp/out"
```

Full pathnames are preferred in **uux** commands, but the special operators **~user** and **~!path** will work in the filename parts of **uux** commands just as they do in **uucp** commands. The **uux** command will fail if any of the files are not found as expected or if the commands are not permitted within the constraints of the **uucp** security rules on the target machine. When **uux** fails, it sends mail to the user who requested the action, on the original machine where **uux** was executed.

The **uux** command can take several command line options. The −**C** (for copy) option causes **uux** to copy local files to the spool directory, which allows you to move or delete any named files before the data transfer is complete. The −**n** (for notify) option causes **uux** to not send the notification mail if the command fails. This is useful for background or automatic **uux** jobs, such as regularly collecting some data from the machines on a local area network. The −**j** (for job) option causes **uux** to display a job id as it queues the action, while −**r** causes the job to be queued but not immediately started. The −**z** option causes mail to be sent to the originator of the job if it succeeds; normally **uux** will be silent if the job succeeds. Finally, the −**x** option takes a digit between 1 and 9 as argument and produces the corresponding level of debugging output to appear as the job is queued.

The uustat Command

Because the **uucp** subsystem performs its file transfer activities in the background, there is no immediate way to tell if transfers are succeeding. Therefore, the **uustat** (for UNIX to UNIX status) command is provided to report the status of the **uucp** file transfer queue. Among other features, **uustat** will provide a short summary of spooled but unsent jobs or the communications status of the machines with which your machine communicates. By default, **uustat** will report only on jobs created by the user who executes the **uustat** command.

```
$ uucp /etc/profile my_sys!~/root/
$ uustat
my_sysN74d6    06/27-18:58  S  my_sys  root 4290 /etc/profile
$
```

Here one job is queued; it has the job id **my−sysN74d6** and was queued at 6:58 P.M. on 6/27. It is directed to machine **my−sys** and was created by user **root**. The file size is 4290 bytes, and the file to transfer is /**etc**/**profile**. The "S" signifies that the request is to *send* a file (an "R" here would have denoted that a file is to be received).

A queued job may have more than one part under the same job id.

```
$ uustat
my_sysN74d7     06/29-17:47  S  my_sys   root 62 D.tune2317f15
                06/29-17:47  S  my_sys   root  rmail jim
$
```

This request results from a **mail** command with a remote addressee. In fact **mail** sends the mail message as one data file, which is the first file in the **uustat** output. The second file is a **uux** command to execute **rmail jim** on the target machine to deliver the message. If multiple files are sent via **uuto** or **uucp**, they will result in multiple files per job id. If more than one **uucp** command is queued, more than one job id will appear in the **uustat** output. When the data transfer is completed, the job id is removed from the **uustat** list, and if no jobs are outstanding, **uustat** will exit silently. Thus no output from **uustat** is good news; it tells you that all queued jobs have been sent.

By default, **uustat** reports only on the jobs queued by the user who initiates the **uustat** command. The −**a** (for all) option instructs **uustat** to display all the queued jobs on the machine, no matter who created them. The −**u** (for user) option takes a user id as argument and produces a listing of queued jobs scheduled by the named user only.

```
$ uustat -u steve
```

This is the same result as would occur if **uustat** alone was executed by user steve.

Reporting on Specific Machines

In addition, **uustat** can display the queue for a specific machine with the −**s** (for system) option. You must enter a machine id after the −**s** option. This command

```
$ uustat -s my_sys
```

produces the listing of queued jobs for the machine **my_sys**.

The **uustat** command can also report on the communications status of transfers from the local machine to any remote machines that have recently been contacted. Use the −**m** (for machine) option.

```
$ uustat -m
my_sys        1C              06/29-17:47 SUCCESSFUL
sys2          1C              06/29-18:20 TALKING
$
```

In this example two machines have recently been contacted. The machine **my_sys** was last contacted at 17:47 on 6/29, and the connection was completed successfully. The machine **sys2** is currently connected with the local machine, and some data is being transferred. Other conditions can be reported in the status field at the end of the line. The **uucp** weekly administrative script deletes the status log, so there will seldom be any output from **uustat** −**m** right after the weekly script executes, until some machines have been contacted.

Deleting a Queued Job

Finally, you can use **uustat** to delete an unsent job from the **uucp** queue. You might need this feature when you change your mind about a data transfer or when the connection is not completing correctly. All **uucp** transfers are available from **uustat**, including those created by **mail** or **uux**. To delete a job, you must know the job id, which is displayed when the job is originally queued or by **uustat**.

To kill a job, use the −**k** (for kill) option with **uustat** and the job id as argument.

```
$ uustat -k my_sysN74d7
Job: my_sysN74d7 successfully killed
$
```

Only one job id is allowed per invocation of the **uustat** −**k** command. If the job has already been completed, it cannot be killed, and **uustat** will return an error.

```
$ uustat -k my_sysN74d7
Can't find Job my_sysN74d7; Not killed
$
```

Lastly, **uustat** cannot kill a job if it is in progress.

Administration of the uucp Subsystem

The **uucp** subsystem is a powerful and extremely flexible data communications tool. However, all this flexibility has its cost; you pay for it when you must *administer* the **uucp** subsystem. Administration of **uucp** has a reputation for extreme complexity that requires the administrator to have arcane skills. This can be true, especially when the machine must be adapted to new communication networks or when it just isn't working. However, **uucp** administration is definitely possible for ordinary users on personal systems, and unless some pathological failure occurs, **uucp** will work correctly without much attention.

A Note on Versions of uucp

The version of the **uucp** subsystem included with SVR3 is known formally as the BNU (for Basic Networking Utilities) and informally as the HDB (for HoneyDanBer) version, after the login id's of its three developers. This version differs significantly both from older releases and from BSD versions. Our discussion will focus on the HDB version, which is far superior to other versions because of its elimination of bugs, its great flexibility, and its freedom from derangement.

uucp Directory Structure

There are three directory structures primarily owned by the **uucp** subsystem: **/usr/lib/uucp** contains the control files used by **uucp** to figure out how to connect to a specific machine; **/usr/spool/uucp** contains the log and status files used by **uustat** and other commands; and **/usr/spool/uucppublic** is the directory used for public transfer of files between machines (**uuto** and **uupick** move files to and from this directory). The latter two directories have large subdirectory structures that are maintained by the **uucp** administrative tools; these should never be manually changed or deleted. The **/usr/lib/uucp** directory contains the control files that you will edit when adding new remote systems or changing the modem or network setup of your machine.

The directory **/usr/spool/uucppublic** contains the public spool for all normal **uucp** transfers. It can have many directories within it, which are usually created with the following command:

```
$ uucp files target!~/dir/
```

The directory **dir** will appear in the **uucppublic** directory on the target system. Each target user has a personal subdirectory within **receive**, and the **uuto** command uses **/usr/spool/uucppublic/receive**. Within this per-user directory, there will be an additional subdirectory named for each source machine, and the actual transferred files appear in that directory. That is, the command

```
$ uuto file1 my_sys!steve
```

if sent from machine **uname**, will cause **file1** to appear in the directory **/usr/spool/uucppublic/receive/steve/uname** on the **my_sys** system. This complex directory structure is designed to prevent files of the same name, sent from different machines, from overwriting each other.

The directory **/usr/spool/uucp** contains **uucp** log files and queued files.

```
$ ls -aFC /usr/spool/uucp
.Admin/     .Log/       .Sequence/     .Workspace/     my_sys/
.Corrupt/   .Old/       .Status/       .Xqtdir/
$
```

These materials are all contained in subdirectories, most of which begin with . (dot), so **ls —a** is needed to see them. The "normal" directories contain temporary information about unsent queued jobs for the machine given in the directory name. These spool directories are created as needed by the **uucp** system and are deleted during the weekly cleanup procedure. The logs and other **uucp** administrative records are kept in the other directories, especially **.Log**. You can browse them if you wish. The file **/usr/spool/uucp/.Admin/xferstats** contains a listing of the communications efficiency of all data transfers, in bytes per second of connect time. A 1200-baud telephone link will average about 105 characters per second, which is highly efficient compared to many other data transfer algorithms. A faster data link has better performance.

The directory **/usr/lib/uucp** contains the executable programs owned exclusively by the **uucp** subsystem, the administrative demons for cleanup and other chores, and the control files that instruct the **uucp** programs on how to make a connection to other machines.

```
$ ls -FC /usr/lib/uucp
Devconfig      Maxuuxqts      Uutry*             uudemon.hour*
Devices        Permissions    remote.unknown*    uudemon.poll*
Devices.cico   Poll           uucheck*           uugetty*
Dialcodes      SetUp*         uucico*            uusched*
Dialers        Sysfiles       uucleanup*         uuxqt*
Dialers.cico   Systems        uudemon.admin*
Maxuuscheds    Systems.cico   uudemon.cleanu*
$
```

The demons are named **uudemon.....** Because these are shell scripts, you can browse them to see their functions. The **uucico** program is the heart of the **uucp** subsystem; it makes the connection and transfers the data. The **uugetty** program is a new version of the **getty** program, which can replace **getty** in

/etc/inittab. Use **uugetty** when you need to allow both incoming and outgoing access over a single **tty** port. It works with the **uucp** and **cu** programs so that incoming calls are handled correctly when the port is idle. When the **uucico** or **cu** program wants to call out over the port, it cooperates with **uugetty** so that **uugetty** is suspended during the outgoing call. When the outgoing connection ends, **uugetty** pops back to allow incoming calls again.

Most of the other files, those whose names begin with an uppercase character, are the **uucp** control files that specify how to make a connection to a remote machine. We will discuss them shortly.

All the materials in the directories **/usr/lib/uucp** and **/usr/spool/uucp** are owned by the administrative login id **uucp** and have group **demon**. These ownerships must be maintained, and the permissions of the files must not be changed from the values set when the files were created. Any changes made to the permissions or ownership of these files or directories will cause the **uucp** subsystem to begin to fail in mysterious ways. When this occurs, it is best to reload the system software from the original disks, restoring everything to its default state. You should back up the control files before reloading, to save the material in them, but be careful not to just rewrite the old files over the newly restored ones, or the incorrect permissions will follow. Extreme care is required when editing anything in the **uucp** subsystem. Only the superuser can edit the files, and he or she is responsible for keeping the permissions and ownership correct.

One additional directory is used by the **uucp** subsystem. This is **/usr/spool/locks**, where the system's lock files reside. The files are created when the **uucico** and **cu** programs are using a device or port. The **uugetty** program also creates a lock file when a user calls into the machine. The presence of such files signals the other programs in the **uucp** subsystem that the port is in use. Other programs respect the lock files and will not contend for the device when it is already in use. The programs remove the lock file when they finish with the device, freeing it for another use. Lock files are deleted during system reboot, so any failed **uucico** jobs that might leave a lock file cannot permanently block usage of a port.

uucp Subsystem Architecture

When a job is queued for transfer with **mail** or one of the **uucp** programs, the **uucp** utilities look in a list of known remote machines. If they find the target system, the programs will create a new file under **/usr/spool/uucp** that contains the data transfer request. If no data transfer to that machine is currently in progress, the **uucp** utilities will execute **/usr/lib/uucp/uucico** (for **uu**-copy-in-copy-out). The **uucico** program will use additional control files to determine the best way to connect to the target system and will try to connect to the remote machine using that pathway. If the connection succeeds, **uucico** will execute the transfer. In fact instances of **uucico** will be executing at both ends of the communications link, and one can often be seen in the output from **ps—fe**. When the transfer is complete, the control file in **/usr/spool/uucp** will be deleted.

If the connection fails, **uucico** may try several different communications paths before it gives up, depending on the administration of the control files.

If the transfer fails, the job will stay on the queue. A **uucp** demon, scheduled via the **cron** timing facility, executes in most systems once each hour. This demon searches **/usr/spool/uucp** and its subdirectories for queued jobs that have not been sent, and it will execute **uucico** to transfer any jobs that it finds. The scheduling algorithm is variable, so recently queued jobs will be retried more frequently than ones that have failed repeatedly. Finally, if a transfer fails repeatedly for a week, the weekly **uucp** cleanup demon will send a warning message via **mail** to the sending user. Usually **uucp** will succeed before this happens, unless the target machine is not in operation or the communications channel is inoperative.

Specifying a Connection Method to a Remote System

Each remote machine that you can access via **uucp** or **mail** must be specified in a **uucp** control file. When the **uucp** tools queue a transfer, they will examine the contents of a control file to see if the remote machine is included. If not, the **uucp** commands will fail with an error message.

```
$ uucp file1 nosys!~/user/
bad system: nosys
uucp failed completely (11)
$
```

You can determine the complete list of available remote systems with the **uuname** command, which produces a list of machine names, one per line. You should **grep** through this list to find a specific machine, because the output may be voluminous.

```
$ uuname | grep nosys
$
```

The list of known machines may differ between **uucp** and **cu**, and you can use the −**c** (for **cu**) option of **uuname** to get the list of machines known to **cu** instead of **uucp**.

The list of known machines is kept in a complex interlocking file structure in the /**usr**/**lib**/**uucp** directory so that administrators can flexibly administer the list of systems available under different situations. The file /**usr**/**lib**/**uucp**/**Sysfiles** gives a table of these files, along with other information.

```
$ tail -7 /usr/lib/uucp/Sysfiles
service=cu       systems=Systems \
                 devices=Devices \
                 dialers=Dialers

service=uucico   systems=Systems.cico:Systems \
                 devices=Devices.cico:Devices \
                 dialers=Dialers.cico:Dialers
$
```

The first part of **Sysfiles** is usually a long comment section describing how to use the file. Browse this file on your machine for more information. Information in **Sysfiles** is divided up for each different *service* available on the machine. These are usually **cu** and **uucico**, as just described. The keyword **service**= starts the description of different services, and each description starts on a new line, though more lines are allowed if you escape the NEWLINE with a \ (backslash). Each service has three different kinds of information that the software needs to make the connection: (1) the *system information*, (2) the *devices information*, and (3) the *dialers information*. Each type has a keyword in **Sysfiles** that specifies one or more additional files in **/usr/lib/uucp** where that information is found. Thus multiple files can hold system information and so on. These files are named after the appropriate keyword following the **service** keyword. Different files are separated with a : (colon) in these lists, and the different keywords are separated from each other with white space. Each service has its own list of control files.

In the previous example the **systems=** sections of **Sysfiles** give the names of files that contain the lists of remote machines that **uucico** (or **cu**) can access. The files **Systems.cico** and **Systems** contain these tables for the **uucico** service. When **uucico** executes, the file **Systems.cico** is consulted; if it does not contain the requested machine, then the file **Systems** is consulted. All these files must be in the directory **/usr/lib/uucp**.

The Systems Files

The contents of the **Systems** files determine how the service will attempt to connect to the remote machine. With different networks, different types of modems, hard-wired data links, and different login/password sequences for different machines, a great deal of information must be encoded in the **Systems** entry for a machine. The file **Systems** normally contains a comment section to explain the meaning of the various fields in the file, and you should browse this section for more information. For example:

```
$ tail -3 /usr/lib/uucp/Systems
my_sys Any ACU 1200 5300548 "" \d ogin:--ogin:--ogin: nuucp
packet Any DIR 300 - "" \d ogin:--ogin:--ogin: nuucp
another Any D2 4800 - "" \d ogin:--ogin:--ogin: nuucp
$
```

Each remote machine has one or more lines in the **Systems** file. The machine name is the leftmost field on the line. The next field gives a range of times when calling is allowed. **Any** means that a call can be placed at any time. The *device* to use for the connection is given in the third field. The name here is a pointer to a device descriptor in the **Devices** file. The fourth field in **Systems** gives the requested speed of the data link, which is matched with the capabilities of the device. **Any** is often used for the speed in the **Systems** file to push the decision on connection speed to the **Devices** logic. The fifth field contains the telephone number if a dial-up modem is used or a *Dialer* name if a network is desired. The − (minus) is a dummy place holder if this field is unused. The rest of the line constitutes a chat sequence that gives a series of hand-shaking strings.

The chat script works like this. While the connection is being made, the local machine waits to hear the first string ("is" a null value that means wait for nothing"). When that string comes across the data connection, the local machine will send the next string, then wait for the next one, and so on in alternating sequence. This allows the service to traverse arbitrarily complex login sequences in making connections to remote machines. The last part usually waits for **login:** at the remote machine and then sends the login id for the **uucico** program: **nuucp**. If the remote machine requires it, the **chat** script might wait for the "passwd:" prompt and then send the password for that machine. Many machines do not use a password for the **nuucp** login because the **uucico** program will get control rather than a normal shell.

In addition to these normal character strings, the **chat** can include some special keywords that have such functions as delaying for a while, sending a break signal, and so on. These special keywords are documented in the comments for the **Systems** file.

A single remote machine may have more than one entry in the **Systems** file if there is more than one way to reach the machine. For example, a machine might be accessible over a local area network or by a dial-up connection. When attempting to connect to such a machine, **uucico** will try the first **Systems** entry, and if that one fails, it will try the second, and so on. Thus a busy data link need not prevent data transfer if another route is available.

The Devices File

As part of the connection, the service (usually **cu** or **uucico**) may need to understand some details of how the local communications *devices* are configured. A device is usually a modem or a network link that has a specific port on the local machine, and it may require a chat to activate it. For example, an autodialing modem with the **AT** command set will be attached via an RS232 connection to a specific **tty** port on the machine; the correct **AT** command must be sent to turn on the autodialing feature, and the telephone number to dial must be sent. The modem responds with ASCII strings after each command. This information is logically associated with the modem, not with the specific system that you access using that modem. So this chat and other device-specific information is kept with the device data, but information that is specific to the system, such as the login sequence, is kept with the system data. The latter is kept in the **Systems** file, as just discussed, while the former is kept in one of the **Devices** files, as specified by the **Sysfiles** list. **Devices** usually contains a long comment section that gives instructions on the use of the file; you can browse it for more information.

During the processing of the **Systems** file entry for a machine, the third field names a device for making the connection. The service will search **Sysfiles** to find a **devices**= entry for the service; then it will search the named files. If it finds a line whose leftmost field matches the third field in **Systems**, it will perform the processing specified in the line.

The other fields in the **Devices** files specify other device-specific information. For example:

```
$ tail -3 /usr/lib/uucp/Devices
ACU tty01 - 1200 hayes
DIR tty00 - 9600 direct
STARLAN,eg starlan - - TLIS \D
$
```

This illustrates three commonly used **Devices** entries. The first is for a modem with **AT** command set, the second is for a machine directly connected via RS232 link on **/dev/tty00**, and the third is an entry for the STARLAN local area network.

If more than one device exists for a specific connection strategy, then more than one line in **Devices** can have the same name. For example, two modems might be attached to the machine on different ports. You seldom don't care which modem is used to make a call, so there might be two **ACU** entries in the **Devices** file, naming the port for each modem separately.

As mentioned, the first field is a token that names a device. These tokens appear in the third field of a **Systems** entry. **ACU** (for automatic calling unit) is usually used for dial-up modems, while **DIR** (for direct) is usually used to name directly connected machines. The second field gives the /**dev** file or port used for the connection. The name is given without the /**dev**/ part. In the previous example, the modem is attached to the COM2 port, which is named **tty01** under the UNIX system naming scheme. The third field can name a dialer device if it differs from the connection device. This field is rarely used in modern hardware and is — (minus), the dummy placeholder, in these examples. The fourth field gives the connection speed. If the speed field in the **Systems** file is **Any**, the speed is determined from the **Devices** entry. Because the speed is usually a function of the device, **Any** is usually used in the **Systems** entry. Otherwise, the **Systems** speed must match the **Devices** speed, or the service will not use the line. The fifth field gives the name of a line in a **Dialers** file, which usually specifies an additional chat script that is unique to that device. In the **ACU** example, the **dialer** entry is **hayes**. Sometimes the **dialer** name specifies a built-in dialer that is specifically associated with some special hardware. The STARLAN entry is of this type because **TLIS** specifies a dialer based on the *streams* I/O mechanism new to SVR3. These built-in dialers will not appear in the **Dialers** file.

In addition, a device-specific chat can follow these required five fields, as in the \D operator in the STARLAN line. This chat is described in the comments in the **Devices** file.

However, the device-specific **chat** is usually included in the **Dialers** file entry rather than in the **Devices** entry.

The Dialers File

The **Dialers** file is also specified through the **Sysfiles** list so that dialers can differ depending on the service. The dialer is the chat script that causes the device to dial the connection. Actually the term *dial* may be misleading because not only dial-up modems use **Dialers**. Many local area networks use complex login sequences to pass network security and address a remote machine on the network, and control for these connections is also included in the **Dialers** file. The file /**usr**/**lib** /**uucp**/**Dialers** includes comments that describe the format and operators available with dialers.

The fifth field of lines in the **Devices** file usually contains a name that matches the first field of the **Dialers** line.

```
$ grep hayes /usr/lib/uucp/Dialers
hayes   =,-,     "" \dAT\r\c OK\r \EATDT\T\r\c CONNECT
$
```

The second field lists tokens that appear in a telephone number in the **Systems** entry, translating the tokens required by the dialer. For example, the **hayes** entry instructs the **uucico** program to translate = into , and − into ,. The = (equal sign) has historically been used to specify a wait for secondary dial tone, and the − (minus) was used to specify a 2-second delay. In this example both are converted to the **AT** modem's delay operator, the , (comma). The rest of the line specifies a chat script that is used to communicate with the modem.

In summary, communication services make connections by consulting **Sysfiles** to determine which files to use for the other operations. Then they consult the appropriate **Systems** file to find out what kind of connection to use for the call, when calls are allowed, and so on. Next, they follow the device name (third field of **Systems**) into the **Devices** file, where they determine which hardware implements that connection method. Then they follow the fifth field of **Devices** into the appropriate **Dialers** file (or use a built-in dialer) to determine how to talk to that specific device. When the call is made using the **Devices** and **Dialers** information, and those chat scripts complete successfully, **cu** will return control to the keyboard, or **uucico** will return to the **Systems** entry and log into the machine using the **chat** given there. When all these steps are complete, then the connection is made and data communication begins.

Going Further

The **uucp** subsystem is a very powerful and flexible communications system that can handle a great many different kinds of networks and devices. Consequently, a great many potential problems and pitfalls are associated with it, especially when you are trying to install a new type of connection. Here we can mention only some of the issues and additional tools that are available in SVR3.

Debugging uucp Connections

The **uucp** subsystem includes excellent debugging tools that can trace the progress of a connection and diagnose failure modes and errors in your chat scripts. The **cu** command includes the −**d** (for debug) option that displays a trace of the connection as it is made.

```
$ cu -d steve
conn(steve)
Device Type ACU wanted
Using hayes caller (dev=tty00)
Use Port /dev/tty00, Phone Number  5554848<
fixline(6, 1200)
getto ret 6
device status for fd=6
```

```
F_GETFL=2,iflag=`12045',oflag=`0',cflag=`2271',lflag=`0',line=`0'
cc[0]=`177',[1]=`34' , [2]=`10' , [3]=`100' , [4]=`1' , [5]=`0' ,
[6]=`0' , [7]=`0' ,
call _mode(1)
Connected
transmit started
_receive started

login:
```

After the connection is complete, the debugging output stops, and you can use **cu** nearly normally. However, more debugging output will appear when you disconnect.

```
~[my_sys].

call tilde(.)
call _quit(0)
call _bye(0)

Disconnected
call cleanup(0)
call undial(6)
call _mode(0)
$
```

Similarly, the **uucp** subsystem includes a tool in **/usr/lib /uucp/Uutry** that also produces debugging output, as shown in Figure 14-1. **Uutry** takes the machine name as argument. Figure 14-1 shows a connection over a STARLAN local area network, including the transfer of one file during the connection.

You should execute **Uutry** on your machine frequently to kick off your **uucp** data transfers. Do you understand each step of the communications process?

When you execute **Uutry** it will appear to hang the machine; no PS1 prompt will reappear. This is normal because **Uutry** uses **tail −f** to display its log file. To return to the shell at any time during or after the execution of **Uutry**, you must press DEL. Your terminal will immediately return to the shell, and the **Uutry** output will end. However, the data connection established by **Uutry** will continue, and it will end normally. This allows you to watch the **Uutry** output during the connection phase and then abandon the display while the (possibly many) files are transferred.

```
$ /usr/lib/uucp/Uutry my_sys
/usr/lib/uucp/uucico -r1 -smy_sys  -x5 >/tmp/my_sys 2>&1&
tmp=/tmp/my_sys
conn(my_sys)
Device Type STARLAN wanted
expect: ("")
got it
sendthem (<NO CR>NLPS:000:001:102^@)
getto ret 6
expect: (in:)
login:got it
sendthem (@nuucp^M)
expect: (word:)
login: @^M^Jnuucp^M^JPassword:got it
sendthem (^M)
Login Successful: System=my_sys
wmesg 'U'eg
Proto started e
*** TOP *** - role=1, setline - X
Request: steve!/usr/jim/s --> my_sys!/usr/steve/root (steve)
setline - S
wrktype - S
 wmesg 'S' /usr/steve/s /usr/steve/root steve -dc D.0 644 steve
rmesg - 'S' got SN2
 PROCESS: msg - SN2
SNDFILE:
mailopt 0, statfopt 0
*** TOP *** - role=1, setline - X
Finished Processing file: /usr/spool/uucp/my_sys/C.my_sysN3f5a
wmesg 'H'
rmesg - 'H' got HY
 PROCESS: msg - HY
HUP:
wmesg 'H'Y
cntrl - 0
send OO 0,exit code 0
Conversation Complete: Status SUCCEEDED
$
```

Figure 14-1.   Sample output from **Uutry**

In both of the previous examples most of the output describes the chat sequence that was executed in completing
the connection. These chats differ significantly in the two examples because the requested networks differ. In the **cu** example a
dial-up connection using an **AT** command modem was used.
The output describes the use of the **ACU** device and then shows
the successful access of the device through the line **getto ret 6**.
More sophisticated networks will show different sequences.
Then **cu** displays its terminal settings for this connection in a

terse debugging format. Finally, it announces that the **cu** transmit and receive processes are started.

In the **Uutry** output in Figure 14-1 more details of the chat are available, and most users prefer **Uutry** over **cu −d** for debugging. However, remember that the **Sysfiles** scheme allows different chats for **cu** and **Uutry**, so some connections may work with one command but not the other. **Uutry** will make a connection even if no files are queued for transfer, to make it easier to debug the chat scripts. Successful file transfer is more than just the connection, however, so be sure to test the link by sending a few files in both directions.

The first part of the **Uutry** output shows the **uucico** command that it is executing and then the device (from the **Systems** and **Devices** files) selected. Next comes a detailed description of the chat, with lines beginning "sendthem" displaying output from the local machine, and lines beginning "expect" displaying what the local machine expects from the remote. This continues until both local and remote machines are talking together; then "Login Successful" is displayed. Next, the file transfer begins (after the "TOP" display). Each file gets "Request" and "SENDFILE" sections. When all transfers are complete, the two sides of the connection signal completion with 'H', and the connection is complete.

When a connection fails, the output will change. Failure is usually caused by an incorrect chat script, in which case the "expect" section will not be fulfilled, and the display will show a "Timeout" message, followed by "Status FAILED." The location of the message will tell you where the **chat** went wrong. Many other types of error codes displayed by **Uutry** indicate various other kinds of failures. Two of the most important are "No Device" and "Can't Access Device," which mean that the **Devices** file entry is incorrect or the physical device is not operating correctly. Sometimes "Permission Denied" will appear in the output for a file transfer, which means that the directory locations for the files, on either the sending or receiving side, do not allow the requested operation. This is under control of **uucp** security, though the public directory **/usr/spool/uucppublic** should always allow access. Most of the other error codes are somewhat self-evident, though a true

uucp expert may be needed to debug complex network connections.

The uulog Command

Even when debugging is not explicitly selected with **Uutry**, the **uucp** subsystem retains a log of some information for all systems that have been contacted since the last weekly cleanup of **uucp** data. The **uulog** command displays this information, giving a full history of all accesses to a machine. Because this information is stored on a per-machine basis, **uulog** command requires a system name as argument, as shown in Figure 14-2.

This example shows the log from remote machine **my—sys** to local machine **steve**. Four calls are represented, the first two of which were initiated by **my—sys**, and each of these resulted in two files being transferred. The call begins with "startup," which indicates that the chat was successful and file transfer began. The call ends at "conversation complete." Two failed calls are included in the last two lines of the log. The first of these ("LOGIN FAILED") reports that the chat was incorrect for that machine, and it was completed correctly. The second ("CAUGHT") results from a *timeout* failure, in which the connection did not complete before **uucico** gave up in fail-

```
$ uulog my_sys
uucp steve  (7/2-9:48:26,12288,0) OK (startup)
uucp steve  (7/2-9:48:26,12288,0) REMOTE REQUESTED (steve!D.steve791d37a
--> my_sys!D.steve791d37a (root))
uucp steve  (7/2-9:48:28,12288,1) REMOTE REQUESTED (steve!D.my_sys2ac61b4
--> my_sys!X.my_sysN2ac6 (root))
uucp steve  (7/2-9:48:29,12288,2) OK (conversation complete tty00 5)
uucp steve  (7/2-14:24:29,21372,0) OK (startup)
uucp steve  (7/2-14:24:29,21372,0) REMOTE REQUESTED (steve!D.steve791f84b
--> my_sys!D.steve791f84b (root))
uucp steve  (7/2-14:24:30,21372,1) REMOTE REQUESTED (steve!D.my_sys2ac7685
--> my_sys!X.my_sysN2ac7 (root))
uucp steve  (7/2-14:24:31,21372,2) OK (conversation complete tty00 4)
uucp steve  (7/2-18:10:07,156,0) CONN FAILED (LOGIN FAILED)
uucp steve  (7/2-18:34:59,206,0) CAUGHT (SIGNAL 15)
$
```

Figure 14-2. Typical output from the **uulog** command

ure. This is likely to happen when the data line is not set up correctly, and signaling between the local and the remote machines is not working as expected.

The log can be very long if two machines converse actively, but it is deleted during the weekly **uucp** cleanup. With luck, a long log for a suspect machine can provide a great deal of information to help you understand why your files do not reach their destination as expected.

The uucp Administrative Demons

Much of the work of the **uucp** subsystem is done on a *schedule*, not under direct command of the user. Once a job is on the queue, **uucp** will keep trying to deliver it until it succeeds or until the job is killed and removed from the queue. No user action is required when a target machine is down or the local machine is rebooted, because the queue stays active indefinitely. Therefore, the **cron** facility is employed to stimulate the **uucp** subsystem into action on a regular basis. The **uucp** tools will search for any queued jobs and will try to send any that they find. In addition, the logs are regularly cleaned, and the **uucp** subsystem can be administered to regularly poll a remote machine to see if any jobs are to be sent to the local machine.

All these activities are managed by the **uudemon** scripts in the **/usr/lib/uucp** directory. They are scheduled from the **crontab** facility, and each demon runs on a different schedule, depending on its function. The **uudemon** tools are usually shell scripts, and you can browse them for more information about their actions.

The **uudemon.hour** script is executed once each hour while the machine is up. It executes the **uuxqt** (for **uu**-execute) program, which looks for any unsent jobs and starts sending any that it finds. Usually **uuxqt** includes a good algorithm for determining if any specific job should be started on its regular schedule. If a job has repeatedly failed, **uuxqt** will not try as often. A commonly used algorithm is: try once each hour for the first day, then once every 2 hours for the next day, then once each 12 hours the third day, then once a day for the rest of the first week. If the job still has not succeeded, **uuxqt** will send a mail message to the user who created the job. Generally, if the job fails for a whole week, either the target machine is non-existent or the chat is wrong for connecting to that machine.

The **uudemon.admin** script is executed once each day, usually in the small hours of the night. It creates an administrative report concerning that day's **uucp** activity. It reports on job transfers, machines contacted, suspected security breaks, and disk space used by the **uucp** queues. It sends its report via **mail** to the **uucp** login id. Many system administrators forward mail for the **uucp** login to their own id.

The **uudemon.cleanu** (for cleanup) script executes once a week. It deletes old log files, informs users of unsent files, and performs other cleanup tasks. Because of the administrative nature of these demons, they should be set to execute at some part of the day when the machine is usually up and running. If the machine is kept off during the nights and weekends, you should change the schedule in the **crontab** to move these de-mons to a time when the machine is usually active.

Polling Other Machines

The **uucp** subsystem can call other machines on a schedule. This is called *polling* the other machine, and you might use it when the local machine is able to contact the remote machine but the remote machine, for some reason, cannot call the local machine. In this case, any jobs queued on the remote to the local will never be delivered unless the local machine calls the remote. You can add the script **uudemon.poll** to the **crontab** to cause regular polling. It is usually scheduled to execute once each hour, a few minutes before **uudemon.hour** runs.

The **uudemon.poll** script consults the file **/usr/lib/uucp /Poll** for a list of systems to poll and the times to poll them. It then sets up a dummy job in the regular **uucp** queue. When **uudemon.hour** runs, it will find the dummy job and call the machine. If **uucp** security is properly administered, the remote machine will send any queued jobs for the local machine during this call. The **Poll** file contains a line for each machine to be polled and a list of hours to poll that machine. You can set it up to poll a remote machine as often as you wish, from once a day up to once each hour. Naturally, it is best to call a machine as rarely as necessary, to reduce traffic on the connection network and on the two machines.

Changing the Data Transfer Protocol

The **uucp** subsystem supports several different data communications *protocols* for moving data across different types of networks. The default is called the **g** protocol, and all **uucp** versions support it; it is an effective error-correcting protocol that has served well for many years. However, faster networks that include their own error-correcting procedures can get better performance if another protocol is used. The **e** (for error-free) protocol is often used with local area networks. When more than one protocol is available, the **uucico** program will automatically *negotiate* with the other end of the connection to choose a protocol that both ends can speak.

You can specify the protocol in the **Devices** files for a specific network type. Following the first field in the **Devices** file that you are using for **uucico** (as specified in **Sysfiles**), add a , (comma) and the names of the protocols that you wish to use on that device. No white space is allowed before the comma. For example, this command

```
STARLAN,eg starlan - - TLIS \D
```

will use the **e** protocol when the remote can support it; otherwise, it will use the **g** protocol. No changes to the **Systems** or other control files are required. Because the protocols are included when the **uucico** program is configured, not all versions of the **uucp** tools can support alternate protocols. Further, you should test your network to be sure that it will really produce error-free data transfer before you depend on the **e** protocol.

The Devconfig File

There are many other features of the **uucp** subsystem that are just too difficult to discuss here in detail. One is the **Devconfig** (for device configuration) file, which is new to SVR3 **uucp**. **Devconfig** is used for data communication dialers based on the streams device driver scheme. When **uucp** wants to use a streams-based device, it consults the **Devconfig** file to determine what streams modules to attach to the data path to the device. Among others, the STARLAN and ETHERNET local area networks use the streams mechanism in their software.

rje and IBM 3270 Emulation

Historically, the UNIX system has been able to connect well to the IBM SNA network, allowing **rje** (for remote job entry) access between mainframes and the UNIX machine. Now, packages for UNIX systems allow IBM 3270 emulation as well. However, both of these features require add-on hardware and special device drivers. These packages are available from several sources but are not a part of the standard UNIX system.

Word Processing

The spell Command
The troff Document Preparation Package
Going Further

The UNIX system was one of the first general-purpose computer systems to include a fully functional *word processing* or *document preparation* subsystem. During the 1970s, the UNIX system was widely used for word processing, but personal office systems based on the UNIX system were nonexistent. The **troff** (for typesetting runoff) package provided very powerful tools for the times. Users could create documents ranging from simple business letters to printer-ready copy for entire books. Indeed most books about the UNIX system were and are produced entirely on the UNIX system. The **troff** package produced output to drive the phototypesetters of the day, to produce camera-ready copy for typeset documents and books.

Even today the **troff** tools are unsurpassed for professional-quality documents. The *UNIX User's Manual* is always produced entirely with the **troff** tools and a phototypesetter. No better tools exist for large-scale, complex documents. However, with the rise of the personal computer in the 1980s and the recent popularity of *desktop publishing* and sophisticated word processors for personal computers, many of the older word processing tools for the UNIX system have become somewhat dated, especially for smaller documents. Nevertheless, the **troff** package and associated tools are still widely used among professional writers. Many experts who have used

troff for several years, and who have learned most of its subtleties, still find **troff** to be the most powerful and flexible word processing package available. These experts never seem to switch to another word processor!

The major drawback (and a major advantage!) of the **troff** package results from its design philosophy: it is intended to be a programming language for manipulating text and driving an output device. It does not use a WYSIWYG (what you see is what you get; pronounced "wis-ee-wig") model for its user interface. Rather, text is created with a normal text editor such as **vi**, and **troff** commands are interspersed with the text to produce an ASCII file containing both the contents (the text) and the form (the commands) of the document. In a separate operation the text file is processed (or compiled) by the **troff** program to produce the final output. This requires a two-step process that is not needed in modern word processors. Like many programming languages, **troff** is very powerful. However, it can be difficult to learn, and you may make several tries before you get the exact commands you need to produce a particular result.

In many versions of the UNIX system, the document preparation tools are sold as a separate add-on software package. If you don't need the specific capabilities of **troff**, or if you already have a favorite word processor from another operating system such as MS-DOS, you needn't purchase this *Documenter's Workbench* software. Most popular word processors for other operating systems are also available for the UNIX system, and they are usually adequate for most types of text processing. In fact modern word processors can outdo **troff** in many areas. On the other hand, recent versions of **troff** can produce output to drive printers that speak the Postscript formatting language.

Of course the basic concepts of filters and tools readily lend themselves to processing words, and many tasks normally associated with word processors can easily be done with filters and shell scripts.

The spell Command

Usually included with the basic system, the **spell** command is an intelligent and powerful spelling checker. It contains a large database of *root words* and has sophisticated algorithms for producing plurals and other endings for the English language. It also has the facility for lists of personal words — words that you define as correctly spelled. You can define acronyms, peoples' names, and unusual technical terms on a per-user or per-system basis to reduce the list of misspelled words that **spell** finds. The **spell** command ignores case in producing its output, treating uppercase and lowercase characters as equivalent. The **spell** command is usually a shell script kept in **/usr/bin/spell**, and it is an instructive script to browse.

The **spell** command reads its standard input or a filename list given as arguments, and it produces on its standard output a list of the words it thinks are incorrectly spelled.

```
$ spell file
```

The input must be a normal ASCII file, so **spell** will not work with most WYSIWYG word processors, which usually encode formatting information in non-ASCII form. The **spell** command will break up the input into a list of words and look up each word in a spelling list. It will ignore the **troff** formatting commands, and it uses a relatively intelligent algorithm for determining if a word is correctly spelled.

```
$ echo behavior behaviour | spell
behaviour
$
```

American spelling rules are used by default, though the −**b** (for British) option instructs **spell** to use British spelling rules.

```
$ echo behavior behaviour | spell -b
behavior
$
```

In addition to the built-in list of words, **spell** allows you to add a personal spelling list from the command line. The + (plus) option precedes a filename that includes a list of words that will be *eliminated* from the **spell** output.

```
$ cat local.spell
behaviour
$ echo behavior behaviour | spell +local.spell
$
```

The local file contains one word per line. You can add as many words as you need to a local file, but only one + option is allowed in a **spell** command. If you need more, you can use a pipeline.

```
$ spell +local.spell in.file | spell +second.local
```

The second **spell** command will filter the misspelled list from the first **spell** command to eliminate the words in both local files.

The −**v** (for verbose) option will display many of the rules that **spell** uses to make its decisions. It shows all the words that are not explicitly in the **spell** word list, and it displays the rules that **spell** uses to build derivative words:

```
$ echo derive derivate derivative deriving | spell -v
-e+ion-ion+ive    derivative
-e+ing    deriving
$
```

The root words *derive* and the more obscure *derivate* are in the **spell** word list, so they cause no output. *Derivative* is constructed by removing the *e* from derivate (−**e**) and adding "ion" (+**ion**). Then the "ion" is removed (−**ion**), and "ive" is added, producing the target word *derivative*. Similar rules are used for *deriving*, based on the root *derive*.

The troff Document Preparation Package

As mentioned, the major word processing tool used with the

UNIX system is the **troff** package. The name **troff** is used to refer to both the programming language as a whole, and to the command in the UNIX system that processes the source documents. The **troff** language produces output that can directly drive most popular phototypesetters and laser printers. It is actually a programming language that is optimized for typesetting. It takes an ASCII input file that contains formatting commands interspersed with the text and then *compiles* this source code into an instruction stream for a specified printer device. The output is no longer in ASCII format because it consists of commands in the control language of the printer device.

The **troff** language cannot produce ASCII output for dot-matrix or other ordinary printers because it produces control data for typesetters. A separate tool called **nroff** (for non-typesetting runoff) formats its input files for output on terminals or simple printers. Output quality is necessarily poorer than **troff** can do, but **nroff** takes the same input files and most of the same command line arguments as **troff**. The **nroff** tool is often used to review the document at the terminal. The **troff** output is of much higher quality and can produce *camera-ready* output for publishing. However, ASCII printer devices are still much more prevalent than laser printers, so **nroff** has an important place in the **troff** family. Many smaller computers support **nroff** only.

The troff Command Language

In general the function of **troff** is to *fill* or *flow* the input text across output lines to fill a page or column, using the character font specified. Larger or smaller character size, different spacing, and so on will change the amount of text that flows onto an output line from the input file. Commands are provided to prevent the filling functions of **troff**, and they are used for creating breaks between paragraphs and for making headings in a document. In addition, **troff** does an excellent job of hyphenation and both left and right justification of output lines, producing an optimal page layout.

The **troff** package includes a powerful *macro* capability that allows complex but frequently used functions to be coded in a simpler form. In fact several popular macro packages have been developed, and few people use the raw **troff** commands directly.

Figure 15-1 shows a short text file that can be read by **troff**. It was created by a normal text editor such as **vi**. Except for the macro packages, no popular tools exist for creating these source files, and users typically create them with their preferred text editors. Of course users must understand the command languages in order to create the source files! Many users have evolved template files that capture the major commands for the kinds of documents that they usually produce, and this template becomes the starting point when they begin a new document. If you are a **troff** beginner, you might ask a friend for a template as your starting point.

After being processed by **troff** and printed on a laser printer, Figure 15-1 looks like Figure 15-2. The commands provide complete control over the font type, the font size, and the placement of characters on the page, including filling and centering. Commands are available to change the page length and to set page headers and footers. Several internal *registers* can be used to count various things and to number footnotes, figures, and the like. The current date and time are available, and you can use the value of any register in the text with special inline commands.

Few operators are available to produce output graphics, and most **troff** documents are text-only. Some logos are available, but general integration of text and graphics is not possible with **troff**.

Most **troff** commands begin on a new line in the source document, interspersed with lines that contain text. These commands are identified by . (dot) as the first character on the line. All **troff** commands consist of lowercase characters immediately following the dot, and some of them can take

```
.sp 12
.ll 5i
.ps 14
.vs 16
This is a sample of \efBtroff\ef source text
.ps 6
and its output.
.ps 14
\efItroff\ef is actually
a \es+6programming language\es-6 that
.ul
fills
text automatically,
and can completely specify \efBfonts\ef and spacing.
Here is a simple equation:
\e(*S(\e*a\e(mul\e(*b)\e(->\e(if
.sp 4
and some other stuff:
\es8\ez\e(sq\es14\ez\e(sq\es22\ez\e(sq\es36\e(sq
\eb'\e(lt\e(lk\e(lb'\eb'\e(lc\e(lf' x \eb'\e(rc\e(rf'\eb'\e(rt\e(rk\e(rb'
.sp 3
.ps 8
\efItroff\ef can produce multi-column output, numbers pages
correctly with headers and footers,
.de bx
\e(br\e|\e\e$1\e|\e\e(br\el'|0\e(rn'\el'|0\e(ul'
..
.br
.ce
.bx "and can even put words in a box."
.vs 14
.br
\efItroff\ef allows extension through
.ps 24
macros
.ps 8
and the box is created by a macro definition.
.ps 10
Here are some more special characters:
\e(34   \e(ct   \e(co   \e(bu   \e(dg
.ps 6
.br
The \efBtbl\ef and \efBeqn\ef tools allow professional
formatting of tables and mathematical equations, respectively.
```

Figure 15-1.   Source document for a **troff** "sampler"

This is a sample of **troff** source text and its output. *troff* is actually a programming language that *fills* text automatically, and can completely specify **fonts** and spacing. Here is a simple equation: $\Sigma(\times | \beta) \rightarrow \infty$

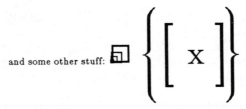

and some other stuff:

troff can produce multi-column output, numbers pages correctly with headers and footers, and can even put words in a box. *troff* allows extension through macros and the box is created by a macro definition. Here are some more special characters: ¾ ¢ © • †

The tbl and eqn tools allow professional formatting of tables and mathematical equations, respectively.

Figure 15-2.   Output from a **troff** "sampler"

additional arguments on the line, with each argument separated from the command and other arguments by white space. Most commands will make permanent changes in the **troff** environment, such as those to change the font style or character size. However, some commands, such as **.ul** (for underlining) refer only to the next line following the command, to change the processing of that line.

In addition, you can embed some commands in a line to affect text in the middle of the output line. These are identified by special *escape sequences* to distinguish them from normal text characters, and they may in turn be escaped to turn them back into normal sequences. Many dot commands have inline equivalents so that some changes can be made in the middle of a word. Many internal **troff** registers are of this form so that the values of the registers can be embedded in "normal" text.

The troff Command Line

The **troff** command reads the input source text from its standard input or from a filename list given as argument.

```
$ troff source.text
```

The **troff** output comes to standard output but is not very useful because it is in a typesetter format. It is usually redirected to a file or piped to another command that controls the printer device. You can use **lp** if the printer can be attached to a serial or parallel port.

The **troff** command can take several command line options, the most important of which specifies the printer type. Modern versions of **troff** use a filter scheme in which output is sent to a device-specific program that converts generic type-setting commands to commands for a specific device. This version of **troff** is known as **ditroff** (for device-independent **troff**), but the command line options are the same for most versions. The −**T** (for typesetter) option takes an argument that names the device.

```
$ troff -Ti300 source.file
```

The "i300" here names the IMAGEN Imprint 300 printer. The filtering is done directly by the **troff** command, from the −**T** option, and users needn't create the pipeline directly. Other command line options allow you to specify the value of some of the internal **troff** registers and can limit the output to some part of the true document. The −**a** (for ASCII) option causes an ASCII approximation of the real output. It is useful if you want to preview the document on a terminal before sending it to the typesetter. These command line options are also used for **nroff**, though devices named in the −**T** option will differ between **troff** and **nroff**.

Macro Packages for troff

Direct use of the **troff** formatting commands illustrated in Figure 15-1 is actually relatively rare. The commands are so difficult and deal with the document at such a detailed level that they are only used by a few experts. Instead, most users rely on the macro packages that encode blocks of **troff** commands for special purposes. The macro packages are themselves based on the **troff** macro definition feature. Macros can be read by **troff** when it begins executing, and whenever a macro name appears in a document, **troff** replaces the name with the full list of **troff** commands associated with that name. For example, *document headings*, such as chapter numbering and font changes for the headings, take many commands in **troff** that are encoded in a few simple-to-use commands in the macro packages. Users can learn the macros for their specific document type, and they never need to use **troff** commands directly.

Many different macro packages have been developed for special purposes, but only three have gained wide popularity. The **mm** (for memorandum macros) package produces business letters and business memos. The **me** (for macros for education) macros are used in universities for technical writing. Finally, the **man** (for manual) macros are used to produce the *UNIX User's Manual* and associated documents. Each defines a command set that is used instead of the direct **troff** commands, although the real **troff** commands can be interspersed with the macros when needed. The macros are usually named with capital letters, whereas the **troff** commands are all lowercase names. This can help you distinguish a **troff** source document from one that uses a macro package.

One of these macro packages can be specified in a **troff** command line. The package name is preceded by − (minus) in the **troff** command line.

```
$ troff -man cmd.1
```

This example selects the **man** macros for formatting the man page **cmd.1**. The macros in the packages differ substantially, and you can select only one for a single execution of the **troff** or **nroff** command. In addition, the different macro packages contain significant overlap of their commands, so it is easy to confuse commands from the different packages. For example, the .P command is used to start a new paragraph in the **mm** package, but .PP has the same function in the **man** package.

The man Macros

Traditionally the *UNIX User's Manual* has been produced with the **man** macro package. Nearly all new software for the UNIX system, both professional and public domain, includes at least one man page to describe its function. When this software is installed on a machine, these man pages are frequently placed on the hard disk, usually in the directory **/usr/man** or a subdirectory. The man pages are usually in **troff** source form, though thoughtful developers also provide versions that can be read with **cat**. If you wish to print this source-form documentation, you need the **troff** package and the **man** macros. In a sense this is a limitation of the UNIX system documentation style because the Documenter's Workbench package is usually a separately priced option in modern UNIX systems. Luckily, most documentation for UNIX systems comes in paper format as well as machine-readable format. If you have man pages but no **troff** package on your machine, you can delete the man pages and save disk space.

The tbl Command

The **troff** package includes several other tools. The **tbl** (for tables) command is a preprocessor for **troff** files that produces formatting commands that generate high-quality tables embedded in documents. Tables can be multicolumn and surrounded by boxes. The **tbl** command automatically produces the correct column positioning for the table, relieving the user of the task of manually laying out the table on the page. A special set of **tbl** macros has been defined, and the **tbl** command is a filter that reads these macros from the source file, figures out the best table layout, and then produces **troff** commands to do the job. The output of **tbl** is then fed to **troff** or **nroff** for printing.

```
$ tbl source.table | troff -mm -Ti10 | lp
```

The **tbl** command is a separate command rather than a macro package because **troff** can effectively use only one macro package at a time. Rather than embed the **tbl** command into every macro package, the **tbl** filter is used.

Formatting Mathematical Equations and Graphics

The **eqn** (for equations) command provides a similar tool for producing high-quality mathematical equations. The **eqn** command is a special-purpose preprocessor for **troff** that has its own set of commands. Figure 15-3 gives an example of **eqn** output. This command is still widely used for equation-intensive documents.

The **troff** package was not designed to allow embedded graphics within a document. However, some phototypesetters and laser printers allow the installation of a special graphics font, and **troff** can use such a font to produce *line graphics* that allow you to draw moderately complex block diagrams and flowcharts. The **pic** (for pictures) tool is another special-purpose preprocessor for **troff** to produce such pictures. Like **eqn**, **pic** has its own command set. Learning to use **tbl**, **eqn**, and **pic** can be as complex as using **troff** itself, but together they make a flexible document preparation system.

$$G(z) = e^{\ln G(z)} = \exp\left(\sum_{k\geq 1} \frac{S_k z^k}{k}\right) = \prod_{k\geq 1} e^{S_k z^k/k}$$

$$= \left(1 + S_1 z + \frac{S_1^2 z^2}{2!} + \cdots\right)\left(1 + \frac{S_2 z^2}{2} + \frac{S_2^2 z^4}{2^2 \cdot 2!} + \cdots\right) \cdots$$

$$= \sum_{m\geq 0}\left(\sum_{\substack{k_1,k_2,\ldots,k_m \geq 0 \\ k_1 + 2k_2 + \cdots + mk_m = m}} \frac{S_1^{k_1}}{1^{k_1}k_1!} \frac{S_2^{k_2}}{2^{k_2}k_2!} \cdots \frac{S_m^{k_m}}{m^{k_m}k_m!}\right) z^m$$

Figure 15-3.　　Typical **eqn** output

Going Further

Like most programming languages, the **troff** tools provide the
opportunity for developing tremendous skill. This discussion
has not attempted to provide a **troff** tutorial. To learn **troff**, you
must study the detailed user's manual provided with the
Documenter's Workbench package. In this section we will just
mention a few more of the issues associated with word
processing.

troff Directory Structure

The **troff** package and its associated commands reside in
several directories within the file system. The macro libraries
are located in **/usr/lib/macros**. However, the **troff** command

does not access this library directly; it does so through short linkage files in **/usr/lib/tmac**. The purpose of this indirect linkage is unclear, but if either directory is corrupted, the **troff** tolls probably will not work correctly. The printer and terminal descriptions used by **troff** reside in **/usr/lib/term** or **/usr/lib/nterm**, depending on which **troff** version is in use. Only one of these directories will be present. Note that the **troff** terminal description files are unrelated to the **terminfo** database used by full-screen applications such as **vi**.

The Writer's Workbench

One of the most interesting add-on tools based on **troff, spell**, and filters is a full-scale "critic" of documents written with **troff**. The Writer's Workbench package provides tools to analyze sentence construction, word usage, prose style, sexist references, and many other facets of documents. Its output is quite readable and can itself help to teach writing skills to students or even professional writers. It can operate in tutorial (voluminous) or summary mode (terse). Table 15-1 gives some summary data from one of the tools in the Writer's Workbench package—the *style analysis program*—for this book. You can compare these numbers against typical values for "good" technical memoranda or "good" training documents.

The Writer's Workbench is just one of many advanced tools that can make professional writing under the UNIX system quick and productive.

The spellhist File

Whenever **spell** executes, it adds all the misspelled words that it finds to a log file. The file **/usr/lib/spell/spellhist** contains this log. The log is a mixed blessing. On the one hand, a system administrator can use it to update the word list with commonly used acronyms and words. Also, the history allows statistical

Measure	Bell Laboratories Technical Memos	AT&T Training Documentation	This Book
Kincaid readability grade	grade 10.1 to 15.0	7.8 to 12.4	10.5
Average sentence length	16.7 to 25.3 words	12.3 to 20.2	20.9
Average length of content words	5.8 to 7.0 letters	5.5 to 6.8	5.85
Percentage of short sentences	29.2% to 38.0%	23.1% to 31.4%	33%
Percentage of long sentences	11.7% to 18.9%	7.3% to 12.8%	13%
Percentage of simple sentences minus the percentage of complex sentences	−24.2% to 30.1%	−28.4% to 56.0%	−3.0%
Percentage of compound sentences plus the percentage of compound-complex sentences	5.7% to 35.2%	4.7% to 25.7%	26%
Passives should be fewer than	28.6%	28.7%	20%
Nominalizations should be fewer than	4.2%	3.4%	2%
Expletives should be fewer than	5.7%	7.2%	2%

Table 15-1.   Readability Analysis of Some **troff** Documents

analysis of misspelled words, a useful feature in an educational setting. On the other hand, the history list can grow very large because there are no automatic administrative tools for truncating it. The system administrator must keep the **spellhist** file from growing too large. You can regularly truncate the spelling history manually, add the operation to a regularly scheduled cleanup script, or change the **/usr/bin/spell** script to stop it from building the history.

Building a New spell Database

If you use **spell** for documents with specialized jargon, you may need to update the **spell** word lists. Also, you can screen out many control commands from word processors other than **troff** if you add these codes to the **spell** database. Browse the **spellhist** file to determine which words should be added for your usage of the **spell** tools.

The word list used by **spell** is stored in an efficient, hashed database of word roots. This database, and most other material used by **spell**, is found in the directory **/usr/lib/spell**.

```
$ ls -FC /usr/lib/spell
compress*       hashmake*      hlistb      spellhist    spellprog*
hashcheck*      hlista         hstop       spellin*
$
```

The spelling lists are **hlista** and **hlistb**, although these cannot be browsed because they are binary files. The American word list is **hlista**; **hlistb** is the British list. The **hstop** file contains a stop list of misspelled words that would otherwise pass the spelling rules, such as "thier." The **spellprog** program is the actual, executable spelling check program called by **/usr/bin/spell** to do the work. The rest of this directory contains tools for updating the word lists. The **hashmake** program reads a list of words from its standard input and writes a list of hash codes to its standard output. The **spellin** program reads a list of hash codes from its standard input and writes a compressed spelling list to its standard output. The **hashcheck** program does the opposite: it reads a compressed spelling list from standard input and writes a list of hash codes to its standard output. The **spellin** program takes a numeric command line argument, specifying the number of hash codes in its input.

To add a new set of words to the **hlista** file, several steps are required. First, the list of new words must be prepared, one word per line. This list must then be given to **hashmake**. Third, **hlista** must be unpacked with **hashcheck**. Next, this output and the hashed list for the new words must be sorted together. Finally, the hash lists must be compressed with **spellin**. These commands will do the job.

```
$ hashmake < new.list | sort > new.hash # create hash file for new list
$ hashcheck < hlista | sort -mu - new.hash > hash.out  # create final list
$ NUM=`wc -l hash.out`                   # count needed below
$ spellin $NUM < hash.out > hlista       # and make new hlista
$
```

Be sure to save the original files until the new versions are tested!

Media

**S
I
X
T
E
E
N**

Disk management is an area of importance in any operating system, and you must work with *media* such as disks and magnetic tape from the first time you load the operating system onto the hard disk through your routine procedures for backing up your data for protection. The UNIX system provides two different basic modes of handling media, and you can use many different types and sizes of disks with UNIX systems.

Disk management can be complex, and there is really no quick way through the issues. UNIX systems differ markedly in the way that disk devices are named, and it is always a challenge to figure out the scheme used in a new release. In this chapter we will review manual access to the disk management tools and discuss some of the issues associated with using disks in your normal activities.

Disk Blocks and Inodes

The UNIX system manages disk space in units of a *block*. There are two different types of disk blocks, *physical blocks* of 512 bytes each, and *logical blocks*, usually of 1024 bytes each. In some SVR3 systems the logical block size is 2048 bytes. Logical blocks are used for file-related operations, but most disk management commands and lower-level disk operations report disk space in physical blocks. Only a few commands, notably **ls**, use bytes directly as a measure of space. For each disk-related command, you must convert the block values to the correct form to determine the correct sizes.

Disk operations are performed on a single logical block. That is, you cannot create a disk file smaller than a single block, even if it contains only 1 byte of data. Similarly, a file of 1025 bytes will take two logical blocks. Directories also use disk blocks, and again the minimum size of a directory is one logical block, even if only one file (or none!) is listed in the directory.

In addition to disk blocks, the file system contains a list of names of all the files on the disk, matched with a pointer to the first disk block associated with each name. Each name and the associated blocks are stored in an entity called the *inode* (for identification node). One element in a directory is the inode used for each file. Whenever a file is updated, the system updates the correct inode. The list of inodes is fixed when a file system is created. You will seldom have reason to deal with inodes, but the inode list can fill up, especially on floppy disks, and you cannot create a new file if no inode is available.

File Systems

The list of disk blocks, inodes, and other information associated with disk usage is maintained separately for each *file system* on the machine. Each physical disk attached to the machine must have its own file system, though you can create more than one file system on a disk. The reverse is not possible: a file system cannot span more than one disk. When your UNIX system was installed, either one or two file systems were probably created on the disk, usually named / (root) and /**usr** (user). Floppy disks and magnetic tapes can also have file systems, although this is not required.

Individual file systems are handled separately within the UNIX system, and you cannot **ln** files across file systems. You must **cp** a file to move it to another file system. If one file system fills up or fails for some reason, it will *not* affect other file systems on the machine.

Hard-Disk Management

Because the primary activity of the UNIX system is on the machine's built-in *hard disk*, you should be especially concerned with its management. Disk space always fills up as time passes, and it is a natural tendency not to delete material from the hard disk. If you understand your disk space budget, you can keep your machine running better and guarantee that enough space is available when you need it.

Disk Free Space — The df Command

You can determine the amount of disk space for each file system on the machine, including both free space and space in use, with the **df** (for disk free) command.

```
$ df
/          (/dev/dsk/0s1   ):    55314 blocks      10115 i-nodes
$
```

The file system location is reported (/ only in this output) in the leftmost column for each file system on the machine. The second column gives the device name of the file system in the /**dev** directory. The number of free blocks is given next, and the number of free inodes is reported in the last column. These blocks in the **df** output are physical blocks of 512 bytes each. To determine the actual amount of free space on the disk, multiply the number of blocks by 512.

```
55314 * 512 = 28,320,768 bytes free
```

The inode count gives the total number of new files that you can create before the file system is full. If you create 10115 files without deleting any, the file system will be full even though there may still be some free blocks.

The **df** command will also report on the *total* amount of disk space in the file system. Use the −**t** (for total) option with **df**.

```
$ df −t
/          (/dev/dsk/0s1   ):    55314 blocks      10115 i-nodes
               total:    105944 blocks    13232 i-nodes
$
```

You can easily compute the percentage of disk space used and can see how fast the disk space is being used up.

Some SVR3 systems include a **dfspace** (for disk free space) command that combines **df** with an estimate of the percentage of disk space used up. Try **dfspace** on your machine to see if it is present.

Disk Space Used — The du Command

The **df** command reports on disk space available in the file system as a whole. In addition, you can determine how much space any files or directories are using. The **du** (for disk usage) command gives this report, for directories given as arguments.

```
$ du /usr/spool/cron
6          /usr/spool/cron/crontabs
1          /usr/spool/cron/atjobs
8          /usr/spool/cron
$
```

The **du** command also counts blocks in 512-byte physical blocks. To determine the true size of the disk usage, multiply the output from **du** by 512, as for **df**.

By default, **du** does not take a filename as argument, only a directory name. It will report on all subdirectory trees within the named directory. The —**a** (for all) option causes an output line to be generated for each file and directory in the named list, instead of just the directories. The —**s** (for summary) option causes only a grand total for each of the named directories to be displayed.

```
$ du -s /etc
5258    /etc
$
```

This can be helpful when you want a quick summary of disk usage.

Finally, **du** will silently ignore files and directories that it cannot open. Use the —**r** (for report) option to make **du** complain when it cannot open a file or directory.

These two commands, **df** and **du**, are invaluable tools for managing your disk space. Execute them regularly, either manually or in a regularly scheduled demon, to track the disk usage on your machine.

Size of Files and the ulimit

Most files under the UNIX system are relatively small; a file of a megabyte or larger is unusual. Internally, however, the system allows programs to take as much disk space as they need. Thus rogue processes or failing applications can incorrectly use all the disk space on the machine. To prevent this, UNIX provides the **ulimit** (for user limit) variable, the value of which is the largest file that can be created within the file system. In most UNIX systems the default **ulimit** is quite small.

```
$ ulimit
2048
$
```

This is the maximum file size in physical blocks. When you try to create a file larger than the **ulimit**, the file growth will stop at the **ulimit**, and the command that creates the file will fail with an error.

The default **ulimit** is set inside the kernel, though it can be changed for an individual login session. Naturally you cannot *increase* your **ulimit**, but you can reduce it. Only the superuser can increase the **ulimit** for a session. You set the **ulimit** by giving the new value as an argument.

```
$ ulimit
2048
$ ulimit 1000
$ ulimit
1000
$
```

This change is active only for your current session, and when the change occurs in a subshell, it will not affect the parent session. Often the system administrator will set the **ulimit** in the system as a whole in a script executed when the machine boots, so it is some reasonable value when you log into the machine. The **ulimit** is frequently set to 1 or 2 megabytes in small machines, so if you use large databases or other large files, be sure that the **ulimit** is not too small for your needs.

Never Fill Up the Hard Disk

Hard-disk space is always limited and always seems to fill up faster than you expect. If the space available for files becomes full, the machine will stop working, either by crashing, or by slowing down so much that the system becomes inoperative. When this happens, you must boot the machine from a floppy disk and manually remove unneeded files from the hard disk, which can be a difficult and complex procedure. Alternatively, you may need to reload the system software, causing all the files on the hard disk to be lost.

Therefore, you should always maintain at least **10 percent** free space on the machine's main hard disk. Use the **df** command regularly to determine the disk space available and delete unneeded files and directories. Many system administrators execute **df** whenever they log into the machine and regularly act to keep the disk at least **10 percent** free.

You can use some routine procedures to reduce disk space usage.

First, back up little-used files and directories to floppy disk and only reload the floppies when needed.

Second, use the /**tmp** directory to store temporary files and intermediate data from your shell scripts. The contents of /**tmp** are deleted every time the machine boots, so its contents will not remain in the file system for too long.

Third, use **find** to routinely search for files that are larger than a selected size and delete files that are growing. For example, this command

```
$ find / -size +200 -exec ls -l {} \;
```

will display the name and size of all files larger than 200 blocks. If you do this, be careful not to delete files that are legitimately larger than the cutoff size, such as **/unix** and many others. Look for files that continue to grow over a period of days and weeks. Files in the directories **/bin**, **/lib**, **/usr/bin**, and **/usr/lib** are usually legitimate, while others may be suspicious.

Fourth, watch for the accumulation of files named **core** in the system with the following command:

```
$ find / -name "*core*" -print
```

These **core** files are produced when a command or application fails for some reason; they are often large and are rarely useful. In fact their presence signals some pathological condition in the machine that may need attention. Sometimes the directory location of **core** files can be a clue to the cause of the failure.

Finally, watch user areas such as HOME directories and subdirectories for cases of "disk-hogging" by users. Users should be considerate of the machine's resources and other users.

Floppy Disk Management

Before you can use a floppy disk, it must be *formatted*. Formatting prepares the disk for use, and you must format all new disks after you buy them. You can also format an old disk to delete its contents and prepare it for reuse.

How a diskette is formatted depends on the type of disk. A *double-sided, double-density* disk can hold 360 or 400 kilobytes (KB) of data. This is the common diskette used in older PC-compatible machines. *High-density* diskettes can hold 1.2 or 1.4 megabytes (MB) of data. These disks are used in AT-class machines. These are the two most common disk types, and you must specify the disk type when buying the disk. Three-inch plastic-cased disks may differ in their capacity.

The type of diskette to use depends on your machine hardware. Most UNIX systems have 5 1/4-inch *high-density* disk drives, and the system software is probably provided on this larger size disk. However, you can format and use 360-KB disks with these drives as long as you select the correct disk format. You cannot use a double-sided, double-density diskette for more than the 360 KB allowed.

Floppy disk formats for the UNIX system are not the same as for the MS-DOS system. Even if your machine can execute a stand-alone MS-DOS system and your disk drives can use MS-DOS disks while MS-DOS is running, most UNIX systems do not allow you to format, read, or write MS-DOS diskettes directly. Do not intermix diskettes for the two operating systems, even if you have a merge feature on your machine. Similarly, you cannot use disks formatted for the UNIX system with MS-DOS. Loss of data on the floppy disk can result!

Once a diskette is formatted, the UNIX system provides two ways to use it. First, you can create a *file system* on the floppy and use it like a hard disk. For example, you can create directories, **cd** around in them, and **cp** files just as you do on the hard disk. To use this form of disk, you must create a file system on the disk and then *mount* it into the hard disk file system at a specific place, or *mount point*. When you have done this, you can use the floppy just like any other directory in the system.

The second way to access a floppy diskette is called *raw access*. Disks used in the raw form will not have file systems associated with them, and you cannot use them like a hard disk. However, this form of access allows you to create more than a diskful of data; when one disk fills up, you can simply go on to a second disk. The raw form of diskette access is usually used for backing up or archiving data.

Another complication arises if you want to be able to *boot* the machine from a floppy disk rather than from the machine's hard disk. Bootable floppy disks are seldom used with UNIX systems, although the first disk of the System Installation Set is a bootable disk. Bootable disks must contain a *boot block* and an executable kernel because the entire operating system must run from the floppy. These additional requirements substantially reduce the disk space available for your data, so unless you have a real need for bootable floppies, you should not use them. The decision on whether a floppy disk is bootable is made when the disk is formatted, but the normal formatting tools do not create bootable disks. You usually must copy the first disk of the System Installation Set and then edit its contents to create a new bootable disk.

Diskette Device Files

Diskettes (and hard disks as well) are managed through the *device file* that names the disk type. These device files specify both the disk drive to use for an operation and the type of format that the disk has. When you use a floppy disk you name the device file that refers to that type of disk on that drive. Table 16-1 lists disk device files for SVR3 systems, both for hard disks (HD) and floppy disks (FD).

All the disk devices are included in the directories **dsk** (for disk) for the mountable disk types, or **rdsk** (for raw disk) for the raw disk types, within the /**dev** directory. Each file in these directories refers to a specific type of device.

Each filename encodes a specific device for that type of access to the disk. For example, in the name **f0q15dt**, **f0** refers to floppy disk drive 0; **f1** is used for floppy drive 1 if it is installed on your machine. The **q15** specifies a quad-density disk with 15 tracks per cylinder. In the name **f0d9dt**, **d9** refers to a double-density disk with 9 tracks per cylinder.

In addition, **dt** specifies a disk with no boot block, while **d** specifies a disk with boot block. Normally you should use the **dt** format because it provides more space on the floppy for your use. However, some application software is shipped on disks in the **d** format, and you must use that format to read them. Experiment with other formats if you cannot read a disk in one format.

Thus **f0q15dt** is a 1.2-MB disk in drive 0, while **f0d9dt** is a 360-KB floppy, also in drive 0. Most disk drives that can use 1.2-MB disks can also format and read 360-KB disks, but drives marked 360-KB cannot use 1.2-MB disks.

Formatting Floppy Disks

To format a disk manually, use the **format** command, which usually resides in the /**bin** directory but is sometimes found in /**etc**. If it is in /**etc**, you will probably need to use the full pathname when you use it, or else add /**etc** to your *PATH*. The **format** command takes a complete pathname of the device you wish to format as an argument.

```
$ format /dev/rdsk/f0q15dt
```

You need a high-density disk and a 1.2-MB drive to use this format. Insert the disk into the drive and close the drive door before executing this command. Be sure that the write-protect tab on the side of the disk has been removed. The floppy will be formatted, erasing any data already on the disk.

The raw device (/**dev/rdsk/**...) is always used in formatting floppies because formatting is a low-level operation that requires basic access to the disk, below the file system level.

Raw Device File	Block Device File	Device	Size	Comment
/dev/rdsk/0s0	dev/dsk/0s0	HD 0	Variable	Entire disk
/dev/rdsk/1s0	dev/dsk/1s0	HD 1	Variable	Entire disk
/dev/rdsk/0s1	/dev/dsk/0s1	HD 0	Variable	root file system
/dev/rdsk/1s1	/dev/dsk/1s1	HD 1	Variable	tmp file system
/dev/rdsk/0s2	/dev/dsk/0s2	HD 0	Variable	Swap area
/dev/rdsk/1s2	/dev/dsk/1s2	HD 1	Variable	Swap area
/dev/rdsk/0s3	/dev/dsk/0s3	HD 0	Variable	usr file system
/dev/rdsk/1s3	/dev/dsk/1s3	HD 1	Variable	usr file system
/dev/rdsk/0s4	/dev/dsk/0s4	HD 0	Variable	usr2 file system
/dev/rdsk/1s4	/dev/dsk/1s4	HD 1	Variable	usr2 file system
/dev/rdsk/0s5	/dev/dsk/0s5	HD 0	Variable	DOS-only partition
/dev/rdsk/1s5	/dev/dsk/1s5	HD 1	Variable	DOS-only partition
/dev/rdsk/0s6	/dev/dsk/0s6	HD 0	Variable	Boot block
/dev/rdsk/1s6	/dev/dsk/1s6	HD 1	Variable	nsr 3 file system
/dev/rdsk/0s7	/dev/dsk/0s7	HD 0	Variable	Alternate tracks
/dev/rdsk/1s7	/dev/dsk/1s7	HD 1	Variable	Alternate tracks
/dev/rdsk/f0d4dt	/dev/dsk/f0d4dt	FD 0	160 KB	Entire disk
/dev/rdsk/f0d4d	/dev/dsk/f0d4d	FD 0	160 KB	All but boot block
/dev/rdsk/f1d4dt	/dev/dsk/f1d4dt	FD 1	160 KB	Entire disk
/dev/rdsk/f1d4d	/dev/dsk/f1d4d	FD 1	160 KB	All but boot block
/dev/rdsk/f0d8dt	/dev/dsk/f0d8dt	FD 0	320 KB	Entire disk
/dev/rdsk/f0d8d	/dev/dsk/f0d8d	FD 0	320 KB	All but boot block
/dev/rdsk/f1d8dt	/dev/dsk/f1d8dt	FD 1	320 KB	Entire Disk
/dev/rdsk/f1d8d	/dev/dsk/f1d8d	FD 1	320 KB	All but boot block
/dev/rdsk/f0d9dt	/dev/dsk/f0d9dt	FD 0	360 KB	Entire disk
/dev/rdsk/fd048	/dev/dsk/fd048	FD 0	360 KB	Entire disk
/dev/rdsk/f0d9d	/dev/dsk/f0d9d	FD 0	360 KB	All but boot block
/dev/rdsk/f1d9dt	/dev/dsk/f1d9dt	FD 1	360 KB	Entire disk
/dev/rdsk/fd148	/dev/dsk/fd148	FD 1	360 KB	Entire disk
/dev/rdsk/f1d9d	/dev/dsk/f1d9d	FD 1	360 KB	All but boot block

Table 16-1.   Disk Device Files for SVR3 Systems

Raw Device File	Block Device File	Device	Size	Comment
/dev/rdsk/f0q15dt	/dev/dsk/f0q15dt	FD 0	1.2 MB	Entire disk
/dev/rdsk/fd096	/dev/dsk/fd096	FD 0	1.2 MB	Entire disk
/dev/rdsk/fd	/dev/dsk/fd	FD 0	1.2 MB	Entire disk
/dev/rSA/diskette	/dev/SA/diskette	FD 0	1.2 MB	Entire disk
/dev/rdsk/f0q15d	/dev/dsk/f0q15d	FD 0	1.2 MB	All but boot block
/dev/rdsk/f1q15dt	/dev/dsk/f1q15dt	FD 1	1.2 MB	Entire disk
/dev/rdsk/fd196	/dev/dsk/fd196	FD 1	1.2 MB	Entire disk
/dev/rdsk/f1q15d	/dev/dsk/f1q15d	FD 1	1.2 MB	All but boot block

Table 16-1.   Disk Device Files for SVR3 Systems (*continued*)

The **format** command will format the named disk type and verify that the format is correct.

```
$ format /dev/rdsk/f0q15dt
formatting...............
Formatted 160 tracks: 0 thru 159, interleave 2.
$
```

Other diskette devices will give slightly different output from **format**, as in this example for a 360-KB, double-density diskette.

```
$ /bin/format /dev/rdsk/f0d9dt
format limited to track: 80
formatting........
Formatted 80 tracks: 0 thru 79, interleave 4.
$
```

The **format** command will complain if the disk is defective or is not the right type, and the operation will fail. If it fails, verify that you are using the correct disk type, in the correct drive, for the device filename you are using. If you cannot format a disk after two or three tries, discard it. Don't take chances with bad disks; the data that you could lose is usually much more valuable than the diskette.

Once a disk is formatted, you won't need to reformat it unless it becomes damaged, or you wish to erase it completely. Part of the formatting operation is a verification step that will find bad blocks on the floppy and mark them as unusable. Occasionally you can improve a questionable disk by reformatting it because a new bad block table will be created on the floppy.

Making a File System on the Disk

After the disk is successfully formatted, you can either use it for raw access or make a file system on the disk. The /**etc**/**mkfs** (for make file system) command will place a file system onto a newly formatted diskette. A file system is required to mount a disk. The **mkfs** command takes the device file as argument.

```
$ /etc/mkfs /dev/rdsk/f0q15dt 2400
```

Use the *raw* device for creating a file system on a floppy disk. Creating a file system on a disk will erase the disk because the table of directories and files will be reconstructed.

Specifying Blocks and inodes

In addition to the device file, **mkfs** requires you to specify the number of blocks to use for the file system. This number follows the device name in the **mkfs** command line and is expressed in 512-byte physical units. Normally you will use the entire disk, so you can compute the number of blocks from the disk size: 1.2 MB divided by 512 bytes per block will be 2400 blocks for a high-density disk, as in the previous example. You can specify fewer blocks, but this will waste the disk space not in the file system. If you specify too many blocks, the **mkfs** operation will fail with an error.

You can also specify the number of inodes to allocate in the file system. If you do not give this number, **mkfs** will compute a default value, usually one fourth of the number of blocks specified. You cannot have more files and directories on the diskette than the number of inodes, but the default value is rarely exceeded.

Because the table of inodes takes disk space, you can reduce the number of inodes and recover a few KB of space on the disk if you are sure that you will keep only a few files on the disk. On the other hand, if you have a great many files on the disk, you can increase the number of inodes. Generally you should not reduce the inode value below 100, and the default value is usually best. Once you have specified the disk blocks and inodes, you cannot change them without losing the data on the disk.

To specify the number of inodes to allocate on the disk, add it following a : (colon) after the block number.

```
$ /etc/mkfs /dev/rdsk/f0q15dt 2400:200
```

No white space is allowed between the blocks, the :, and the inode count.

The **mkfs** command reports on the values it is using and allows you to abort the operation before it starts.

```
$ /etc/mkfs /dev/rdsk/f0q15dt 2400
Mkfs: /dev/rdsk/f0q15dt?
(DEL if wrong)
```

Press DEL immediately to prevent the **mkfs** operation. Be sure to check the device again at this opportunity, because you can destroy your hard disk or other file system if you mistakenly give the wrong device name and make a new file system over your valuable data.

If you accept the values as prompted, do nothing, and **mkfs** will continue.

```
bytes per logical block = 1024
total logical blocks = 1200
total inodes = 336
gap (physical blocks) = 7
cylinder size (physical blocks) = 400
mkfs: Available blocks = 1176
$
```

The new file system is now usable.

Mounting a Floppy Disk

Once the disk has been formatted and the file system created, you can *mount* the disk. Mounting a disk links its file system with the normal file system on the machine's hard disk. After you have mounted a floppy disk (or any other file system), you can **cd** into it, **cp** files to and from its directories, and use all the normal file system commands.

You can think of a file system as a part of a directory hierarchy that extends below a specific directory. Like the normal *root directory* /, each file system has a root directory, and all its subdirectories fan out from this root. When you mount a floppy disk, you are actually attaching its root directory into a place in the normal file system. This place, called the *mount point*, is a normal directory in the hard-disk file system. That is, you can create a directory on your hard disk and mount the floppy at that point. Then you can **cd** into the directory on the hard disk, and you will be in the root directory on the mounted file system.

For example, most systems provide a default mount point at /**mnt** (for mount) in the / directory. Normally this directory is empty.

```
$ ls -a /mnt
$
```

When you mount a floppy disk at that point, the root directory of the floppy becomes the contents of the /**mnt** directory.

```
$ /etc/mount /dev/dsk/f0q15dt /mnt
mount: warning: <> mounted as </mnt>
$ ls -a /mnt
data
sample
$
```

When you *unmount* the floppy disk, the mount point becomes empty again.

```
$ /etc/umount /dev/dsk/f0q15dt
$ ls -al /mnt
$
```

If any files exist in the mount point directory before the floppy is mounted, they will be hidden by the mount and will not be visible until the mounted file system is unmounted. The files will not be lost or disturbed, but it is best to use an empty directory as a mount point.

The mount point can be any directory location that you choose within the file system, though a standard mount point is used most often. SVR3 systems provide the directory /**mnt** to mount floppy disks or tapes. You can mount only one file system at any mount point, so you will need another one if you have more than one file system mounted, perhaps by two floppy disk drives. Create the directory /**mnt2** as this second mount point if it does not already exist in your root directory.

When you create the file system on the floppy with the administrative user agent, you can specify a *file system name*. If you do not mount the disk at this mount point, the **mount** command gives the error message

```
mount: warning: <fsname> mounted at <mount-point>
```

where **fsname** is the file system name and **mount-point** is the mount point. This is a friendly warning and is not really an error.

While mounted, the UNIX system will follow normal procedures to keep the floppy up to date with the changes that you make, and it will act just like the hard disk in all ways. The **mount** operation will add an entry to the *system mount table* in /**etc/mnttab**. The mount table is read by several system programs that work with mounted devices, such as **df**. However, no permanent record is made of which file systems are mounted, so if you reboot the machine while a floppy disk or tape is mounted, it will not be mounted after the reboot. Shutting down the machine while a floppy is mounted is safe only if you use the **shutdown** command. It is best to mount media only while they are in use and to unmount them when you are through using them.

Using the mount Command

The **mount** command is used to mount a file system at a specific mount point. Give the device file to mount as the first argument and the mount point as the second argument. Use the block device name, not the raw device.

```
$ /etc/mount /dev/dsk/f0q15dt /mnt
```

This will mount the 1.2-MB floppy at /**mnt**. You cannot remove the diskette from the drive until you have unmounted it.

Once the device is mounted, you can **cd** to the directories through the mount point and use it as a normal directory.

```
$ cd /mnt
$ ls -FC
data        file1       file2
$
```

The mounted file system is writable as well as readable, so you must remove any write-protect tab from the disk before you mount it. The mount will fail if a disk is write-protected unless you specify that the diskette be mounted *read-only*, which means that you can read the disk but cannot write it. You should mount your precious archive disks read-only to guarantee that you cannot accidentally destroy them. Use the −**r** (for read) option with **mkfs** to mount a diskette as read-only.

```
$ /etc/mount /dev/dsk/f0q15dt /mnt -r
```

On SVR2 systems **mount** requires the −**r** option *after* the device file and mount point. With SVR3, however, you should use the −**r** in its normal spot.

```
$ /etc/mount -r /dev/rdsk/f0q15dt /mnt
```

You cannot write a file or change anything about a file system that was mounted as read-only.

The **df** command can report on the capacity of a mounted diskette.

```
$ /etc/mount /dev/dsk/f0q15dt /mnt
mount: warning: <> mounted as </mnt>
$ df -t
/        (/dev/dsk/0s1   ):      55314 blocks     10115 i-nodes
               total:    105944 blocks   13232 i-nodes
/mnt     (/dev/dsk/f0q15dt):       2358 blocks       286 i-nodes
               total:     2400 blocks     288 i-nodes
$
```

This can help you track the use of space on your mountable media. The **du** command will also work as expected on directories in mounted file systems.

In addition, the −**d** option is available for mounting *remote resources*. These are associated with the *Remote File Sharing (RFS)* feature of SVR3 and cannot be used with floppy disks or tape. We will discuss RFS in Chapter 22.

Unmounting a Diskette

When you are through using a mounted diskette or tape, you must unmount it before you can remove it from the drive. Use the **/etc/umount** command, with the device file as argument.

```
$ /etc/umount /dev/dsk/f0q15dt
$
```

In SVR3 you can also use the mount point as argument instead of the device file.

```
$ /etc/umount /mnt
$
```

These commands will remove the diskette or tape from the system, and you can then remove it from the drive. You must unmount the same device that you have previously mounted. If the operation succeeds, **umount** will return silently to the shell.

If any user has an open file in the mounted file system or has used **cd** to enter the file system, **umount** will fail. All the files and directories on the disk must be free before **umount** will work.

```
$ /etc/mount /dev/dsk/f0q15dt /mnt
mount: warning: <> mounted as </mnt>
$ cd /mnt
$ /etc/umount /dev/dsk/f0q15dt
umount: /dev/dsk/f0q15dt busy
$ cd /
$ /etc/umount /dev/dsk/f0q15dt
$
```

All users must be free from a resource before it can be unmounted. Luckily, this protects you from unmounting your default hard disk!

Reporting on Mounted Media

If you give the **mount** command with no arguments, it will report on the devices that are currently mounted on the machine.

```
$ mount
/ on /dev/dsk/0s1 read/write on Wed Aug 26 10:45:03 1987
$ mount /dev/dsk/f0q15dt /mnt
mount: warning: <> mounted as </mnt>
$ mount
/ on /dev/dsk/0s1 read/write on Wed Aug 26 10:45:03 1987
/mnt on /dev/dsk/f0q15dt read/write on Wed Aug 26 12:46:11 1987
$ umount /mnt
$ mount
/ on /dev/dsk/0s1 read/write on Wed Aug 26 10:45:03 1987
$
```

This report changes to read-only when the diskette is mounted with the **−r** option.

Copying Floppy Disks

The UNIX system provides two different procedures for copying floppy disks. In both cases, you must format the new floppy before copying to it. You must also be sure that the type and format are the same for both the original disk and the copy.

Manually Copying a Mounted Disk with cp

First, you can mount the floppy disk as just described and copy all the files individually from it to a temporary directory on the hard disk. You can use the **cp** command, perhaps in a shell script to make it easier to use. Alternatively, you can use the **cpio −p** command, discussed at the end of this chapter.

Then you can mount a new formatted floppy, with file system, and copy the files from the temporary directory to the new disk with the same commands that you used to create the temporary directory. If you have a second floppy drive, you can mount the new formatted floppy, with file system, on the second drive (at a different mount point) and copy the files directly from the source to the target directory.

This procedure is tedious and can lead to errors. Take care to copy all the subdirectories and files whose names begin with . (dot) correctly. In addition, it only works with mountable media. However, when you wish to delete or change the files during the move, this is the only procedure to follow.

The dd Command

The UNIX system provides another command that makes an *exact* copy of a floppy disk, whether it is mountable or not. As usual, the new disk must already be formatted and must be the same size and type as the original disk that you are copying. However, you needn't make a file system on the new disk because the copy procedure will do that as part of the exact copy.

Use the **dd** command to copy media exactly. By default, it copies its standard input to its standard output, so you can copy a file with the following command line:

```
$ dd < in.file > out.file
```

If one of the files is a device, you can give the device pathname.

```
$ dd < /dev/rdsk/f0q15dt > /tmp/out.file
2400+0 records in
2400+0 records out
$
```

The **dd** command reports on the number of blocks it reads and writes. The number following the + is a count of bytes in any partial blocks that were copied.

To copy a floppy disk, use **dd** to copy the disk device file into a temporary file, as in the previous example. Next, replace the diskette with a new formatted floppy of the same type; then use **dd** again to copy the temporary file out to the disk.

```
$ dd < /tmp/out.file >/dev/rdsk/f0q15dt
```

This procedure uses the raw device file to guarantee a complete, exact copy of the entire floppy disk. To complete the operation, delete the temporary file.

This procedure will work regardless of the floppy type or the number of files and directories on it because the device as a whole is treated as a single large file. When the entire disk is copied, the end-of-file marker is read and the operation ends.

The dd Command Line

The **dd** command line syntax differs significantly from that of most other commands. You give options to **dd** as *keyword=value* pairs, where *keyword* is the option to set and *value* is the value to use for that option. For example, you can give the input filename after the **if=** (for input file) option and give the output filename after the **of=** (for output file) option. If given, these options will replace the standard input and output.

```
$ dd if=/dev/rdsk/f0q15dt of=/tmp/out.file
```

By default, **dd** will make its copy by reading a 512-byte block, then writing it, then reading another, and so on. This can be slow, so options are provided to increase the block size (in multiples of 512 bytes for best performance). Significantly faster operations can be performed if you use a block size of 5120 bytes. You specify block size with the **bs=** (for block size) option.

```
$ dd bs=5120 </dev/rdsk/f0q15dt >/tmp/out.file
240+0 records in
240+0 records out
$
```

The block size is changed for both input and output operations, and the number of records copied will change because the block size changed. This is the most efficient form of the **dd** command.

You can also specify the block size separately for input and output operations. The **ibs=** (for input block size) and **obs=** (for output block size) options are used to set input and output block size, respectively.

```
$ dd if=/dev/rdsk/f0q15dt ibs=5120 of=/tmp/out.file obs=51200
240+0 records in
24+0 records in
$
```

When **ibs** differs from **obs**, **dd** will give a different count of records in from records out, which is relatively inefficient because **dd** must construct the output blocks before writing them. If you are making a copy of a floppy, use the same block size for all four reads and writes, preferably with **bs=**.

In addition, **dd** provides tools to change data formats during the copy. The **conv=** (for convert) option specifies a conversion algorithm to use. Allowed are **ascii**, to convert files from EBCDIC to ASCII; **ebcdic**, to convert from ASCII to EBCDIC; **lcase**, to make all lowercase characters in the copy; and **ucase**, to make all uppercase characters. In addition, the **swab** option allows you to swap the order of each pair of bytes in the file. This can be very useful when you are porting files from other machines that use a different byte-ordering system than yours. Any of these options can be combined on the **conv=** option if they are separated by a , (comma).

```
$ dd bs=5120 conv=ascii,swab < in.file > out.file
```

These conversion options are useful for file-to-file copies but less so for file-to-disk copies.

Finally, **dd** allows you to skip some blocks on the input or output before beginning the copy. Use **skip=n** to skip the first n blocks of the input file before copying and **seek=n** to skip the first n blocks of the output file before beginning the output. Use these options with care; they can easily destroy a file system if you misuse them.

Raw Device Access — The cpio Command

The **mount** procedure allows the convenience of file system access to floppy disk and tape devices. But mounting a diskette is relatively slow, and the standard file system takes disk space that you might wish to use for your data. Further, you cannot expand your files beyond the disk space available on the mounted disk. A complete file must fit onto the mounted disk; you cannot split files across multiple file systems.

To solve these problems, the UNIX system provides the **cpio** (for copy in/out) command to give you raw access to the diskette without mounting it. This is actually an archiving program that copies a list of files into a single large output file, creating headers between the files so that you can recover them individually. The **cpio** command has options that allow you to create archives and others that let you read the archives and reload the files from the archives. You can use **cpio** to create archives directly on the machine's hard disk, though it is most often used to create archives on a floppy disk or tape.

The **cpio** archives can span multiple diskettes, allowing efficient backup of large directory hierarchies. In addition, **cpio** preserves file ownership and modification times, and it can archive both text and binary files. Use of **cpio** is the most efficient way to store files on a floppy disk, and a **cpio** archive is usually somewhat smaller than the original files that make up the archive. The system software and most installable disks are usually in **cpio** format.

Using Media for cpio Operations

Before you use **cpio** with a floppy disk or tape, you must format the media as usual. However, you do not need **mkfs** because **cpio** will overwrite the file system as it creates its archive on the floppy. In fact, once you have used a diskette with **cpio**, you will need to create a new file system on the disk before you can mount it. The **cpio** disks are not compatible with file system diskettes, so creating a file system with **mkfs** will destroy any data stored in **cpio** format.

You must use the raw device file for **cpio** operations because **cpio** does not use the file system. Because **cpio** sends its archive to its standard output, you should use a command of this form when writing to a floppy disk.

```
$ echo filename | cpio -o > /dev/rdsk/f0q15dt
```

Before executing this or any other **cpio** command line, be sure that you have a formatted floppy disk in the correct drive with the drive door closed. The diskette must be write-enabled to allow output, but it can be write-protected for reading.

Creating cpio Archives

When creating an archive, **cpio** takes a list of files or path-names on its standard input and writes the archive on its standard output. This output is nearly always redirected to a normal file or a device file. You must give the filenames one per line in the standard input stream. The −o (for output) option instructs **cpio** to create an archive from a list of files.

```
$ echo "$HOME/myfile\n$HOME/yourfile" | cpio -o > output.file
```

The **ls** command is often used to archive a complete directory.

```
$ ls | cpio -o > output.file
```

You can also execute **cpio** with the filename list redirected from a file.

```
$ cpio -o > output.file < file.list
```

A single output file is created that contains all the files in the input list.

Several other command line options are often used with **cpio** −o. The −a (for access) flag resets the file modification times associated with each file. By default, the original time stamps are preserved on all the files.

The −c (for character) option causes **cpio** to produce its internal headers in character form instead of binary format. This is required for portability and should be the default. You should always use the −c option with **cpio**. Most **cpio** files you receive will also use it.

The −B (for block) option instructs **cpio** to create data blocks rather than a data stream. If the **cpio** file will reside on the machine's hard disk or will be moved via **uucp**, the −B option is not required. But if the archive will reside on a floppy disk or tape, you should use the −B option. This speeds up access to the disk.

The −v (for verbose) option tells **cpio** to echo the names of all files as it reads them. This output comes to standard error.

Using cpio

Frequently **cpio** is paired with the **find** command to generate archives. The **find** command will search a directory for files that meet its command line arguments and write the pathnames to its standard output. This output is piped to **cpio** for archiving.

```
$ cd
$ find . -print | cpio -oc >/tmp/home.cpio
113 blocks
$
```

The **cpio** command reports on the number of blocks written if there are no errors. The command in the previous example creates an archive containing all files and subdirectories in your HOME directory and leaves the archive in **/tmp/home.cpio.**

You could write the output to a diskette file by naming the correct device file instead.

```
$ find . -print | cpio -ocvB >/dev/rdsk/f0q15dt
```

Of course you can vary the **find** part of the command to change the filename list that is included in the archive. For example, to create a **cpio** file with only files that have changed within the last week, use the following command:

```
$ find . -mtime -7 -print | cpio -ocv > /tmp/home.cpio
```

Be sure to include the −**print** on the **find** command line, or no names will be written to **cpio** for archiving.

You can use **cpio** to archive a file that is already a **cpio** archive, and **cpio** can keep track of the levels correctly. However, you must not create an archive by redirecting the output into a file in the same directory that you are archiving. This will create an infinite loop and a very large archive! The following command is allowed but is seriously wrong.

```
$ find . -print | cpio -oc > ./arch.cpio
```

Do you understand why this command is incorrect?

Reading a cpio Archive

The **cpio** command provides the −**i** (for in) option to read the archives produced by its −**o** option. The archive to be read is the standard input to **cpio**, which re-creates the files according to the pathnames given when the archive was created.

```
$ cpio -icv < /tmp/home.cpio
```

If the archive was created with relative pathnames, such as with **find . −print**, the input files will be built as a directory tree within the current directory when **cpio −i** is executed. If the archive was created with absolute pathnames (beginning with /), however, that same absolute path will be used when re-creating the file. Using absolute pathnames can be dangerous because you cannot easily move the input directory tree, and so your **cpio −i** operation may attempt to overwrite the original files.

The −**c**, −**v**, and −**B** options have the same meaning for input as for output. If you created the archive with the −**c** or −**B** option, you must use it when the archive is read back in or **cpio** will fail.

```
$ find . -print | cpio -o >/tmp/home.cpio
113 blocks
$ cpio -ic </tmp/home.cpio
cpio: ERROR: This is not a cpio file. Bad magic number.
$
```

If you don't know which **cpio** options were used when the archive was created, experiment with different combinations of −**c** and −**B** until **cpio** reads the file correctly.

When you direct a **cpio** archive to a device, you must specify the correct raw device file according to the diskette format used. Similarly, when you read the archive back in, you must use the same device.

```
$ find . -print | cpio -ocB >/dev/rdsk/f0q15dt
113 blocks
$ cpio -icB </dev/rdsk/f0q15dt
113 blocks
$
```

When files are reloaded, their original permissions are retained. However, the owner and group of the file will be changed to your user id and group unless you are logged in as superuser. If so, the original owner and group are retained. These are encoded as the numeric user and group id, so you must take care when moving files from one machine to another as superuser because the same user and group id's may belong to a different user on the other machine. After loading an archive with **cpio** −**i**, check the permissions with **ls** −**l** to be sure that they are correct, and reset them if needed. Things can get quite confused if the user and group id's are incorrect, especially when you are moving important system files such as **/etc/passwd!**

cpio Command Line Options for Input

The **cpio** command provides many options to control the reading of files from the archive. By default, it will not create directories needed to rebuild the pathnames of files in the archive. The −**d** (for directory) option forces **cpio** to make any necessary directories for the files that it is reading in.

```
$ cpio -icBd </dev/rdsk/f0q15dt
```

Existing directories will be used, but if needed, **cpio** will make new directories to complete the specified path.

Similarly, **cpio** will not overwrite an existing file with the same name as a file read from the archive unless you give the —**u** (for unconditional) option. Use this option with great care because the archive might contain a corrupt or out-of-date version. Usually you will wish to create archives with relative pathnames and then reload the archives into a temporary directory to avoid clashes with existing files.

You can also avoid this problem with the —**r** (for rename) option. As **cpio** reads each file out of the archive, it will prompt you for a new filename. You can enter a pathname if you wish, or you can enter NEWLINE and the file will be skipped.

```
$ cpio -icBr </dev/rdsk/f0q15dt
Rename <data1>
```

Each file on the archive is prompted in this way, so it may be tedious to reload a large archive.

The —**m** (for modification) option instructs **cpio** to retain the file modification time of the original file. By default, the file is created with the current time.

Displaying a Table of Contents
for an Archive

You can examine the contents of a **cpio** archive without actually reloading it. Although this can save disk space, it is no faster than completely reloading the archive because the entire archive must be processed. Use the —**t** (for table) option with —**i** to list the filenames and other information. No files are created when —**t** is given. As usual, the —**c** and —**B** options must be correct to read the archive.

```
$ ls -l
total 128
-rw-rw-rw-  1 root     users        526 Aug 27 18:20 data1
-rw-r--r--  1 root     users       6404 Aug 27 18:20 data2
-rw-rw-rw-  1 root     users      57856 Aug 27 17:53 xx
$ find . -print | cpio -ocv >/tmp/arch.cpio
xx
data1
data2
128 blocks
$ cpio -ict </tmp/arch.cpio
.
xx
data1
data2
128 blocks
$ cpio -icvt </tmp/arch.cpio
40777  bin        0  Aug 27 18:20:53 1987  .
100666 root    57856  Aug 27 17:53:13 1987  xx
100666 root      526  Aug 27 18:20:42 1987  data1
100644 root     6404  Aug 27 18:20:52 1987  data2
128 blocks
$
```

The output differs significantly when you use the —**v** option with —**t**. The leftmost column gives the numeric value of the file permissions, while the next columns give the owner, the size in bytes, the file modification date and time, and the filename, respectively. This information is stored in the archive for use when the files are restored.

Selecting a Subset of Archived Files

Finally, you can instruct **cpio** to reload only a subset of the files in the archive. After the command line flags, you can give a pattern in the format of shell wild-card operators. The **cpio** program will find all files whose names match the pattern and reload only those files. You should quote the patterns to prevent the shell from expanding them before **cpio** sees them.

```
$ cpio -icvB "*file" < /dev/rdsk/f0q15dt
```

This command will reload all files with pathnames ending in the string **file** from the archive on the 1.2-MB floppy disk.

Multiple patterns are allowed, but you must surround each with double quote marks.

```
$ cpio -icvB "*file" "*[0-9]hello*" </dev/rdsk/f0q15dt
```

In addition to files with pathnames ending in **file**, this example will reload all files with the digits 0 through 9 followed by "hello" anywhere in the pathname.

Archiving to a Floppy Disk or Tape

When you create a **cpio** archive to a diskette or tape, the archive can be larger than the capacity of the medium because **cpio** will detect this condition and prompt you to replace the diskette with another (formatted) one. You can continue your archive onto a second diskette (or even more) in this way.

When the diskette is full, **cpio** will prompt you to replace it with another of the same format.

```
$ ls | cpio -ocB >/dev/rdsk/f0q15dt
Reached end of medium on output.
If you want to go on, type device/file name when ready.
```

You must enter the full pathname of the device to use. Normally you will use the same device that you started with. If so, replace the diskette with another of the same type, formatted correctly. Then type in the full pathname of the device file and press NEWLINE. The **cpio** operation will continue. With this style of **cpio** prompt, you can mix diskettes of different formats, switch between two drives, and so forth. However, it is wise to keep the media format constant for an entire archive. If you switch formats in the middle of a **cpio** operation, carefully mark each diskette with its format.

In recent SVR3 systems you can also use the −**O** (uppercase *o*) or −**I** (uppercase *i*) option, followed by the device name, to cause **cpio** to use the device named instead of the standard output or input, respectively. For example:

```
$ find . -print | cpio -ocvB -O /dev/rdsk/f0q15dt
```

This option has another effect as well: it causes **cpio** to give a different prompt when the diskette is full.

```
$ find . -print | cpio -ocB -O /dev/rdsk/f0q15dt

Reached end of medium on output.
Change to part 2 and press RETURN key. [q]
```

To continue, insert a formatted disk of the same type and then press NEWLINE. You can repeat this step until the archive is complete. Be sure to mark and number the media correctly.

Similarly, when you read a **cpio** diskette, you must feed the media in the correct order as written, replacing a disk with the next one as needed. You will be prompted to change disks or to give the device name, as previously.

```
$ cpio -icBd -I /dev/rdsk/f0q15dt

Reached end of medium on input.
Change to part 2 and press RETURN key. [q]
```

You must match the devices and the order of diskettes that you used when creating the archive.

If you wish to stop the **cpio** −i operation in the middle, press DEL at the prompt; the **cpio** operation will end, and return you to the shell. Files already copied in will be retained. However, you cannot begin reading in the middle of a sequence of floppies; you must start from the first disk each time. Similarly, you can end your **cpio** −o operation in the middle but cannot restart where you left off. In each case a partial file may be in the archive when the **cpio** operation does not complete normally.

Backing Up and Restoring Your Files

Though you can archive your data with the **mount** procedure, most routine backups use the **cpio** mechanism, which allows more data on a floppy and will correctly write or read as many floppies as needed.

Figure 16-1 gives a sample shell script that will back up a list of files and directories, taking all the files in any subdirectories of the named directories. This script will back up files to a high-density diskette.

You can edit this script to include the files and directories you wish to back up routinely. The command needed to read the archive is given at the beginning of the script.

Many users have several scripts like the one shown in Figure 16-1 to back up the different areas of their work. The files in the figure are a sample of system files that might be modified on a machine. Other scripts might back up individual user HOME directories or databases for an application.

In general it is better to use several smaller backups than a single larger one; smaller backups are quicker and easier to use, and you will be less likely to neglect them. Even more important, if the first or second disk in a large multidisk **cpio** archive goes bad for some reason, the remaining disks will be unreadable. Thus the use of several smaller archives significantly improves the reliability of your backup procedure and reduces the loss when a catastrophe occurs.

However, the most important thing about backing up data is to do it early and often. You cannot back up your data too often! Make backups at least daily, and on busy days, perhaps even hourly. You need not back up inactive data as often, but try to reload your backup media occasionally, because the disks might be writable but not readable. If so, you can create the backup successfully, but you may not be able to read it. Remember, floppy disks and tape do wear out after frequent use. A disk might stop being readable after a few months of use.

On a multiuser machine where you do not have access to the backup facilities as often as you wish, you can sometimes copy your files onto another file system on another physical disk. Thus your files are still protected if one disk fails. Consult with the system administrator to discuss procedures and security considerations.

System failures have an annoying tendency to occur only when you are not backed up well enough, causing painful loss of data. Even if the failure never occurs, frequent backups will give you confidence that your valuable files are safe. Remember, the cost of creating the files and data is always much higher than that of the disks and time used in regular backups. A little paranoia in backing up your data may save months of work when the disaster happens.

Care of Floppy Disks

Floppy disks are not immune from damage. Magnetic fields are their most dangerous enemy. Keep your diskettes well away from large electric motors, magnets of all sorts, and magnetized tools. In addition, you can destroy a diskette by heating it or freezing it. Don't leave media in the sun or in a hot car. Keep diskettes in their paper envelope and store them in a clean, dust-free place. Of course you should not spill food, liquids, or ashes on a diskette, and you should never remove the disk from its plastic cover.

Backup archives are usually stored at a site well away from the machine they are backing up to prevent loss in case of a fire or other site-related disaster. Large corporations store their data in special environment-controlled vaults. This level of security is seldom needed for smaller machines, but you should keep your backup data from office machines at home, and vice versa.

Going Further

As you might expect, a great many more issues are associated with media. Though our discussion has focused primarily on diskettes, many different types of media are used with UNIX systems. After disk, the most common is magnetic tape. However, except for specific device pathnames associated with them, these media usually act just like disks, with associated **mount** and **cpio** operations.

```
echo "Backing up key system files...."
echo "Restore with:  'cd / ; cpio -icvBdu </dev/rdsk/f0q15dt'"
echo "Insert formatted high-density floppy and hit return."
read DUMMY
cd /

find . -name \
usr/lib/uucp/D* \
usr/lib/uucp/Permissions \
usr/lib/uucp/Systems \
usr/lib/crontab \
.ksh.aliases \
bin/ksh \
etc/suid_exec \
etc/passwd \
etc/inittab \
etc/gettydefs \
etc/profile \
etc/cleanup.wk \
etc/rc2 \
-print | cpio -ocBv > /dev/rdsk/f0q15dt
```

Figure 16-1.   Sample shell script for backing up a list of files and directories

Moving a Directory Hierarchy as a Unit

The **cpio** command also allows you to copy a list of files from one location in your file system to another. Use the −**p** (for pass) option instead of −**i** or −**o**. Instead of making an archive, this option just *passes* the files through the **cpio** command. This command takes a pathname as a target directory rather than the redirected standard output used by the other two **cpio** options.

```
$ ls | cpio -p /tmp/myfiles
```

As usual, **cpio** −**p** takes a list of files on its standard input. All the files in the current directory will be copied to the directory **/tmp/myfiles**, if it exists.

This command also works with **find** to copy an entire directory hierarchy with one command line.

```
$ find . -print | cpio -p /tmp/myfiles
```

This command differs from the previous one in that the entire directory tree under the current directory will be moved.

Use the normal **cpio** options −**a**, −**d**, −**u**, −**v**, and −**m** with −**p** to reset the file access times, create subdirectories as needed, overwrite existing files of the same name, display filenames as copied, or retain the original file time.

Note that **cpio** −**p** will actually make a copy of the files, so large directory structures can take a lot of disk space to copy. Use the −**l** (for link) option to instruct **cpio** −**p** to *link* the files together rather than copy them, where possible. This can save significant disk space. Of course you cannot link files across different file systems.

Creating Unusual File Systems

The **mkfs** command can create many different types of file systems. It can create special forms of interblock gap, and it allows you to select the number of blocks per disk cylinder.

You can specify the interblock gap and the number of blocks per cylinder with additional command line arguments. These parameters, which can improve the efficiency of disk I/O, are usually used only with hard disks. After the *blocks: inodes* arguments, add the gap size and the number of blocks per disk cylinder.

```
$ /etc/mkfs /dev/rdsk/1s1 130000:30000 10 144
```

This will create a gap size of 10 and specify 144 blocks per cylinder. These values are optimal for a Micropolis 67-MB hard disk. Consult the documentation to find the best values for your disk.

You can also specify a *prototype file* as an argument to **mkfs**. This file gives the details of the file system that you wish to specify. The prototype can contain names of directories to create on the file system, along with their permissions. Further, you can name specific files that are included on the file system. Finally, you can name a file to be copied onto the boot block of the disk if you use a device file that includes a boot block. This form of the **mkfs** command gives the pathname of the prototype file instead of the block count.

```
$ /etc/mkfs /dev/rdsk/f0q15d /etc/vtoc/myformat
```

Consult the **mkfs** man page for details on using the prototype file.

Mounting a Second Hard Disk

Most small UNIX systems are supplied with a single hard disk, but you will probably wish to expand your disk space eventually. You can buy a larger hard disk to replace your original, but you can also add a second hard disk. Be sure that the disk you buy is supported by the hard-disk controller card that you are using. Consult your hardware vendor to get the correct disk and cables, and install the cables carefully on the controller card.

When the disk is operating correctly, you can format it with the **format** command just as you do with a floppy disk. Use the raw device associated with the lowest numbered partition on hard disk 1.

```
# format /dev/rdsk/1s0
```

You can then make a file system on the disk. Compute the number of 512-byte blocks needed to fill the disk and use that number as the argument to the **mkfs** command. Use the raw device associated with the file system part of the disk.

```
# /etc/mkfs /dev/rdsk/1s1  74000:15000  7 14
```

This is typical for a 40-MB hard disk. You may need to experiment with the block number for your disk because different disks format to different useful sizes.

Now you can mount the hard disk at a chosen mount point. Don't use /**mnt** for a permanently mounted hard disk; it is used for mounting floppies. Instead, you might use /**usr/src**.

```
# mkdir /usr/src
# mount /dev/dsk/1s1 /usr/src
```

The second disk is now usable.

Finally, you can set up the machine so that the second disk is mounted at boot-time and **fsck** operations are done on it (if needed) when the machine boots. The file /**etc/fstab** contains a list of file systems to be mounted at boot-time, one per line.

```
$ cat /etc/fstab
/dev/dsk/1s1 /usr/src
$
```

The default hard disk is not included in the list, only additional file systems to mount. Each line contains up to four fields, separated from each other by white space. The first field is the device to mount (the block device), and the second is the mount point. These two fields are required. If present, the third field can either be −r (for read-only), which specifies that the file system will not be writable, or −d for a remote mount (RFS). The fourth field is the *file system type*, which can be used by the **mount** command. Edit this file to add your new disk.

File System Checking

The /**etc**/**fsck** (for file system check) command lets you check the correctness of a file system and repair it if needed. This is a complex command that can damage a file system if used incorrectly but can also save some data on a damaged disk. Use of **fsck** is limited to the superuser. It is usually used to repair a hard disk after a system failure, as discussed in Chapter 19, though it can also be used to repair a mountable floppy disk or tape.

If you suspect that a floppy disk with file system is damaged, you may be able to salvage some of its files with **fsck**. The **fsck** command works only on mountable media, not on **cpio** archives. If possible, always copy a diskette before using **fsck** with it, using the **dd** command. You will always lose some data when you repair an inconsistent file system, but **fsck** does a good job of reducing the losses.

The **fsck** command takes a raw device name as argument and checks that file system.

```
# /etc/fsck /dev/rdsk/f0q15dt
```

Typical output from **fsck** is given in Figure 19-5.

The incorrect "pieces" of files found by **fsck** are linked into the corrected file system in the directory **lost+found** below the root directory of the file system being checked. You can browse these files after **fsck** completes to see if any are of value.

By default, **fsck** is an interactive tool that prompts for confirmation before making changes to the named file system. The —**y** (for yes) command line option instructs **fsck** to answer all its questions itself, choosing good answers. We recommend this option because the built-in **fsck** rules are excellent. The —**n** (for no) option instructs **fsck** to check the file system but make no changes. This can be used to test the correctness of write-protected media.

The **fsck** command has many other options, but they should not be used in most situations. Experiment with these options on a file system that you don't mind losing!

Magnetic Tape

We have used the term *media* to refer to both diskettes and magnetic tape because some magnetic tapes can contain file systems and can be mounted just like a disk. The only differences will be in the names of the device files used for the tape drive.

However, some tape units are not mountable and can be used only as raw devices. The manufacturer will include this information in the user's manual for the tape drive, and you must use the mode of access defined there. Usually cartridge tape drives will be mountable, while large 9-track reel tape units will not.

Cartridge tape units are often supplied with a version of **cpio** that was created specifically for that tape unit and cannot be used for disks. Larger tapes usually use the normal **cpio** command, but this depends on the device driver associated with the device. The device driver will be specific to your machine and to your version of the UNIX system, so consult your vendor's documentation for details on how to access the tape unit.

The tar Command

In addition to **cpio**, the **tar** (for tape archive) program is also available. The **cpio** command is limited to one archive per disk because you cannot update an archive once it is created. That is, **cpio** does not let you *replace* a file in an archive with a newer version of the file without completely re-creating the archive. The **tar** command, however, allows you to *add* new files to the end of an existing archive and *replace* files in the archive. You implement replacement in **tar** by writing the new file at the end of the archive. Then, when files are reloaded from the archive, the last file overwrites all the other files with that name. This feature is valuable when you have very large media such as 9-track tapes. In fact, **tar** was originally developed to support large tapes, though it can also be used with floppy diskettes or smaller tapes.

The **tar** command is a little more difficult to use than **cpio** because you must manage the archive on the media yourself. That is, if you create an archive with three versions of a file, you must take care that the last is always the one you want because **tar** cannot easily extract any but the last occurrence of a file. Of course in backups the last is usually the one you want because it is the most recent.

Further, the **tar** command is noticeably slower in operation than **cpio**. Though it can use either the raw device or the block device for its archives, the raw device is noticeably faster. Finally, **tar** cannot overflow onto a second disk when the first fills up, so its archives are limited to the maximum size of your media.

The **tar** command is located in the /**bin** directory on some SVR3 releases and in /**etc** on others. Check your machine to determine which is used.

The tar Command Line

The **tar** command takes a filename as its first argument and treats it as the name of the archive to create. It can be a normal file or a device file. If it is not a tape device, you must specify the command line argument −**f** (for file). Arguments following the archive name are treated as filenames to archive. Unlike **cpio**, **tar** will automatically take all subdirectories of named directories. For example, this command will archive the directory trees /**usr**/**steve** and /**usr**/**src**, with all their subdirectories, to a high-density floppy.

```
$ tar -fc /dev/rdsk/f0q15dt /usr/steve /usr/src
```

If − (minus) is used as the archive name, **tar** will use standard I/O, so redirection is allowed. Use the −**f** argument with −. The only time you do not use the −**f** argument is when you are writing to a tape on a device in the directory /**dev**/**mt**, which contains devices for 9-track magnetic tape drives.

The **tar** command can create, read, and update an archive. The **tar** options −**c** (for create), −**x** (for extract), and −**r** (for replace), respectively, control these operations. To create a new archive, give the −**c** option along with −**f** and the archive device and input files. This command line will destroy the previous contents of the archive.

```
$ cd /
$ tar -fc /dev/rdsk/f0q15dt usr/steve usr/src
$
```

If successful, **tar** will return silently. Like **cpio**, **tar** stored the pathname that you used when the archive was created. Thus you should take care when using absolute pathnames because when you *extract* files from the archive, they may incorrectly overwrite existing files. It is usually better to use only relative pathnames in your **tar** command lines.

To reload the archive, use the −**x** option and give the name of the archive you wish to reload.

```
$ tar -xf /dev/rdsk/f0q15dt
Tar: blocksize = 20
$
```

The **tar** command reports the block size in use when the archive was created.

If used with a list of filenames following the archive name, **tar −x** will reload only the named files.

```
$ tar -xf /dev/rdsk/f0q15dt usr/src/steve/bsplit.c
```

Use the exact pathname given when the archive was created.

Use the **−r** option to replace a file or to add new files without destroying the existing archive.

```
$ tar -fr /dev/rdsk/f0q15dt usr/src/steve/bsplit.c
```

The **−x** option will find the newest version of a file when more than one is present in the archive.

You can display a table of contents of the archive with the **−t** (for table) option.

```
$ tar -ft /dev/rdsk/f0q15dt
usr/steve/data1
usr/steve/data2
usr/steve/cpio.out
usr/src/bsplit.c
usr/src/bsplit
$
```

The **−v** (for verbose) option produces a list of files written to or read from the archive. Use it with the **−t** option to produce a table of contents similar to the **ls −l** output.

Finally, the **−w** (for what) option instructs **tar** to prompt the user before taking any action. If you press y, the action is taken; if you enter any other character, the action is skipped and **tar** continues.

```
$ tar -fxw /dev/rdsk/f0q15dt usr/src/bsplit.c
x usr/src/bsplit.c:
```

The x at the beginning of the prompt tells you that **tar** wants to extract the named file from the archive. You can retrieve an older version of a file with the **−w** option if you accept the version you want and reject the later ones.

Mounting Your Hard Disk from a Bootable Floppy

Occasionally you may wish to boot your machine from a floppy disk. This might be required, for example, if you forget the **root** password on the machine. You can boot the machine off a floppy disk, mount the file system on the hard disk, and edit the **/etc/passwd** or **/etc/shadow** file to remove the **root** password. Then you can reboot from the hard disk and log in without difficulty. The floppy boot procedure is discussed in Chapter 19.

Once the machine is running from the floppy, you can mount the default hard disk and examine or repair it. Use the following command:

```
# mount /dev/dsk/0s1 /mnt
```

In this example you are mounting the file system part of the hard disk onto a mount point on the floppy. All the files on the hard disk will be available for use.

# SEVENTEEN

Running MS-DOS
Under the UNIX System

**S
E
V
E
N
T
E
E
N**

One of the most interesting recent innovations in the UNIX system is the ability to use the MS-DOS operating system on UNIX machines. That is, machines based on the Intel 80286 and 80386 CPU chips have the intrinsic ability to execute both operating systems independently. Tools have now been invented that allow executing MS-DOS *while* the UNIX system is running.

MS-DOS applications are often notoriously selfish about how they use such machine resources as RAM, console display, and disk. They seldom allow the kind of cooperative sharing of resources that is required in a multitasking system. Thus it is amazing that it is possible to use MS-DOS under the UNIX system.

In its best form this feature is currently limited to machines based on the 80286 or 80386 microprocessors. However, some other machines allow the execution of MS-DOS on *coprocessor boards* that contain MS-DOS-compatible microprocessors. In this section we will discuss only those implementations that allow MS-DOS to *share* the same CPU with the UNIX system. The 80386 running SVR3 is an example of this class, and several vendors of the UNIX system provide *MS-DOS merge* packages that allow at least one user to execute MS-DOS while the UNIX system is running.

In the 80386 versions of the UNIX system, the MS-DOS capability is significantly expanded over 80286 versions. Because of the internal architecture of the microprocessors, only one session of MS-DOS can run on 80286 machines at any time. The 80386 machines, however, allow *multiple* MS-DOS sessions at the same time, though only one of these sessions can access the hardware devices, such as the console or the diskette drives, at any time.

While MS-DOS is running, you can switch to the UNIX system at any time and execute commands from the shell as you normally would. Then you can switch back to the MS-DOS session and continue under that operating system. When you are through with MS-DOS, you can kill that process and return your machine to the normal UNIX system. The MS-DOS process lets you share files and directories between the two operating systems, so you can create files under one system and read them under the other.

These features can be extremely useful to users of one of the operating systems who have wished that some of the functions of the other were available. One commonly used capability lets you easily use MS-DOS floppy disks while your primary interactive session is with the UNIX system.

To use MS-DOS under the UNIX system, you will need to purchase a special software package. You can also use MS-DOS as a stand-alone operating system, not running under the UNIX system, without harming the UNIX system on your hard disk. We will discuss these issues in this chapter.

A Note on Variability

The merge capability is the newest of all major UNIX system features, and it has been independently marketed by at least two vendors. In addition, the 80386 CPU has significant internal improvements over the 80286 systems, in which the merge feature first appeared. As a result, there are noticeable differences between the various implementations of the merge feature. Some releases provide a user agent for accessing merge functions, or you can use the commands as discussed below.

In this section we will only survey the major features and pitfalls of a typical merge subsystem. Much of the information is drawn from the Locus DOS Merge package for the 80386, which is sold with the Microport release of SVR3. The releases issued by Interactive Systems, AT&T, and others may differ in some details. You should consult the documentation specific to your merge package for more information.

Starting and Stopping MS-DOS

The MS-DOS capabilities on SVR and SVR3 machines are simple in concept: under the UNIX system a process provides a working environment in which MS-DOS applications believe they have complete control of the machine. The interface between this process and the underlying hardware is through a special linkage or *bridge layer* of software that usually guarantees the two systems see no contention for resources.

To use MS-DOS applications, you must first *start* this MS-DOS control process. This will give you access to the normal MS-DOS **command.com**, its "shell." Then you can execute MS-DOS programs as you would with a stand-alone

MS-DOS system. When you are through, you can *stop* the MS-DOS process and return to the UNIX system.

From the shell, start an MS-DOS process with this command.

```
$ dos
```

dos is a UNIX system command that links to the MS-DOS system. It executes under the UNIX system, but results in an MS-DOS session. This MS-DOS session executes as a normal process within the UNIX system. Following some banner material and copyright notices, you will see the **command. com** prompt ("C>").

```
$ dos
 .
 .
 .
C>
```

The banner material is omitted in this example.

This particular invocation will create a *foreground* MS-DOS session that acts like many other commands with built-in subcommands, such as **vi** and **cu**. The entire MS-DOS system is available from the "C>" prompt, and you can enter any MS-DOS commands or applications.

When the MS-DOS session starts, it will read your **config.sys** and **autoexec.bat** files, and then initialize your MS-DOS session just as if you had booted a stand-alone MS-DOS system. Thus you can use the **profile** features of **autoexec.- bat** to set up your environment within the MS-DOS session as you like it. Consult the MS-DOS documentation for more information on starting MS-DOS. You can include MS-DOS *device drivers* such as **ansi.sys** or **TSR** (for terminate and stay resident) applications in your **config.sys** as desired. These configuration changes are local to your MS-DOS session and will not affect any UNIX session in progress. Some merge releases require that **config.sys, autoexec.bat**, and any device drivers be in the root directory on the file system, or in some special directory specified by the merge feature, while other releases expect to find them in your HOME directory. Be sure to follow the instructions specific to your merge implementation.

To kill the MS-DOS session and return to the shell, use the **quit** command at the MS-DOS prompt.

```
C> QUIT
$
```

The MS-DOS session will end. Unlike the shell session, you cannot end the MS-DOS session with CTRL-D, CTRL-C, or CTRL-BREAK, because MS-DOS treats these keys differently than the UNIX system. In many implementations of the merge feature you can end the MS-DOS session by pressing CTRL-ALT-DEL. You hold down the CTRL and ALT keys and then press DEL. This may not work with all implementations of the merge feature, so you should experiment on your machine.

Background Execution of MS-DOS

We just discussed the most straightforward use of MS-DOS under the UNIX system. In addition, you can use a *hot key* to immediately switch between an active MS-DOS session and a shell without stopping the MS-DOS process. To use this feature, you must start the MS-DOS session in the *background* with the following command:

```
$ dos &
```

This invocation differs from the previous one because the shell is still active, sharing your login session with the MS-DOS process. When the background MS-DOS process starts, it takes control of the keyboard and display, and the shell is temporarily suspended. Thus the first display from this command will be the same as for the foreground execution of the **dos** command.

You can use this MS-DOS session as expected and then use **quit** to kill it and return to your normal session under the UNIX system. However, you can use the hot key to immediately switch back to the UNIX system at any time, keeping the MS-DOS session active. You can use most commands under the UNIX system as normal, and the MS-DOS session will move into the background. When you are ready, you can immediately switch back to the MS-DOS session.

Switching Between Sessions

The hot key used to switch between the two sessions is usually a multiple-key combination such as the CTRL-SYS REQ or ALT-SYS REQ key sequences, or sometimes CTRL-ALT-SYS REQ. The latter is entered by holding down the CTRL and ALT keys, then pressing SYS REQ. Some releases may use CTRL-ALT-BACKSPACE, and some keyboards use a special key marked *window* (because different OS sessions are called windows, even though they are all full screen). Finally, you can usually configure your system to use another combination of keys.

In some merge systems, when you press the correct key sequence the display will immediately be re-drawn for the new operating system. In others, you may see a pop-up menu of available sessions that you have created, and you select the session you want. When you make your selection the screen will switch to that session. When you switch back, the former contents will be re-displayed. The contents of the screen will not be lost when you switch sessions.

You can switch sessions while a command is executing in either operating system. That is, you needn't be at the command prompt to switch sessions, because the hot key is interpreted at a very low level of the machine, not at the shell level. In this sense the hot key is similar to the CTRL-Z operation of the **shl** program within the UNIX system, except that the merge hot key causes the screen to be re-drawn when the session changes, and **shl** does not.

If a command is in progress when you switch sessions, output from that command may *block;* that is, the program will stop executing and wait until you return to that session. Often the type of display you are using will determine whether the suspended session blocks or continues to run. With an EGA display, suspended sessions will usually block, while the older CGA displays allow the background session to continue. Some merge releases allow you to control whether the background session blocks as an option when you start the MS-DOS session. Blocking guarantees that no output is lost when you switch away from an active program, but it may not be what you want in all cases.

Of course, in both cases the application in the background will stop when it expects user input. When the session is blocked or waiting for your input, you can start it again by switching back to that session.

Changing the Hot Key

Some merge implementations allow you to change the hot key to another keystroke combination as long as it includes CTRL and ALT. That is, if you don't like CTRL-ALT-SYS REQ, you can use another key instead of the SYS REQ. In all cases but the window and CTRL-SYS REQ keys, the CTRL-ALT part is required. To change SYS REQ to another key, use the **doskey** command (called **dosscreen** in some implementations). The

doskey command takes a *scan* code for a key as argument.

```
$ doskey 50
$
```

Scan codes are arbitrary numerical codes sent to the CPU by the keyboard when a key is pressed. Scan codes are usually a count of keys that starts at ESC at the left side of the keyboard, moves across the first row, then the second row, and so on. Consult the **doskey** documentation for a complete table of scan codes. In the previous example CTRL-ALT-M became the new hot key.

You can display the current hot key definition by giving **doskey** with no arguments.

```
$ doskey
50
$
```

Changes to the hot key with **doskey** do not survive a system reboot; you must reenter them after the machine comes up. You can add the **doskey** command to your **.profile** if you want to permanently change your hot key.

Invoking MS-DOS Programs Directly from the Shell

In addition to the screen-switching access to MS-DOS, you can execute MS-DOS commands and applications directly from the shell. There are two different procedures.

The first is to give the name of the MS-DOS application as an argument to the **dos** command:

```
$ dos ws.exe
```

This will execute the MS-DOS system and immediately start the WordStar application program. You can also start the MS-DOS session in the background.

```
$ dos ws.exe &
```

In both cases, when you quit from the named application program, you will remain in the MS-DOS session, where you can start another command or exit to the shell.

The second procedure is to type the name of an MS-DOS command just as you would name a command under the UNIX system. The MS-DOS *environment* will start, and the named application will execute. When the MS-DOS command completes, you will return to the shell, and the MS-DOS session will disappear. For example:

```
$ ws.exe
```

will run the WordStar application. To do this, the named program must be in one of the directories named in your PATH.

This indirect invocation of MS-DOS is simpler but less efficient than the first procedure, since the MS-DOS environment must be started each time that you execute a command; it does not "live" between commands.

When using the second procedure, give pathname arguments in the UNIX system format. That is, specify pathnames with the / (slash) character separating directory elements; and you should not use the \ (backslash) separator used in MS-DOS. For example, you can use the MS-DOS **copy** command from the shell

```
$ copy /usr/steve/file /tmp
```

This command is equivalent to the **cp** command.

When you use an MS-DOS command directly from the shell, you must take extra care that any "special" characters are quoted to protect them from the shell. This applies to special characters for both the MS-DOS and UNIX systems, since they could be interpreted or expanded by the shell before being passed to the MS-DOS system. For example, you might use

```
$ copy *.dat mydir
```

to move several files to another directory. This is a correct command when executed directly from MS-DOS. However, when it is entered from the UNIX system, the shell will expand the wild-card character * before passing the command to MS-DOS. This will be an error since the copy command allows only one name as source file. You can prevent this type of problem by quoting command line arguments that contain any special or wild-card characters.

```
$ copy "*.dat" mydir
```

Be careful. Mistakes that you make with these special characters can easily destroy files.

MS-DOS Command Extensions

There is one important consideration when you execute MS-DOS commands from the shell. In an earlier example, the **ws** command included the MS-DOS *filename extension* **exe**. Other MS-DOS commands have the extension **com**. These extensions need not be present when you name the commands under MS-DOS. But when you use these commands from the shell, you must include the correct extension or rename the application. Otherwise, the shell will be unable to locate the correct command.

```
$ ws
ws: not found
$
```

Unfortunately, there is another exception to this rule because MS-DOS includes some *built-in* commands that have no extension. Table 17-1 lists them. When you use one of these commands from the shell, you cannot give a filename extension.

```
$ copy.com file1 file2
copy.com: not found
$
```

cd	mkdir
chdir	rd
cls	rem
copy	ren
date	rename
del	rmdir
dir	time
echo	type
erase	ver
for	vol
md	

Table 17-1.   MS-DOS Built-in Commands

To relieve this confusion between commands with and without extensions, you can rename your favorite MS-DOS applications, without the extension. Use the **ln** command to link a file with an MS-DOS extension to another name without the extension. Then the shell can find the name without the extension, and things will work correctly. Be sure to link the application into one of the directories in your PATH.

```
$ ws
ws: not found
$ ln /usr/dbin/ws.exe /usr/dbin/ws
$ ws
```

Find the commands that you wish to change in the MS-DOS **bin** directory on your machine with the **find** command under the UNIX system; then do the **ln** operation within that directory.

Some implementations of the merge feature supply these links for the "normal" MS-DOS commands such as **edlin**. Usually you will only need to worry about these extensions when you install MS-DOS applications yourself.

You can include MS-DOS programs in shell scripts or other programs. The rules described in this and following sections also apply within scripts. Take care when using the "dos &" syntax within a shell script, however, because the hot key will be available and a user can switch back to the UNIX system while the shell script is running—probably not what you intend.

Pipelines

You can sometimes create pipelines that contain a mixture of UNIX and MS-DOS commands. If the MS-DOS command is well behaved, it will read its standard input and write to standard output, just like most programs under the UNIX system. If so, you can combine commands from both operating systems into a single pipeline.

```
$ dir a: | sort
```

This will use the **sort** command under the UNIX system on the directory output from the MS-DOS **dir** command. *Ill-behaved* programs, ones that do not use MS-DOS standard I/O, should not be used in pipelines. Any program that reads or writes directly to the machine's hardware, without using the MS-DOS BIOS conventions, will be ill behaved.

SVR2 merge implementations allow only one MS-DOS session per machine, which means that you can execute only one MS-DOS command at any time. Thus, you can execute only one MS-DOS command in a pipeline, and only one user can execute the pipeline at any time. In SVR3 implementations, more than one MS-DOS command can appear in a pipeline. Of course, such pipelines can be quite inefficient because the whole **dos** environment must start when the MS-DOS command is executed.

Executing UNIX System Programs
from the MS-DOS Session

A parallel facility called **on unix**, or sometimes **rununix**, allows you to execute some UNIX system commands under the MS-DOS session. The feature differs significantly between merge implementations, so you should take care when using it. Specifically, the treatment of output, the command names, and whether the session blocks may differ between implementations. Some merge releases may allow you to name the UNIX system command directly, without preceding it with the **on unix** command. Consult your release's documentation for more details.

Give the UNIX system command line after the command **on unix**.

```
C> ON UNIX CAT DATA.FILE
```

Use the file naming conventions of the UNIX system for commands and arguments. Output comes to the MS-DOS session.

In some implementations, the **on unix** procedure can be used only with commands and pipelines that are noninteractive. That is, you may not be able to execute any command that requires user input with this mechanism; you must return to the normal UNIX system with the hot key.

You can execute background jobs with the **on unix** facility by adding the **&** operator to the end of the command line.

```
C> ON UNIX CAT DATA.FILE &
```

You must put a space before the **&** or the **on unix** command will treat it incorrectly. This is called a *detached* job.

When you create these detached tasks, the MS-DOS "C>" prompt will reappear, and you can continue with your session or create more detached jobs. Some merge implementations provide a pop-up menu to *reattach* a detached job. Other releases provide the **jobs** command from the MS-DOS session to list the detached jobs that you have created, along with their current status.

```
C> JOBS
    JOB     STATE     EXIT STATUS     COMMAND
    [1]     Running                   cat data.file
    [2]     Done      exit(0)         ps -ef
C>
```

The **jobs** command will return silently if there is nothing to report.

The job identifier is given in the JOB column as a small *job number.* The STATE column gives the current status of the job, which can be **running**, **exit**, **unknown**, **signal**, **coredump**, or **err3**. **Running** and **exit** are normal; **signal** reports that the command exited after receiving a signal; **coredump** implies an error in the command that caused it to fail; and **unknown** and **err3** are errors internal to **on unix**.

Completed jobs continue to appear in the **jobs** output until you flush them. Use − (minus) as the argument to **jobs** to clear completed jobs.

```
C> JOBS -
```

Once you have cleared a job from the list, you can no longer access it or its output.

You can use the job number to reattach a detached job in order to view its output. Use the **jobs** command with the job number as argument to request that the job be reattached. Precede the job number with the % (percent) operator.

```
C> JOBS %1
```

To save the output of a job that has completed, redirect the output from this **jobs** command to a file.

```
C> JOBS %2 > OUTPUT
```

To kill a detached job before it has completed, use the **kill** command from the MS-DOS session, with the job number as argument.

```
C> KILL %1
```

This command acts like the **kill** command under the UNIX system, and it can take a signal number if you wish.

```
C> KILL -9 %1
```

The **on unix** facility has many more features. Consult the documentation with your merge system for more details.

Disk Usage Under the Merge Session

The two operating systems will normally share the system's hard disk; that is, both sessions can use it simultaneously. The full file system is visible to both sessions. The drive designations often vary dramatically between implementations of the merge feature, but usually the system's default hard disk will be accessible under the merge session as **drive C**, or sometimes as **drive U**. The first floppy disk will be **drive A**, and a second will be called **drive B**.

You can navigate the file system with either the **cd** command under the UNIX system or the equivalent MS-DOS command. However, if you change your working directory under one operating system and then use the hot key to switch to the other system, the directory change will *not* follow.

In most implementations the starting directory for a new MS-DOS session will be the directory that is current when you start the **dos** session. You can include a **cd** command in your MS-DOS **autoexec.bat** file to change this to your HOME or some other place.

By default, the **dos** command will look on the system's hard disk for any commands given as its arguments. This command

```
$ dos ws.exe
```

is equivalent to

```
$ dos c:ws.exe
```

You can execute programs from a floppy disk with this procedure by explicitly naming the drive where the program resides. This command

```
$ dos a:123.exe
```

will run the Lotus 1-2-3 program from floppy disk drive A. You can use this procedure to run copy-protected applications that have a *key disk*, such as Lotus 1-2-3. Alternatively, you can sometimes copy the application to the hard disk and then insert the key disk in the floppy drive before starting the application. Some applications will read the key disk correctly when it starts.

File and Directory Conventions

The two operating systems share the standard file system, and you can move around the directory hierarchy as expected. The **cd** command is available to both operating systems. However, remember to use the / (slash) character to separate directory tree arguments when you are under the UNIX system, and the \ (backslash) when you are under MS-DOS.

A more serious problem is the filenaming scheme used in the two environments. Filenames under the UNIX system can be up to 14 characters long, while MS-DOS filenames can be no more than 11 characters, with an 8-character limit in the *name* section and a 3-character limit in the *extension* section. Also, some legal characters in filenames under the UNIX system are not allowed under MS-DOS rules. Thus, when you use the MS-DOS **dir** command to view a directory created with the UNIX system, the filenames may not be acceptable under the MS-DOS rules. All legal filenames under MS-DOS, however, are acceptable under the UNIX system rules.

Because of these problems, the merge system changes "incorrect" filenames according to **conversion rules**, which guarantee that all filenames acceptable to the UNIX system will be unique under the MS-DOS session. Thus, all files are accessible under both the MS-DOS and UNIX systems. When you use a file or directory under MS-DOS, it may have a name different from its name under the UNIX system. When you use a file under MS-DOS, you must give its name as displayed in the **dir** command. Sometimes unusual characters or numbers will appear in converted names. The following conversion rules apply to SVR3 systems; older versions may have different rules.

First, all filenames that contain lowercase characters are converted to uppercase. Next, UNIX system filenames shorter than eight characters will be the same under MS-DOS. If the name has no more than eight characters, followed by a . (dot), and then no more than three characters, it will be the same under the MS-DOS rules (but uppercase). However, longer filenames in the UNIX system will be changed. If the "bad" name contains a ., the rules are applied separately to the parts before and after the dot. Simply, the **dos** linkage layer looks at all the filenames in the directory and finds a new combination of characters in the name that is unique and also follows the MS-DOS rules.

For example, this directory might be present in the UNIX system:

```
$ ls -C /tmp/SS
1234567890.dat        2234567890.dat        short.txt
1234567891.dat        longerthan8           small.large
$
```

When viewed under the MS-DOS system, it might look like this:

```
C> dir \tmp\SS'DLN
 Volume in drive C is steve
 Directory of  C:\TMP\SS'DLN

             <DIR>        9-25-87    9:59a
 ..          <DIR>        9-25-87    9:57a
 1234'DLO DAT      0      9-25-87    9:45a
 1234'DLP DAT      0      9-25-87    9:45a
 2234'DLQ DAT      0      9-25-87    9:59a
 LONG'DLR          0      9-25-87    9:44a
 SHORT    TXT      0      9-25-87    9:44a
 SMAL'DLT LAR      0      9-25-87    9:45a

       8 File(s)    3567616 bytes free
```

You can see that the names can be changed substantially when they violate the MS-DOS naming rules.

Take special care that directories you create within the UNIX system are also legitimate under MS-DOS. Otherwise, you may have trouble using **cd** under MS-DOS to change to the directory if the conversion rules are invoked on the name. In the previous example, the name **SS** was changed by the **dos** linkage to **SS'DLN**. This can occur because the conversion rules change lowercase characters under the UNIX system to uppercase characters under MS-DOS. Thus a name in the UNIX system that contains uppercase characters will be converted. If you create a directory or file named **SS** under MS-DOS, it will display as **ss** under the UNIX system.

If you create a file under the MS-DOS rules, its name will not differ when you use **ls**. Similarly, if you edit or otherwise use a file whose name has been changed under the MS-DOS session, its name will not change when you return to the UNIX system. However, if you delete a file under MS-DOS and then re-create it under the name that **dos** uses, the *new* name will appear under the UNIX system.

A new MS-DOS command, **udir** (for UNIX system **dir**) will list both the unconverted and converted file names, so that you can check the conversions performed.

```
$ udir

 Volume is drive C is steve
 Directory of c:/tmp/SS

           root    drwxr-xr-x  <DIR>       9-25-87   9:59a
```

```
..            ..            sys    drwxrwxrwx  <DIR>      9-25-87   9:57a
1234567890.dat  1234'DLO.DAT  root   -rw-r--r--        0 9-25-87   9:45a
1234567891.dat  1234'DLP.DAT  root   -rw-r--r--        0 9-25-87   9:45a
2234567890.dat  2234'DLQ.DAT  root   -rw-r--r--        0 9-25-87   9:59a
longerthan8     LONG'DLR      root   -rw-r--r--        0 9-25-87   9:44a
short.txt       SHORT.TXT     root   -rw-r--r--        0 9-25-87   9:44a
small.large     SMAL'DLT.LAR  root   -rw-r--r--        0 9-25-87   9:45a

       8 File(s)    3567616 bytes free

C>
```

Files on the machine's hard disk are usually visible to both MS-DOS and UNIX system programs. Neither operating system protects you against editing a file in one system and then switching sessions before the changes are written out. If you then edit the file in the other operating system, you will see the original file unchanged. That is, there is no *concurrency control* between changes to the file in the two sessions, so you must be sure that files are *consistent* between the sessions. It usually is sufficient to be sure that you write a file back to disk from your editor before you switch sessions. In more complex cases you could set up application programs in both operating systems that can process a file at the same time. It is easy to forget that you have such tools, and your files can become corrupted.

MS-DOS Directories

The MS-DOS commands and tools have their own **bin** directory within the merged file system. This may be **/usr/dbin** or **/usr/vpix/dosbin**, depending on your merge release, though some older implementations use **/osm/bin** instead. Locally installed applications may be in **/usr/ldbin**, **/usr/vpix/dosapps**, or **/osm/lbin**, and other supporting materials may be in other subdirectories of **/usr/vpix** or in **/usr/lib/merge**. The / directory often contains the **autoexec.bat** and **config.sys** files and any device drivers that are installed by **config.sys**.

PATH and Other Environment Variables

Both the MS-DOS and UNIX systems use a PATH environment variable to define the directories to search when a command is typed. Because the normal UNIX system **bin** differs from the MS-DOS **bin**, the PATH variables will also differ. The **dos** command will usually create a PATH variable for you when you start the MS-DOS session. You should usually not delete any directories from either PATH when using the merge feature, or commands may not be located correctly.

The **dos** command creates the MS-DOS PATH by figuring out an equivalent of the UNIX system PATH. If this is not satisfactory, you can set the PATH environment variable in your **autoexec.bat**, so that it will be picked up when your MS-DOS session starts. Take care not to remove any of the merge directories from your PATH, or the linkage to the UNIX system may not work as expected. In addition, some merge releases provide a *DOSPATH* environment variable under the UNIX system that will become your PATH under MS-DOS.

Some releases allow you to pass other environment variables to the MS-DOS session if their names are the values of the *DOSENV* environment variable. That is, **dos** looks at the contents of the variable DOSENV, and puts any named variables into the MS-DOS environment:

```
$ PROMPT="hello:"   ; export PROMPT
$ TERM=AT386        ; export TERM
$ DOSENV=PROMPT,TERM  ; export DOSENV
$
```

The variables PROMPT and TERM will be added to the MS-DOS environment when the **dos** command starts. Use the DOSENV feature carefully because environment space may be limited in the MS-DOS session.

Converting Files to the Other OS

The format of disk files differs between the MS-DOS and UNIX systems. These differences, caused by conventions for ending text lines, are usually most noticeable with text files, but binary files and executable programs can also differ.

Binary files that contain text lines, such as some word processor document files, may also cause problems.

In the UNIX system each text line ends with the NEWLINE character, which is actually the ASCII character CTRL-J, or *linefeed*. Under MS-DOS, however, each line ends with the *carriage return* and *linefeed* pair, or CTRL-M followed by CTRL-J. Thus, when you edit an MS-DOS file under the UNIX system, you will see a spurious CTRL-M at the end of each line. Similarly, when you use an MS-DOS command such as **type** to examine a file created under the UNIX system, each line ends with a linefeed, but the next line will not begin at the left margin. For example,

```
$ cat data
123 456 789
987 654 321
hello goodbye
$ dos "type data"
123 456 789
           987 654 321
                       hello goodbye
$
```

Each line in the file went to a new display line, but the missing carriage return did not return the cursor to the left margin.

Two utilities are provided to convert files to the format of the other operating system: **unix2dos** and **dos2unix** convert a file from UNIX to MS-DOS format and from MS-DOS to UNIX format, respectively. These command names and the specific options they provide may differ, but the conversion operation is usually required when you are moving files between operating systems. Both programs can execute under either the MS-DOS or UNIX systems.

By default, both commands read their standard input and write the converted data to standard output.

```
$ unix2dos < unix.file > dos.txt
$
```

The filters return silently if there are no errors.

If you give one filename as argument, that file is used as the input file, and output comes to standard output.

```
$ dos2unix dos.txt > unix.file
```

If you give two filenames the first is the input file and the second is the output file.

```
$ unix2dos unix.file dos.txt
```

If you use one of the filters on a file that is already in the target format, the file will not be changed.

Several command line options are supported. Remember that options under the UNIX system begin with the − (minus), while arguments under MS-DOS begin with a / (slash).

By default, these programs make the output data 7-bit ASCII characters. Use the −**b** (for binary) option to preserve any 8-bit characters in the data. You can also convert files to all uppercase or all lowercase with the −**l** (for lowercase) or −**u** (for uppercase) option. The −**b**, −**l**, and −**u** options are mutually exclusive; you can use only one of them on a single command.

Both programs will remove any *extra* NEWLINE characters at the end of each line. When converting UNIX system files, this will make all output files single spaced. If you wish to convert all NEWLINES to return-linefeed pairs and preserve the spacing of the input file, use the −**f** (for force) option.

```
$ unix2dos -f double.space > double.spc
```

Remember, use these programs only on 7- or 8-bit ASCII text files, not on binary files; there is no way to convert binary files. Some word processors in both operating systems use binary files for their document files, and these will not convert correctly with **unix2dos** or **dos2unix**. Experiment on copies of your word processor files before trusting that you can convert them successfully from one format to the other.

MS-DOS Memory Allocation

When the MS-DOS session starts, some of the random access memory (RAM) in the machine will be allocated to that session. In many merge implementations, an MS-DOS session cannot be swapped or removed from memory until it ends. Thus memory given to MS-DOS may be unusable by the UNIX system, which can create problems if you have too little real memory on your machine. If you have too little memory, the UNIX system will run dramatically slower when the MS-DOS session is running than when it isn't. In severe cases your UNIX system commands will appear to not start correctly. If you use the hot key to switch back to the MS-DOS session and quit the session, programs will begin to act normally under the UNIX system. If this happens, you must add more memory to the machine to improve its performance.

The amount of real memory "grabbed" by the MS-DOS session is an argument to the **dos** command. You can instruct **dos** to take only the memory you need, up to the MS-DOS maximum of 640 KB. Use the −**m** (for memory) option on the **dos** command line.

```
$ dos -m400 &
```

This will allocate 400 KB to the MS-DOS session. You can ask for any amount between 64 KB and 640 KB. The **dos** command will try to allocate that much memory, and if it is not available, **dos** will do the best that it can. Typically, if you ask for a large amount of memory, **dos** may allocate somewhat less. You can sometimes get more memory for the MS-DOS session by reducing the number and size of processes running in the UNIX system when you start the MS-DOS session. If you have plenty of memory and ask for 640 KB, the **dos** program will probably give you only about 600 KB, because the *linkage* between the MS-DOS and UNIX systems requires some memory.

Most MS-DOS applications can determine if the amount of memory available is inadequate and, if so, will display an error message. Use this information to determine the correct value for the −m option. Usually you should use the minimum necessary because the UNIX system will suffer if it does not have enough memory for its needs.

The default memory allocation when you give no −m option is a configurable parameter that you can set according to your needs.

Other Command Line Options for the dos Command

In addition to −m, the **dos** command supports many more command line options to configure the MS-DOS session and regulate the MS-DOS environment. The options vary widely among implementations of the merge feature, so consult the **dos** man page for details on your machine. These often follow the format −x to turn the option off and +x to turn the option on. You can usually use +h (for help) to display a list of options available to your version of the **dos** command.

You can "grab" hardware devices (see the next section) with the +a (for assign) option and release them with −a. You can send the **dos** arguments directly to **command.com**, without interpretation, with +c (for command). The +u (for UNIX system) option changes the meaning of the pathname separator and switch character to the UNIX system equivalents. The / (slash) character under MS-DOS becomes −, and the \ (backslash) character becomes / in command lines. This will not work with all MS-DOS programs, so use +u with care.

Device Sharing Between the MS-DOS and UNIX Systems

When the operating systems have full control of the machine, they each allow you to access any hardware devices. However, because the rules for device management differ between the two systems, occasional problems arise with devices when both systems are running simultaneously. These problems do not arise with the hard disk, but floppy disks, printers, and communication ports will show some unusual behavior at times.

Floppy Disk Management

Both operating systems allow you to use the floppy disk drives, but the systems cannot share the floppy disk. The diskettes themselves differ in format, and the low-level device drivers to read and write the diskettes also differ. Thus only one system can use the disk drives at any one time.

When MS-DOS starts, it will not grab the floppy drives until you use them under the MS-DOS session. That is, you can switch from the MS-DOS session back to the UNIX system and use normal media commands to access the floppy under the UNIX system.

If you use the drives from MS-DOS, however, the MS-DOS session will grab the drives. If the drive is in use under the UNIX system, the MS-DOS command that accesses the drive will fail. If the drive is idle in the UNIX system, the MS-DOS session will use the drives as expected. In some merge implementations, the drive will remain "owned" by MS-DOS after it is used, and the UNIX system will no longer have access to it until the MS-DOS session is killed. To release the disk drive back to the UNIX system after it has been used under the MS-DOS session, you may need to quit from the MS-DOS session. Then you can restart the MS-DOS session, and the disk drives will again be accessible by the UNIX system. In other merge implementations, you can release the drive back to the UNIX system without killing the MS-DOS session.

Printing under MS-DOS

A similar situation arises with attached printers because both systems could simultaneously try to send output to the printer. There are two solutions to this problem in most merge implementations.

If the **lp** subsystem is in use, the MS-DOS **print** command will send output to the **lp** print queue instead of printing directly by the MS-DOS print spooler. This prevents conflicts because **lp** manages the spool intelligently. Similarly, the MS-DOS **print screen** function works as expected by sending the screen dump into the **lp** print queue. In both cases the default printer specified in the **lp** configuration is used for the output.

Alternatively, you can specify that the normal MS-DOS printer drivers are used instead of the **lp** queue. A special MS-DOS command is provided that grabs the printer from the **lp** spooler and reserves it for the MS-DOS print utilities. From the MS-DOS session, use this command

```
C> PRINTER DOS
```

to grab the printer for the MS-DOS session. You can return the printer to the UNIX system with the following command:

```
C> PRINTER UNIX
```

After assigning the printer to the MS-DOS session, you may need to use the **mode** command to set the printer configuration correctly, especially if you are using a serial printer.

While the printer is grabbed by MS-DOS, the **lp** spool will be *disabled* so that the queue can grow even though output will not be printed.

Going Further

As you might imagine, a great many more issues are associated with sharing a single machine between two different operating systems. It is a fine achievement that the merge facility is available at all!

Unusable MS-DOS Commands

While the merge feature is running, MS-DOS commands that can destroy the merge environment are prohibited. Do not use the MS-DOS commands **fdisk** or **ship**, or any other commands that park the fixed-disk heads. Further, do not use the MS-DOS **chkdsk**, **format**, or **sys** commands on the shared hard-disk partition, though you can use them on floppy disks.

Multiple Sessions

With SVR3 implementations of **merge**, you can run multiple sessions with both the MS-DOS and UNIX systems. Some releases provide a pop-up menu that lets you start a new session, or you can return to the UNIX system with the hot key, then execute another **dos &** command. Alternatively, a synonym for the **dos &** command is **newdos**, which can create a new MS-DOS session from either the MS-DOS or UNIX systems:

```
C> newdos
```

This will start a new MS-DOS environment directly from the MS-DOS session.

You can also start a new session with the UNIX system with **newunix**, which also works from either the MS-DOS or UNIX system. Each session will have its own screen. The **newdos** and **newunix** commands may not be available in all merge implementations.

In both cases all other sessions will still be active, and you can sequence through them by repeatedly pressing the hot key until you find the one you want, or possibly by using a pop-up menu that appears when you press the hot key. There is an implementation-dependent limit on how many of these sessions are allowed, so consult the documentation for your system. Also, in many implementations each MS-DOS session will take its own "private" memory away from the system's available RAM, causing the UNIX system to slow down when its needs are no longer met.

Communications and Interrupts

Because the MS-DOS session runs as a process under the UNIX system, it does not really have full access to the hardware resources of the machine. In fact, the UNIX system monitors hardware events and interrupts even while the MS-DOS session is active. Interrupts are passed through this linkage level to the MS-DOS session. This has several implications. First, communications devices that cause frequent interrupts cannot run as fast under the merge session as under a stand-alone MS-DOS session. Usually 4800 or 9600 baud is as fast as a serial device can run under the MS-DOS session. Second, MS-DOS programs that turn off interrupts for too long can cause a fault in the linkage level, because the UNIX system must have interrupts enabled. The **dos** command solves this problem by killing the MS-DOS session when interrupts are either disabled for too long or are set to some unacceptable state. Deranged MS-DOS applications are sufficiently protected that they cannot damage the executing UNIX system.

Stand-Alone MS-DOS on a UNIX Machine

If you have configured your machine with a separate MS-DOS partition (as discussed in Chapter 21), then you can use MS-DOS as a stand-alone system without the merge feature. When MS-DOS is running as a stand-alone system, you cannot access the hard-disk partition used by the UNIX system, but will use the separate MS-DOS partition that was established when you formatted your hard disk. This lets you use the full speed and power of the MS-DOS system, when needed, without the UNIX system sharing the CPU.

There are two ways to use stand-alone MS-DOS. First, you can boot the machine from a floppy MS-DOS *system* disk. When you do this, the MS-DOS-only partition of the hard disk will be known as **drive C**. This is not the same partition as the drive C or drive U known to MS-DOS while it is running in the merge session. The latter is the normal file system shared by the MS-DOS and UNIX systems, while the former is the stand-alone MS-DOS partition.

Before you can use this stand-alone drive C, you must format it as normal for MS-DOS disks. This format operation is done only once, the first time you use the partition. After booting the machine from an MS-DOS floppy disk, enter

```
A> FORMAT C: /S
```

to prepare the partition for use. This format command may give an error message, such as the following:

```
Warning:  this will destroy all the data on the hard disk.
```

In fact, you will erase only the files in the MS-DOS-only partition, not all the data in the merged partition.

After formatting, you can load the MS-DOS operating system or applications onto this drive C as usual, and the files will not clash with the UNIX system on the merged file system. When you reboot the machine from the hard disk, the UNIX system will come up as usual.

The second way to access the MS-DOS-only partition is to use the **fdisk** command from the UNIX system to change the *active partition* to the MS-DOS-only partition. Execute **fdisk** from the UNIX system, not from the MS-DOS session. You should never use **fdisk** from the MS-DOS session within the merge system. When you reboot the machine, the MS-DOS partition will have control, and the machine will boot under MS-DOS. Whenever you subsequently reboot the machine, the MS-DOS partition will be active. When you wish to change back to the UNIX system, use **fdisk** under the stand-alone MS-DOS system to change the active partition back to the merged partition. Then the UNIX system will start at boot-time.

The E Drive

When you are using the merged session, you can access the MS-DOS-only partition with some logical drive letter. In some implementation, drive E is used by default. In others you may name it as you wish. This is possible only under the MS-DOS session within the merge system. You cannot access the MS-DOS-only partition from the UNIX system, nor can you access the merged partition from the stand-alone MS-DOS system.

The D Drive

Another logical disk drive is also available when you start the MS-DOS session. This is drive D or drive Y in some releases. Unlike drive E, drive D *can* access the shared disk partition. It differs from drive C (or drive U) in one respect: the root of drive D is your HOME directory, not the real root of the shared file system. You cannot see "above" your HOME directory in drive D. You can switch to drive D like this:

```
C> D:
D>
```

Drive D is useful for applications that try to create files in the / (root) directory. When you install these applications in drive D, they will make their files in your HOME directory instead of the real / directory, thus avoiding conflicts when more than one person uses these applications.

The J Drive

In addition to drives D and E, the **dos** command may give you a drive J when it starts. Drive J is available when you execute an MS-DOS command directly from the shell.

```
$ ws.exe document
```

Drive J will have as a working directory the directory in which the executable program was found. This can differ from the working directory under the UNIX system, which will be drive C. Some versions of MS-DOS applications, especially older programs, require that your data files be in the same directory as the executable program. Drive J will point to the executable program, while drive C will point to the data file. Thus these programs will work correctly. Drive J is not otherwise very useful, and it usually points to the MS-DOS **bin** directory.

Booting the MS-DOS Session from a Floppy Disk

When you execute the **dos** command, the MS-DOS session starts from the *MS-DOS image* on the system's hard disk. This is fastest and is usually what you want. Occasionally, however, you might want to boot the MS-DOS system from a floppy disk. Some applications cannot be installed on the hard disk, and some games are configured on stand-alone floppy disks that do not have a true MS-DOS system. You can use these applications with the merge feature by booting the MS-DOS session directly from a floppy disk.

Place the bootable diskette in drive A and execute the command **dosboot** from the UNIX system.

```
$ dosboot
```

The merge system will start from the floppy disk, and the session will act just as if you had booted the machine from the floppy.

You can use this feature to boot other operating systems as well, such as CP/M-86 or even OS/2.

Using MS-DOS as a Login Shell

You can set up users' login id's so that they get an MS-DOS session instead of a normal shell when they log into the machine. Just use the **dos** command as the shell field of the /etc/passwd line identifying those users. For example,

```
jim:x:103:100:Jim J.:/usr/jim:/bin/dos
```

The shell field contains **/bin/dos**, so the MS-DOS session will start when the user logs into the machine.

When you use **/etc/passwd** in this way, the **dos** command may not use the normal **autoexec.bat** file when it starts. A special profile, often called **dosenv.def** is read first, then a profile in your normal HOME directory called **dosenv**. The **dosenv.def** file is a system-wide profile, and **$HOME/dosenv** is specific to each user. These profiles may differ in their name and in their directory location, so consult the documentation for your specific merge release to take advantage of this feature.

These profiles can contain anything you would normally put into **autoexec.bat**. The default PATH is probably insufficient, so you should include a PATH= line in the **dosenv** file to set it as you wish.

The dosopts Command

When you start an MS-DOS application directly from the UNIX system, the **dos** program runs first to create the MS-DOS environment. Because you do not run **dos** directly in this case, you cannot specify any command line options for that invocation of the MS-DOS session. The **dosopts** (for MS-DOS options) command is used to permanently associate some **dos** options with an application program so that they will be in effect when the command is executed directly from the UNIX system. Some implementations include a special full-screen version of the **dosopts** function called **dosadmin**. Use **dosadmin** if it is present; otherwise, use

```
$ dosopts [options] command
```

to install the named options with the command.

The list of options is the same as for the **dos** command. For example, to set the largest possible memory size when you execute the Lotus 1-2-3 application, use the following:

```
$ dosopts -m640 123.exe
```

Then, when you execute

```
$ 123.exe
```

it will be allocated the maximum available memory space. This command may vary among merge implementations, so check the documentation for your system.

Installing the Merge Feature

Another area of great variability is the installation of the merge feature. In most cases the UNIX system vendor will provide a special user agent that will prompt you through the installation procedure. Consult the documentation provided with your merge system for the exact procedures to follow.

The procedure may be quite simple because the MS-DOS system is usually included with the merge installation diskette and does not require separate installation. In older releases you might have to use a temporary diskette to save some of the system files during the process. You might also have to feed this temporary disk several times during the installation procedure and reboot the machine a few times. When the installation is completed, you can load the standard MS-DOS system into the merged partition.

After loading the merge utilities and MS-DOS system software, you can install MS-DOS application programs onto the hard disk. You must install applications with the merge feature. Do not use the installation procedures provided with the application software unless you are installing the application into the stand-alone MS-DOS partition. Instead, use the user agent provided with the merge system.

The MS-DOS Image

The *MS-DOS image* is a file that contains the exact configuration of the MS-DOS session that is started when you execute the **dos** command. It is a snapshot, stored on disk, of the **dos** session that exists when it is running. This file allows fast startup of the MS-DOS session because it is already configured and can be loaded quickly into the machine's memory when you start MS-DOS.

The MS-DOS image is created when you install the merge feature. However, the MS-DOS image must change whenever you change the hardware configuration on the machine by adding or removing disks, display cards, system ROMs, and the like. You can remove the merge feature before changing the hardware configuration and reinstall it after you have upgraded the machine.

Alternatively, you can use the **dosadmin** command to create a new MS-DOS image. After all the hardware changes are completed, enter

```
$ dosadmin
```

from either the MS-DOS or UNIX system. A menu item named **Create MS-DOS Image** will create the new image for you. If you neglect this operation, the MS-DOS session will not work correctly after you make hardware changes in your machine.

MS-DOS Device Drivers and TSR Applications

Finally, there is usually an updating procedure which you should use when you change the contents of your **config.sys** file so that the **dos** command knows how to load the MS-DOS device drivers you have specified. Follow documented procedures carefully when you add MS-DOS hardware or change your software configuration. You might have to insert a copy of your merge diskette for updating. You should also follow this procedure if you add **TSR** (for terminate but stay resident) applications and desk accessories.

Timing and Scheduling

Scheduling of tasks is an important area in any multitasking operating system. For multiple processes to receive fair access to the single CPU of the machine, *timing mechanisms* within the operating system must allow switching to a new process when another has used its share of CPU resources. Indeed, the UNIX system includes excellent tools for timing and scheduling, with a time scale that ranges from milliseconds through years. The basic timing mechanisms are built into the operating system itself, and the commands and tools based on these mechanisms regularly perform administrative functions without much attention from the user or system administrator.

Timing is so important under the UNIX system that nearly all UNIX machines have built-in, battery-operated clock/calendar hardware that keeps time correctly while the machine is turned off. However, the correct operation of administrative functions usually depends on the machine being "up" nearly 100 percent of the time. Many functions are scheduled by the system to run once a day, usually in the small hours of the night. Other functions are scheduled to execute once a week, and some may operate only once or twice a year. In this chapter we will review some of the user-level timing considerations and mention some of the administrative operations that are scheduled by the UNIX system.

The UNIX System is Designed to Operate All the Time

Historically the UNIX system was used on time-sharing systems with nearly 100 percent availability. In these machines the only available CPU time was late at night, when few users were active on the system. Therefore, a lot of background administrative tasks were scheduled for these late-night hours, and over the years tools evolved to provide for their automatic scheduling. In fact many machines were turned off only for occasional hardware maintenance. Over time many subtle assumptions concerning high availability have crept into the UNIX system, and today it is preferable to keep machines powered on, and operating, as much as possible. In addition, high availability allows your electronic mail and **uucp** data transfers to take place at night, when telephone rates are low and the machine is lightly loaded.

Of course the UNIX system will run successfully if it is only turned on occasionally; keeping the machine up and running is not truly required. However, if the machine is in daily use, it is better to keep it powered up all the time rather than shutting it down overnight. In our discussion of the **cron** function you will learn when activities are scheduled on your machine; you can tune the machine to do its administrative work at a time of day that you usually have it turned on.

The date Command Revisited

The UNIX system maintains an internal date that is available to users. In its raw form this date is actually a count of the total number of seconds that have elapsed since January 1, 1970, which (at least in myth) marks the dawn of the UNIX system era. Times longer than 1 second are kept in this format within the UNIX system. There is no easy way to get at this "raw" time value from the command line, but in fact this number is fairly large, at least 560000000, and growing fast!

Most commands that use the current time convert the raw value into a friendlier format. We have already discussed the basic functions of the **date** command in Chapter 6: **date** provides the basic user-level access to the timing functions. This command

```
$ date
Wed Jun 10 18:50:06 EDT 1987
$
```

will display the current date and time as known by the machine.

In addition, **date** can format its output differently when you wish. You specify the format as the argument to **date**, beginning with + (plus). Nearly any output format is possible if you define *fields* in the argument. The % (percent) operator introduces a field, and a single character following the % describes the date element desired. For example, **m** requests the month of the year (1 through 12).

```
$ date +%m
06
$
```

In this case the month is 06, or June. Other operators following the % are **d** for day of the month (1 through 31), **y** for the last two digits of the year, **H** for hour of the day, **M** for minute, **S** for second, **w** for day of the week (Sunday through Saturday), **h** for month (Jan through Dec), and **r** for time in AM/PM notation. These formats can follow the % operator. Characters that do not follow % in the argument are treated as normal characters, so **date** can print complex expressions involving the date and time. For example:

```
$ date "+Today is %h %dth.  The time is now exactly %r"
Today is Jun 10th.  The time is now exactly 06:26:32 PM
$
```

In addition, you can use **%n** to request a NEWLINE, allowing multiline date output.

```
$ date +"Month: %m%nDay: %d%nTime: %T"
Month: 06
Day: 10
Time: 19:02:58
$
```

These specially constructed **date** commands are often used in shell scripts to produce a display or to assign environment variables. The possibilities are limited by your imagination; 15 different % operators are allowed with the **date** command.

Setting the System Date

The superuser can also use the **date** command to *change* the system's idea of the current date and time. If **date** is given an argument that is not preceded by +, that argument will be interpreted as a current date and time to set the system date. This argument must be of the form **mmddhhmm**, where the first **mm** is a two-digit month, **dd** is a two-digit day of the month, **hh** is a two-digit hour of the day in 24-hour format, and the second **mm** is the minute of the hour. The command

```
# date 06071647
Sun Jun  7 16:47:00 EDT 1987
#
```

will set the current date to June 7, 4:47 P.M. The new date is returned to verify the change. If needed, you can add a two-digit year to the end of the argument to also set the year. This command

```
# date 0607164788
```

will set the same date in the year 1988.

In practice, don't change the date unless you must; discontinuities in time counting can cause problems with some software. Change the system date only when the system is lightly loaded. The best time is immediately after a reboot. In machines with built-in clock/calendar hardware, you rarely need to reset the system date. However, the correct time is important for correct operation of the system, so you should keep the system time accurate.

The Time Zone and Daylight-Saving Time

The date command works in local time, and correctly converts the date and time to GMT, the internal time format of the system. The local time zone and the difference in hours between it and GMT is stored in the file **/etc/TZ**, and is usually also available in the environment variable **TZ**. These entries have a form like that of **EST5EDT**, where the time zone name is first (EST), followed by the number of hours away from GMT (5), followed by the name of the time zone if daylight saving time is used (EDT). Usually the **TZ** environment variable is set by the system from the **/etc/TZ** file, so if you move your machine you can change the **/etc/TZ** file and then reboot. However, to be safe you should set time zone through the administrative user agent provided with the machine.

The system provides a built-in algorithm for switching between standard time and daylight saving time, and this algorithm may not be completely correct, since governments often change the daylight saving time rules. Be sure to check your system's time after daylight saving time begins and ends.

File Times

The UNIX system maintains several time stamps for all files in the system, and one of these is displayed for each file with the output from **ls −l**. This is the *modification time* of the file—the time at which the file was last changed. Several commands use this time to determine if a file is up to date, and some commands will detect if a file has changed since the last time the command looked at the file. In addition, the system keeps two other times associated with a file: the *creation time* and the *access time*. The creation time records when the file was originally created, and the access time records the last time a user or program read the file. The creation and access times are not easily displayed by user commands, but commands such as **find** and **test** can key on these times if you wish. Normally you will be most interested in the modification time.

The touch Command

The **touch** command is used to change the time stamp associated with a file. It takes a filename list as argument and by default will change the access and modification times of a file to the current time.

```
$ ls -l old.file
-rw-rw-rw-  1 steve      users        539 Jan 15 04:15 old.file
$ touch old.file
$ ls -l old.file
-rw-rw-rw-  1 steve      users        539 Jun 10 21:02 old.file
$
```

The **−m** (for modification) option causes **touch** to change only the modification time, while **−a** (for access) causes **touch** to change only the access time.

The **touch** command can also set the times of a file to any other time if you give an additional argument.

```
$ ls -l old.file
-rw-rw-rw-  1 root      users        539 Jun 10 21:02 old.file
$ touch 03211541 old.file
$ ls -l old.file
-rw-rw-rw-  1 root      users        539 Mar 21 15:41 old.file
$
```

The new date follows any flags but precedes the filename list. This new date is set in the same format as the system date: **mmddhhmm**, where the first **mm** is a two-digit month, **dd** is a two-digit day of the month, **hh** is a two-digit hour of the day in 24-hour format, and the second **mm** is a two-digit minute of the hour. You can append an optional two-digit year to the end of the new date string.

The **touch** command can also be used to create an empty file that did not previously exist.

```
$ ls -l new.file
new.file not found
$ touch new.file
$ ls -l new.file
-rw-rw-rw-  1 root      users          0 Jun 10 21:06 new.file
$
```

This procedure is often used in shell scripts to assure that a file exists. You can also create an empty file with your favorite editor or by giving the shell command > (right caret) alone on a command line.

```
$ >new.file
```

The −**c** (for create) option prevents **touch** from creating a file if it did not previously exist.

Like other aspects of time control under the UNIX system, it is undesirable to change the times associated with files unless it is really necessary. Some procedures, such as automated backup tools, may not work as expected if you change the modification times of files.

The at and batch Commands

The **at** command provides the facility to schedule jobs for later execution. Any command line or shell script can be *queued* with the **at** facility. If needed, the shell script can include another **at** command within it, allowing scripts to reschedule themselves. The **at** command is intended for normal users of the system and includes appropriate security to allow or deny its use by individual users. The **at** command works in addition to the system-wide scheduling mechanism called **cron**, which is intended for use by system processes and the system administration facilities. The **at** command is present in SVR3 and other recent releases, but some older versions may not include it.

Execute **at** by giving a time and date as command line arguments. The **at** command reads its standard input for the text of the command or script to execute at that time.

```
$ at 11:45 < script
job 550414980.a at Thu Jun 11 11:45:00 1987
$
```

This example will execute the commands in the file **script** at 11:45 A.M. today. The **at** command responds with a job id and the time it will execute the job, written to its standard error.

The job will be executed at that time even if you log off the machine or the machine is rebooted before the scheduled time. You might recognize the job id number as an example of the magic "seconds since 1970" time format that the system uses. Of course, if the machine is not turned on when the scheduled time arrives, the command will not be executed.

The **at** command is fairly intelligent about the shell environment in which the script is executed. It will provide the same environment variables that were exported when the **at** command was executed, and the current directory, the **umask**, and the **ulimit** will be restored for the script. The standard output and standard error for the shell script will be sent as mail to the user after the script is executed, allowing you to see its messages and output. If the script reads from its standard input while it is running, it will see an immediate end-of-file indication.

Specifying a Date for the at Command

The **at** command allows several different formats for the time specification, including ones that specify a date later than today. You may specify a time as an hour with one or two digits. This command

```
$ at 17
```

will execute the command at 5:00 P.M. local time. The 24-hour time format is assumed unless "am" or "pm" follows the time. This command

```
$ at 5pm
```

will also cause the script to be executed at 5:00 P.M. No space is allowed between the numeric value of the time and the **am** or **pm** string. In addition, a four-digit time is allowed with a : (colon) between the hour and minute.

```
$ at 4:35pm
```

If you omit the **am** or **pm** string, the time will again be interpreted in 24-hour format. The special strings **now**, **noon**, and **midnight** are also allowed.

```
$ at noon
```

A job can be executed at an increment in time if you include the + operator after the time. This command

```
$ at now + 15 minutes
```

will execute the job in 15 minutes. In addition to **minutes**, the time specifiers **hours**, **days**, **weeks**, **months**, and **years** are allowed with the + operator. This command

```
$ at 3:15pm + 6 months
```

provides an alarm clock six months from 3:15 P.M. today!

In addition to the time, you can add a date after the time for execution on that date. This command

```
$ at 2:15pm Jul 16
```

will cause the job to be executed on July 16. After the time, the optional date is composed of a month name and then a day of the month. A day of the week is allowed instead of the month and day. The month name and day of the week must be either fully spelled out or abbreviated to three letters. If desired, a year can follow the month if you insert a , (comma) after the date.

```
$ at 2:15pm Jul 16, 1989
```

The + operator is allowed with these longer date specifications if it follows the rest of the date. This command

```
$ at 2:15pm Jul 16, 1989 + 3 years
```

will execute the job three years after July 16, 1989, if the machine is still running!

These date specifications seem complex, but actually the format is fairly natural and intuitive, and most normal ways of writing a date will work as expected. If not, **at** will provide a terse error message.

```
$ at 6:15 pm Satur
at: bad date specification
$
```

Displaying the at Job Queue

The **at** command provides two options for managing the list of jobs you have scheduled. Use −l (for list) to list all your jobs by their job id number, giving the date and time they are scheduled.

```
$ at −l
550503300.a      Fri Jun 12 09:35:00 1987
550503360.a      Fri Jun 12 09:36:00 1987
$
```

Use −r (for remove) with a list of job id's as arguments to remove the named jobs from the queue.

```
$ at −r 550503300.a
$ at −l
550503360.a      Fri Jun 12 09:36:00 1987
$
```

Of course you can remove only the jobs that you have created. Only the superuser may remove any job on the queue. Jobs created by **at** are stored in the directory **/usr/spool/cron/atjobs** until they are executed, and you may delete a specific job directly from that directory instead of using **at −r**.

The contents of the shell script that **at** will execute are determined by your needs, but only scripts that you can normally execute from the shell are allowed. That is, because **at** executes the script with the execution environment in force when the **at** command was given, you cannot do more from **at** than you are normally permitted at the terminal.

Further, **at** executes the script only *once*, at the specified time. However, if you wish to create a script that executes regularly at a specified time, such as once a day or once each hour, include a new **at** command in the script so that the script will effectively *reschedule* itself for execution. Normally the relative time operators available to **at** are used, such as the following:

```
$ at now + 1 day
```

This command will execute a script tomorrow at this time. If you include this command in the script that **at** executes, you have created a command that runs once each day. An easy way to do this is with

```
at now + 1 day < $0
```

near the end of your script. The **$0** is evaluated by the shell to be the name of the script. This will work if the **at** command that starts the schedule is executed from the directory in which the script resides. If not, **$0** will not work, and a full pathname will be needed.

      Self-scheduling jobs like this can cause many headaches in your system if they are incorrect. You must carefully debug the script before allowing it to be self-scheduled. Further, if the script ever disappears from the disk or its pathname changes, **at** will fail and the job will no longer be rescheduled, possibly producing extremely large log files in the process. The **crontab** facility, discussed shortly, is generally preferred for regularly scheduled jobs.

The batch Command

A command related to **at** is **batch**, which acts like

```
$ at now
```

except that the job will be scheduled to run as soon as the system load is low enough. (In addition, **at now** will respond too late, while **batch** will work as expected.) The **batch** command uses an internal algorithm to decide when the job will be executed. It is useful when you wish to execute many large jobs at the same time. If these jobs are simply executed in the background with the **&** command line operator, they will all try to execute at once, possibly clogging the CPU. They will all take longer to execute because each will get only a small time-slice from the operating system, and then another will take control. The **batch** command can prevent this *thrashing*. It allows you to schedule all the jobs at once but have only a few start at a time. The first jobs will complete relatively quickly, and later ones will be spaced as the system load permits. The overall time for completion of all the jobs will actually be slightly shorter with **batch**, and total CPU usage will be lower.

The **batch** command takes no command line arguments because the job will always be executed as soon as it is practical. Like **at**, **batch** reads the script from its standard input and sends the standard output and standard error from the script to the user as mail.

```
$ batch < script
job 550501560.b at Fri Jun 12 09:06:00 1987
$
```

The **batch** command writes the job number to its standard error in the same format used by **at**. You can also use the **at −r** command to delete a job scheduled by **batch** if you catch it before it has begun to execute.

Security Considerations with at and batch

Both **at** and **batch** provide security mechanisms that prevent users (except the superuser) from scheduling jobs without prior authorization. If you try the previous commands on your system, you might be prohibited.

```
$ at 16:35 < script
at: you are not authorized to use at.   Sorry.
$
```

Users can be individually authorized or prohibited from using these tools.

The list of authorized users is maintained in the directory **/usr/lib/cron**.

```
$ cd /usr/lib/cron
$ ls -FC
FIFO        at.deny      cron.deny     queuedefs
at.allow    cron.allow   log
$
```

FIFO is used as a communications channel between the **crontab** and **cron** programs, and **queuedefs** contains information used internally by the **cron** facility. The two files of interest here for **at** and **batch** are **at.allow** and **at.deny**, which contain a list of user id's allowed to use or prohibited from using these commands, respectively.

```
$ cat at.allow
root
sys
adm
uucp
steve
jim
pat
$
```

User id's are listed one per line in the file.

Only the superuser may modify the **at.allow** and **at.deny** files, so the system administrator must keep this file up to date with changes in the users id's on the machine. However, administration can be simplified with some additional rules. If the file **at.allow** is present, then only users listed in the file may execute **at** and **batch**; this rule is observed whether or not **at.deny** exists. If **at.allow** is not present, then **at.deny** is checked to see if a user is explicitly prohibited from using the commands; that is, any user not listed in **at.deny** may execute the commands. If neither file is present, only the superuser may execute the commands. So, to open up **at** usage to all users, delete the file **at.allow** and then be sure that **at.deny** is empty but present. The user id's **root**, **sys**, **adm**, and **uucp** should always be included in the file **at.allow**, if the file is present.

The cron Facility

The **at** and **batch** commands use the services of a more fundamental scheduling mechanism that is always running within the UNIX system. This is the **cron** (for chronograph) facility, which you have already met in the output from **ps —e**. The **cron** command is the name of a system demon that is executed early in the boot-up sequence of all UNIX systems. Once every minute it wakes up, looks in a control file to see if there are any jobs to be executed at that minute, and then executes them. If no jobs are scheduled for that time, **cron** goes back to sleep until the next minute. This powerful scheduling mechanism depends on the multitasking nature of the UNIX system. Fortunately, though always present, **cron** does not use many CPU resources.

The **cron** command is kept in the file **/etc/cron** and is executable. However, **cron** is not a user command and should not be executed directly, even by the superuser. If two copies of **cron** are running on the machine, the system will be quite deranged. If **cron** is not running on your machine, reboot the system rather than executing cron directly. If **cron** is still not running after a reboot, something is seriously wrong with the machine. Usually you will need to reload the operating system from the original disks to repair the problem. However, some versions of the UNIX system include timing mechanisms with a different name than **cron**, so if a machine is not running SVR3, there may be no process named **cron** in the output from **ps —ef**. However, the functions performed by **cron** are basic to the operation of all UNIX systems, and it will always be present under some name unless the machine is deranged.

In addition to the system-wide use of **cron** functions, mechanisms allow individual users (in addition to the superuser) to schedule jobs for regular execution at intervals of one minute or longer. While **at** schedules a job for one-time execution, the **cron** facility schedules jobs to execute regularly at some specified interval.

crontab File Format

The control file used by **cron** is known as the **crontab** (for **cron** table), and it was originally a single file with the pathname **/etc/crontab**. Only the superuser was permitted to modify this file and thus change the system schedule. Some older releases still use this file location. However, SVR3 and other recent versions of the UNIX system provide an expanded **crontab** facility within the directory **/usr/spool/cron/crontabs**.

```
$ ls -FC /usr/spool/cron/crontabs
adm        root      sys       sysadm
$
```

Each user who has specified some jobs for scheduling by the **cron** facility will have a file in this directory, named for the login id of the user who created the file. The files listed in this example will be present on nearly all SVR3 systems, and each is intended for a specific system-wide scheduling application.

Often the **sys** file is used to collect system performance data if the **sar** performance analysis tools are installed on the machine. The **adm** file is usually used to schedule performance profiling from **sar** data. The **root** file is often used to collect accounting data associated with use of system resources by individual users. In a public UNIX system, where users are billed for their use of the machine, the **root** file often contains several scheduled jobs. In small personal UNIX machines, however, these three **crontab** files are probably empty or not present on the machine.

Most system-wide scheduling usually appears in the **sysadm** file, which often contains several comments describing the format for all **crontab** files. In some releases the contents of **sysadm** have been moved to the **sys** file, and **sysadm** does not exist. Figure 18-1 shows a typical **sysadm crontab** for a small SVR3 system. Though yours will probably differ from this example, the figure does show the required file format and some of the administrative tasks scheduled in the system as a whole. We will discuss how individual users can create scheduled jobs shortly.

```
# This file will be scheduled via the cron command
#
#       Format of lines:
#min  hour  daymo  month  daywk    /etc/ckbupscd >/dev/console 2>/dev/console
#
#       min  - time(s) of day
#       hour
#       daymo - day(s) of month (1, 2, ... 31)
#       month - month(s) of the year (1, 2, ... 12)
#       daywk - day(s) of week (0-6, 0 = sun)
#
#       Example:
#00 17 *  *  1        /etc/ckbupscd >/dev/console 2>/dev/console
#
#       At 5:00pm in the evening on mondays during any month of the year,
#       check to see if there are any file systems that need
#       to be backed up.
#
#----------------------------------------------------------------------
#
#       Default backup schedule calls for checks mon through friday
#       at 5:00pm.
#
00 17 *  *  1,2,3,4,5 /etc/ckbupscd >/dev/console 2>/dev/console
0  4  *  *  *         /bin/su uucpadm % /usr/lib/uucp/uudemon.admin > /dev/null
30 5  *  *  1         /bin/su uucpadm % /usr/lib/uucp/uudemon.cleanu > /dev/null
30 5  *  *  1         /bin/su root % /etc/cleanup.wk > /dev/null
34 *  *  *  *         /bin/su uucpadm -c "/usr/lib/uucp/uudemon.hour > /dev/null"
```

Figure 18-1.   Typical **sysadm** or **sys crontab** for a small SVR3 UNIX system

Comment lines in the **crontab** files begin with the # (pound) operator. These lines are ignored when **cron** reads the file. Lines that do not begin with # name commands to be scheduled, one request per line. If you escape the NEWLINE with \ (backslash), the command can continue onto subsequent lines. The first five fields of the line give the date and time to execute the command. Each field is separated by white space from the others. A number in a field gives the date or time to schedule the job, and entries consisting of * (star) are translated to "every" by **cron**. The first field in the line specifies the minute of the hour to execute the job: 00 means on the hour, 30 means 30 minutes after the hour, and so on. The second field of the line specifies the hour of the day in 24-hour format: 2 is 2:00 A.M., 14 is 2:00 P.M., and so on. The third field specifies the day of the month, from 1 through 31. The fourth field gives the month of the year, from 1 through 12, and the fifth field gives the day of the week, from 0 for Sunday through 6 for Saturday.

You can combine these time specifications, so that

```
30 5 * * * 1
```

is interpreted as 5:30 A.M. on every Monday, while

```
30 5 * * *
```

means 5:30 A.M. every day of the week, and

```
30 * * * *
```

means 30 minutes past every hour, every day.

Lists of times are allowed within each field, separated by a , (comma),

```
00 17 * * 1,2,3,4,5
```

if there is no white space between entries in the same field. This example specifies a command to run at 17 minutes past midnight, Monday through Friday.

The rest of the line after the schedule is the name of the command to execute, along with any redirection of input or output. In the first noncomment line in Figure 18-1 the command /etc/ckbupscd is executed 17 minutes after midnight, with its standard output and standard error redirected to the system console. The other entries on the line show a more complex syntax in which the commands are executed under a specific user id instead of **bin**, the real owner of /etc/cron. The **su** command is used to switch the user id to its first argument, usually **uucpadm** in Figure 18-1. The % (percent) operator has a special meaning to **cron**: it instructs **cron** to take the rest of the line as the standard input of the command named before the %. In Figure 18-1 the line beginning "0 4 * * *" uses the contents of the file /usr/lib/uucp/uudemon.admin as a script of commands given to **su** as its standard input. By using the \ operator to escape NEWLINE, you can include large shell scripts directly within the **crontab** files, although this is rarely done, and most scripts live in their own files.

The first command in Figure 18-1 is simply a reminder, directed to the console, that some file systems may need backup. If the redirection to the console is deleted, this reminder will be sent by mail rather than written directly. The **cron** command, like **at**, will use electronic mail to report the standard output and standard error of the commands back to the user.

The next two commands, and the last, are administrative tasks performed regularly by the **uucp** communications programs. These run at different times, depending on their function. The **uudemon.admin** generates a weekly status report; it is scheduled for 4:00 A.M. every Sunday. This script usually reports on possible **uucp** security violations and jobs that have been queued for sending during the past week but have not yet been sent.

The next line, scheduled for 5:30 A.M. every Monday, is a weekly cleanup script that usually flushes old jobs and log files from the **uucp** system. It is scheduled a day after the status report so that the system administrator can take action based on the status report, if necessary, before the **uucp** logs are deleted.

The last line in Figure 18-1 is the hourly **uucp** schedule, which looks for unsent outgoing jobs and attempts to send them, if needed. Because **uucp** uses an incremental algorithm to determine if a connection to a remote machine should be attempted, the hourly demon may not always cause a connection to be attempted even though a job might be waiting. These **uucp** schedules should be present in a system **crontab** file if you use the **uucp** or **mail** facility to communicate with other machines. If they are not present, your mail may not be sent correctly.

The last line in Figure 18-1 is also executed at 5:30 A.M. each Monday. It executes a script to perform some weekly cleanup tasks that are unrelated to the **uucp** system. This entry, or one like it, is usually present on active UNIX systems, but its contents may differ depending on the work usually done on that machine. Some routine administrative tasks, such as the deletion of old log files in **/usr/adm**, the deletion of old core files, and so on, are usually delegated to **cron**.

The crontab Command

Skilled administrators will often edit these **crontab** files directly to make changes to the system schedules. However, individual users can create scheduled jobs with the **crontab** command, which is provided to help you create and change individual **crontab** files.

To create a new **crontab** schedule, create a **crontab** file with your editor or copy an existing one to a new file for editing. When the file is correct, you can add it to the **crontab** directory with

```
$ crontab filename
$
```

where "filename" is the name of the new file you have created. As usual, the command will return silently if the installation was successful. The schedule is created under the id of the user who executes the command, so different users can have their own schedules without interfering with each other. Only one **crontab** file is allowed per user.

The **crontab** command can also read its standard input for the schedule, so redirection is allowed. However, if you enter the **crontab** command with no filename and no redirected file for input, you must exit with the DEL key rather than with CTRL-D because the end-of-file mark will cause **crontab** to load an empty file in your schedule, probably not what you intended.

The **crontab** command will remove a schedule if you give the −**r** (for remove) option.

```
$ crontab -r
$
```

The **crontab** command will complain if there is no file to remove. In addition, the −**l** (for list) option will list your **crontab** if one has been created.

cron Permissions and Security

The materials associated with use of the **cron** facility are located in two directories. The directory **/usr/spool/cron /crontabs** contains the **crontab** files, while **/usr/lib/cron** includes the control information for the scheduling mechanisms. The files **cron.allow** and **cron.deny** in this directory serve the same functions as **at.allow** and **at.deny** as discussed earlier. If **cron.allow** is present, it is checked for a list of users authorized to use the **crontab** command. If **cron.allow** is not present, **cron.deny** is checked to see if a user is prohibited from using the **crontab** command. If neither **cron.allow** nor **cron.deny** is present, then only the superuser may use the **crontab** command. User id's in both **cron.allow** and **cron. deny** are listed one per line in the files.

Going Further

Many of the timing-related tools in the UNIX system are designed for developers to use in optimizing the system and its applications. These are of little use to most users, so here we will just mention some of them.

The cron Log File

The **cron** facility maintains a log of all jobs executed with **at**, **batch**, or **cron**. On SVR3 systems this is the file **log** in the directory **/usr/lib/cron**. However, older versions of the system may have another location for this file, often **/usr/adm/cronlog**. The log file can help you trace mysterious problems associated with scheduled jobs. The file format is not particularly verbose, but it can be understood.

```
$ tail log
<   sysadm 229 c Wed Jun 10 17:00:02 1987
<   sys 230 c Wed Jun 10 17:00:02 1987
! *** cron started ***   pid = 75 Thu Jun 11 08:18:45 1987
>   CMD: /usr/lib/sa/sa1
>   sys 86 c Thu Jun 11 08:20:00 1987
```

```
<   sys 86 c Thu Jun 11 08:20:01 1987
! *** cron started ***    pid = 75 Thu Jun 11 08:41:45 1987
>   CMD: 550414080.a
>   root 98 a Thu Jun 11 08:48:00 1987
<   root 98 a Thu Jun 11 08:48:03 1987
$
```

Log file format may differ on older releases from this SVR3 example. The lines containing "**cron** started" are generated by the **cron** program when the system is rebooted and **cron** starts up. A date stamp is included. Each command executed by the **cron** demon, either via **at** or a **crontab** file, has a section beginning with "CMD:" and the name of the command to execute. The last entry here, "CMD: 550414080.a", is a familiar name for a command scheduled by **at**. All the lines following the "CMD:", until the next command, are log entries produced by **cron** as it executes the commands. In fact **cron** executes commands by forking another copy of itself, and the child process actually executes the commands. However, both write to the log: lines beginning with > (right caret) are written by the original **cron** program before the command is executed, and lines beginning with < (left caret) are written by the child process, one per additional program executed by **cron**. The effective user id for the process is given first, followed by the PID of the process. Next is the job type, **a** for an **at** job or **c** for a job scheduled by **cron**. The date and time that the process was executed appears last on the line.

This log information can be useful if you suspect **cron** of creating or changing files incorrectly. Often the date or ownership of a file as revealed by **ls −l** can be traced back to an entry in the **cron** log and then associated with the **CMD** that changed the file. You only need this in those rare cases when scheduled jobs are causing problems. You might suspect these problems when mysterious changes in your machine or the file system occur at regular times but are obviously not under user control.

The log file is often not truncated by the default system administration procedures, so you should occasionally examine it to be sure that it is not growing too large. You should probably truncate it once or twice a month unless you think that some problem exists with scheduling on a machine. This is a good job for a custom **cleanup.wk** script that you can schedule in a **crontab** file.

Measuring Command Execution Time

When creating new shell scripts or executable programs, you often want to estimate the system resources used in the command. This information can help you better understand the relative expense of commands and thus optimize them. However, in a multitasking operating system the real (clock) time that a command takes may not be a good estimate of the system resources it consumes. Consequently, the UNIX system provides several tools for computing how much time a command takes to execute.

The simplest one is the **time** command. You give a command or pipeline that you wish to measure as an argument to the **time** command.

```
$ time sleep 100

real      1:39.4
user        0.0
sys         0.1
$
```

This example simply "sleeps" for 100 seconds. The **time** command writes its output to standard error, and this output gives the amount of system resources, expressed in seconds and tenths of seconds, used by the **sleep** command. The *real time* is the total elapsed time from the beginning of the command execution until it ends. In this case 1 minute, 39.4 seconds has elapsed. You know that **sleep** can be inaccurate by up to 1 second, and here it is 0.6 second off. The *user time* is the amount of time that the program spends executing its own code, which in this example is below the limits of measurement. The **sys** time is the amount of time used directly by the UNIX system in the service of the command, 0.1 second in this example.

The CPU time used by a command is actually the sum of the **sys** and **user** time measurements, but the **time** command shows them separately so that developers can determine whether the program is using kernel resources or is spending time within its own code. The difference between the real time and this sum is a measure of the CPU time that is going to other programs executing on the machine while you are making the measurement. It is apparent that the CPU time used by a command can be much less than the real elapsed time. Under lightly loaded conditions, most commands will show real time as very close to the sum.

```
$ time cat /unix >/dev/null

real        6.5
user        4.5
sys         1.0
$
```

This command takes 5.5 seconds of CPU time and completes in 6.5 seconds. One second went to other work in the system. In a heavily loaded system, this same command will take almost the same amount of **user** and **sys** time but much more real time.

The sync Operation

For purposes of internal efficiency, the UNIX system keeps data in *buffers* in its memory and updates the buffers to disk only when necessary. That is, you might edit a file, write it, and then quit back to the shell. The file actually may not have been written to the disk, so that if you immediately turn off the power to the system, your changes may not be preserved when the machine is turned on next. SVR3 systems include special processes to occasionally update the changed buffers to the system hard disk. These processes, called **bdflush** (for buffer to disk flush) and **bmapflus** (for buffer map flush), are present in the output from **ps −e**, and they update the disk regularly, often every 30 seconds. Older releases of the UNIX system may not include this automatic update procedure, however, so you must be careful that the disk is correct with respect to the system buffers before shutting down the machine. A special program called **sync** (for synchronize) allows you to manually update the memory buffers. You can execute this program whenever you want to force a buffer update, though in SVR3 systems it is rarely necessary.

```
$ sync
$
```

The **sync** program may return to the shell before its job is done, so you should normally execute **sync** two or three times to assure that the disk is updated correctly before you turn off the system power.

```
$ sync
$ sync
$
```

System Usage Accounting for Individual Users

Large public UNIX systems often include accounting procedures so that individual users can be charged for their connect time, CPU usage, and disk space usage. When installed, these tools are usually kept in the directory **/usr/lib/acct**, and a log file of all processes executed is kept in **/usr/adm/pacct**. Additional data is kept in **/etc/utmp** and **/etc/wtmp**. If accounting is used on a machine, the system administrator must take care that the accounting summary tools are executed regularly, perhaps through the **cron** facility, or these data files may grow too large. You should routinely check these files and truncate (but not delete) them when they grow large.

Many commands are available, and the accounting tools make a coherent package that allows professional billing of resource use by individual login id's.

```
$ ls -FC /usr/lib/acct
acctcms*      acctmerg*     chargefee*   holidays     prdaily*     runacct*
acctcon1*     accton*       ckpacct*     lastlogin*   prtacct*     shutacct*
acctcon2*     acctprc1*     diskusg*     monacct*     ptecms.awk   startup*
acctdisk*     acctprc2*     dodisk*      nulladm*     ptelus.awk   turnacct*
acctdusg*     acctwtmp*     fwtmp*       prctmp*      remove*      wtmpfix*
$
```

You can turn accounting on and off with these tools. They allow detailed analysis of system use by time of day, disk and process use, and connect time use. Only a skilled system administrator can fully use the tools, and they are not widely used with smaller personal UNIX systems.

Process Accounting with the sar Package

Finally, fully configured systems include the **sar** (for system activity reporting) package, which gives a complete *profile* of all activity in the UNIX system during an interval of time. The **sar** package includes data logging tools for CPU and disk utilization, buffer usage, activity counters for disk and tty devices, file access measures, and other internal measurements. Understanding this data is a task for an expert, but if present, the **sar** tools will be located in the directory **/usr/lib/sa**, and the various logs produced by them will be in the directory **/usr/adm/sa**. Browse these directories occasionally to assure that the log files do not grow too large and consume excessive disk space. The **sar** tools are usually executed via the **cron** facility, and the **crontab** files may include one or more commands related to **sar**. Usually the **sys crontab** is used, and lines executing the commands **sadc**, **sa1**, and **sa2** are related to the **sar** tools. You can turn off **sar** activity logging by commenting out the appropriate lines in the **crontab** files, if they are present.

The **sar** package includes another timing program like **time**, called **timex**, which provides better diagnostic information than **time**, especially for shell scripts that spawn child processes. However, the **sar** package must be present on the machine for **timex** to provide this detailed output. By default, **timex** will produce the same real, user, and sys time that you saw with **time**. Use the −**p**, −**o**, and −**s** options with **timex** to display the process accounting data, disk block usage, and total system activity, respectively, associated with the command executed after **timex**.

```
$ timex -o cat /etc/profile >/dev/null

real        0.93
user        0.00
sys         0.26


CHARS TRNSFD = 145216
BLOCKS READ  = 76

$
```

The other options are correspondingly more verbose.

# NINETEEN

Boot and Shutdown

Several processes are usually executing in a UNIX machine at any one time, so it is very dangerous to simply turn off the machine's power when you are done using it. The UNIX system provides tools expressly designed to create an orderly sequence of events when you wish to turn off the machine. This is known as the *shutdown procedure*, and you should follow it carefully to assure system sanity when you start the machine again. The startup procedure is also complex, and tools are provided to *boot* the machine correctly when you turn it on. In this chapter we will review the steps the system goes through during the power-off and power-on procedures and briefly mention some of the possible *system states* and some of the more common problems that can result from boot procedures.

The Ongoing System Environment

When the UNIX system is running correctly, there are likely to be many processes active on the machine. Of course the system demons will always be running, and a system administrator logged into the system console will have a shell and possibly some other programs associated with the session. In addition, other users may be logged into the machine from remote terminals, and they may be executing programs. Also, background electronic mail or **uucp** data transfers may be running at any time, and print jobs may be in progress. Finally, lack of synchronization between the *in-memory buffers* and the system hard disk means that the "real" contents of the disk and the "logical" contents will often differ. That is, when you write a file from the editor, that file will probably not be updated to the disk until seconds or minutes after the write operation is completed and you are back at the shell executing new commands.

All these factors (and several others discussed shortly) make it important that you take care when shutting down the machine. Whenever possible, use the tools that are provided to help in these tasks. Of course, sometimes the power to the machine will go off inadvertently, such as when the building power is interrupted. Modern versions of the UNIX system can withstand such power outages and incorrect shutdowns, though with some risk of failure to the system or the contents of the system disk. You will avoid problems by reducing the occurrence of inadvertent shutdowns to the minimum possible.

Shutting Down the Machine

In principle a correct shutdown will warn other users to log off before the system goes *down*, carefully kill all nonessential processes, update various system files and logs, synchronize the disk with the in-memory buffers, and, finally, kill the rest of the processes. Some systems can automatically park the disk heads as part of the shutdown. In fact some UNIX machines include a software-controlled power switch so that the last step of the shutdown procedure is physically turning off the machine.

The shutdown Command

You can use several different tools to shut down the machine, and all are preferable to simply turning off the power. One of these tools is safest, though also the slowest. This is the **shutdown** command, which is a shell script located in **/etc/shutdown**. You can browse it to better understand its actions. Like all the tools related to turning the machine on and off, **shutdown** is reserved for the superuser. It can be run only at the system console, and only from the root directory (/). The **shutdown** command will complain and refuse to act if these conditions are not met.

The shutdown procedures, and the messages displayed during shutdown, vary widely among different versions of the UNIX system. Many systems have a menu-oriented tool available to the root login id, and the output from the **shutdown** script can differ. The examples given here are taken from an SVR3 system.

The **shutdown** command was originally intended to be interactive, with the superuser controlling the actions taken during the shutdown procedure. It can still be used interactively, but recent releases of the UNIX system provide the **−y** option, which instructs **shutdown** to answer all questions itself.

```
# shutdown -y
```

This form is much easier to use than the command without the **−y** option. Before running this command, it is courteous to check with other users to be sure that they are not doing something critical. The **who** and **ps −af** commands will determine the current system activity. In addition, you should check that no job is being printed and no **uucp** data transfers are in progress because these activities will restart from the beginning after a reboot if they are interrupted by the shutdown.

When executed, **shutdown** will warn all users that the

machine will be coming down soon and they should log off before the machine dies. Figure 19-1 shows a typical console display during a shutdown sequence. Some of these messages are sent to all current users of the system, and others are limited to the system console. The two warnings beginning "The system will be shut down" and "THE SYSTEM IS BEING SHUT DOWN NOW" are *broadcast messages* sent to all users currently logged into the machine. They are sent by the **/etc/wall** (for write to all) command directly to the terminals of all users. The first is sent soon after the shutdown process begins. The **shutdown** command will sleep for 60 seconds, and then the second message will be sent. Users are expected to respond immediately to the first message by closing any open files, securing their session, and then logging off. The second message is a last warning before **shutdown** begins the final shutdown procedures. All users (except the root login on the system console) must take immediate action.

Following these messages, the **shutdown** command will stop all active processes, update the disk correctly, and gracefully bring the operating system to a stop. Finally, the system will be brought down to a point where the power can be turned off or a reboot initiated. Always wait for the "Reboot the system now" message, or its equivalent, before actually turning off the power or rebooting the system. This assures that the shutdown process has completed successfully.

By default, **shutdown** allows 60 seconds between the first and second warning messages. You can change this interval by adding the −**g** (for grace) option to the **shutdown** command line. The number of seconds to wait before really beginning the shutdown sequence follows the −**g** option. This command

```
# shutdown -y -g300
```

```
# cd /
# shutdown -y

Shutdown started.    Mon Jun 15 20:29:49 EDT 1987

        The system will be shut down in 60 seconds.
        Please log off now.


        THE SYSTEM IS BEING SHUT DOWN NOW ! ! !
        Log off now or risk your files being damaged.

The system is coming down.  Please wait.

The system is down.
Reboot the system now.
```

Figure 19-1.   Typical console display during the shutdown sequence

will cause **shutdown** to wait 5 minutes during the "warning" period. You can lengthen this period to allow any users to complete their activities before the shutdown begins or shorten it to allow a faster shutdown when it is safe. In extreme cases you can select −**g0** to reduce the waiting interval to nothing. This may be dangerous if there are many active terminals because the warning message may not be displayed to all terminals before the system is brought down. Sometimes the shutdown will fail, if all user processes are not completed before the shutdown procedure begins, and −**g15** is the shortest safe interval in busier machines.

The Boot Sequence

When the power is turned on, the machine goes through a complex process to start up. This boot sequence can take several minutes depending on the hardware and software installed on the machine and cannot be made faster. The boot process includes several *sanity checks*, and it will often try to repair any damage found, especially damage to hard-disk files. Most UNIX machines have built-in procedures that minimize this error checking if the previous shutdown was completed correctly. Thus the boot sequence following a power outage or other inadvertent shutdown will probably be more complex and complete than a reboot after a normal shutdown. In any case the boot sequence will often help repair system problems. Usually your first response to any derangement of the machine should be to reboot it.

Figure 19-2 shows a typical boot sequence as displayed on the system console. This output will vary depending on the CPU type in use, the version of the UNIX system installed, and any additional hardware or software on the machine. Not shown in the figure is the initial hardware test that most small computers will make before beginning the boot. This may include a memory test and display of installed hardware and is already familiar to most PC users. This test comes from the system ROM hardware and does not depend on the operating system in use.

The first message, "Primary boot-strap" (a row of dots on some releases), is displayed by the *ROM loader*, which loads the first parts of the operating system off the disk. In fact the ROM will load another "loader" program that loads the UNIX system itself. This additional *software loader* is stored on the system disk, so it must be loaded by hardware and ROM that exist permanently. Different operating systems keep their loader programs at the same relative disk location within their disk partition so that the ROM loader can find the software loader. This allows you to switch between operating systems by simply changing the default partition from which the ROM loads the software loader.

```
Primary boot-strap

Booting UNIX System...

total real mem  = 4194304
total avail mem = 3059712

UNIX System V Release 3.1

Copyright (c) 1987 AT&T
ALL RIGHTS RESERVED

386/ix Drivers Copyright (c) 1986 Interactive Systems Corp.
ALL RIGHTS RESERVED

The date is Thu Oct 15 13:19:07 EDT 1987
The system is coming up. Please wait.
The system is ready.

Welcome to the 'my_sys' 386 UNIX System
System name: my_sys

Console Login:
```

Figure 19-2.   Typical console display for a simple boot sequence

The software loader is brought into memory, and the ROM turns control over to it, starting it executing. The machine is now committed to running the UNIX system because the software loader can only deal with its own operating system. When the software loader begins, it displays the message

```
Booting UNIX System...
```

and then loads the operating system *kernel*, which is normally /unix. You can press a key on the keyboard while the "Booting ..." prompt is displayed, and the loader will let you enter the pathname of an alternate kernel to load.

On other releases, the message will be the following:

```
boot:
```

You can type in the name of an alternate kernel if you wish. Normally you do nothing or just press NEWLINE, and after a short interval, the loader will display the default kernel.

```
boot:   /unix
```

Then it will begin to load the UNIX system.

This file, **/unix**, is visible on the hard disk in the root directory. It is the kernel, the actual memory-resident portion of the UNIX system. The software loader will read it from disk and install it into the machine's memory. The software loader then gives control to the newly loaded kernel, and the UNIX system begins to initialize itself.

First is a display of the UNIX system version, in this case SVR3, Release 3.1. Another version of SVR3, Release 3.0, may be displayed instead.

As part of the initialization sequence, the kernel may display its idea of how much real memory is installed in the system. Older versions often required compiling the memory information into the system like the default **uname**, but SVR3 can configure itself depending on how much memory is actually installed. If you add more memory, the display will change, and the UNIX system should correctly adapt itself. If the "Total real memory" display differs from the physical memory that you know is installed in your machine, you must repair some hardware problem before you use the machine. "Available memory" displays the real memory that the system can make available to normal processes after the UNIX system takes what it needs. It appears that the difference between these two numbers is the real memory used by the kernel. But in fact this number, over 1 megabyte in this case, is much larger than the size of the file **/unix** as revealed by **ls −l**. The difference occurs because the UNIX system allocated significant amounts of memory for its *buffers*, which act somewhat like a RAM disk.

Some releases of SVR3 will actually display the number of buffers allocated at this point in the boot sequence. If present, a line of this form will appear in the display.

```
buffers=900K
```

The number of buffers allocated during the boot sequence is a *tunable parameter* in SVR3 that you can change if necessary. However, the default value is appropriate for most needs.

Normal programs can use the available memory when they execute. However, modern UNIX systems can *swap* or *page* segments of memory from RAM to disk when the system needs more memory. Thus many more programs can be executing than you might expect from the "Available memory" display. As usual, the more real memory that is available, the more effective the UNIX system can be because swapping to disk is reduced.

Next, the UNIX system begins to initialize itself and any installed hardware devices. The series of copyright notices in Figure 19-2 comes from this device initialization, and additional, or at least different, copyright notices will probably appear on other versions with different software and hardware installed.

When initialization is complete, the UNIX system is actually up and running, though much more must be completed before the system is ready for users to login. The material in Figure 19-2 from the display of the current date and time until the appearance of the "login" prompt results from boot-time shell scripts that you can browse. We will discuss these after a short digression.

In a correctly operating system no action is required between turning on the power and the eventual appearance of the "login" prompt. However, if the machine came down with a crash just prior to your rebooting it, an additional prompt will often appear in the boot sequence.

```
There may be a system dump memory image in the swap device.
Do you want to save it? (y/n)
```

This memory dump or *core image* is for debugging the kernel. Press N to bypass this step.

init States

The boot procedure for the UNIX system is complicated by the possibility of bringing up the system in different *states*. That is, the system can take several different modes of operation. These are known as the different *init states*, after /**etc**/**init**, which is the program responsible for keeping the system running correctly. These states are very different from each other, and the system can be "in" only one of them at any time. The shutdown and reboot procedures actually control which state the machine is in.

The most commonly used state is called *multiuser mode*. This system state is used for nearly all the interactions discussed in this book and is the only one that allows more than one user. Another state that was historically important but is seldom used in small modern systems is called *single-user mode*. This state is a multitasking version of the UNIX system, so that multiple processes are allowed, but it is not multiuser. That is, only the system console is active when the machine is running in single-user mode. It is usually a mistake when the system gets into single-user mode. The *UNIX User's Manual* recommends that such tasks as setting the system date and time be executed only in single-user mode, but in modern UNIX systems these can be done in multiuser mode.

There are several other states besides the single-user and multiuser modes. All of them are named by special identifiers, as shown in Table 19-1. Init state **0** is used to bring the machine down and stop the UNIX system. Single-user mode is known as init state **1** or as **s** or **S** depending on whether the single active terminal is the system console or a remote terminal. Multiuser mode is known as init state **2**, and **3** is used in SVR3 systems when the Remote File System (RFS) feature is active. State **4** is almost never used, but states **5** and **6** are used on some machines to mean "shutdown and reboot," and "shutdown to the boot ROM," respectively. Most SVR3 machines based on the Intel 80386 will not use states **4**, **5** or **6**.

State	Function
0	Power off the machine
1	Single-user mode
2	Multiuser mode
3	Multiuser with RFS
4	Not used
5	Shutdown and reboot (usually not used)
6	Shutdown to ROM (usually not used)
s	Single-user mode
S	Single-user mode with remote console

Table 19-1.   **init** States for SVR3 UNIX Systems

Changing the init State

The **shutdown** command is useful for more than simply turning off the machine; it is really designed to change the init state. By default, **shutdown** will take the machine to state **0**, thus preparing to turn off system power. However, the −**i** argument is provided to explicitly set the init state, and the desired init state is given after the −**i**.

```
# shutdown -y -g45 -i0
```

This will take the system down, while

```
# shutdown -y -i1
```

will take the machine into single-user state. Normally the system will be in state **2** unless you are using the **RFS** facilities, in which case it will be in state **3**.

These states are important to understanding the boot process because the shell scripts that are executed during the boot procedure will differ depending on which state the system is going into.

The /etc/inittab File

After the completion of the internal initialization, the system will start the /**etc**/**init** (for initialization) demon, which takes control of the boot-up sequence. The **init** process, which will remain active for as long as the system is running, serves a very important function: it makes sure that all other system demons are executing when they should be. For example, when you login to the machine your shell replaces the **getty** program so that **getty** no longer exists for the terminal. However, when you log off the machine, your shell will die, leaving a dead terminal port that cannot be used. The **init** process most recognize when your shell dies and *respawn* the **getty** for your terminal port. This results in a new display of the "login:" prompt at the terminal. Actually **init** is informed via a system signal when the shell dies, and it then takes appropriate action. In fact **init** has this effect on several other system demons as well, and it generally assures that important system processes are running. Of course, if **init** itself dies, no process will be around to respawn it, and the system will gradually become more and more deranged until it crashes. Luckily, it is very difficult to kill **init**.

The **init** process takes its instructions from the file **/etc/ inittab** (for init table). The contents of this file control all the **init** states, and the file also controls which processes get respawned when they die. The **inittab** file is a typical UNIX system database, with lines consisting of several fields separated by a : (colon). Figure 19-3 shows a typical **inittab** from a small SVR3 system. Its contents will differ greatly depending on the software installed in the machine, the number of remote terminals allowed, and the version of the UNIX system itself. When **init** starts up, it reads each line of the file and takes action depending on the contents of the line.

The first field of each line is an identifier that effectively "names" each line, and it should be unique. The second field defines the **init** states for which the line is active. This can be more than one state, as in **23**, which defines the line as active in **init** states **2** and **3**. If this field has no contents, the line will be active in all **init** states, as in the first two lines in Figure 19-3.

The last field on the line gives a command line that is executed by **init** when the machine is in the states named in the second field. This is a normal shell command line, and redirection of input or output is supported, as in several of the lines in Figure 19-3. Because **init** creates a shell process to execute the command, either shell scripts or executable programs are allowed, and command line expansion is performed if necessary.

init Actions

The third field describes the action that **init** should take when it is in one of the states given in the second field. There are several possibilities: **off** instructs **init** to kill the named command if it exists, while **once** instructs **init** to execute the program when it enters the named state but not to wait for it to complete. The **init** process will continue with its work, not noticing whether the command exits or continues to execute. The **wait** command causes **init** to execute the program when it enters the named states but to wait until the process completes before continuing. Thus you can execute commands in a specific sequence through **init** because the **wait** operator causes the command in one line to finish before the next line is executed. Commands that you specify with **boot** and **bootwait** are executed only when **init** reads the **inittab** file at boot-time — not when it reads the file at other times. These commands differ in that **bootwait** causes **init** to wait for the command to complete, while **boot** does not. The **initdefault** command has special meaning and will not include a command field. It instructs **init** to enter the named state when it first starts up. Finally, **respawn** instructs **init** to start the process when it enters the named states and to restart (respawn) the program whenever **init** detects that the program is no longer running. Several other commands are possible in the second field, but these are rarely used in most machines.

Boot-Time Processing

With this information, you can read the **inittab** file to see how the boot-up process and the normal activity of the ongoing UNIX system will work. Because **init** reads the file sequentially, the entire boot sequence can be understood. In the example in Figure 19-3 the first line (**bchk**) begins the boot

```
$ cat /etc/inittab
bchk::bootwait:/etc/bcheckrc </dev/console >/dev/console 2>&1
brc::bootwait:/etc/brc 1> /dev/console 2>&1
mt:23:bootwait:/etc/brc </dev/console >/dev/console 2>&1
is:s:initdefault:
r0:0:wait:/etc/rc0  1> /dev/console 2>&1 </dev/console
r1:1:wait:/etc/rc1  1> /dev/console 2>&1 </dev/console
r2:23:wait:/etc/rc2 1> /dev/console 2>&1 </dev/console
r3:3:wait:/etc/rc3  1> /dev/console 2>&1 </dev/console
00:23:respawn:/etc/getty tty00 9600 # the COM1 pcrt
01:23:off:/etc/getty tty01 9600
co:12345:respawn:/etc/getty console console
sl:23:respawn:sh -c "exec /usr/net/slan/lib/admdaemon"
$
```

Figure 19-3.   Typical **/etc/inittab** file for a small SVR3 system

sequence by executing the script in **/etc/bcheckrc** (for boot check run control; you might see the **rc** in other contexts as well). This is used in all **init** states and is executed only at system boot-time. The **bchk** command checks the file system for sanity before turning the operating system loose with it. Because of a preliminary test to determine whether the file system is thought to be sane, this script will not have much effect when the system was shut down correctly. However, if the system went down because of a power outage or because of some internal error, the **fsck** (for file system check) command will be executed to clean things up. We will discuss **fsck** shortly.

The second line (**brc**) is also executed at boot-time. It is not executed until after **bchk** is completed, and the system will not proceed until it is completed. The **brc** command is responsible for initializing the *active* file systems for the machine. This includes the standard file systems, often /**root** and /**usr**, as well as the remote file systems available under the RFS feature. The **brc** command is executed again in the boot sequence by the **mt** line if the system is heading for **init** state **2** or **3**, the multiuser modes.

The next line (**is**) tries to tell **init** to enter single-user mode when it starts up (at boot-time). If an **initdefault** line is not present, **init** will prompt at the system console for a state to enter. Because this is usually undesirable, the **initdefault** entry is nearly always present. There is a slight trick here because **init** will refuse to enter state **1** from an **initdefault** entry. Thus this line has the single effect of suppressing the prompt for *run-level* that **init** would otherwise make at boot-time. Then **init** heads for state **2**—multiuser mode.

rc Scripts

The next few lines specify scripts to execute when specific states are requested. They are all shell scripts, and you can browse them if you wish. Usually /**etc**/**rc2** (for run control for state **2**) will be executed because state **2** is most often used. Again, **init** will wait for the script to be completed before it will continue. The script /**etc**/**rc2** contains much of the specific initialization code to create the normal operating environment. The contents of this script differ among different versions, but in SVR3 systems its primary function is to examine the directory /**etc**/**rc2.d**.

```
$ ls -FC /etc/rc2.d
K30fumounts*    S01MOUNTFSYS*    S21perf      S70uucp*
K40rumounts*    S05RMTMPFILES*   S22acct      S75cron*
K65rfs*         S20sysetup*      S67starlan   xK67nls*
$
```

Yours will probably differ from this example. The /**etc**/**rc2** script will execute the scripts in that directory in a specific order: all files with names beginning with **K** are executed first, in sequence sorted by their names. Then all files with names beginning with **S** are executed, also in sorted order. This procedure allows developers to add new functions that are active during **init** state changes by simply adding new files to the directory **/etc/rc2.d**. You can browse this directory to get an understanding of the normal boot process on your machine.

In this machine the **K** scripts will unmount any shared resources created by the **RFS** feature. This is required because you might have been at state **3** previously. **S** scripts remount the local file systems, clean up files in the system temporary directories, start the system user and process accounting, clean up the **uucp** directories, set up the STARLAN local area network on this machine, and start the **cron** program running. These functions are usually more complex than simple command lines in the **inittab**, and they are given the status of complete shell scripts instead of single lines with the **bootwait** action in the **inittab** file. Only files beginning with **K** or **S** are executed, so the file **xK67nls** is ignored by **/etc/rc2**. The numbers in the filenames provide sequence information so that **/etc/rc2** knows the order in which to execute the scripts.

This same scheme is used when **init** enters states **0**, **1**, and **3**. The script **/etc/rc0**, **/etc/rc1**, or **/etc/rc3** is executed in the appropriate case, which in turn scans the directory **/etc/rc0.d**, **/etc/rc1.d**, or **/etc/rc3.d**, as appropriate. By following the sequence of these scripts and the contents of the directories, you can trace the complete sequence of actions that the UNIX system goes through when it changes state.

getty Processes

When these scripts are completed, **init** will continue to scan the **inittab** file. Usually the only thing left is to define standing demon processes that respawn if they are killed for some reason. The last four lines in Figure 19-3 are of this type, although there may be a great many of these in a large installation. They will probably be **getty** (for get **tty**) processes, which listen on an idle communications port for a connection from a terminal or modem. One **getty** process is required for each communications port at which login is allowed. When a user logs into that port, the **getty** will disappear, although **init** does not treat it as killed until the user logs off the port and hangs up the terminal. Then **init** will respawn the process. Lines 00 and 01 in Figure 19-3 are examples of **getty** entries, though only 00 is active; 01 is set to **off** so that port COM2 is disabled. COM1 will allow logins from either an attached terminal or modem. These terminal ports are only active in multiuser mode. Line **co**—the **getty** for the system console—is required to provide superuser access to the machine, so it is active for all **init** states. The final line, **sl**, is a special line required for the STARLAN local area network software.

Making Changes to the inittab File

You will often make changes to the **inittab** file when you change the system configuration. For example, to disable the **getty** for a remote port, change the **respawn** action to **off**, or change the action from **off** to **respawn** to start it. Also, you will often change the default speed in the **getty** line as you change the devices attached to a port. These changes can be made by the superuser, who can edit the **inittab** file as desired.

In newer SVR3 releases changes to /etc/inittab will not survive the addition of hardware/software packages that require *relinking* the kernel to install new device drivers. After adding new packages, you should check that /**etc/inittab** has retained the changes you have made, and add them again if they are lost.

The **init** program reads the **inittab** file only once, when it starts up. If you make changes to the file, they will not take effect until you inform **init** that the file has changed. Use the **telinit** (for tell init) program for this.

```
# telinit q
```

The **q** argument for **telinit** instructs **init** to reread the **init-tab** file and take actions based on the *changes* in the file since the last time **init** examined it. No change in the **init** state takes place. The **telinit** program is reserved for the superuser.

In addition, you can use the **telinit** command to change the **init** state. This is rarely done in modern systems, and it should be done with care. In addition to **q**, **telinit** can take an argument for a new **init** state, one of the actions listed in Table 19-1. This command

```
# telinit 1
```

will bring the system into single-user mode, while this command

```
# telinit 0
```

will bring the system down to power-off. But this use of **telinit** is not recommended. From single-user mode, you should bring the machine down completely and reboot it to change to multiuser mode.

Going Further

The boot and shutdown procedures for the UNIX system can be very involved. When things are just slightly wrong, the system as a whole will not act correctly. Rather than manually debugging the boot procedure and going through the sequence of events needed to change **init** states, it is usually easier to reload the system software from the original disks. If your data is backed up correctly when a reload is required, nothing important will be lost. Luckily, the boot sequence is usually quite robust, so things rarely get deranged unless you experiment too much with the **inittab** file or the boot-time scripts **rc0**, **rc1**, **rc2**, and **rc3**. The only changes normally required to the **inittab** file are changes to the **getty** lines, and the system administration menus can do this without your direct intervention.

A Shorter Shutdown Procedure for SVR3

You should rarely try to speed up the boot-up procedure, though you might often wish that it took less time. Indeed, by appreciating the many complex tasks being done at boot-time, you can to tolerate the relatively long boot-up sequence. You can, however, speed up the shutdown procedure. Often no users are on the machine, and you may understand the processes on the machine well enough to know that none will be affected unduly by being abruptly killed. If you know that the machine is in a relatively quiescent state, you can bypass the **shutdown** command and bring the machine down very quickly. Three different actions are required. First, the UNIX system buffers must be synchronized to the disk so that the disk is up to date. Second, you should unmount any additional file systems beyond the root file system. Third, the disk sanity marker must be correct so that the file system check will not be required when you restart the machine. This procedure is only available to SVR2 and SVR3 systems, not to earlier versions.

The first requirement is handled by the **sync** command, which updates the machine's hard disk so that the disk is correct. This command is normally executed two or three times in succession.

```
# sync
# sync
#
```

The **sync** command is reserved for the superuser.

Second, you can unmount any mounted file systems beyond the root file system with the **umount** or **umountall** commands. This safely removes the additional file systems.

The third action is handled by the **uadmin** command. The **uadmin** command takes an argument that specifies the action to take, and the argument **2** is used to shut down the machine immediately, after marking the disk as sane.

```
# uadmin 2
Reboot the system now.
```

When the "reboot" message appears, you can shut off or reboot the machine. This usually takes only 2 or 3 seconds. The argument **2** is not an **init** state but a special code used only by **uadmin**. Use this shutdown sequence with care and only when you know that the system activity is extremely low, with no users, no print jobs, and no remote data transfers in progress.

The fsck Command

One more important action is usually associated with the boot-up procedure. This is *file system checking*. Because the UNIX system depends so much on the sanity of the file system, a special tool exists to check and repair it. This is the **/etc/fsck** (for file system check) command, and it is reserved for the superuser.

Its functions are many, and its use is complex. At boot-time the **/etc/bcheckrc** script tests whether the file system sanity flag was written as part of the shutdown sequence. The **shutdown** command will write this flag correctly, but unexpected shutdowns will not. When the flag exists, the boot-up procedure will assume that the file system is correct (even if it is not!). The **fsck** command will not be executed, and the boot-up sequence will be noticeably faster. If the flag is not set correctly, the **bcheckrc** script will assume that the file system may have been *damaged* and will automatically execute **fsck**. When **fsck** is executed, additional output will appear in the boot-time console display, as shown in Figure 19-4.

The **fsck** command can also be executed at the console by the superuser, with a file system name to check as an argument (as in Figure 19-4), but it can cause great damage to the file system in unskilled hands. You should reboot the machine when a file system check is desired unless you known *exactly* how to use **fsck**. When you use **fsck** manually, execute it on an *unmounted, raw file system* rather than on an actively mounted file system.

The **fsck** command executes five different *phases* of the file system check. First, it checks the internal tables of file sizes with the actual size of the files on the disk. Second, it checks the sanity of the pathnames of directories and files. Next, it checks for correct connectivity between files and their parent directories. Fourth, it checks the link count between files and their names to be sure that the files are correctly referenced. Last, it checks that all unused disk blocks are correctly entered on the file system *free list*. When errors appear, **fsck** displays an error message or prompts the superuser to dispose of the file in some way, by either deleting it or relinking it into the file system. The y responses to the questions shown in Figure 19-4 are examples of manual responses to these prompts. When you execute **fsck** as part of the boot-up procedure, it makes intelligent guesses about the action to take in each case and will not prompt for your assistance. The boot-time **fsck** procedure is usually executed on *each* file system that was in use when the system went down.

When **fsck** finds a file or part of a file that is not correctly linked into the file system, it relinks that file into the system at a special place. This is the **lost+found** directory, and one such directory should appear in the root directory of each mounted file system. These will usually be /**lost+found** and /**usr/lost+found** if the machine has two file systems. After the boot-up has completed, the superuser can browse these files or parts of files to be sure that nothing of value is there. Any files in these directories were put there when **fsck** found the files to be in error. Thus you should watch for files

```
# fsck /dev/rdsk/0s1

  /dev/rdsk/0s1
  File System: rootus Volume: disk0

  ** Phase 1 - Check Blocks and Sizes
  ** Phase 2 - Check Pathnames
  ** Phase 3 - Check Connectivity
  ** Phase 4 - Check Reference Counts
  UNREF FILE I=2680  OWNER=listen MODE=20000
  SIZE=0 MTIME=Jun 22 08:22 1987
  CLEAR? y

  UNREF FILE I=3540  OWNER=listen MODE=20000
  SIZE=0 MTIME=Jun 22 08:22 1987
  CLEAR? y

  UNREF FILE I=3541  OWNER=listen MODE=20000
  SIZE=0 MTIME=Jun 22 08:22 1987
  CLEAR? y

  FREE INODE COUNT WRONG IN SUPERBLK
  FIX? y

  ** Phase 5 - Check Free List

  SET FILE SYSTEM STATE TO OKAY? y

  3560 files 61968 blocks 40310 free
  *** FILE SYSTEM WAS MODIFIED ***
#
```

Figure 19-4.   Typical output from **fsck**

appearing in the **lost+found** directories because they came from some other place in the file system. Sometimes they are stray linkages with no useful contents, but they could be critical system files that were being updated by the system when the machine went down. Treat the **lost+found** files very carefully; it is always difficult to determine what they mean and where in the file system they came from. However, **lost+found** directories can get big, so you should browse them occasionally and delete unknown files.

Security

Because it is designed to support multiple users, the UNIX system provides many ways for users to access the system, as well as many different tools for communication between users and between different machines. However, in today's world, unauthorized persons break into a computer system for a variety of reasons, from simply the thrill of the hunt to malicious damage to commercial theft of data and programs. Thus, the many communications-related tools in the UNIX system provide a mixed blessing, since you must balance ease of access for your "friends" with preventing access to your "enemies."

The UNIX system was originally developed to serve small groups of people who fully shared the machine. There were no rigid limitations on the access of one user to the files and commands of other users, or even to the most sensitive data used to keep the UNIX system running. If they so desired, any users could easily delete or change files, or even bring down the system.

Over the years the philosophy toward greater security has definitely changed, and the SVR3 release can be made quite secure. A skilled system administrator can totally control access to the system, and the UNIX system is now as secure as most operating systems. However, the issues of security are complex because of the existence of so many subsystems. Everything must be correctly tuned for optimal security.

This chapter reviews the issue of computer security and examines some of the tools and commands related to system security. As you grow more and more dependent on your UNIX machine (and the files and data it contains), the security of the system becomes more important. You can take steps to prevent unauthorized access, but the natural tendency of a complex operating system will be toward less security over a period of time. You must be constantly alert for security loopholes, and vigilant to defend your system by plugging the holes.

A Security Policy

Within a machine (or network of machines), the system administrator (or the user group as a whole) should establish a consistent security policy to guide the assignment of new user id's, the amount of password protection required within the system, and the default permissions as new files are created. The policy should be published for new users, and regular *sweeps* of the file system should be made to assess compliance with the policy. If the system is relatively isolated from the outside world, and has a small group of users with the same community of interest, then the security policy can be relatively lax.

On the other hand, if the system is large, has several different user groups, has a high public profile, or contains especially sensitive (or proprietary) data, then the security policy must be more restrictive. The primary responsibility for compliance belongs to each individual user. However, a responsible system administrator can develop a procedure of regular audits, with feedback provided to the user community.

Security issues fall naturally into several general categories. The first category is protection of your private files and data from other users. Second, the key operating system files must be protected from damage, either intentional or accidental. Third, the physical security of the machine must be maintained. Finally, the system must be protected against determined attacks by skilled hackers bent on breaching or destroying the system. Each of these topics is examined in detail in the sections that follow.

Protection of Data from Other Users

When you share a machine with other users, you must make decisions concerning how much you want the other users to share your data. As discussed in Chapter 4, files in the file system have three levels of permission: those that refer to the individual user, the *group* that the user belongs to, and all the other users on the machine. Normally, in a small machine where users share a strong community of interest, the system administrator establishes a single group for all users. In this environment, users can share files at the group level, while individual users can protect files for their own uses. In larger installations where several unrelated communities exist, there may be many different groups.

As you recall from Chapter 4, the command **ls −l** displays the permissions on a file or directory:

```
$ ls -l /etc/inittab
-r--r--r--  1 root    sys        526 Apr 10 19:49 /etc/inittab
$
```

The file has three sets of permissions for each of the three different security levels: read, write, and execute access for the owner, the group, and all other users. Each file is owned by a login id, and belongs to a group. In the previous example, the file owner is **root** and the group is **sys**. The file is readable by all, but not writable or executable by anyone.

When you create a new file, you are made the owner of the file, and your group is assigned to the group id. You can give away ownership of the file with the **chown** command, and you can give away the group of the file with **chgrp**, but only if you own the file. Normally you cannot take back ownership once you have given it away. However, if a file is readable, you can make a new copy of the file with your ownership restored. Only the superuser can change the permissions of any file in the system.

Default Permissions for File Creation

After you have created a file, you should check the permissions with **ls −l** to ensure that the permissions are what you want. Is it acceptable if everyone in your group has access to the data? Should anyone else be allowed to read or write the file? You must ask these questions and set the permissions on each file after you create it.

The UNIX system creates a file owned by the creator of the file (and the group of the creator), and this cannot be changed. However, you can set a system variable associated with your login id that will set the *permissions* of a file without explicit action on your part. This system variable is called the *umask* (for user file-creation mask), and is accessed with the **umask** command. You can determine the current value of the **umask** by executing the command with no arguments:

```
$ umask
000
$
```

The result is three octal digits that refer to the owner, group, and other permissions (from left to right). This number is called a *mask* because each digit is subtracted from a system-wide default permission that all new files get. Normally this system-wide permission is **−rw−rw−rw−**, but individual systems and programs may differ from this default. Because the user's **umask** is subtracted from this default value, you cannot turn on permissions with the **umask** that are normally turned off. But you can turn off permissions that are normally turned on. Of course, you can explicitly turn on permissions with **chmod** if you own the file.

Each octal digit in the **umask** contains a binary bit that clears a permission: a 1 will clear the execute permission, a 2 will clear the write permission, and a 4 will clear the read permission. Thus, if a digit is 0, then the default is used. For example, the **umask** given previously (000) means not to change any of the default values. If the **umask** value were 022, then files would be created with no write permission for the group or for others. For example,

```
$ umask
000
$ > def.perm
$ ls -l def.perm
-rw-rw-rw-  1 steve      users         0 May 10 14:57 def.perm
$ umask 022
$ umask
022
$ > no.write
$ ls -l no.write
-rw-r--r--  1 steve      users         0 May 10 14:58 no.write
$ umask 777
$ > no.perm
$ ls -l no.perm
----------  1 steve      users         0 May 10 14:58 no.perm
$
```

With the default **umask** of 000, files are created with the default permissions. When you reset your **umask** to 022, you create files with no write permission for other users. A setting of 777 turns off all the permissions for all users, so the last file is not accessible at all.

Normally the **umask** is set in your **.profile**, or perhaps in the system-wide **/etc/profile**, according to the security policy at your site. Thus, you do not need to think of the permissions for each file you create.

File Encryption

You can further protect files that need special treatment by *encrypting* them. Most UNIX systems in the U.S. provide tools to scramble files according to a password that you provide. Only by re-entering the correct password can you correctly access this file. File encryption is not available in implementations sold outside the U.S.

Editors such as **ed**, **vi**, and **emacs** provide the ability to create and edit encrypted files. You can tell your editor to *decrypt* a file when it loads it, and encrypt it again when you write the file out to disk. The −**x** option specifies encryption:

```
$ vi -x crypt.file
Key:
```

The editor is prompting for the encryption password or *key*. Enter the key just as you enter your password when you login. As usual, the key is not echoed. If you enter the password correctly, the file is decrypted and comes up in your editor. When you write the file back out during or after your editing session, the file will be encrypted again. You can use this procedure to create a new file or edit an existing file.

Versions of the UNIX system sold in the U.S. also provide a filter to perform encryption and decryption. The **crypt** command reads its standard input and writes to its standard output. If the input is in *plain text*, the output will be encrypted. If the input is encrypted, then the output will be decrypted. Like the editing procedure, **crypt** prompts for a password:

```
$ cat plain.text | crypt
Enter key:
```

As usual, the password is not echoed.

Unfortunately, the algorithm by which files are encrypted under the UNIX system is somewhat too well-known, and programs are available that can break the encryption algorithm. Thus, putting excessive trust in encrypted files is not safe, especially in a hostile environment. The **crypt**-breaker programs work by analyzing the character frequencies in normal English text, and analyzing the frequencies of characters in the encrypted files. To defeat them, you can change the character frequencies of the plain text before encryption with another filter, such as **pack**:

```
$ pack plain.text
$ cat plain.text.z | crypt > out.file
```

The packed file cannot be analyzed by any known **crypt**-breaker. Of course, when you decrypt the file you must remember to unpack it:

```
$ cat out.file | crypt > plain.text.z
$ unpack plain.text.z
$
```

You must pack before encrypting, and unpack after decrypting.

The **pack** command is also useful to reduce the size of any file. This command generally results in savings of 20%-40% of the original file size.

Of course, the most successful file-protection scheme involves writing the file to a floppy disk or tape, deleting the file from the machine, and keeping the magnetic medium with you.

Login Id's and Passwords

The heart of the security scheme in the UNIX system is the login id and password of each user. If potential attackers can be completely kept off the system, they can cause no damage. Unfortunately, password security is so poor in many machines that even an unskilled attacker can get to a shell. Each user has the responsibility to defend passwords and to change passwords regularly.

Many user id's on a typical small system have no password at all, or the user's password is so similar to the login id as to be ineffective for security. Unfortunately, most users do not want to remember the kind of difficult-to-figure-out password that is really required. Thus, over a period of time, passwords become detectable. Every user should be forced to have a password, and the password should be *aged* so that the user is forced to change it regularly. Since the password is stored in encrypted form, the system administrator cannot determine what it is. Luckily, the letter-frequency attack mentioned previously is not possible with a short sample of text like a password.

The tool for changing your password is the **passwd** command. As discussed in Chapter 2, this command prompts you for your current password before allowing you to change it. Then you must enter the new password twice before it takes effect.

Most UNIX systems have rules that describe an acceptable password. Even if these rules are not enforced by the system software, they make good guidelines for creating your own password. A good password has at least six characters, of which at least one (preferably two) is a numeric or other nonalphabetic character. A mix of uppercase and lowercase characters is good, and any unusual or nonintuitive sequence of characters is helpful. Some examples of unacceptably trivial passwords are your login id, your name, your child's name, your room or telephone number, your astrological sign, your address, and so forth.

Login History

Some SVR3 releases provide a display of the *last* time your login id was used. This feature is not supported in all SVR3 systems, so your machine may not have it. The display appears when you log into the machine:

```
login: steve
Password:
Login last used: Wed Oct 28 15:11:02 1987
$
```

This display is intended to notify you if someone else is using your login id. If the time differs from your recollection of your last login, then your login id is being misused. You should immediately take steps to change your password.

This feature is maintained by the **login** program when it verifies your password. It keeps a zero-length file that is called **.lastlogin** in your HOME directory. The last login date and time are the modification date of this file. The **.lastlogin** file is owned by the system, not by the individual user, and its permissions make it difficult to change:

```
$ ls -l $HOME/.lastlogin
-r--------    1  root    sys           0 Oct 28 15:11 .lastlogin
```

This is not a strong security feature, but it can warn you if your login id is compromised.

The Superuser

Normal users are restricted to their own files and data, and those of their group. However, the **root** login id is provided on all UNIX machines to allow full read, write, and execute access to all files and directories. This user is known as the **superuser** (for super permissions). In addition, you can use the **su** (for superuser) command to switch to superuser status without logging off and logging in again as **root**:

```
$ /bin/su
Password:
#
```

The superuser is discussed in detail in Chapter 11.

The Password File

The critical information that controls user logins is maintained in a simple database file called /**etc/passwd**. This file is readable by all users, but is not writable:

```
$ ls -l /etc/passwd
-r--r--r--  1 root     root       526 Apr 10 19:49 /etc/passwd
$
```

These permissions should be carefully maintained because if the file is writable by anyone, then system security is easily breached.

Each user has a line in the password file, and also several standard system-wide login id's are needed for correct functioning of the system. A sample **passwd** file for an SVR3 system is shown in Figure 20-1. Each line in the password file

```
$ cat /etc/passwd
root:x:0:3:0000-Admin(0000):/:
daemon:x:1:12:0000-Admin(0000):/:
bin:x:2:2:0000-Admin(0000):/bin:
sys:x:3:3:0000-Admin(0000):/usr:
adm:x:4:4:0000-Admin(0000):/usr/adm:
uucp:x:5:2:0000-uucp(0000):/usr/lib/uucp:
nuucp:x:6:1:0000-uucp(0000):/usr/spool/uucppublic:/usr/lib/uucp/uucico
sync:x:67:1:0000-Admin(0000):/:/bin/sync
lp:x:71:2:0000-lp(0000):/usr/spool/lp:
listen:x:72:4:0000-NETWORK:/usr/net/nls:
install:x:101:1:Initial Login:/usr/install:
jim:x:103:100:jim:/usr/jim:
pat:x:104:100:Pat:/usr/pat:
steve:x:105:100:Steve:/usr/steve:/bin/ksh
$
```

Figure 20-1.   A typical **/etc/passwd** file

consists of several fields, delimited by a colon. The user's login id is first on the line, and a placeholder for the user's password (x) is the second field. Third is the numeric representation of the *user id*, and fourth is the numeric representation of the *group id*. These two fields work with file permissions to determine who can access each file in the system. The fifth field is a *comment* that usually contains the user's name and address. The next-to-last field contains the user's HOME directory, and the last field contains the full pathname of the user's login shell. If the last field is blank, it defaults to /**bin/sh**.

In older releases of the UNIX system, the second field contained the actual encrypted password for each user. In newer SVR3 releases, however, a second file was introduced into the system to contain only the encrypted password. This file is /**etc/shadow**, and it should be readable only by **root**:

```
$ ls -l /etc/shadow
-r--------  1 root      root         187 Apr 10 19:49 /etc/shadow
$
```

The /**etc/shadow** file contains the user's login id, an encrypted password, a numeric code that describes when the password was last changed, and the minimum and maximum number of days required between password changes:

```
# cat /etc/shadow
root:dskrOdkwc24Kw:6491::
daemon:NONE:6480::
bin:NONE:6480::
sys:NONE:6480::
adm:NONE:6480::
uucp:NONE:6480::
nuucp:NONE:6480::
sync:NONE:6480::
lp:NONE:6480::
listen:NONE:6480::
install:NONE:6480::
jim:lftgKW03qFGwe:6523:7:120
pat:wouOQWqw34fgeu:6621:7:120
steve:qUWmdk4ROSqwe:6496:7:120
#
```

One line in **/etc/shadow** will be for each line in **/etc/passwd**. When **/etc/shadow** is present, the password field in **/etc/passwd** is replaced by the single character x. Otherwise, the second field in **/etc/passwd** will look like the second field in the previous example of **/etc/shadow**.

The **/etc/shadow** file is created by the command **pwconv**, which reads **/etc/passwd** for the information. Whenever you manually change **/etc/password**, you should immediately execute **pwconv** to be sure the changes are updated to **/etc/shadow**. Since the password and shadow files should be only readable, only the superuser can change them.

A Typical /etc/passwd File

Figure 20-1 provided a typical **/etc/passwd** file for an SVR3 machine. The default system includes several login id's, even before you begin adding users. These login id's are required for the correct operation of the machine. You cannot delete them or change them substantially without causing damage to the system. In most cases, you can change only the password (or disable it) without causing problems. The login id's, the user and group id's, the HOME directory, and even the default shell should not be changed on any login that does not belong to a real user.

The login **root** is the superuser. This is user id zero, and its HOME directory is the root directory / (slash). The root login should *always* have a password. An unprotected root login is the worst possible security violation in the UNIX system, since the root user has complete access to everything in the system. The next few login id's are for other administrative tools. In large installations, these id's are used by individuals who might have responsibility for administration of the different subsystems. Normally on a small machine with a single system administrator, you can disable these login id's by editing the string NONE or some other plain-text string into the password field in /etc /passwd, or in /etc/shadow if it is present.

Since the password is decrypted from the entry in /etc /shadow or /etc/passwd, a plain-text string here will be decrypted into a nonsense string that users will not be able to guess when they try to login.

The functions of these disabled login id's should be performed by the **root** user. All the login id's with a password of NONE in the previous /etc/shadow example are of this type. These may differ depending on the hardware setup on a machine. For example, the **listen** login is associated with the STARLAN local area network, and will not appear if no STARLAN network is installed.

The login **nuucp** is used by remote machines when they login to send you mail. The shell for this login is /**usr/lib/ uucp/uucico**, the program that handles data transfer for the **uucp** subsystem. Since this is not a normal shell, and since the **uucico** program is secure, you need no password for the **nuucp** login. The similar login id **uucp** is for administration of the **uucp** subsystem and should be disabled.

The three individual users (pat, jim, and steve) are listed near the bottom of Figure 20-1. These users each have their own user id number in field 3, but all belong to the same group—group 100 (field 4). These users should all have passwords (in /**etc/shadow**). Note that pat and jim use the default shell, but steve gets a different shell when he logs into the machine.

To reiterate, all login id's in /**etc/passwd** should have passwords except **nuucp**. These are either a legitimate encrypted password for the real users and **root**, or a plain-text password for all other logins.

Adding and Deleting Users

It is usually easy to add a new user, but this procedure is limited to the superuser. First you need to create a HOME directory for the user. This is normally in the directory /**usr**, but many installations create separate user file systems such as the /**u** directory. Where the HOME directory is in the file system does not matter. However, if the machine includes an administrative tool to create login id's, then you should use the same directory location when you manually add a user.

The HOME directory is normally owned by the user, with group set to the group of the user you are creating. The permissions of the directory should be −**rwxr**−**xr**−**x**. This allows other users to **cd** through the directory, and read the files in the HOME directory, but they cannot write in the directory. More restrictive permissions can be used according to the machine's security policy.

After you create the HOME directory, you can then add a line to /**etc**/**passwd** for the user, according to the rules previously described. When you are finished with /**etc**/**passwd**, run **pwconv** to update the /**etc**/**shadow** file if it is present on your machine. Often the password field is left blank until the user logs in the first time (when the user creates an individual password). However, this is unsafe, since frequently the user will not login for a while and thus leaves an unprotected login id. A safer procedure is to create an unprotected login id, immediately login using that login, and set up a password using the **passwd** command. Then you can tell the user what the initial password will be. If password aging is in force, you can set the password so that it expires the first time users log into the system. This procedure requires the user to change the password immediately. Of course, the same rules of trivial passwords apply to this initial password you set (no login id, name, telephone number, and so forth).

When you manually create an entry in /**etc**/**passwd**, you must take care to use a new numeric user id in field 3. Each user should have a unique user id. Often these start at 100 for normal users, and you should assign them to individual users on a one-by-one basis. Furthermore, the numeric group id in field 4 should be established in accordance with your security policy, but you cannot establish new groups without updating an additional file (/**etc**/**group**, discussed in the next section). If the user wants a different shell than the normal, you can put its full pathname in the last field of the **/etc/passwd** entry. If the user is to be restricted, you can use **/bin/rsh** (discussed later in this chapter).

To permanently delete a user, simply reverse the procedure. That is, delete the user's HOME directory, delete the lines in **/etc/passwd**, and execute **pwconv** (if your machine has it).

You can disable the login id without actually deleting it from the machine. This might be useful when the user's files must be saved, but you do not want the user to log into the machine. Two different procedures are used for different versions of the system. If your machine has the file **/etc/shadow**, then you can use the **passwd** command with the −**l** (lock) option:

```
# passwd -l steve
#
```

You must be a superuser to use this **passwd** option. The only way to unlock a password is to delete it with the −**d** (delete) option:

```
# passwd -d steve
#
```

Of course, then the login is completely unprotected, and you should immediately add a new starting password.

If your machine has no **/etc/shadow** file, you can edit the password field in **/etc/passwd** to insert the string NONE (or some other plain-text string) in place of the encrypted password. Later, the user can be re-enabled (if needed) by deleting the entry in the password field and establishing a new password for the user.

You must take care to keep up-to-date with the deletion of users. Often a user will leave the system (for whatever reason) and you do not immediately disable the login id. This often happens in large systems with hundreds of users. This is a bad security risk, since ex-users may harbor a grudge and can cause serious damage to the machine. You must take unusual care to regularly peruse the password file, and to delete those users who are no longer active.

Adding Groups

When you add a new user to an existing group id, no further activity is needed after you create the entries in **/etc/passwd** and run **pwconv**. However, if you wish to create a new group for the user, you must add that group to the file **/etc/group**. Some systems include the commands **addgrp** (add to group) and **delgrp** (delete from group) to rearrange users between groups. However, you usually must manually edit the file **/etc/ group** to change groups and membership in groups. The format of the file **/etc/group** is

```
# cat /etc/group
root:NONE:0:root
other:NONE:1:
bin:NONE:2:root,bin,daemon
sys:NONE:3:root,bin,sys,adm
adm:NONE:4:root,adm,daemon
mail:NONE:6:root
rje:NONE:8:rje,shqer
daemon:NONE:12:root,daemon
users:NONE:100:jim,pat,steve
#
```

This file contains a single line for each group defined on the machine. As usual, the fields are separated by a colon. The first field of the line is the group name that will appear in the **ls −l** output and other places. The second field is a password that must be given if a user attempts to change groups with the **newgrp** (new group) command. Normally users should be prohibited from changing groups, so this field should contain the plain-text string NONE to prevent this access. The third field contains the numeric group id that appears in **/etc /passwd**. Usually the first user group is 100 and increases as you add new groups. The last field (with entries separated by commas) contains the id's of users who are members of that group. The file **/etc/group** should be readable by all, but not writable or executable by anyone. When you add a new user to the system, you should verify that the group id is correct, and add the user's id to /**etc**/**group**.

Password Aging

The password scheme allows the system administrator to set up a *password aging* procedure in which all users must regularly change their passwords. When a password is established, a clock is started. When the established interval passes, then the password is discarded and users are required to use different passwords. The superuser can turn on the password aging feature with the **passwd** command if the system has the file /**etc**/**shadow**. If the system does not have this file, the superuser may edit the password field in a user's entry in /**etc**/**password**. The notation can be complex, but must be done only once per user.

If your machine has the /**etc**/**shadow** file, the **passwd** command can enable password aging. Several command line options are provided to manipulate the passwords. Use the −**d** (delete) option to delete a user's password:

```
# passwd -d steve
#
```

To set the maximum number of days that a password can be active before it must be changed, use the −**x** option with a number of days:

```
# passwd -x 120 steve
#
```

To set the minimum number of days that a password must be active before it can be changed, use the −**n** option:

```
# passwd -n 7 steve
#
```

All of these options will return silently if no error exists. You must set the maximum interval before you are allowed to set the minimum interval. The **passwd** command can also report on the status of a user's password with the —s (status) option:

```
# passwd -s steve
steve  NP  10/10/87  7 120
#
```

The user id is first, followed by a status (NP means "no password"), then the date at which the password was last changed, followed by the minimum and maximum intervals as previously set.

If your machine has no **/etc/shadow** file, password aging is enabled by manually editing the password field in **/etc/passwd**. After the existing password (or in the empty password field if there is no password), add the comma character, then a string that describes the password-aging parameters. For example, this **/etc/passwd** entry contains no password aging:

```
steve:oQPCEmQL38t6E:105:100:Steve:/usr/steve:/bin/ksh
```

However, this entry does contain password aging:

```
steve:oQPCEmQL38t6E,f4:105:100:Steve:/usr/steve:/bin/ksh
```

The comma and the characters following it in the password field are the keys to the password-aging scheme. The first character following the comma encodes the maximum number of weeks the password will be valid. The second character following the comma encodes the minimum number of weeks before the user is allowed to change the password. Any additional characters following the comma are used by the system to encode the date at which the password was last changed. Normally you do not add these additional characters after the first two, but instead allow the system to do it.

The encoding scheme used by this password-aging option is as follows: week 0 is denoted by . (dot), week 1 by / (slash), weeks 2-11 by the digits 0-9 respectively, weeks 12-37 by the uppercase characters A-Z, and weeks 38-63 by the lowercase characters a-z. For example, if you want users to change their passwords at least every 26 weeks, but no more often than every 10 weeks, you can add the string ,O8 after the users' passwords.

The system will automatically prompt the users to change their passwords when the time has expired.

Password aging generally is helpful for maintaining security. Users' passwords do tend to become publicly known after a while. Requiring users to regularly change passwords can reduce security violations. Requiring the users to change their passwords two or three times a year is usually sufficient. One drawback to password aging is that users often tend to have two favorite passwords and they alternate between them. These two passwords are often trivial permutations of each other. For the reasons previously discussed, this practice should be discouraged.

After changing the files **/etc/shadow**, **/etc/passwd**, or **/etc/group**, you should verify that the permissions and the ownership of the files are correct. The files should be readable by all, except the file **/etc/shadow** (which should be readable only by **root**). These files should not be writable or executable by any users, and they should be owned by **root** with group **root**.

The Restricted Shell

The standard shell provides many capabilities that allow a user to move around in the file system, execute many commands, change the PATH, and so forth. However, an additional shell called **rsh** (restricted shell) is provided in all UNIX systems. This is actually the same executable program as the normal shell, which exists under two names in the **/bin** directory. This program just acts differently depending on the name used to invoke it. The **rsh** program allows fewer capabilities than the normal shell. If you set **/bin/rsh** as the user's shell in the last field of the entry in **/etc/passwd**, then users get this shell instead of the standard shell.

The **rsh** program differs from the normal shell in the following ways:

1. The user cannot use **cd** to change directories. The user is limited to the HOME directory.

2. The user cannot change the PATH variable, so only commands in the PATH set up by the system administrator are allowed.

3. The user cannot name commands or files by using a complete pathname. Only files in the HOME directory and subdirectories can be accessed.

4. The user cannot redirect output with > or >>.

These restrictions are enforced after the user's **.profile** is executed. The system administrator will set up a restricted environment in the user's **.profile**, including a PATH that points to a limited **bin** directory. The system administrator then will change the ownership of the **.profile** to **root** and make it readable by all, but writable or executable by no one. Now the user with the restricted shell will be limited to the HOME directory and the commands allowed in the PATH.

The **rsh** program limits naive users from straying too far away from their intended environments into the system files. Normally **rsh** is given to users who have limited reasons to login to the machine. For example, a bulletin-board system might use **rsh** for its users, or a word processing clerk might be limited in this way. Usually you do not want to limit skilled users with **rsh**, since it needlessly interferes with their work. Also, the **rsh** is not completely secure, and any skilled attacker can easily break through it into the normal shell. You cannot depend on **rsh** as a security tool for hostile attackers, but it is useful to keep unskilled users from inadvertently injuring themselves or the system.

Protection of the UNIX System and Files

Even skilled users can damage the UNIX system if they have too much access to key files (such as /**etc**/**passwd** or the **uucp** data). You must take care to prevent security reduction of the system as a result of the normal changes that occur during the lifetime of the system. The solution is easy to explain, but difficult to accomplish: simply keep all file permissions and ownerships the same as when the system was installed. Normally the initial load of a UNIX system sets all the files and directories to the correct, secure permissions. The only exception to this may be the system login id's in /**etc**/**passwd**, which usually have no passwords by default. However, over time the permissions gradually will become less secure just because no one is perfectly attentive to security. Files become more accessible, passwords disappear, inactive user logins accumulate, and so forth.

Since no one is perfect in this regard, a good policy is to regularly reload the machine from the original system software. This is a burden on users, and on the system administrator who has no doubt *customized* the machine. However, when security violations are suspected, this policy is the only way to assure a safe system. Once or twice a year is normally sufficient for most machines. When you do this, you can be sure that the password file is current. You can also clean up unsuspected disk clogging with unused commands and files. Of course, a good data back-up procedure makes reloading the system much simpler.

Physical Security

The previous discussion focused on user login id's and how to establish security for normal users. However, many more potential security hazards exist than those caused by users you allow into the system. You must also be concerned with direct access to the machine by people who can walk up to it in your absence.

In all cases, the primary form of security for a UNIX system is physical security. If you can prevent access to the machine either by keeping it in a locked room or having no external connections (such as modems or local area networks), you can guarantee that security cannot be breached. A truly secure system has no external data connections except for hard-wired terminals in locked rooms. If all login id's are correctly protected with passwords, then no unauthorized access is possible.

However, all UNIX systems are accessible by rebooting them from a master floppy disk or tape. An attacker who is able to get to the machine can reboot it and enjoy full privileges from a version of the operating system on the bootable disk. Therefore, you must also take care that the machine itself is not accessible.

A second form of *physical security* concerns the software and applications that you load. Any disk or application package that you load onto the machine may have security traps added by the developer or by an enemy who might hold the software before you receive it. A typical scenario is that the software is loaded correctly, but some part of it contains a security breach. When the command is executed, the breach is activated. Either the program itself causes damage to the machine, or some modification is made to the system so that an attacker can break in.

These problems usually do not occur with commercially available packages, but any uncertified software is suspect. Free software available from bulletin boards or pirated software circulated by hand are especially suspect.

Usually you cannot detect these problems until after the damage is done. You should be extremely wary of adding unknown software to your machine. In the worst case, security-conscious system administrators should demand access to the source code for applications, examine it carefully in a secure environment, and then compile it directly for the target machine. This usually is not possible, but you can sometimes spot suspicious behavior by your sources of software.

Local Area Networks

Environments in which many machines are connected by way of a local area network (LAN) are especially dangerous security risks. If attackers can get into any one machine on the network, they can usually "jump" to the other machines. Users of all machines on a network should understand the importance of secure passwords.

Since LAN users are usually associated with a single project, they develop tools that allow easy sharing of files and data between machines. For example, many networks of UNIX systems contain remote execution tools so that a user of one machine can execute commands on other machines in the network. Naturally this is risky, but can usually be acceptable if the individual machines are kept secure.

Sometimes an additional password is required before access to the network is allowed. This may slow down users in their daily activities, but can be an additional protection when security is a major issue.

uucp Security

The **uucp** data-communications subsystems are a potential security risk, since these tools are designed solely to *allow* remote access. When **uucp** works, it connects to another machine and executes commands remotely on that machine by reading and writing files as requested. If security is poor, then an attacker (or even an honest mistake in the use of **uucp**) can cause serious damage to your machine. However, the modern **uucp** software is secure and robust *if security precautions are observed.* Like other aspects of the UNIX system, the **uucp** security naturally degrades over time. You must be vigilant in monitoring the **uucp** tools.

The major security issue associated with **uucp** is the permissions of the **uucp** files. The materials in the directory **/usr/lib/uucp** must keep the permissions that they had when you initially loaded the software on the system. You should list these files with **ls −l** soon after you load the machine, and take care to check correctness of the files whenever you change anything in the **/usr/lib/uucp** directory.

The **uucp** system is designed so that a machine has a public directory hierarchy in which all **uucp** activity normally occurs. This public area is required if you allow any **uucp** activity on the machine. In addition, a list of commands can be executed by a remote machine running the **uux** command. Normally the public directory location is **/usr/spool/uucppublic** and the command list available remotely is only the mail command **rmail**. You cannot receive mail from remote machines unless you allow other machines to execute your **rmail** command.

uucp Permissions File

Permissions that are **uucp** related can be customized as you wish. The control data is kept in a file that is read by the **uucp** programs when they are executed. If a request is made that is not allowed by the control data, the request is refused and the **uucp** connection is broken. If the request is within the acceptable list, the request is honored. The file **/usr/lib/ uucp/Permissions** contains this information, but only the superuser and the **nuucp** login should be able to read it.

The permissions can vary from quite open to quite restrictive. Usually the default (as established when the machine is loaded) is quite limited. A typical wide-open **Permissions** file is as follows:

```
# cat /usr/lib/uucp/Permissions

# This entry is wide-open....

LOGNAME=uucp:nuucp  REQUEST=yes SENDFILES=yes READ=/ WRITE=/

MACHINE=OTHER COMMANDS=ALL REQUEST=yes READ=/ WRITE=/
#
```

The format is a normal ASCII file, with lines beginning with # (pound) treated as comments and the other lines containing the data. The basic layout is a series of lines containing *keyword=value* pairs, where the keywords describe the capabilities to be controlled, and the values set the permissions allowed. Should more than one value exist for a keyword, separate the items with a colon, as shown previously in the LOGNAME=... entry. Each line can control a specific set of permissions. Each line controls either how the machine acts when it calls other machines or how other machines are treated when they call your machine. You will often need several lines of both types to tailor your **uucp** system for your needs.

The Default Permissions

By default, **uucp** permissions are relatively restricted, so a simple entry will provide good security. You can use only

```
LOGNAME=nuucp
```

as the entire contents of the **Permissions** file. The keyword LOGNAME is used to refer to the login id's that may request **uucp** services. This is not for real users on a local machine, but rather refers to remote machines that may call your machine and request **uucp** services.

The simple entry LOGNAME=nuucp restricts remote **uucp** system access to the login id **nuucp**, which is normal. Recall that the default shell for this login is **/usr/lib/uucp /uucico**, which is a secure program for data communications. With this simple **Permissions** file, the **uucp** system is restricted to file transfer to and from the public directory **/usr /spool/uucppublic**. Only the **rmail** command is allowed to remote machines.

Customizing the Permissions File

You can add more lines to the **Permissions** file to customize **uucp** security to your needs. Two different types of lines are in a more complex **Permissions** file—those that modify the actions of the system for incoming calls, and those that modify the actions for connections to specific machines you call. The line that begins LOGNAME=... affects all incoming calls, and any line that begins MACHINE=... refers to specific machines when you call them. Only one line that begins LOG-NAME=... can be in your **Permissions** file, but as many MACHINE=... lines as you need can be included. As you are modifying these **Permissions** lines, add additional keyword= value pairs on the same line. If the line is longer than you want, you can continue it by ending the line with \ (backslash) to escape the NEWLINE.

Controlling Incoming Calls with the LOGNAME Line

When another machine calls you, you can send jobs that are queued to it, or you can force your machine to call that machine before outgoing jobs are sent. This is secure since a calling machine may lie about its **uname**, and may take files not intended for it. This lying is called *spoofing* the **uucp** system, and the only way to truly prevent spoofing is to make your machine call another machine whenever you have jobs spooled for the other machine. Add the keyword SENDFILES=... to the LOGNAME=... line to control whether jobs are sent when your machine is called. The entry

```
LOGNAME=nuucp SENDFILES=yes
```

allows such transfer, and

```
LOGNAME=nuucp SENDFILES=no
```

prevents the transfer in all cases. The default **SEND-FILES=call** means that files will only be sent to another machine when your machine calls it, not when the other machine calls you.

Similarly, you can add the keyword REQUEST=... to control whether your machine allows a remote machine to request files from your system. The entry

```
LOGNAME=nuucp SENDFILES=yes REQUEST=yes
```

allows a remote machine to "grab" files from you, whether or not you have queued them for sending. This feature can be dangerous and should usually be set to REQUEST=no.

You can also specify what directories you allow remote machines to use when they read or write files by adding the READ=... and WRITE=... keywords to the LOGNAME=... entry. The specified directory names a complete substructure, so that any directory under the named directory can also be written or read. If you use READ=/ and WRITE=/, you allow reading and writing from all directories on the machine. This practice is definitely not recommended. The values READ= **/usr/spool/uucppublic** and WRITE=/**usr/spool/uucppublic** are used by default. This is the recommended public directory.

When a machine calls you, you can set the **uucp** system to refuse to accept the call, but to trigger your machine to immediately call back that machine. Use CALLBACK=yes on the LOGNAME=... line to force this callback behavior. By default, callback is not required (that is, CALLBACK=no).

Controlling Outgoing Calls with the MACHINE Lines

Permissions for outgoing calls may be modified for a specific machine or list of machines when you call them, by your use of the MACHINE=... entry at the beginning of the line. All changes to the command list from the defaults are associated with specific machines that you must name explicitly in the MACHINE=... entry. If you want all calling machines to have the same permissions, you can use the special string OTHER following the MACHINE=... entry to refer to all machines, or you can name specific machines if you wish. The REQUEST=..., SENDFILES=..., READ=..., and WRITE=... keywords can appear in the MACHINE=... line, as well as in the LOGNAME=... line.

In addition, you can change the list of commands that other machines can execute on your machine, either when you call them or when they execute **uux** requests on your machine. To change the commands, add the keyword COMMANDS=... to the MACHINE=... line, with a list of commands separated by colons.

```
MACHINE=OTHER   COMMANDS=rmail:news:lp
```

In this example, incoming **uux** jobs can use the **rmail**, **news**, and **lp** commands. The **rmail** command is always required, but in this example you can allow the **lp** command so that remote machines can send jobs to your printer. All commands given in the COMMANDS list must be located in the directories /**bin** or /**usr**/**bin**. You can use COMMANDS=ALL if you want to allow a remote machine full access to all commands. Use of COMMANDS=ALL is not recommended unless you completely trust the remote machine, and surely should not be used with MACHINE=OTHER.

The uucheck Command

The **Permissions** file setup can be verified with the /**usr**/**lib** /**uucp**/**uucheck** command, which checks the **uucp** subsystem for correctness and pays special attention to the **Permissions** data. The **uucheck** command is restricted to the superuser, since **uucp** permissions should be kept secret. Use

```
# /usr/lib/uucp/uucheck -v
```

to see a verbose display of how the **uucp** permissions are configured. The **uucheck** command is a useful tool that can substantially reduce confusion in establishing **uucp** permissions. Figure 20-2 shows typical output from the **uucheck** command when executed on the **Permissions** setup given in the wide-open **Permissions** file previously listed. The check is run in two phases. First, the correctness of the **uucp** files and directories is checked, and no output is provided in Figure 20-2 since it is correct. The second phase lists the **Permissions** data in an easy-to-understand, verbose format.

```
# /usr/lib/uucp/uucheck -v
*** uucheck:   Check Required Files and Directories
*** uucheck:   Directories Check Complete

*** uucheck:   Check /usr/lib/uucp/Permissions file
** LOGNAME PHASE (when they call us)

When a system logs in as: (uucp) (nuucp)
        We DO allow them to request files.
        We WILL send files queued for them on this call.
        They can send files to
            /
        They can request files from
            /
        Myname for the conversation will be my_sys.
        PUBDIR for the conversation will be /usr/spool/uucppublic.


** MACHINE PHASE (when we call or execute their uux requests)

When we call system(s): (OTHER)
        We DO allow them to request files.
        They can send files to
            /
        They can request files from
            /
        Myname for the conversation will be my_sys.
        PUBDIR for the conversation will be /usr/spool/uucppublic.

Machine(s): (OTHER)
CAN execute the following commands:
command (ALL), fullname (ALL)


*** uucheck:   /usr/lib/uucp/Permissions Check Complete

#
```

Figure 20-2.   Sample output from the **uucheck** command

Unknown Remote Machines and Polling

If an incoming call is identified to be from a machine that your system does not have in its **Systems** files, it can be accepted as normal, or a shell script can be executed by the **uucp** system. This shell script is often used to log calls from unknown machines, or for similar security precautions. This capability is not supported in the **Permissions** file, but works somewhat differently. If the file **/usr/lib/uucp/remote.unknown** is executable, the incoming call from a remote machine is terminated and the **remote.unknown** script is executed. If the file is not present or is not executable, the call is accepted in the MACHINE=OTHER category. Normally you disable the **remote.unknown** feature because you want to receive mail from machines that might know about your machine, but which you do not know. However, when security breaches are suspected through the **uucp** system, this feature can be enabled by making **remote.unknown** executable. Examine the file on your machine for ideas if you want to change the script.

In addition, the **uucp** subsystem can be configured to *poll* another system. This means that one machine can call another system and request any jobs that are intended for it. This feature is often used when a machine cannot call yours for some reason, but you can call it. For example, a machine may have only incoming call support.

When a machine calls another, the "callee" can transfer any waiting outgoing jobs for the "caller." Usually this capability is disabled by the default value SENDFILES=no in the **Permissions** file of the recipient machine. When SEND-FILES= no, a machine that wishes to send data must call the recipient machine, and the recipient cannot "pick up" messages when it calls the sending machine. Set SENDFILES= yes on a machine if you wish to allow it to transfer outgoing jobs when it is called.

You can administer a machine to regularly poll another machine. The shell script /**usr**/**lib**/**uucp**/**uudemon.poll** controls this polling, and it reads the file /**usr**/**lib**/**uucp**/**Poll** for a list of machines and times to start a poll. Usually the **Poll** file includes comments that describe how to set it up. You must then add an entry to /**usr**/**lib**/**crontabs**/**uucp** to regularly execute the **uudemon.poll** script (usually once an hour). The machines you are polling must be administered with SEND-FILES=yes.

Going Further

The security issues previously discussed are central to any well-run public UNIX system. Security precautions can be quite strong if administered with care and attention, but they really cannot defeat a skilled, devious, malicious attack. An amazing amount of UNIX system skill is in the world, and some of it is directed solely toward unauthorized entry to UNIX machines.

System Attacks

Usually a malicious attack starts with "hackers" who only wish to stretch their skills at your expense. Frequently an attacker will break into the machine, snoop through the file system, get bored quickly, and leave without damage. However, attackers occasionally want to steal your data or simply damage the system.

Typically an attack scenario goes like this. An attacker gets a telephone number of your modem (or your LAN) through a network of other attackers, or even by randomly dialing telephone numbers. The attacker experiments until an unprotected login id is discovered, thus providing access to the machine. The attacker can then browse the password file and the rest of the system at leisure, until an opportunity is found to switch to the **root** login id. Often system files are changed, permissions are rearranged, and corrupted commands are added to the system to make it easier to break in later. Network connections are then explored to find "nearby" machines to attack. When your machine has been digested, the attacker often causes some damage just for fun. Finally, the access information is passed to another attacker and the problem starts again.

You can learn about malicious attacks from this scenario. First, password security is critical to stopping entry at the beginning. Second, once an attacker gets into the system, detecting and preventing the attack can be extremely difficult. Third, once the system is violated it is very likely to be attacked again. Attacks will often spread to "nearby" machines. Finally, if you take inadequate action against an attack, the attacker will learn of your changes, and continue to defeat them.

Defender Behavior

Almost invariably the first reaction to a suspected attack on your machine is to deny that it happened. You can usually think of good rationalizations as to why file permissions were changed, or even how your password file was suddenly modified. Often you really do not remember what the system should look like. Naturally, a malicious attacker will take advantage of this confusion (and denial) to dig deeper into your machine.

When you are sure that an attack has occurred, you frequently deny its importance. Even when unknown logins are active, you often will try to contact the users with **mail** or **write** to politely ask why they are using your machine. Of course, this warning is just what attackers want. In the next stage, you might announce to all users (usually by **news**) that your machine is under attack. Again you have warned attackers that they are no longer unknown. Next you may take some tentative steps to improve your security, such as changing your passwords (usually to another trivial password similar to the one that the attacker probably used to break into the machine). Finally, after repeated attacks, you may overreact and totally close down all connectivity to the machine.

Obviously, this defender behavior only trains a more skilled attacker. You have repeatedly warned attackers that you know the machine is compromised, and you have made security changes at such a slow pace that attackers can usually keep ahead of your precautions. If they want to, attackers can plant some "Trojan Horse" software that can trap passwords as people login, change file permissions, and so forth. Finally, you may take such drastic action against the attack that it hinders your own use of the machine.

Far better behavior has been described previously in this chapter. Usually if you detect an attack, you should not change the system at all while you plan your defense. Putting up a news announcement describing the changes you will make is especially unwise. You should suddenly and completely change the system: change the telephone numbers for modems, reload the system software from the beginning, change all the passwords and login id's, and then re-establish your **uucp** connections with other machines. If your defense is silent and strong enough, you have solved the problem. In no case should any evidence of the changes (or even that you are aware of an attack) appear on the machine under attack.

Detecting an Attack

Unfortunately, detecting an attack can be difficult, since most attackers are more skilled than most defenders. Key places to look for an attack are the following: changes to permissions of security-related files discussed in this chapter, as well as changes to **/etc/inittab**, **/etc/profile**, the **cron** data files, **/bin/ login**, and **/etc/getty**. Any changes to the contents of any of these files is suspicious, especially **/etc/passwd**, **/usr/lib/uucp /Permissions**, the **uucp** Systems files, and **/etc/profile**. The **uucp** log files can provide information on unusual **uucp** connections to other machines that may be unknown. Unusual users logged into the machine during late-night hours is also suspicious. The file **/usr/adm/sulog** contains a record of all uses of the **su** command, which is often used by attackers.

Attackers usually try to cover their tracks. A skilled attacker can edit files like **sulog** to remove their traces, but the permissions and modification date of the files may give away the fact that they were changed.

A security-conscious system administrator could develop a shell script that searches through the file system to look for changes in file permissions and sizes of executable programs. Such a tool would be specific to each release of the UNIX system and the specific hardware, but could potentially capture some of the search process involved in detecting an attack. If the tool is kept on floppy disk rather than on the main file system, then it will be relatively secure from attack itself.

Trojan Horses

The most devious and unpleasant form of attack occurs when the attacker changes your machine by replacing some key pieces of software with corrupt copies that allow access for the attacker. This usually only happens when you have warned attackers that you know they are present on the machine, but can be very difficult to detect.

You might use your routine back-up procedures to copy the corrupt program to your archive. When you rebuild the system in defense, the natural tendency is to restore the backup rather than to reload the system from scratch. This often just restores the corrupt program, and again you have only helped to train the attacker. Sometimes software received from bulletin boards contains these Trojan Horse programs.

When you suspect an attack, your back-up data may be suspect. You must take care when you restore this material. You should back up only your user data, and not back up the system software. When you reload the system, you should use the original system software that was purchased with the machine.

System Configuration

Hardware and the UNIX System
A Minimal Configuration
Setting Up the System
Testing the Initial Configuration
Hard Disk Partitions
Swap Space
File Systems
Loading the System Software
Terminals and getty
Going Further

When you acquire a new computer and a UNIX software package, the first step is to *load* the software onto the machine's hard disk. During this loading process, several decisions must be made, decisions that affect the *tuning* of the machine. Modern releases of the UNIX system simplify this loading process, and all decisions can be made by accepting the suggested default values during the loading process. However, the default values tend to be compromises to cover the majority of situations. You can change the defaults to tune your machine to your specific needs.

This chapter discusses the issues concerned with *building* a UNIX system, which includes both hardware and software configuration. This chapter focuses primarily on SVR3 systems running on powerful microcomputers, but most of the issues (if not the exact numbers) can be useful for other releases on other hardware.

Hardware and the UNIX System

Since the UNIX system was originally designed for large minicomputers and only recently ported to microcomputers, the system makes significant demands on the computer hardware environment in which it runs. For this reason, implementations of the UNIX system on the smallest machines have not been an outstanding success. True, Microsoft XENIX can run on the original IBM PC, but even there a hard disk is required. Also, performance is usually not acceptable on these original PCs and other small machines. Only with the continuing drop in prices for hardware has the UNIX system really become viable on personal computers. The SVR3 release is a large and complex operating system that requires significant machine resources.

The 80386 and Other Machines

The Intel 80386 processor provides an ideal hardware environment for the UNIX system. It provides the raw CPU speed a sophisticated system requires, and includes efficient support for *virtual memory* and other features needed for optimum performance. However, the SVR3 release can also run well on the Motorola 68020 processor, as well as on other microprocessors.

Of course, you must buy the correct software for a specific machine. Versions of the UNIX system designed for 80386 machines will not work with 68020 or other machines, and vice versa. However, versions of the UNIX system designed for the 80286 processor might run on 80386 machines, but performance will not be equivalent to a native 80386 implementation. Before you buy a machine, consult your vendor to make sure that the correct software is available for it.

Memory (RAM) Considerations

The UNIX system requires significant *real memory* (or RAM) to be installed in the machine. The SVR3 version requires at least 2.0 megabytes of real RAM, and more memory is desirable. The true potential of the system does not become apparent until 3.0 or 3.5 megabytes of real memory are installed. For very heavily loaded file servers or multiuser systems, even more memory is desired. A busy system can contain 8 or 12 megabytes of real memory. This much memory is not needed for a typical personal system, of course, but at least 2.0 megabytes is always required to successfully run SVR3.

The UNIX system can determine the amount of memory installed on the machine when the system boots and will automatically use all the memory available. Make sure that any switches are set correctly so that the power-up diagnostics can find all the memory in the machine.

Memory for the UNIX system is not the *paged* type of memory used under MS-DOS for expanding beyond the MS-DOS 640-kilobyte limit. The UNIX system uses a *linear* type of memory management. Thus, any switches on expansion memory cards should be set at *nonpaged* settings. If switches are set to allocate any memory to the paged type, the UNIX system will not use that memory and the memory will be wasted. Often hardware retailers correctly set up the memory when you buy the machine, provided you tell them that the machine will use the UNIX system.

Disk Considerations

At least one *floppy disk* is usually needed for the initial load of the system software. In addition, a floppy disk is useful for backing up your data and allowing you to move files easily from machine to machine. Several current formats of floppy disks include 5 1/2-inch floppies and 3 1/2-inch microfloppies in plastic cases. Before buying a machine, you must verify that the UNIX system is provided on the disk format for your machine. Generally you cannot copy the UNIX system floppies from one format to another because the *floppy boot* procedure that starts the UNIX system from a floppy disk is usually tied to a specific disk format. For all UNIX systems, this floppy boot procedure is needed at least once, when the machine is initially loaded with the system software.

The UNIX system requires at least one *hard disk* to operate as designed. The UNIX system is installed on a hard disk, and the system boots and runs primarily from the hard disk. Floppy disks are used primarily for initial software loading and for backup of your data. The UNIX system can read and write from floppies just as it can from hard disks, but the system is optimized for hard disks. Floppy access is painfully slow by comparison.

The larger the hard disk installed on the machine, the better. Experience shows that disk usage eventually rises to fill all the available space. Buying a larger hard disk early is cheaper than changing the hard disk later. The SVR3 system requires at least 20 megabytes of hard disk space for its own uses (this is the bare minimum required). A 40-megabyte or larger disk is preferred. Most 80386 systems designed for use with SVR3 are sold with a 60- to 70-megabyte hard disk. The 130-megabyte and larger hard disks are not unusual in busy machines. The UNIX system can support all the available disk space, and has no artificial limitations.

In addition, the UNIX system allows multiple disks. Large minicomputer versions of the UNIX system may have three or four disks, each with 400- to 600-megabyte capacity. However, smaller personal computers may be limited to a single hard disk controller card, which in turn may be limited to controlling only two hard disks. Again, consult your hardware vendor for more information about a specific machine. Two large hard disks are usually sufficient for most needs. You can buy this second hard disk when the first disk fills up, and cable it to the existing hard disk controller without reloading the first disk.

The hard disk is controlled by a software *device driver* that is specific to the hard disk controller. The controller may not be able to access some disks. Adding a new hard disk controller card to an existing UNIX system is usually futile unless you are sure that the correct device driver is included with the card. Disk-controller software designed for MS-DOS or other operating systems will not work with the UNIX system. Before buying an add-on disk, you should consult a reputable dealer to determine that the disk is usable with your controller.

The Console and Monitor

All UNIX systems must have a *system console*. On larger systems this is usually an inexpensive printing terminal that is permanently attached to the machine and rarely used. On smaller personal machines, however, the built-in console is configured as the system console. This console serves double duty, both as the system console and as a user's terminal. The system console is used to display boot-time messages and system error messages. Furthermore, SVR3 restricts the use of the **root** login id to the system console.

A device driver is also used to control the console, so you probably cannot change the display adapter and monitor without installing a new display driver. For example, the 80386-based UNIX machines usually have drivers to support the CGA and EGA display standards, and the display adapter must support one of these standards. Again, the best solution is to consult your hardware vendor to be sure that a machine is compatible with the version of the UNIX system you are using.

Ports and Terminals

Remote terminals used for UNIX machines are generally serial, ASCII, character-only devices that can attach to a **tty** *serial port* (usually called COM1 or COM2 in PC/AT style machines). These asynchronous communications (serial) ports cannot support graphics terminals without special device-driver support. However, many different types of ASCII terminals can be attached to UNIX machines if the TERMINFO database includes a description of the terminal. In addition, external modems can be attached to these ports so that remote users with modems can dial into the UNIX system. In either case, no additional software or device drivers are required.

Most microcomputers include a single serial port, and many add-on cards provide a second serial port. You should definitely have at least one serial port with your UNIX system to take advantage of its best features.

The presence of only one or two asynchronous communications ports may prevent you from attaching your machine to some local area networks that use the machine's serial port because these networks will take one of the two available ports. Similarly, a serial printer will use one of these communications ports if it is installed. You should carefully analyze your expected use of serial ports before investing in a machine or a specific implementation of the UNIX system. Experienced users of the UNIX system find that there are never enough serial ports on a machine to allow freedom of expansion. Some "multiport" add-on cards that may include four or eight ports per card are available. However, you should consult with the vendor to make sure that the implementation supports a particular *ports card* before you buy the system.

SVR3 Licensing Restrictions

Microcomputer versions of SVR3 are sold in two forms: a two-user version and a more-than-two-user version. That is, the operating system software is restricted in the two-user version so that only two users may be logged in simultaneously, though more than two ports are allowed. One user may be on the console and the other on a serial port. Alternatively, two users may simultaneously use the machine through serial ports if the console is unused. To support two simultaneous remote logins, you need two serial ports. The two-user version is less expensive and is usually adequate for personal UNIX systems.

The larger, *unrestricted* version allows as many simultaneous users as there are ports on the machine. The restricted two-user license does not limit the ports for printers, local area networks, and so forth, but does limit simultaneous user logins.

Printers

Because of this (potential) shortage of serial ports, most microcomputers using the UNIX system utilize *parallel printers* rather than serial printers. Most modern microcomputers include a parallel port, and a second parallel port can be added with an expansion card (LPT1 and LPT2, respectively). These parallel ports cannot be used for terminals, so only one is usually needed unless you have more than one printer on the machine. The **lp** system can support many different types of printers, both parallel and serial. However, this is another area in which you should confirm that the UNIX system and the machine hardware can support the specific printer devices you want to use. Common dot-matrix or letter-quality printers generally are supported without difficulty, but sophisticated laser printers or other uncommon devices may need expert coaxing to make them operate correctly.

Networking

Because of the economies associated with sharing printers and other devices, many modern UNIX systems are attached to local area networks. Many networks use their own plug-in cards and special device drivers, and so these networks do not use either parallel or serial ports. This setup can save these ports for other uses. In addition, some networks allow incoming telephone calls to a special network modem, which can then switch the caller to a specific machine on the network. This setup can be noticeably less expensive than providing extra communications ports and modems to each machine. A network allows the establishment of file-server machines with larger disks than most machines on the network, which results in additional savings. These file-server machines can be used to store large databases or data backups from the "personal" machines. However, local area networks that use serial ports on the attached machines may be more expensive than buying modems and communicating at lower speed over dial-up telephone links.

A Minimal Configuration

Based on these notes, a stand-alone personal UNIX system can be configured with a single serial port and attached modem, and with a parallel printer. The serial port with modem will allow both incoming and outgoing telephone calls, though not both at the same time. One remote user can call in while a user is active on the console, and printing is supported simultaneously on the parallel port. Recall that at least 2.0 megabytes of real memory, and at least 40 megabytes of hard disk space are required. Later you may be able to add additional ports or network cards if you have verified that your machine and implementation of the UNIX system can support them.

Setting Up the System

Physically attaching the parts of the system together is so dependent on the specific machine and associated devices that little of value can be stated here. You should generally lean heavily on your hardware vendor to be sure that the correct cables are provided for attaching your devices. Great differences exist in the cabling needs of various devices, and even "standard" RS232 cables and devices can differ in many frustrating ways.

Experts usually set up a machine with the minimum hardware configuration, load the software, and get the machine running before trying to attach additional devices (like printers or terminals). This incremental approach enables you to become familiar with the machine before introducing new problems with recalcitrant cables or the **lp** subsystem. The best advice is to get something working first, slowly add to it, and keep it running all the time, until the full configuration is achieved.

One issue to watch for is the "sex" of the connectors on the machine and the peripheral devices. Compatible cables should be purchased after examining the machine and peripherals. This practice prevents having to use special "gender-bender" plugs to achieve cabling compatibility.

In addition, cables designed for attaching an external modem to a serial port may not work when attaching a hard-wired terminal instead. This is because the modem and the terminal use different pins to signal that they are active. A special *null modem cable* may be needed when attaching a terminal to a port designed for a modem. Again, consult with your vendor for the correct cables to reduce unnecessary frustrations.

Finally, do not neglect the human factors of your working position at the computer. Arrange the display screen, the floppy disk mechanism, the keyboard, your chair, and your work table for your comfort. This seems obvious, but it is amazing how many uncomfortable and even painful work-stations are built around computers. If you get stiff, sore, or suffer headaches from your use of the machine, it is probably because your chair is the wrong height for your keyboard rather than because the UNIX system is so difficult.

Testing the Initial Configuration

Before loading any software on the hard disk, you should verify that the machine is operating correctly. Most machines are sold with a *diagnostics disk*. You can boot the machine with this disk in the floppy drive. If the machine comes up to a diagnostics prompt on the display, you can be sure that the machine is at least partially working. However, before proceding, you should exercise many (if not all) of the different tests available through the diagnostics procedure. Convince yourself that things are working correctly at this level before loading software.

Usually the diagnostic disk boots up to a menu that allows you to select among several tests, including floppy-disk formatting and hard-disk surface test.

Figure 21-1 shows a typical display after the diagnostics menu comes up. If the diagnostics disk does not boot, then the system is probably deranged beyond recovery, though the diagnostics disk itself may be bad.

In this diagnostics menu, options 1 and 2 allow formatting and copying of floppy disks. These features can be used to copy the *floppy boot disk* (the first disk of the System Installation Set) before loading the UNIX system for the first time. This is required because the floppy boot disk must be write-enabled and can be destroyed by careless handling.

Option 4, "Setup," allows you to set the system date and time. This is redundant with better tools in the configuration procedure and in the running of the normal UNIX system.

```
SELECT AN OPTION

0 - SYSTEM CHECKOUT
1 - FORMAT DISKETTE
2 - COPY DISKETTE
3 - PREPARE SYSTEM FOR MOVING
4 - SETUP
9 - END DIAGNOSTICS

SELECT THE ACTION DESIRED
?
```

Figure 21-1.   Typical display from diagnostics disk

Option 3, "Prepare System for Moving,"is used to *park* the heads on the hard disk (that is, to secure the hard disk from damage when the system is to be moved or disassembled). This is most important in preventing damage to your disk. You should use this option *whenever* you move or disassemble your machine. Do not take chances with disk damage.

Option 1, "System Checkout," is used to examine the installed hardware and the switch settings used to enable RAM memory, disks, and other hardware. Select this option to verify the system's idea of your hardware configuration. Usually a mismatch is a result of incorrect switch settings on the machine's system board (or in a software-controlled ROM, if your machine has one). If you have changed the machine's hardware configuration (including adding new RAM), you will probably need to change the switch settings on the system board to reflect the new hardware. Some machines no longer use physical switches for hardware configuration, but have a software-controlled ROM that can be set from a Setup option on the diagnostics disk. Carefully follow the vendor's instructions when changing the switches.

Occasionally some hardware will be inoperative. If the "System Checkout" option works at all, then the fundamental hardware configuration is operating correctly. However, it does not completely guarantee correct operation of the machine, and does not test the integrity of the software in any way. Usually failures in the "System Checkout" will require you to return your machine for repairs, unless you can fix things by changing switch settings on the system board or on an add-on card.

An especially important part of the diagnostic procedure is the *hard disk surface test*. This test verifies that all parts of the disk are working correctly, writes data to each disk block, and then reads back the data. Any failed operations mean that a particular disk block is bad, and the bad area will be added to a *bad track table* on the disk. These bad blocks will not be used while the machine is running. The disk surface test may take an hour or two to complete, but it is strongly recommended whenever you reload the system software. The UNIX system can become seriously deranged if bad disk blocks are available for its use. Many problems can be avoided if you take care to keep the disk's bad block table up to date. Perform the surface test every time you reload the system software.

When you are finished with the diagnostics disk, the machine will be shut down. Remove the diagnostics disk and then reboot the machine, either from the UNIX system (if it is installed) or from the floppy boot disk (if you are just beginning the software installation).

Hard Disk Partitions

Once the hardware is configured and correctly connected, you must load the UNIX system onto the machine's hard disk. Several decisions are involved with loading the system software, and these revolve around the configuration of the hard disk.

A hard disk can be divided into several separate parts (or *partitions*) that can be used for different operating systems (such as the UNIX and MS-DOS systems). Usually these separate partitions are not "visible" from each other. That is, when you are using one part of the disk with one operating system, the other parts cannot be accessed. The **fdisk** command is provided to change the *active* partition. After a reboot, the selected partition will be used, allowing another operating system to be booted. The partitions are established when the machine is first set up, and cannot be changed without erasing the hard disk. Consequently, you must decide how many disk partitions to establish on your machine before loading the UNIX system.

Most SVR3 versions for the 80386 machines allow multiple partitions. One partition can be used for the UNIX system and another for the MS-DOS or MS-OS/2 operating system. A second partition will be needed if you want to use any other operating system in addition to the UNIX system. The disk space used for any additional partitions will not be available for the UNIX system, so you must be sure that enough space is available on your hard disk for additional partitions. About 5 to 10 megabytes are generally reserved for an MS-DOS partition (or more if you have large storage needs under MS-DOS). If you rarely use any other operating system than the UNIX system, then you will not need a second partition.

This additional partition dedicated to MS-DOS or MS-OS/2 is separate from (and in addition to) a merge capability that might allow you to use the MS-DOS operating system under the UNIX system. That is, the merge software shares the file system between the UNIX and MS-DOS systems, so an additional partition is not required. Only if you plan to execute MS-DOS or MS-OS/2 as a stand-alone system will you need a separate partition for it.

Swap Space

Another consideration in disk configuration is *swap space*. When processes fill up the entire available real memory, the UNIX system automatically *swaps* some idle processes to disk in order to free real memory for active processes. This swapping is done without user intervention, and the disk space used for swapping does not come from the normal file system. Swap space is in the partition used by the UNIX system, but is a logically separate disk area.

The desirable amount of swap space depends on the amount of real memory installed, as well as how heavily the machine is used. The more real memory, the less swap space is needed. If the machine is heavily used (with many processes active simultaneously), more swap space will be needed. Disk space devoted to swapping is not available for files, even if it is not used for swapping. Since the UNIX system crashes heavily when swap space becomes full (with a *panic* error message directed to the console), you should have too much swap space rather than too little. Most SVR3 systems will default to about 6 megabytes of swap space, and this is a good compromise for most situations. If you have a heavily used server machine with insufficient real memory, perhaps more swap space is desired (up to 8.0 megabytes), but this is an unusual situation. If 8.0 megabytes of swap space is insufficient, then the machine as a whole is probably inadequate for your uses, and may need replacement.

File Systems

The disk space available to files can be further subdivided into separate *file systems*. The concept of file systems is really intended for machines with two or more hard disks. One file system is usually installed on each disk. This allows the UNIX system to efficiently manage access to the separate physical disks. On machines with only one disk, it is usually better to configure a single file system that fills the disk.

However, some advantages are associated with separate file systems, since a general corruption of one file system will not affect the others. For example, if one file system fills up, it will not steal space from the others. On the other hand, the **ln** command will not work across separate file systems, since a physical copy of a file must be made to create it in another file system. The configuration process may establish two file systems on a single hard disk by default, and you will need to take action during the installation process to make only one.

Loading the System Software

With this background, you can configure your machine to your needs as you load the UNIX system from floppies. Some differences exist between the installation procedures of different implementations of the UNIX system (even within SVR3) and several steps in the installation may differ from the following examples.

The basic scenario is to boot the machine off the first floppy disk in the *System Software Set*. The installation procedure prompts for disk configuration information, formats the hard disk correctly, and then loads a kernel from the floppy. You must then remove the floppy disk and reboot off the hard disk. The installation process continues by loading the remainder of the UNIX system from the other floppy disks, and then reboots the machine.

You are then led through an initial setup for the UNIX system that allows you to set the machine's date and time, install passwords for the system logins, and add new login id's for the system's users. You can log into the machine and load any add-on software packages by using the normal system administration tools.

When this process is completed, you can load the **merge** software and the MS-DOS operating system (if you have it). If you have established an MS-DOS partition, you can reboot from an MS-DOS floppy, access the dedicated MS-DOS partition on the disk, and load the MS-DOS operating system for the stand-alone version of MS-DOS. The entire load procedure can take several hours, especially if you include a disk surface test at the beginning of the procedure.

Begin the installation by inserting the first floppy disk in the machine's drive and turn on the power. The correct disk is called the *System Installation Disk* or the *Floppy Boot Disk*. This may be the first disk of the *Base System Package*. In most versions of the UNIX system, the Floppy Boot Disk must not be write-protected (that is, no label should cover the notch in the right-hand side of the disk). Always use a copy of your boot disk, not your only original disk. You can copy the disk with a procedure on the diagnostics disk supplied with the machine.

A special *installation* version of the UNIX system will boot off the floppy and prompt you through the rest of the installation procedure. Do not remove the floppy until prompted to do so.

fdisk Installation Procedure

In some releases, the first display is from the **fdisk** (fixed disk) command, which is used to manually configure the partitions on the hard disk. In other releases, an initial series of prompts determines the partitioning information. The **fdisk** command is then executed automatically by the installation scripts to set up the partitions.

Before continuing, you should map out your intended use of the machine's hard disk. If you want some space for a stand-alone MS-DOS or MS-OS/2 partition, you must decide how much space to devote to each. Usually only a few megabytes are devoted to the MS-DOS partition, especially if you have a merge package that can share the file space between the UNIX and MS-DOS systems. Simply think of the different disk partitions in terms of the *percentage* of the disk they will use. For example, if you have a 67-megabyte hard disk, you may wish to devote 10% for exclusive use by MS-DOS and the rest for the UNIX system. This gives a stand-alone MS-DOS partition of about 6 megabytes, which is plenty for most uses.

If your Floppy Boot Disk starts with the **fdisk** program, some initial copyright notices appear, followed by the message

```
Strike ENTER to install the UNIX System on your hard disk.
```

You should press NEWLINE at this point to continue, or you can immediately reboot if you want to prevent the reloading of your hard disk.

After you press ENTER, your screen will resemble Figure 21-2. Figure 21-2 shows two partitions already established. However, in your initial load, the partition table will probably be empty. This example is for a 67-megabyte disk. The number of cylinders will differ for different disk sizes.

You can select an operation from the menu to proceed with the partitioning of the disk, or you can select 5 to exit without changing anything. Make your selections by typing the selection number followed by NEWLINE.

```
       Total hard disk size is 1024 cylinders

                                        Cylinders
   Partition   Status    Type      Start   End   Length    %
   =========   ======    =========   =====   ===   ======   ===
       1                 DOS           1    100      100    10
       2       Active    UNIX        101   1023      923    90



SELECT ONE OF THE FOLLOWING :

     1.    Create a partition
     2.    Change Active (Boot from) partition
     3.    Delete a partition
     4.    Exit (Update disk configuration and exit)
     5.    Cancel (Exit without updating disk configuration)
Enter Selection:
```

Figure 21-2.   **fdisk** display for disk partitioning

To create a partition, select option 1. The **fdisk** menu prompts you for the starting and ending cylinders for the partition. Use the total disk size as displayed at the top of your screen and your selected disk percentage for the partition to compute the size to enter. The first partition should always start at cylinder 1 or 2 (never at cylinder 0), and the last should end at one less than the total hard disk size as displayed for your system. Each partition after the first should start at the next cylinder following the end of the previous partition. When creating partitions, use partition number 1 for MS-DOS or MS-OS/2, and the UNIX system should be on the last partition you create, as shown in Figure 21-2.

If you make an error in setting up a partition, you can delete any or all partitions with option 3, then start again. Be sure to get the partitions correct at this point, since once they are established you cannot change them without destroying the contents of your hard disk.

The *active partition* is the one that will boot when you turn on the machine. If you want the machine to start in the UNIX system, then it should be the active partition. If you want the machine to boot under MS-DOS, then it should be the active partition. Select the active partition with option 2 on the menu. When the MS-DOS partition is active, you can only use the UNIX system if you execute the MS-DOS version of the **fdisk** command to set the active partition to the UNIX system and then reboot.

After creating a stand-alone MS-DOS partition with **fdisk**, the MS-DOS partition will not be formatted. To use it, you must enter MS-DOS and follow normal procedures there for setting up the hard disk. The partition devoted to the UNIX system will be formatted as part of the load procedure.

Prompted Installation Procedure

In some versions of the UNIX system, the configuration is prompted and **fdisk** runs automatically. If so, the initial display after booting the Floppy Boot Disk will resemble Figure 21-3. The copyright notices may differ on your machine. After loading, the system will pause at the "Do you wish to proceed" prompt. Presumably you will enter "y", and press NEWLINE. The system will respond with "Do you wish to (re)format your hard disk?" You should select "y", since this guarantees a clean disk for the installation. The system will next prompt with "Do you wish to do a complete surface analysis?" Again, you should respond "y" here to verify that all the bad blocks are included in the disk's records. The surface test is not actually done at this time, but later in the installation process.

Figure 21-4 continues the configuration dialogue. The *Disksetup* program allocates the various disk partitions and subpartitions. When the program begins, it first reads information directly from the disk and reports on the disk sector parameters with the message "This system uses...." This example is for a 67-megabyte hard disk. The numbers may

```
. . . . . . . . . . . . . . .
boot: /unix


UNIX System V/386 Release 3.0
Node intel
Total real memory  = 3801088
Available memory   = 2748416

Copyright (c) 1986 AT&T
All Rights Reserved

386/ix Drivers Copyright (c) 1986 Interactive Systems Corp.
All Rights Reserved

About to install UNIX on your hard disk.  This process will destroy
any and all data currently on that disk, INCLUDING DOS FILES!
If you have DOS files you would like to back up before proceeding
with system installation, enter n<RETURN> to the following question.

Do you wish to proceed with UNIX installation (y/n)?
y

Do you wish to (re)format your hard disk (y/n)?
y

Do you wish to do a complete surface analysis?  Answer 'y' to write
and read every sector, 'n' to just read every sector.  NOTE: writing
the whole disk takes a while... (y/n)?
y
```

Figure 21-3.   Prompted configuration procedures

vary if you have a different type of hard disk on your machine, but usually you can trust the displayed message. However, if you are sure that the disk parameters are reported incorrectly, you can change them if you respond "n" to the prompt "Is this correct (y/n)?" If the reported values are incorrect, usually some mismatch exists between the hard disk's *low-level format* and the disk controller card. You may need to change the firmware on the controller card if you suspect the disk size

```
Welcome to the Disksetup program.  This program will allow you to
specify certain parameters about your hard disk, as well as partitioning
the disk into Unix volumes and a DOS area (if desired).

This system uses 17 512-byte sectors per track.

Disk parameters currently configured are as follows:
Number of heads: 8.  Number of cylinders: 940.
Is this correct (y/n)? y


Your disk drive will have 1 cylinder used for alternate sectors.

This leaves 939 cylinders (65384448 bytes) available, 69632 per
cylinder.

Do you wish to allocate any of your disk to exclusive use by DOS (y/n)? y

Enter number of cylinders for DOS (0-577): 50

FDISK will be run to create the following disk allocation:
DOS starting at cylinder 1 for 50 cylinders, and
UNIX starting at cylinder 51 for 889 cylinders.

Is this the partitioning you want (y/n)?

You will now have the opportunity to enter known bad areas on
your disk.  To do this, you will need to know the cylinder, head,
and byte offset from the index mark of each defect.  This data
can usually be found on a label on the disk drive or on a defect
list which is shipped with the drive.  If you have no such list,
only those sectors found to be bad during surface analysis will
be marked.

Do you wish to enter any more defect information (y/n)? n
Are you sure you've entered all defects (y/n)? y
```

Figure 21-4.   Prompted system-installation dialogue (Part II)

information to be incorrect as reported. Normally, however,
you should accept the values by responding "y" to the prompt.

The next prompt allows you to dedicate some disk space for
exclusive use by MS-DOS. If desired, enter "y" at this prompt,
and the system will prompt you for the amount of disk space to
reserve, as shown in the example. You enter disk space by
giving a number of *cylinders* to reserve. Compute this number
from your chosen disk percentage devoted to MS-DOS by

dividing the total disk size (in cylinders) by your percentage. Only 50 cylinders (3.48 megabytes) is reserved in this example. This machine will only be used for simple stand-alone MS-DOS applications (such as copying disks or running games) so little space is allocated. The system will report on its computations and prompt you again to verify the results, with "Is this the partitioning you want?" If you enter "n" here, then the prompts will be repeated from the beginning.

The next section allows you to manually enter bad blocks. These are blocks listed as bad in addition to the bad blocks found by the surface test. You should probably enter the bad blocks listed on a label attached directly to the hard disk case (inside the machine's cover). The blocks listed there are the result of a rigorous disk test given at the factory where the disk was produced. Many of the listed bad blocks are only marginally bad. Most users let the surface test find real bad blocks. In some installation procedures, the original bad block table on the disk is retained, and you do not need to manually enter the list from the top of the disk itself. However, this is *not* true for SVR3 on the 80386. To be completely safe, enter the bad block list manually, *and* perform the surface test. You are better safe now than sorry later. In this example, the entry of bad blocks is bypassed by responding "n" to the prompt. Another verification prompt is given, and you can enter "y" if you are really finished entering bad blocks.

File-System Partitioning

For both the manual and prompted configurations, the installation procedure continues with the partitioning of the file system, as shown in Figure 21-5. By default the installation procedure will make two separate file systems on a 67-megabyte disk, but only one on a 40-megabyte disk. On 130-megabyte disks, three file systems are created by default. However, a single file system is usually much easier to handle, and so you should answer the first prompt with "n" to refuse the default partitioning. You can also see that about 7.3 megabytes are reserved for swap space in the default partition.

```
The following seems like a reasonable partitioning of your Unix
disk space:

A root filesystem of 195 cylinders (13578240 bytes),
a usr filesystem of 588 cylinders (40943616 bytes),
and a swap/paging area of 106 cylinders (7380992 bytes).

Is this allocation acceptable to you (y/n)? n

Do you wish to have separate root and usr filesystems (y/n)? n

One megabyte of disk is approximately 17.7 cylinders.
How many cylinders would you like for swap/paging (1-535)? 106
The remaining 783 cylinders will be assigned to root/usr

You have specified the following disk allocation:
A single root/usr filesystem of 783 cylinders (54521856 bytes),
and a swap/paging area of 106 cylinders (7380992 bytes).

Is this allocation acceptable to you (y/n)? y

Installation of your Unix system will now proceed automatically.
Thank you.
```

Figure 21-5.   File-system partitioning

The next prompt enables you to select single or multiple
file systems. You should refuse the separate file systems by
responding "n" to this prompt. This prompt will not appear
on systems with a 40-megabyte hard disk. The system will
then go on to describe the swap area and provide you the
opportunity to enter the number of cylinders you want. Usually 110 to 130 cylinders is adequate, but be sure to compute
the number of cylinders from the bytes-per-cylinder
numbers rather than just entering 110 here. Your disk may
differ in this number, but the swap space should be 6 to 8
megabytes regardless of how many cylinders are required.
Retaining the default is recommended in most cases.

The system then displays the partitioning it will use, and provides you one more chance to reject the results. Enter "y" to accept the disk allocation.

With the prompted configuration procedure, **Disksetup** now automatically configures the disk according to your instructions, with both the **fdisk** part and the file-system parts combined. You may be entertained by watching the automatic process proceed, but soon it begins the disk surface test that takes at least one hour to complete. During this time, the system displays rows of dots on the console, one dot for each cylinder that is verified. Any bad disk blocks that are found during the verification procedure are displayed on screen and added to the disk's bad-block table.

In both configuration procedures, the first system files are loaded from the System Installation disk onto the newly formatted hard disk when the formatting process is finished. When this is completed, the system prompts you to remove the floppy and reboot the machine:

```
Please remove the floppy disk from the drive and strike
CTRL-ALT-DEL to reboot from the hard disk.
Reboot the system now.
```

The message may differ on your machine.

Loading the Foundation Set

When the system reboots, it will be executing a special "installation" version of the UNIX system. The first prompt after the reboot resembles the following:

```
Please insert the UNIX system "Base System Package"
Floppy Disk 2 of 8 and then strike ENTER.
```

Different releases differ in the message. However, all releases start with the first disk in sequence *after* the Boot disk. You now feed the rest of the system software floppy disks into the machine one by one. The system reads each disk and then prompts for the next. While a disk is being copied in, you cannot remove it. Do not interrupt the load procedure in any way or you must start the installation process from the beginning. Many SVR3 systems are divided into several software *sets* that can be installed separately. This initial load is for the *Base System Package* or the *Foundation Set* only. After the Foundation Set is loaded, the system will be self-sustaining, and the other sets can be loaded by using the System Administration tools.

When all disks in the Foundation Set have been loaded, the system prompts you to reboot from the hard disk:

```
Unix has been installed on the hard disk.
The system will now be shut down.  Re-boot to run.
Reboot the system now.
```

Do not reboot until you see this message. Remove the last floppy disk and reset the machine.

The Setup Procedures

The system reboots from the hard disk, and first comes up in a special "setup" environment. This allows you to perform the initial administrative tasks needed for a well-behaved machine. These procedures are well-prompted and are quite straightforward, but can differ significantly between releases of the system. In some releases, you may need to log into the system with the special **setup** login id. In other releases, the setup procedures are automatic after the Foundation Set is installed. You should complete the setup procedures now while they are prompted rather than going back to them later with manual procedures.

The first part of the setup sets the date and time in the internal clock of the system. UNIX systems generally depend on the correct time, so this must be set correctly. If you follow the prompts, you can change the system's date and time (if they are not correct already). Each prompt or menu displays a default that is the current value for that data item. You can accept the default instead of changing the value.

The next prompts in the **setup** procedure enable you to create new login id's and passwords for yourself and other users. You should at least create a login id for yourself, since the **root** login should be reserved for system administration and maintenance tasks. Each new login id includes several items of information, including the desired login id, the user's name, and a starting password. You can use any login id you wish, as long as it begins with a lowercase letter (a to z) and contains from 2 to 8 characters. Most users use their names or initials, or a whimsical name chosen by them. You should usually accept the default values for the user id number, group id number, and user's HOME directory, since the system can do a better job at determining correct values. All login id's should always have passwords, so you should always select an initial password when you install new login id's. The password must be entered twice to guard against errors. Be sure to follow good security practice (as discussed in Chapter 20) when creating new passwords.

After you are finished entering new login id's for your users, the setup proceeds to installing passwords for the **system** login id's required for the correct functioning of the UNIX system. You should create passwords for all of these users, or better yet, manually, go into the **/etc/passwd** file (or **/etc/ shadow** if you have it) to edit NONE into the password field. This prevents these login id's from being used.

The final step in the setup procedure is to establish a unique system *name*. This is known as the *node name*, or system **uname** (UNIX name). The machine name should be unique so that other machines can easily send you mail. A default **uname** may be hard-coded into the kernel, but you should always change this name to something unique. Select a machine name of 4 to 8 characters, beginning with a lowercase letter (a to z).

You will need to set the machine name only once, and you should rarely change it, since users on other machines may begin to send mail to your machine. If the name is changed, the **uucp** subsystem will not work correctly unless all your correspondents make matching changes to their **uucp** data.

The **uname** is the last item in the setup procedure. You may now log into your login, and can begin to use the machine.

Installing Additional Software Packages

If your release of the UNIX system has been divided into several software packages, you can load them now. Log into the machine as **root**, and execute the command **installpkg**. If the **installpkg** command is not present, you may need to use the following commands instead:

```
# cd /usr/admin
# sysadm installpkg
```

Which command is correct depends on the release of the UNIX system you have.

The **installpkg** procedure prompts you through the installation procedure for the software package you are installing. Consult the specific documentation for your machine and for the software package to determine any special or additional steps needed.

Terminals and getty

One additional capability is often configured immediately after setting up the system. This is the establishment of **getty** (for get tty) or **uugetty** processes so that users can log into the system from remote terminals over the asynchronous communications ports. Usually the **uugetty** program is used instead of the older

getty, since **uugetty** allows two-way communications over the device and **getty** allows only incoming calls. Establishing **getty** processes is discussed in Chapter 11.

After you are finished, the terminals or modems will be active for incoming connections. Also, you will probably want to configure the **uucp** subsystem to allow your machine to call out to other machines. This is discussed in detail in Chapter 14.

Going Further

System configuration is properly an expert's job, since tuning the system for optimal efficiency is a complex task. However, most microcomputers are not sensitive to configuration and tuning, so the exact sizes of disk partitions are not critical. You can usually accept some small reductions in system performance, and in return do not need to be concerned much about the details of system configuration. However, some other issues should be addressed.

Panic Messages

When the UNIX system and the kernel are not operating correctly, the system can occasionally crash unexpectedly. This is not a normal event, and only occurs as the result of a bug or problem in the deepest parts of the operating system. You should never see this condition when things are operating correctly, though the condition sometimes appears when you have incorrectly added new hardware or expansion cards to your machine.

When a crash happens, the system displays a message at the console and then dies:

```
PANIC: system error type 0x0e
Attempting to dump 512 pages.....
```

The machine is then inoperative until rebooted.

The specific message may differ, but the key word *PANIC* will appear somewhere in the message. You should record the message completely, then reboot the machine. If it does not reboot, then you probably have encountered a failure of some hardware (such as the disk or motherboard).

If the machine boots but the panic message reappears, it is usually the result of some switches or jumpers on some add-on boards being set incorrectly. Be sure that all your additional hardware is operating correctly. Determine this either by removing the cards one by one and watching the state of the system, or by carefully examining the card's documentation and switch settings.

If the panic message appears only once and does not recur, then you usually need not worry. You have uncovered a (rare) bug in the UNIX operating system. Historically, experts judged the quality of a release of the UNIX system by the frequency of panics. Modern UNIX systems should *never* panic unless hardware has failed.

Booting from a Floppy Disk

While the UNIX system is running correctly, the machine will boot from the hard disk whenever no floppy is in the floppy drive. However, if a floppy disk is in the drive and the drive door is closed, the machine will try to boot off the floppy. Usually if the floppy in the drive is not *bootable*, then the boot procedure will switch back to the hard disk and the machine will come up as normal. However, in some cases the machine will hang and the boot will not complete. If this happens, just remove the floppy and try rebooting again.

In addition, the system can intentionally be rebooted off the System Installation disk if needed. You might do this when the system will not boot correctly from the hard disk, and manual repairs to the hard disk are needed. This is done by booting off the System Installation disk just as you would if you were reloading the UNIX system. Be sure to use a copy of the disk and not your original.

The first time the floppy boot procedure pauses for a prompt, you must immediately press the DEL key. This will abort the installation process, and you will be left in a normal shell. However, instead of running the system off the hard disk as normal, the system will be running off the floppy disk.

There are several differences in the environment while running from the floppy disk. First, the system is much slower than normal, since the fast hard disk is not in use. Second, you cannot remove the floppy without crashing the system and destroying the contents of the floppy disk. Third, the list of available commands is considerably reduced because all commands are coming from the small floppy disk. Fourth, the system is running in Single-User mode, and so the process environment is much different than normal. This floppy boot procedure is not intended for regular use of the machine, but rather for rare tests and repairs by a skilled user.

Once the machine is running, you may be able to mount the hard disk to give you access to its files and directories. On most SVR3 machines, the command

```
# mount /dev/dsk/0s1 /mnt
```

will mount the hard disk partition with the UNIX system. You can then **cd** to **/mnt** to access the root directory on the hard disk, and can move around the hard disk file system from that point. You can execute commands from the hard disk by giving their full pathnames (including the leading **/mnt**) and can repair any files that are suspected to be bad. Unfortunately, you cannot remove the floppy to copy files from a back-up floppy onto the hard disk, nor can you use the **uucp** subsystem to move files over a network. So the floppy boot procedure is quite limited. This procedure may have more value for maintenance if you have a system with two floppy drives.

When you boot from a floppy disk this way, you must take care to correctly shut down the machine, or you risk destroying the contents of the floppy boot disk. The **shutdown** command will probably not be available on the floppy disk, but the following short procedure will work:

```
# umount /mnt
# sync
# sync
# uadmin 2
Reboot the system now.
```

You then can power off the machine or reboot from the hard disk as usual.

Upgrading from Older Releases to SVR3

If you are currently using an older version of the UNIX system, you should plan carefully before beginning an upgrade to SVR3. You will need to reinstall the system software, and probably repartition the disk for the additional swap-space requirements of SVR3. Therefore, you will probably want to reformat the hard disk and rebuild the disk from scratch. Furthermore, many of the key system files will have changed (sometimes markedly) between older releases and SVR3.

Therefore, the first step in upgrading is to scrupulously back up your system to some safe medium (such as disk or tape). Back up the complete system, since if the upgrade fails for some reason, you will want to reinstall the older version. For example, the upgrade might fail if one of the floppy disks containing the new release is bad and will not load correctly. Be sure to back up ALL your files and materials that you will want later. The best way to do this is to back up each individual directory onto a separate floppy disk. Later, when you want to bring the materials back in the new release, you can load each disk separately into a temporary directory, carefully move the files into their destination, and then delete the copies.

This procedure will keep the "excess" disk utilization to a tolerable level (since you probably cannot support two separate versions of the entire system on your machine at once). Furthermore, you cannot simply overwrite the older version of the system onto the SVR3 release because this will corrupt the system. At least you should back up your personal files (and those of other users) separately from system files since you cannot restore ANY system files or directories safely. This includes **uucp** files and anything in the **/etc** directory, including **/etc/profile**, **/etc/passwd**, **/etc/shadow**, **/etc/inittab**, or **/etc/rc**.

After backing up everything, begin the load as previously described. When the load is complete, you can log into the system and begin to restore your backed up materials. If you are now using SVR2, the conversion is relatively straightforward. Releases older than SVR2, or older XENIX releases, will require substantial changes. In these cases, trying to save any older materials is probably not worthwhile, but you will have to build up the machine as you discover things that are not to your taste. However, your text files, spreadsheets, databases, and so forth, can be reloaded without harm, though the executable programs to support them may require upgrade.

You must restore the old system into a temporary directory, manually examine the materials, and use **mv** to put them into the target directory location.

If you are not sure, DO NOT overwrite existing system files outside your HOME or other private directories. You must carefully examine each file and decide how to treat it. Usually you cannot restore system files from older releases.

If moved from an 80286 machine, SVR2 executable applications and data files *may* continue to work correctly on the SVR3 system, but you should carefully test them. If possible, you should recompile any applications moved from the SVR2 to the SVR3 machines.

Tunable Parameters

Many UNIX systems allow a skilled system administrator to vary some of the *tunable parameters* within the kernel. These are variables that specify the size of some key data areas within the operating system. If necessary, their values can be set for special purposes. Microcomputer versions of SVR3 usually provide some tools to change a few of these tunable parameters.

Often **nbuf** (the number of system buffers), **ulimit** (the maximum file size limit), **nclists** (the number of system character I/O buffers), **nproc** (the number of simultaneous processes allowed for a user), and **nfile** (the number of open files a process is allowed) are tunable on small SVR3 systems. However, these should not be changed from their default values unless you are installing a special application package that requires them to be changed.

Carefully follow the vendor's instructions, and do not change these values unnecessarily.

Going Further

Games and Toys
The Worldwide User Community
Software Development
The Expanding Influence of the Unix System
The Remote File Sharing Subsystem
Using RFS
Administering RFS
Setting Up RFS
Books and Bibliography
A Few Last Words

The title of this book may be *The Complete Reference*, but you have seen that the UNIX system provides an extraordinarily rich and varied computer environment. No single book can *completely* cover the UNIX system, or even adequately survey the entire range of commands and associated lore. This book has discussed the *Foundation Set* in enough detail that a moderately experienced microcomputer user can become a competent user and administrator of a personal UNIX system.

In addition to the Foundation Set, several other pieces of the UNIX system are in the complete SVR3 release. The *Documenter's Workbench* and the *Software Development Package* are two of the most important of these.

Many *semi-standard* packages are also part of the official AT&T SVR3 software release, but are not usually included in the products of most vendors. The *Writer's Workbench* (a package of additional tools built on top of the *Documenter's Workbench*), the *System Activity Reporting* (**sar**) tools, and the *Remote Job Entry* tools are examples of this class.

A third type of add-on software is the applications supported by the legions of UNIX system devotees in the world. The C and Korn shells, the EMACS text editor, and some popular games are examples of this class. These programs are available for nearly all versions. However, in some cases they are not available for purchase, but only in source-code form. Many public-domain bulletin boards provide executable or installable versions of popular programs, and a little exposure to the *UNIX system community* will provide information for finding them.

Finally, a great many commercial software products are available for the UNIX system. Contrary to the popular impression that no software exists for the UNIX system, many thousands of popular applications are, in fact, available. These include many different spreadsheets and word processors, a large number of sophisticated scientific and engineering programs, and a rich set of communications packages. Most software and hardware vendors today are writing their applications in the C language, and most support the UNIX system. With the growing popularity of the UNIX system, more applications are appearing on the market regularly. Since developers usually prefer to work within the UNIX system over any other operating system, this rich and varied software base will continue to grow.

This chapter mentions some of the most popular nonstandard software and discusses one of the newest (but most powerful) features—*Remote File Sharing*.

Games and Toys

One of the most popular unofficial areas of software is *games and toys*. Over the years, a great many innovative games have been developed for the UNIX system. These are almost all character-oriented toys (that adhere to the philosophy of supporting remote ASCII terminals). The best of the games are almost legendary in the computing world. It is often said that these games have consumed more CPU resources on UNIX machines than any other category, including software development and word processing.

The games (when they are available) are usually kept in the directory **/usr/games**. The contents of this directory vary widely on different machines, since games are no longer delivered as an official part of the UNIX system. However, the UNIX system did include some games at one time, and Section 6 in the manual is reserved for games and toys. This original set of games still forms the foundation for the **/usr/games** directory. The original games are mostly simple children's toys (such as tic-tac-toe and hangman), but several excellent games are included. The UNIX system chess game can beat average chess players, but it has been superseded in recent years by state-of-the-art programs.

The most popular game in the original set is **adventure**. Known by the name "Zork" in the MS-DOS world, **adventure** is one player's exploration of a predefined "dungeon." The user interface for this game is not graphical, but rather language-oriented. That is, the user moves around in the dungeon by entering short command sentences such as "go west" or "pick up the knife."

The **adventure** game was displaced as the king of the UNIX-system games during the early 1980s by **rogue**. The **rogue** game is also a dungeon-oriented game, but is improved over **adventure** in many ways. The **rogue** game includes a full-screen display of the dungeon being explored, has many different dungeon levels, and the "hero" must fight 26 different kinds of monsters in the quest for gold and the fabled Amulet of Yendor. The **rogue** game is so difficult that only a few players have been able to win, but playing it is a peculiarly fascinating and addictive pastime.

In the mid- and late-1980s, **rogue** spawned several popular games, each with more complexity and more features than the last. The **hack** game is a sort of super **rogue** with many more complexities, but with the same basic style of play as **rogue**. The **larn** game is a freer adaptation of **rogue** that requires a different strategy.

Finally, games with bit-mapped graphical user interfaces are beginning to appear for UNIX systems that can support them. Multiplayer games are also appearing. In some cases, these are high-action games based on real-time communications between users. In other cases, these are strategy games (such as chess) that take special advantage of the multitasking features of the UNIX system. A space attack game, **empire**, is the foremost example, but many more are available. These graphical and multiplayer games will surely predominate over the next several years. Some of the best creativity in the computer business is devoted to games and toys, and these games are well worth trying. Generations of users have been enchanted by them.

The Worldwide User Community

Over the history of the UNIX system, a tightly knit *user community* has appeared. This community has been fostered in part by the ease of communication with **uucp**, and in part by the mystique that the UNIX system has always held for developers. Several independent *users' groups* exist, the foremost of which is appropriately called */usr/group*. In addition, several national conventions and meetings are devoted to discussions of the UNIX system, the largest of which is the *Usenix* meeting held regularly. Both of these organizations are excellent sources of information and contacts. Most of the real advances in UNIX system technology have been originally disseminated by word-of-mouth (or electronic-mail) between interested users. These alternatives were brought into the official releases only after the innovations were well accepted by the users.

Users of the UNIX system support a worldwide *bulletin board* and electronic-mail system that serves several thousand machines and hundreds of thousands of users. Known by various names (such as *netnews*, *usenet*, *readnews*, or simply the *net*), this network is based primarily on dial-up access between nearby machines, which exchange electronic-mail messages known as *news items*. The news items can be grouped into more than 100 different categories, or *news groups*.

Nearby machines *feed* the messages to other machines, and thus a message propagates eventually from its originator to all the other machines in the network. A user on one of the machines uses special *news reader* software to see the messages, and can set up a profile to limit retrieval to only as many of the news groups as desired. Users can browse, save, or reply to the messages. The news network has *gateways* that link it with several other popular networks, such as the ARPANET (which primarily connects computers involved in military research) and BITNET (which is a network of computers in colleges and universities).

More than 1000 messages per day cross the news network, on every subject imaginable. Especially fertile subjects involve UNIX system and C language lore. New public-domain source code for everything from games to new algorithms and full-blown expert systems constantly flows across the network. Interesting discussions of new technologies and new products are conducted. Nontechnical news groups discuss politics, music, sports, as well as many other topics.

The news network is a completely self-sustaining operation and is supported by each machine, which pays the telephone bills associated with forwarding messages to its neighboring machines. However, a recent experiment with a satellite-based communication scheme for communications between central *hub* machines may change the free-lance character of the net (satellite costs cannot be shared easily by the individual machines). Netnews software is provided in the public domain by creative developers who are constantly improving the tools. Several popular news readers are available, but they are usually distributed in source-code form.

To add your machine to the news network, you need news-management software for your machine, and the normal **uucp** package. Also, you must locate a nearby machine that is willing to *feed* your site and dedicate a significant amount of hard disk space for the news messages. As much as 2 to 3 megabytes of news per day can be delivered to your machine if you take all the different news groups. Once you are receiving a news feed, you can be attached by a multihop connection to nearly every other UNIX machine in the world.

Software Development

The richest area within the UNIX system is *software development*. The C programming language and the excellent support environment make the system quite popular with developers. While development under the UNIX system is beyond the scope of this book, a great deal of literature discusses it. If you have any interest in programming, you will find the UNIX system well suited to your needs.

The Expanding Influence of the UNIX System

In addition to the software development tools themselves, the UNIX system has proved to be an extremely fertile source of ideas and algorithms for developers. Most modern microcomputer software has borrowed liberally from ideas that first appeared in the UNIX system. For example, the MS-OS/2 operating system learned a lot from the UNIX system, from its kernel through **cmd.exe** (the MS-OS/2 version of the shell). You will find that a knowledge of the UNIX system simplifies your use of nearly all other computer systems. Occasionally, however, you may be frustrated when familiar tools and procedures from the UNIX system are not available in other computing environments.

The Remote File Sharing Subsystem

One of the most interesting new features in the SVR3 release of the UNIX system is *Remote File Sharing* (RFS). Remote File Sharing is the ability for users of one machine to **mount** directory substructures of other machines, and to access the remote directories just as they would normal directories. The commands **mv**, **cp**, and **ls** are allowed as normal. Programs can open remote files, or you can redirect input or output to a remote file just as you would a local file. In multimachine environments, this opens a whole new domain of file use and file sharing, and can significantly reduce disk costs. Appropriate controls, administrative tools, and security features are provided to support RFS and make it a useful and versatile new addition to the bag of tricks.

The RFS is built on another new feature, the *File System Switch* (FSS). The FSS is a general capability within the kernel that allows mapping between any file-system types. That is, you can set up an MS-DOS file system as a file-system type, and you can use this "foreign" file system just like a normal file system (including redirection and the rest of the commands). All the complexity is hidden within the kernel and is not visible to users. Unfortunately, the general features of FSS are still under development, and the only application in SVR3 that uses the FSS is RFS. In later releases of the UNIX system, the FSS is expected to come into its own as an outstanding capability.

The RFS feature is functionally similar to the *NFS* (Network File System) that is available for BSD releases. However, RFS is not compatible with NFS, and machines using RFS cannot share files with machines running NFS.

To use RFS, you must have SVR3 machines at all the *nodes* that wish to share files. Since the RFS feature is new to SVR3, older releases do not support it. In addition, machines must be connected by a high-speed local area network such as STAR-LAN or ETHERNET. If your network is set up to allow **uucp** traffic over the LAN and between SVR3 machines, then you can use RFS over the network as well. This section assumes that the LAN is up and running between your machines. The discussion centers only on the issues directly related to RFS.

RFS Basics

After setting up the SVR3 machines on the LAN, you can configure them into several *domains*. A domain is a group of machines that allow RFS between them and may exclude other machines that are not *domain members*. A large LAN with many machines can have several separate domains that will not conflict with each other. A machine may participate in more than one domain, but machines in one domain usually do not access files on machines in another domain.

Each domain has exactly one *primary name server*. This machine is responsible for administering the domain as a whole, and it usually belongs to the network or domain administrator. In addition, you can establish one or more *secondary name servers*. These are usually not used for administration of the domain, but can take over routine name-server duties if the primary machine is down for some reason. The primary name server executes special demon processes that manage the domain and its activities.

Other machines can join the domain as *clients*. Clients can access files on other machines, but cannot authorize other machines to access their files. Only servers can provide resources, but nonservers in the domain can use resources provided by servers.

Each server and client in the domain must bring up the RFS facilities for that machine. This is an administrative procedure to configure RFS management processes on the machines. Servers can establish security that limits access to designated domain members.

Next, each server can *advertise* specific directories that other machines are allowed to access. These directories can then be used by clients when they *mount* the advertised resources of another machine.

When directories are mounted this way over the LAN, they are effectively available at all times, just like a local directory. This connection is called a *permanent virtual circuit*, since the connection between the machines is permanent, even though the network is being used for other traffic at the same time. When a user is finished with the directory, the resource should be *released* by *unmounting* it. This reduces network load and the chances for derangement because of failure of the network or failure of one of the machines in the circuit.

Only a few machines in the domain need to be servers and the domain can be organized with many client machines. Alternatively, a peer-based domain might have many servers, so that any machine can access resources on all the others. Usually network policy determines whether the network has a few or many servers. The policy is determined by the needs of the users and the security considerations. In a friendly environment where everyone needs access to the data of other users, most machines will probably be set up as servers. In a more secure environment where public data is controlled in a small directory tree, only a few machines might be servers. Remember, once a server machine advertises a resource, any machine on the network can join the domain and access those resources (unless the advertisement is restricted to a specific set of machines). Also, servers have several permanent administrative processes, and the primary server has even more processes. If a machine is already heavily loaded, you may wish to evaluate whether it should be made a server.

Using RFS

If a resource has already been mounted on your machine, you do not need to do anything special to use a file or directory from a remote machine. You can use normal file-system and redirection commands with remote files. An administrator will normally establish a common file-system location for remote resources so you can find remote files easily, but this is not needed. Remote files can be mounted anywhere in the file system, and theoretically you cannot tell the difference between a local and remote file. This also applies to many types of *device* files (special files in the /**dev** directory). You can usually open, read, and write to a remote device just as to a local device, once it has been mounted. However, all devices in SVR3 do not support remote access, so you should experiment with specific devices to see how they act under RFS.

Mounting Remote Resources

To mount new remote resources, or to use any of the RFS administration commands, you must be superuser.

If the RFS feature is already running on your LAN, and your machine is a member of a domain, you can determine what resources are available with the **nsquery** (name server query) command. The **nsquery** command lists resources, permissions, host machine, and a comment for each:

```
$ nsquery
RESOURCE         ACCESS        SERVER              DESCRIPTION

DATA             read/write    local.my_sys        Real data base
DATA_BKUP        read-only     local.my_sys        Backup data base
SCRATCH          read/write    big.my_sys          reserved for temp moves
STEVE            read/write    big.steve           steve's public dir
BILL             read-only     local.protol        bill's public dir
$
```

This output is built from the resources that each member of the domain has advertised as available to your machine, but they may not be currently mounted.

Each advertised resource has a *name*, a set of *permissions* that describe whether it is writable or read-only, and a *description* that provides a comment concerning the contents of the resource. The **nsquery** output also reports the server on which the resource resides. The naming for server machines follows the format

```
domain.server
```

where "domain" is the name of the domain and "server" is the machine's *uname*. These elements are separated by a dot. In the previous example, three machines are in two different domains. The domains are called "local" and "big," and the machines are **my_sys**, **proto1**, and **steve**.

All advertised resources from all servers in all domains on the LAN will be reported in this default command form. A resource will appear in the **nsquery** output if it has been advertised by its server, even though RFS security may be set up to prohibit your machine from using the resource. You must try to mount it to determine if access is allowed from your machine.

You can limit the **nsquery** output to resources on a specific server by naming the server as an argument:

```
$ nsquery local.my_sys
RESOURCE         ACCESS       SERVER               DESCRIPTION

DATA             read/write   local.my_sys         Real data base
DATA_BKUP        read-only    local.my_sys         Backup data base
$
```

Alternatively, you can see a report on all resources on a specific machine by giving the machine name as argument:

```
$ nsquery my_sys
RESOURCE         ACCESS       SERVER               DESCRIPTION

DATA             read/write   local.my_sys         Real data base
DATA_BKUP        read-only    local.my_sys         Backup data base
SCRATCH          read/write   big.my_sys           reserved for temp moves
$
```

Finally, you can see all the resources available in the domain by giving the domain name and trailing dot:

```
$ nsquery big.
RESOURCE         ACCESS       SERVER               DESCRIPTION

SCRATCH          read/write   big.my_sys           reserved for temp moves
$
```

The dot is necessary when naming a domain.

The Mount Command

You can gain access to advertised resources on another machine in the domain with the **mount** command. This command has a slightly different syntax for remote mounts than for normal local mounts. Mounting local resources is discussed in Chapter 16. Each remote resource requires a *mount point*, which is a directory within the local file system. You should normally create a permanent empty directory to use as a mount point, but temporary remote mounts can use the normal /**mnt** directory if you desire. Many RFS installations define a special parent directory that contains empty subdirectories named for each server in the domain. For example,

```
# pwd
/usr/rfs
# ls -FC
guest/        protol/        steve/        my_sys/
#
```

If several resources are available on a server, you may want to create another level of subdirectories within the **server-name** directory so that you can mount more than one resource from the server at the same time. Nearly any scheme is allowed, but a consistent policy is best for all machines in the domain.

To mount a remote resource, use the **mount** command:

```
# mount -d DATA /usr/rfs/my_sys
#
```

DATA is the name of an available resource as determined from **nsquery**, and the local directory location is the last argument. If the operation succeeds, **mount** returns silently. The −**d** (domain) flag signals that this is a remote mount and is required in the command line. Add the −**r** option if you want to mount the resource with read-only permissions:

```
# mount -dr DATA /usr/rfs/my_sys
```

You can mount resources in another domain if RESOURCE includes the domain name:

```
# mount -dr big.SCRATCH /usr/rfs/guest
```

You can examine mounted resources (both local and remote) with the **mount** command with no arguments:

```
# mount
/ on /dev/dsk/0s1 read/write on Tue Jul 28 16:56:04 1987
/usr/rfs/my_sys on DATA read only/remote on Tue Jul 28 17:54:13 1987
#
```

This reports on local mounted disks (**/dev/dsk/0s1**), and on the remote mounts (**/usr/rfs/my‗sys**). The *remote* keyword is present to distinguish local from remote resources.

Unmounting Remote Resources

To unmount a previously mounted resource, use the **umount** command:

```
# umount -d DATA
#
```

The −**d** option is required to signal a remote resource.

If the unmount is successful, **umount** returns silently, but a resource cannot be unmounted if it is in use:

```
# umount -d DATA
umount: DATA busy
#
```

A resource is in use if any user has a directory of the resource as a current directory, or if any program is using one of the files in the resource.

Determining Resource Use

Before attempting to unmount a resource, you can verify that no users are accessing that resource. The **/etc/fuser** (file system users) command is designed for this task. The **fuser** command takes a directory or resource name as argument, and reports the process id's of processes that are using the resource. Use the **−u** (users) option to list the login id's of those people who own the processes:

```
# /etc/fuser −u DATA
DATA:    121c(steve)    123p(jim)    135c(jim)
#
```

Three processes are using the resource DATA, and their PID's are 121, 123, and 135. The user id's are given in parentheses after the process. The letter **c** (current directory) signals that the users have the resource as their current directory. The **p** (parent) marks the resource as the parent directory for the process, and **r** (root) marks the resource as the root directory for the process. For remote resources, the report is for any file within the mounted resource. The **fuser** command can also report on use of local resources (such as mounted file systems). This can help identify users of floppy disks and other removable media.

Forcing an Unmount

In an emergency, you can force a resource to be unmounted even though users are accessing the resource. This procedure is a bit rude to the remote users, so it should be used with care.

The **fumount** (forced **umount**) command is used. The **fumount** command takes a resource name as argument, and an optional delay if the **−w** (wait) flag is given with a number of seconds:

```
# fumount −w 30 DATA
```

The **fumount** command given on a server starts an **rfuadmin** (remote file **uadmin**) process on each client machine that is using the resource, which has the task of unmounting the resource from that machine. The **rfuadmin** process gives a warning prompt to client users with the **wall** command if the

—**w** option is given. The **rfuadmin** process waits the delay time, then uses **fumount** locally to unmount the resource.

Processes accessing the resource will be killed, so if you are a client user and receive a message such as

```
DATA is being removed from the system in # seconds.
```

you should immediately release your use of the resource by ending programs that access the resource or by using **cd** to move out of the resource directory. This procedure is also executed automatically when the server machine is shut down.

Automatic Remote Mounts

You can set up your machine so that some resources are automatically mounted when the machine boots. The file **/etc/fstab** (file-system table) contains this information. When the machine boots, the file is examined for lines of the form

```
name directory -d
```

where **name** is the resource name, **directory** is the local directory at which to mount the resource, and the —**d** (domain) flag identifies the resource as a remote directory. You can use —**dr** (read-only) to mount the resource as read-only. No administrative tools support this file, so you must manually edit it to add automatic mounts. The **/etc/fstab** file contains information on local file systems to mount as well as remote resources. When you edit this file, take care not to change any existing entries.

Administering RFS

A few more procedures are required to administer an RFS site. Before remote resources are mounted, the RFS feature must be started. This involves changing to a new *init state* that allows RFS activity, both for client and server machines. Your machine may also join a domain. For servers, some local demon processes must be started, and local resources must be *advertised* as available to other machines. Several security-related procedures may also be required, depending on how your domain is configured. Similar, but inverse, procedures are required to stop RFS.

Starting RFS

Administrators must make sure that the RFS feature is *running* on their machines before RFS can be used. RFS is implemented by putting the machine into *init state 3*, and is required for both server and client machines.

The **rfstart** (remote file start) command is used to turn on the RFS system, and **rfstop** (remote file stop) is used to stop the service:

```
# rfstart
Password:
#
```

The **rfstart** command prompts for a password before it takes any action. This password is *verified* against the password stored on the primary name server when the domain was established. The **rfstart** command assumes that the domain name servers have already been established, and the machine will be a member of a "known" domain.

You can specify that all clients attempting to mount resources on your server will be verified against your RFS password file. Use the −**v** (verify) option with **rfstart**:

```
# rfstart −v
Password:
```

If the −**v** option is given, all clients must be registered on the local server as members of their domain, and their passwords will be checked. If the −**v** is not given, any client who is not listed in the domain password file on the server will be allowed access, while those in the password file will be verified. You should always use the −v option, unless you allow guests to use your server extensively.

You must have a working LAN before you can turn on the RFS feature. Remember that both client and server machines must have RFS running.

When RFS is started, it will continue to run following a system reboot. The **rfstart** command implements this by changing the boot-time procedures so that the system enters state 3 rather than the usual state 2. Some of the /etc/rc3.d procedures will automatically bring up RFS at boot time.

Advertising Resources

After the machine is established as a server with the RFS feature running, you may want to advertise resources that other machines can use. The advertised resources appear in the **nsquery** list, and clients can mount them if they wish. Servers usually have some advertised resources available to other machines, but that is not required.

The **adv** (advertise) command is used to announce resources to the domain. The primary purpose of advertising resources is to restrict their uses as the server desires, and **adv** allows resources to be restricted in several different ways. The **adv** command takes a resource name and a pathname as arguments:

```
# adv DATA /usr/steve/my.data
```

The resource name is assigned when the resource is advertised, and the pathname is the local directory that you want to share. The pathname must reside on the local server. That is, you cannot mount a remote resource, then advertise it under a new name.

The **adv** command can also take command line arguments. Use −**r** (read-only) to specify that the resource cannot be changed by the clients who mount it. Use −**d** (description) followed by a character string (quoted if white space is included) to give a description for the resource:

```
# adv -r -d"my data archive" DATA /usr/steve/my.data
```

The **adv** command causes new resources to appear in the **nsquery** output. The command also enters the resource into a table on the name server for the domain.

You can restrict access to the resource to a selected list of clients. Enter the list of client machines after the other command line arguments if you want this restriction:

```
# adv -r RESTRICT /usr/steve/my.data my_sys steve
```

You can also use a domain name in the list to limit access to all the members of the named domain.

If you issue the command **adv** with no arguments, it displays a list of resources that have been advertised from the local machine. You can also automatically advertise a list of resources when the machine enters init state 3. The file **/etc/rstab** contains a list of **adv** command lines that you would enter manually to advertise your resources.

Unadvertising Resources

You can remove a resource from availability with the **unadv** (unadvertise) command. The **unadv** command prevents new users from mounting the resource, but does not unmount resources that are currently in use. Use

```
# unadv resource
```

where "resource" is the name given when the resource was advertised:

```
# unadv DATA
```

If an **adv** command has been included in the **/etc/rstab** list, you may want to remove the line to prevent the resource from being advertised again on the next reboot of your machine.

Stopping RFS

You can turn off RFS on your machine with the **rfstop** (remote file stop) command. Before RFS can be stopped, all users must unmount the resources they are using on other machines. If the local machine is a server, client machines must unmount the resources they are using, and you must unadvertise any local resources. These steps will happen automatically when you leave init state 3. The **rfstop** command will take all the necessary actions, use **fumount** if necessary to force remote users off your resources, and return your machine to init state 2:

```
# rfstop
```

However, as a courtesy, you should unadvertise your resources first and give users a chance to unmount them before you stop the RFS feature.

Setting Up RFS

Before any of the RFS procedures can be used, you must *configure* the domain and your machine's appearance in the domain. For example, your machine may be a primary or secondary name server, a normal server (host), or a client only. You can limit your machine to a specific domain on the network, or protect access to resources by passwords. Since many optional procedures are associated with RFS and its domains (including sophisticated security considerations), you should consult the RFS documentation before configuring a domain or starting RFS on your machine for the first time. The discussion here is only a survey of the RFS setup procedures and is based on a STARLAN network. Procedures for other types of networks will differ.

Starting the Network

Before you can use RFS, your machine must be correctly configured on the local area network, able to connect by way of **uucp**, and able to exchange mail across the network. This verifies that the network and supporting software are operating correctly, but RFS does not use **uucp** facilities when it is operating. In fact, on most networks that support RFS, **uucp** traffic can coexist with remote mounts.

Start the network with the **nlsadmin** (network listener service administration) command. This need be done only once for a machine, when the network is first installed. Use the −**i** (initialize) option followed by the network name:

```
# nlsadmin -i starlan
```

If the network is already running, this command will not hurt anything.

Next you must install RFS as an available *service* for your machine on the network. Use the following command:

```
# nlsadmin -a 105 -c /usr/net/servers/rfs/rfsetup \
-y "rfsetup" starlan
```

This command announces that service code 105 is available to the network, and that **rfsetup** is the command to be invoked when a remote machine requests that service.

Next you must announce your *network address* to the demon process that will listen to network traffic and respond to messages to your address. Use

```
# nlsadmin -l "uname.serve" -t "uname" starlan
```

where **uname** is your unique machine's name.

At this point, you can determine whether the network is running with the following:

```
# nlsadmin -x starlan
starlan network ENABLED
#
```

If the response is DISABLED, you must start the *listener* process with the following:

```
# nlsadmin -s starlan
```

Afterward, the listener will be started automatically at boot time.

Establishing a Domain

If you are establishing a new domain, you must first set up the primary name server. If you are joining an existing domain, no more steps are needed. However, you should ask your domain administrator to add your machine to the domain database if your machine is to be a server or if client verification procedures are in force in your domain. Then you can start RFS with **rfstart** as previously described, and mount remote resources as needed.

However, if you are starting a new domain, more setup steps are required. Establish the *domain name* with

```
# dname -D domain
```

where domain is the unique domain name you have chosen. A domain name must be 14 characters or fewer, and must be unique on your network. You must then assign a network to the domain. Since a machine can be attached to more than one network, you must assign a network for the domain:

```
# dname -N starlan
```

In this example, **starlan** is the special file in /**dev** that connects to the network you wish to use, not necessarily the name of the network.

The **dname** command can also report on the domain name and network type on a machine. Use

```
# dname -a
```

(all) to see this information after the domain is created.

Establishing Name Servers

Next you must create a file that contains a table of name servers for the domain. A domain must have only one primary name server, but can have several secondary name servers. The name server executes administrative demons that manage the domain and perform security checks. The secondary name servers take over these tasks when the primary name server is down. Since name server duties add additional load to the machine, only a few secondary name servers are usually specified on a domain.

On the machine to be designated as the primary name server, use a text editor to create or edit the file /**usr**/**nserve**/ **rfmaster** (remote file master). This is the master list of name servers for the domain. When RFS is running, this list will appear on all the other servers in the domain. However, at this point you must create the list on the machine designated as the primary name server.

The **rfmaster** file contains a list of the name servers, whether the machine is a primary or secondary name server, and the network address of the server:

```
$ cat /usr/nserve/rfmaster
# the primary and secondary name servers are listed first
local p local.steve
local s local.my_sys
# the domain and network addresses follow
local.steve a steve.serve
local.my_sys a my_sys.serve
$
```

Each line consists of three fields separated by one white-space character. Some releases allow only a single blank or tab; multiple white-space characters may cause the file to be processed incorrectly.

Two different types of lines are in the **rfmaster** file: those that describe name servers and those that give network addresses for the other servers. The first field is the domain or machine name, the second is an action code, and the third is a network or domain address. The name servers are listed first. In the previous example, the domain is called "local," and the primary (p) name server is the machine **steve** at domain address **local.steve**. The machine **my—sys** is the secondary (s) name server, and its network address is **local.my—sys**. You can have only one p line, but several s lines if desired.

Network addresses are mapped to domain addresses (a) in the rest of the lines. Only name servers need to be mentioned in the a lines. The first field is the domain address and the third field is the network address. Network addresses of the form **uname.serve** are typical of STARLAN networks. Comments are allowed in the **rfmaster** file (comment lines begin with # or pound sign). When **rfmaster** is correct, write it and leave your editor. Verify that **root** owns the file, and the permissions are 0644.

Adding Servers to the Domain

At this point, you can add server machines to the domain. Use the **rfadmin** command with the —**a** (add) option.

```
# rfadmin -a domain.uname
Password:
```

where "domain" is the domain name and **uname** is the name of the server you wish to add. The **rfadmin** command prompts for a password, which must be entered by the administrator on the **uname** machine when **rfstart** is used to start RFS on that machine. Just press NEWLINE to skip the password, but be sure to respect your network security policy when adding servers.

You can remove a server from the domain with

```
# rfadmin -r domain.uname
```

(remove). Use

```
# rfadmin
```

with no argument to display the current name server for the domain. This must be your machine, or you cannot perform any of the domain administrative tasks.

Now you can start RFS on the primary name server with **rfstart**. Then start the RFS feature on the secondary name servers. Your domain is then up and running. Normal hosts and clients can now use the domain. Use **adv** and **mount** to work with remote resources.

Changing an Existing Domain

You can switch the primary name server responsibilities to a secondary name server with the following:

```
# rfsadmin -p
```

You might do this before bringing down the primary for maintenance. This is intended as a temporary change in name servers. As soon as the primary is up again, execute

```
# rfsadmin -p
```

on the current name server to restore responsibilities to the primary. To permanently change the primary name server, you must again edit the file **rfmaster**. Be sure to stop RFS on all primary and secondary name servers in the domain with **rfstop** before changing name servers. Then edit **rfmaster** on the new primary, start RFS there with **rfstart**, and finally start the secondaries.

When the name servers are operating correctly, the primary regularly distributes the key administrative files to the secondary name servers. If the primary name server crashes unexpectedly, responsibilities automatically pass to the first secondary name server in the **rfmaster** file. This will not affect any mounted resources in the domain (unless they resided on the crashed machine). However, the secondaries cannot perform the full name-server duties, so if the primary does not come back online soon, you should switch the primary responsibilities to another machine (usually one of the former secondaries). Carefully check the **rfmaster** file and the advertised resources for errors because the secondaries do not always have administrative files that are completely current.

More RFS Issues

RFS allows *mapping* of users on remote machines into user id's and group id's on the server machines. Thus, you have complete control of permissions that remote users have on your resources. Mapping can be complex, and you should study the RFS documentation before using it.

Finally, several tools measure the use of RFS, and *tune* its performance to your needs. You can use the **fusage** (file usage) command to study how clients are using your resources, and the **sar** (system activity reporting) command will report on how much CPU time is being used for remote-file access. You can change the servers and their responsibilities to minimize the use of CPU time on the domain as a whole. You can also set the values of RFS *parameters* to control maximum users of your resources, the maximum number of processes associated with RFS, and other limits. These are all complex topics that should be used with care.

Books and Bibliography

If you wish to pursue any UNIX system issue in more detail, many other sources of information are available. Over the years, the user community has voted for some documents over others. Some of the best are listed here.

UNIX System V Release 3 User's Manual. AT&T, 1987.

The official reference manual for all commands in the UNIX system. Be sure to get the version prepared explicitly by the vendor for your release of the system.

Nutshell Handbooks, published by O'Reilly & Associates, Inc., 981 Chestnut St., Newton, MA 02164 (1-800-338-NUTS).

Each of these short essays covers a specific topic of the UNIX system. You can order one or more from the publisher. Call for a current list.

Kernighan, B. W., and Ritchie, D. M. *The C Programming Language.* Englewood Cliffs, NJ: Prentice-Hall, 1978.

This is the final word on the classical C language. However, it does not cover the latest ANSI specification for C or the new variant C++, which are used by an increasing number of C compilers.

Harbison, S. P. and Steele, G. L., Jr. *C: A Reference Manual,* 2d ed. Englewood Cliffs, NJ: Prentice-Hall, 1987.

Excellent coverage of the C language, including the proposed ANSI specification. It is somewhat more accessible than Kernighan and Ritchie.

Kernighan, B. W., and Pike, R. *The UNIX Programming Environment.* Englewood Cliffs, NJ: Prentice-Hall, 1983.

This book is an excellent description of the UNIX system interface to the developer.

UNIX System V Release 3 Programmer's Guide. AT&T, 1987.

The official AT&T document for programming in SVR3.

Wood, P. H., and Kochan, S. G. *UNIX System Security.* Indianapolis: Hayden Books, 1985.

Excellent coverage of security issues, though it does not review topics unique to SVR3.

Bach, M. J. *The Design of the UNIX Operating System.* Englewood Cliffs, NJ: Prentice-Hall, 1986.

This is the definitive look at system internals, including a lot of detail on the kernel and its design.

Moore, M. L. *Working with Xenix System V.* Glenview, IL: Scott, Foresman and Company, 1986.

This book gives a user-level view of the XENIX version of the UNIX system.

Of course, many other books and documents on the UNIX system are available. Local bookstores and libraries usually have a selection.

A Few Last Words

Finally, you have reached the end of the book. If you have arrived here the hard way (through all the intervening chapters), you are surely a competent user who can stand on your own to make the UNIX system work for you, now and in the future. We hope that you have become as enthusiastic about the UNIX system as the rest of the worldwide user community. Remember, learning the UNIX system is a continuing process, and even the best "guru" can only know a part of its rich environment. You can continue to develop your skills if you are not afraid to experiment with new ideas and procedures on your own machine. As you join the community of users, be sure to pass your skills on to the next beginners you meet, and help to make others as skilled as you have become. See you on the net.

68020™	Motorola Corporation
AT&T®	American Telephone & Telegraph
Apple®	Apple Computer, Inc.
DEC™	Digital Equipment Corporation
DOS®	International Business Machines Corporation
Diablo®	Xerox Corporation
Ethernet®	Xerox Corporation
HP®	Hewlett Packard Company
Hayes®	Hayes Microcomputer Products
Hewlett-Packard®	Hewlett Packard Company
IBM®	International Business Machines Corporation
IMAGEN®	Imagen Corporation
Intel®	Intel Corporation
LOTUS 1-2-3®	Lotus Development Corporation
MAC™	Apple Computer, Inc.
Microsoft®	Microsoft Corporation
MS-DOS®	Microsoft Corporation
Macintosh™	Apple Computer, Inc.
Multiplan™	Microsoft Corporation
IBM AT®	International Business Machines Corporation
OS/2™	International Business Machines Corporation
PDP®	Digital Equipment Corporation
Symphony®	Lotus Development Corporation
Teletype™	Teletype Corporation
UNIX®	AT&T Bell Laboratories
WordStar®	MicroPro International
XENIX®	Microsoft Corporation
Zork™	Infocom

TRADEMARKS

The manuscript for this book was prepared and submitted to Osborne/McGraw-Hill in electronic form.

The acquisitions editor for this project was Jeffrey Pepper. The project editor was Lyn Cordell.

The text is set in Century Expanded. Display is set in Eras Demi.

Cover art is by Bay Graphics Design Associates. Cover supplied by Phoenix Color Corporation. This book was printed and bound by R.R. Donnelley & Sons Company, Crawfordsville, Indiana.